SECURING PARADISE

NEXT WAVE
NEW DIRECTIONS IN WOMEN'S STUDIES

*A series edited by Inderpal Grewal,
Caren Kaplan, and Robyn Wiegman*

SECURING
PARADISE

✳

*Tourism and
Militarism in Hawai'i
and the Philippines*

VERNADETTE VICUÑA GONZALEZ

Duke University Press
Durham and London
2013

© 2013 Duke University Press

All rights reserved

Printed in the United States of America on acid-free paper ∞

Designed by Heather Hensley

Typeset in Whitman by Tseng Information Systems, Inc.

Library of Congress Cataloging-in-Publication Data

Gonzalez, Vernadette Vicuña, 1973–

Securing paradise : tourism and militarism in Hawai'i and
the Philippines / Vernadette Vicuña Gonzalez.

pages cm. — (Next wave)

Includes bibliographical references and index.

ISBN 978-0-8223-5355-3 (cloth : alk. paper) —

ISBN 978-0-8223-5370-6 (pbk. : alk. paper)

1. Tourism—Hawaii.   2. Tourism—Philippines.

3. Militarism—Hawaii.   4. Militarism—Philippines.

I. Title.   II. Series: Next wave.

G155.U6G625 2013

338.4'791599—dc23

2013010097

CONTENTS

ACKNOWLEDGMENTS

This book represents a decade of research that was, from the beginning, supported by the intellectual generosity of my mentors and colleagues, the unstinting encouragement of family and friends, and timely funding from a variety of sources. The encouragement, steadfast commitment to this project, and warm companionship I have received have made the labor of this book truly collaborative. During my graduate studies at uc Berkeley, I had the wonderful fortune of having as my intellectual guides Jose Davíd Saldívar, Elaine Kim, and Caren Kaplan. Their patience and incisive questions pushed my dissertation into an entirely new direction long after it was filed. I owe Caren Kaplan special thanks for recommending this manuscript to Duke University Press. She has been a model of rigorous scholarship and feminist teaching whose mentorship has continued to inspire. My first writing group with fellow graduate students Kathy Yep, Jeffrey Ow, Steven Lee, and Mimi Nguyen provided critique, commiseration, and engaged collegiality. Early collaborations with Nerissa Balce and Robyn Magalit Rodriguez gave me insight to the questions in this book and introduced me to the kind of scholarly work that I like doing. Mimi Nguyen, in addition to offering formidable intellectual support, was the most dependable and caring of friends who also earned her godmother title even as her goddaughter Inez was still in utero. Her work continues to serve as a touchstone, and her generosity as a colleague is unsurpassed.

At my first tenure-track position at St. Lawrence University, Margaret Kent-Bass was the staunchest of champions, assisting junior faculty with funding and intellectual community formation. In Hawai'i, which has been home for the last seven years, I have been most fortunate in the form of political and intellectual friendships that have both nurtured and unsettled my thinking in the best of ways. My colleagues in the American Studies department are the best ones I could ask for. In particular, Mari Yoshihara, Theo Gonzalves, Robert Perkinson, and David E. Stannard welcomed me as a fellow instigator from the start. Their humor and warmth helped me through various stages of this project. I especially thank David E. Stannard for coming up with creative ways to give me time to do research and write. I thank Mari Yoshihara and the graduate students from our joint grant-writing workshop for comments on my book proposal. I have also had the privilege of working with graduate students who have taught me so much: Mo Wells, Angela Krattiger, Miguel Llora, B. Cheryl Beredo, Eriza Bareng, Kim Compoc, Yu Jung Lee, Ruth Craft, and Sanae Nakatani. I hope to see your work in print soon.

My writing hui has changed membership over the years, and I would like to acknowledge the readers who braved their way through the very rough early drafts: Ty Kawika Tengan, Katharina Heyer, Rod Labrador, Lisa Fa'anofo Uperesa, and Brandy Nālani McDougall. I especially thank a trio of amazing women who helped this book become better in so many ways, especially in the home stretch, when schedules were tight and time was especially precious: Pensri Ho, for asking the right questions even when I wished she wouldn't, and who, even in the worst of times, would always make the time; Hokulani Aikau for sharing insights that sharpened my thinking, and being a wonderful friend with whom to share child-care, gossip, food, and complaints about sore muscles; and Jonna Eagle, for being such a generous colleague and friend right off the bat, for reading with incredible attention to detail, and for making the best chocolate cake ever. Writing group has never been so much fun with their humor, sustaining support, uncompromising critique, and kind offers to read and reread. I plan someday to be able to repay this debt.

I am profoundly grateful (and fortunate) to have readers whose generous and incisive suggestions pushed me to make the book stronger. I am even more glad to be able to thank them by name. Allan Punzalan Isaac and Cynthia Enloe, I owe you dinner and drinks, at the very least, for your careful, encouraging, and critical interventions in this book through various stages. All of your ideas compelled me to make this book better in every way, and I appreciate the time you took for your comments over the entire process. Thanks also goes to Sarita See, for sharing detailed comments on the manuscript and being a supportive colleague from afar, and to Vicente Rafael, whose encouraging words helped when they were needed the most.

Over the course of writing this book, I've relied upon the expertise and assistance of many people. I am grateful for the administrative assistants in my life, who have eased my way through the bureaucratic maze of academia and who have, on top of that, been stellar human beings and friends: Jahleezah Eskew, Joyce Sheridan, Sandy Enoki, and especially Lori Ann Mina. Jodie Kakazu Mattos has been the librarian whom researchers dream of, and I am particularly indebted to her research assistance above and beyond the call of duty. I also thank Waldette Cueto, who curates the Ateneo de Manila University's American Historical Collection; the staff at the Hawaiian and Pacific collection at UH Mānoa's Hamilton Library; and Maria Elena Clariza, who heads the Philippine collection.

The research for this book has taken me from the continental United States to Hawai'i and the Philippines, and I am deeply indebted to the following people who have supported my research, extended their hospitality, and made doing my job truly a privilege: Oscar Campomanes and the Kritika Kultura series at Ateneo de Manila for taking in a visiting scholar and making me feel right at home; Gary Devilles; Erlyn Alcantara, for all her help with Kennon Road fieldwork; F. Sionil José and Teresita José; Dean Alegado and Emmy Alegado; Cynthia Franklin; Laura Lyons; Ruth Hsu; Kath Sands; Karen Kosasa; Bill Chapman; Dennis Ogawa; Dylan Rodriguez; and Setsu Shigematsu. A much earlier version of chapter 3 appeared as "Touring Military Masculinities: U.S.-Philippines Circuits of Sacrifice and Gratitude in Corregidor and Bataan" in *Militarized Currents: Toward a Decolonized Future in Asia and the Pacific* (2010), and I would like to thank the University of Minnesota Press, Setsu Shigematsu, and Keith Lujan Camacho for including an earlier version of my work in that volume.

The research funding for this book has come from a variety of sources: the Ford Foundation, in the form of a predissertation fellowship; and faculty research grants from St. Lawrence University and the University of Hawai'i at Mānoa Research Council. I would like to thank Harold McArthur for all his help and support with shepherding grant applications through the Research Council.

To Ken Wissoker, who from the start has been the most encouraging and sympathetic of editors, I owe special thanks. He took this project under his wing and helped it come to fruition. I also thank the wonderful team at Duke University Press, especially Jade Brooks and Christine Dahlin, for their patience, support, and amazing professionalism; Heather Hensley, for the perfect cover design; and Jessica Ryan, who guided this book through the last stages. You have made the whole process so easy I feel like I want to do this again!

Finally, to my family and friends—I can now show them evidence that I have been truly working all this time. My gratitude goes out especially to Jean and Bill Anderson, the most supportive and loving of in-laws, and to my parents, Vivian and Ernesto Gonzalez, who have let me forge my own path even when it diverged from theirs. They have spent so much of their well-deserved retirement caring for my family so I could write. Thank you for providing me with that precious resource and peace of mind. For my daughter, Inez, who has grown up with this book, and who has been the most patient and understanding of children, I promise that the next book is the one we'll write together. You have been the best of café companions. Thank you for being understanding with your mother even if she is a slow writer. Noah, now I can finally teach you how to read, my dear illiterate son. Now you get lots of bedtime stories. This one's for Evan, who sticks around and always reminds me of what is truly important and absolutely indispensable in life. Your love and support have made this all possible.

MILITARY-TOURISM PARTNERSHIPS IN HAWAI'I AND THE PHILIPPINES

"Joe" is an identity that is almost automatically attributed to young white men of a certain age in the Philippines, regardless of whether or not they are American soldiers. The insistent hail "Hey, Joe!"—in city streets, at markets, or at the beach—while a somewhat awkward attempt at intercultural communication, evokes a long history of U.S. military occupation in the islands that established Joe as a regular fixture. Joe's history militarizes his status as a visitor: his practices of leisure (and by extension, those of civilians) were secured by the labor of his military tours. As symbolic and material evidence of the promise of U.S.-Philippine fraternal collaborations, Joe as tourist and soldier embodies the masculinized mobilities of American-style modernity. His is the ambassadorship of military protection intertwined with the pleasurable cosmopolitan possibilities of stability and security.

Joe's reception, of course, is uneven: in places where massive military installations dominate the landscape, he is welcomed for the income that base economies bring and resented for the sexual trade and erosion of local sovereignties fostered by his presence. In Mindanao, where the U.S. military has waged a century-long pacification campaign against Muslims, Joe might be greeted as a savior or reviled as a violent interloper. My own initial encounters with Joe were largely benign. Growing up on the Visayan island of Negros, where Spanish hacienda culture and American missionary efforts are dominant cultural influences, I was insulated from the realities of military occupation even as I was its indirect subject. Although Joe was only an occasional presence in my town, the United States had an oversized effect on everyday life in the Cold War Philippines. As Martial Law babies, my friends and I played war games, terrorized each other with stories of nuclear annihilation, and, of course, dared each other to greet the occasional white man at the beach with the requisite "Hey, Joe!" Despite its associations with war and militarization, America was invariably the good guy in these scenarios. To us, America was the stalwart liberator of World War II—exemplified by General Douglas MacArthur, who kept his promise to return. My attitudes and feelings about this abstract America were reinforced by the material largesse of care packages sent by stateside relatives, the lessons taught in church and school (both founded by American missionaries), and a fantasy life fostered by television and the movies. I grew up thinking about the United States as a benevolent and generous presence, the guardian of my playground.

Following the family migration trail opened up by Cold War immigration reform and pushed out by a stagnant Philippine economy, my family moved to the United States and settled in upstate New York in 1984. Aside from the traumas of cultural collision, one of my strongest adolescent impressions came from the new experience of traveling for leisure and not solely for family or work obligations. My first experience as a tourist in the United States was a visit to the Douglas MacArthur Memorial in Norfolk, Virginia, close to where my father's older sister had settled. My father, a World War II buff, brought the whole family to the rotunda where MacArthur—the archetypal Joe—was buried. This trip was a pilgrimage to a hero held in great esteem by many Filipinos, but also a confirmation of my family's rise in social status. I still have the photograph of my family posing in front of MacArthur's 1950 Chrysler Imperial limousine, as if to say, "We have arrived." The photograph was souvenir proof not merely of a family holiday but also of a middle-class American leisure practice that was simultaneously an act of identification with militarized U.S.-Philippine relations.

In many ways, this book is an exploration of the enduring childhood memories and feelings about the United States that were generated and deflected by the figure of Joe. How was it that despite the massive scale of violence the U.S. military had carried out in Asia and the Pacific since the turn of the nineteenth century, a child growing up in the Philippines had such positive associations with the United States? What alchemy transforms the terror of imperial violence and American postwar occupation to deeply felt understandings of American rescue, liberation, and benevolence? How are allegiance and love nurtured against and alongside the threat and reality of war and warmongering? While the United States has "formed states and territories, tested weapons, recruited soldiers, exploited resources, induced dependencies, displaced populations, and ruptured cultures," it has done so with little long-lasting damage to its own reputation and with minimal inconvenience to the vast majority of its citizens' consciences.[1] Somehow, the violent aspects of U.S. interventions have been absorbed into an alternative narrative of American benevolence: once-rival Japan has been transformed by virtue of nuclear annihilation, occupation, and reconstruction into a cooperative ally; the trauma of the Vietnam War is today rearticulated as an economic victory for capitalism; and the Asia Pacific Economic Cooperation carries out the neoliberal dictates of Washington, D.C., in the region it comfortably refers to as the site for its "Pacific Century."[2]

Against and in tandem with this sustained record of diplomatic, economic, and military intervention in Asia and the Pacific, *Securing Paradise* highlights imaginative and affective interventions as loci of power. Joe's doubled subjectivity as tourist and soldier gestures to the effects that naturalize and even obscure systematized acts of violence. As a tourist—insisting on a register of human connection and empathy—he invited hospitality, rather than domination or coercion, blunting the more brutal aspects of his mission. In beginning with Joe and the identifications and emotions he provokes, I emphasize not the authenticity of these attachments, but their manufacture. That the subjective authorizes truth as reliably and convincingly as official policies suggests that rather than working in opposition, their mutual entanglements exemplify the complex interrelationships of power. In other words, this book is interested in understanding regimes of feelings not as examples of false consciousness but as essential elements of a garrison state. Their transmission to juvenile citizens testifies to the appeal of pleasure, love, and identification in contrast to and in collaboration with pain, hate, and alienation.

Securing Paradise explores the relationship between tourism and militarism in Hawai'i and the Philippines, the "historical and present-day tropics" of the United States.[3] While other sites host larger American military installations today, Hawai'i and the Philippines represent the first and most sustained American military occupations in Asia and the Pacific: they remain the linchpins of American domination in the region. This book interrogates how the roots and routes of the U.S. military in these sites are foundational to tourist itineraries and imaginations, as well as how the desires and economies of modern tourism are central to American military dominance in Asia and the Pacific. In my childhood recollections, American militarism is an obvious presence, but tourism—with its structuring ideas and practices of mobility and consumption—is *the* perfect partner to militarism's claims to security. The two forces work together to produce gendered structures of feeling and formations of knowledge that are routinized into everyday life and are crucial to the practices and habits of U.S. imperialism in the region.[4] As an American soldier and a sunbathing tourist, Joe is understood to be the product of a modernity to which colonial subjects aspire but inevitably fall short. His masculinized mobilities describe the privileges of imperial governance and desire that positioned me—and Filipinos in general—as his de facto hosts, playing out a familiar and enduring relationship of accommodation.[5]

As the book's title suggests, by placing tourism and militarism within the same analytic lens, I seek to elucidate their mutual constitutions and dependencies. This is a particularly urgent project today in light of tourism's emergence as the savior of developing economies, and the realignment of U.S. military policies in favor of greater flexibility in order to best protect its interests abroad. Tourism and militarism are today interwoven into the everyday and taken-for-granted routines and logics of local and global life, becoming matter-of-fact explanations for themselves and each other. In describing the reach of militarization in the nuclear age, Donna Haraway points to the "incidental" interchangeability of tourism and militarism's technologies of "ultimate mobility and perfect exchange."[6] Yet this overlap between militarism and tourism is better characterized as a strategic and symbiotic convergence. It is by no means only "incidental" that the technologies of one merge so neatly with the other. In Asia and the Pacific, they constitute two of the most dominant apparatuses by which the United States extends its reach, and their convergent cultures, histories, and gendered logics suggest a more mutually constitutive relationship. *Securing Paradise* departs from existing studies in tourism and militarism because it foregrounds how tourism and militarism's *mutual* work produces the possibilities for American historical and contemporary dominance in the region. The same logics that rationalize the uneven economic and cultural landscapes resulting from unregulated tourism also justify the continuing presence of the American military in the Pacific: jobs, stability, protection, and foreign exchange. As Cynthia Enloe suggests, "Militarism and tourism . . . may be kin, bound together as cause and effect."[7] Militarism and tourism, and the ways they serve each other, illustrate the sometimes brutal and sometimes supple work of U.S. domination in the region: they demonstrate the manifold and overlapping circuits and modes of administrative control, ideological frameworks, and territorial occupations that are part of an American project of domination.

In the title of this book, the concept of *securing* is meant to invoke multiple and intersecting ideas that are at play: the economic security promised by tourism's quick exchange and militarism's infusion and protection of capital; a militarized notion of national security that gained intensity during George W. Bush's "global war against terror"; the politics of travel security invoked by tourism economies against other nation-states; the work involved in guaranteeing and assuring outcomes and relationships between actors, institutions, and states; and the act of taking into custody or acquisition, all of which have historical and present-day resonance with regard to the relationships of the United States with Hawai'i and the Philippines. As such, securing is not only a job for the disciplining arm of the military but also an achievement in tandem with and through the pleasures of consumer practices such as tourism. The Cold War era naturalized the massive buildup of the military-industrial complex and, just as importantly, blurred the distinctions between military and civilian life and politics, particularly in the United States.[8] The ideological frameworks of developmentalism and security that characterized U.S. foreign economic and military policy during the Cold War period merged seamlessly with the booming projects of tourism and militarism in American areas of interest. As a developmental strategy that also began during the Cold War, the promotion by tourism of multiculturalism and its updated message of economic uplift personified "liberalization with a human face," softening the austere policies dictated by supranational lending organizations such as the World Bank and International Monetary Fund, which exploited and produced neocolonial economies while ventriloquizing postcolonial homilies.[9]

Even as tourism appears as the "softer" colonial apparatus, as I discuss in the first chapter, its extractive logics and damaging epistemologies are no less hard edged than the kind militarism puts into play. Tourism's amenability to delivering the values of consumer culture across borders made it an ideal Cold War ambassador.[10] It secured, through paternalistic demands for structural adjustments and the exploitation of a feminized service industry, the exploitative conditions and habits of extraterritorial control that serve the New World Order, all the while masking these relations of power through the seductive romance of uplift and development. Indeed, sometimes militarism works best when it has saturated the consumer practices and ideologies of tourism to the point of disappearance, as I discuss in my chapter on helicopter tours. Folded and woven into the fabric of consumer tourist practices, the inextricability of militarism from the consumer culture of capitalism camouflages how it has become a matter-of-fact part of security. Tourism—with its ties to consumer freedom and unfettered mobility—establishes a certain ideological, political, and cultural order that normalizes the presence of the military, prioritizes its needs, and defends its central role in defining "national security."[11] In its articulations with militarism, tourism is more than "just" a consumer practice: its most enabling conditions—that of mobility and modernity—are guaranteed by, at the very least, a racialized and gendered *idea* of security.

These multiple senses of *securing* thus also amplify the gendered logics that structure militarism and tourism. Invoking the ideas of domestic, personal, and national safety, and stability guaranteed by masculine labor and sacrifice, securing takes the form of guardianship and assumes a heroic modern state as the protector of weak and feminized territories and peoples. Asymmetrical imperial relations among the United States, Asia, and the Pacific produce and rely on an "invitation to conquest" as the necessary foil for the implied masculine thrust (discovery, pacification, liberation, development) of the United States.[12] Both militarism and tourism rely on sedimented notions of colonized land and people (especially women) as passively there for the taking. This sexualized metaphor— what Anne McClintock has called "porno-tropics"—does not merely describe the character of broader international relations, or attitudes about the exploitability of land, natural resources, and people; it also represents how these claims are staked out in real-life terms.[13] For instance, the robust militarized "rest and recreation" industry is both made imaginable through fantasies of the eroticized exotic feminine serving the "needs" of men in uniform and coauthorized by the lopsided fraternal alliances of occupying and occupied states.[14] *Security*, then, is a fiction of masculinized rescue and protection that is belied by the realities of state-sanctioned violence against women: the nature of security generated simultaneously by and in the convergences of militarism and tourism is akin to a perverse romance negotiated between masculine heads of state and procured by the currency of women's bodies and feminized lands.[15]

While the products of the mutual labors of tourism and militarism are most starkly illuminated by this systematized state-level gendered violence, the so-called legitimate and self-legitimizing forms of tourism and militarism that tend to escape political and academic condemnation are the objects of this study. These tolerated and even desired military-tourism assemblages, just as powerfully as their illicit siblings, generate more conventional familial and state romances that critically reinforce the racialized and gendered relations of the New World Order. These romances run the gamut from the pilgrimages of fraternal soldierhood in the transnational itineraries of war memorialization to the insistent radioactive blindness of the Western heterosexual tourist gaze as it encounters bikinis in the Pacific.[16] As more legitimate forms of "militourism," tourist acts such as visiting historic battlefields or even sunbathing on the beach are always already refracted through desires to identify with masculinities that have been mobilized in the service of extraterritorial domination.[17] In Asia and the Pacific, these "militourisms" take place on terrains that have long felt the impact of being objects of imperial desire.

In articulating *securing* to *paradise*, I want to emphasize the generative role played by masculinized and militarized desires for security in America's broader imperial project. *Paradise* is not a generic or static term—it specifically refers to an idea of passivity and penetrability engendered by imperialism as an alibi for domination, as Edward Said and others have so ably demonstrated.[18] The profoundly gendered and racialized tropics referenced by contemporary tourist usages of paradise— timeless, passive, island spaces with beaches ringed by palm trees, blue waters, warm sun, and welcoming, sensual yet innocent natives—have their roots in European fantasies of the New World.[19] Driving colonial desire was the idea of a premodern and pristine paradise—a virgin terrain ripe for economic exploitation and for masculine dreams of discovery and exploration. In her political history of tourism in Cuba and Hawai'i, Christine Skwiot suggests that for the United States paradise was a racialized political myth born of an intense process of social and economic collaboration and conflicts over power and land.[20] In other words, paradise is by no means natural—it is conjured through imaginative labor, sustained by such economic apparatuses as plantation and tourism industries and the hierarchized societies they engender, secured through the threat and reality of violence or the promise of rescue, and continually contested by the people who live there.[21]

Locating "paradise" in the nexus of American touristic and militaristic designs on Asia and the Pacific makes visible the maneuvers of U.S. imperialism that have profoundly shaped life in the region, particularly in the last century.[22] Focusing on the neocolonial spaces of Hawai'i and the Philippines, and their central roles in the American militarization of Asia and the Pacific, *Securing Paradise* offers an analysis of tourism's and militarism's articulations in the region by examining how they jointly enable overlapping projects of colonialism, developmentalism, and neoliberalism.[23] I use *neocolonial* as an umbrella term here not to connote a break with an officially imperial past, but as a way to capture how colonialism has been "rearticulated, muted, and unmoored through discourses of neoliberalism, postmodernism, postcolonialism and 'antiterrorism,'" as well as to recognize the enduring and adaptive struggles of Filipino and Native Hawaiian peoples to counter the devastating effects of U.S. interventions in Asia and the Pacific.[24] At stake in this project is a refusal to abandon the narrative of American imperial history and desire to the joint fictions of security and paradise that tourism and militarism coauthorize.

LINKED GEOGRAPHIES AND HISTORIES OF PARADISE

Less than two years after we moved to the United States, the People Power Revolution ushered out the Marcos dictatorship. My family watched on television as, a world away, hundreds of thousands of Filipinos took to the streets to protest the irregular and fraudulent results of a snap election. Led by the widow of the assassinated former senator Benigno Aquino, Jr., and backed by the Catholic Church, the revolution teetered on the edge of violence until finally successfully ousting the Marcos regime.[25] Apart from the indelible image of Imelda Marcos's three thousand pairs of shoes, one of the most arresting moments of the revolution materialized when the Marcoses were granted safe passage and escorted from Malacañang Palace by four American helicopters. They were taken to the U.S. Air Force's Clark Air Base, just eighty-three miles north of Manila. Minutes later, at 9:52 p.m. on February 25, 1986, the radio station DZRH announced, "The Marcoses have fled the country." The helicopters, their flight to Clark, and the base's extraterritorial status illuminated—for a brief but power-ful moment—how U.S. political and military machinations had played an outsized role in the domestic matters of the Philippines. Further, the Marcoses' escape route—to the American base in the Philippines, then to Guam en route to Hawai'i—mapped out the tropical cartography of American desire, showing how American militarism and the economies of tourism incorporated far-flung places into the same circuits.

In Asia and the Pacific, Hawai'i and the Philippines are pivotal Ameri-can tropics. As sites of fantastical imaginings and military occupations, they mark the uneasy tensions between America and its others, American republican ideals and the U.S. state's imperial historical record, and the voyeuristic and violent fantasies of the tourist and the soldier. In contrast to the types of American militarism and tourism that exist elsewhere in the world, such as battleground sites in Europe, U.S. occupations of and with Asia and the Pacific are specifically about the control and occupation of land.[26] Today, although Japan has the largest contingent of tourists in the region, it is the peculiarly American strain of Orientalism that Paul Lyons has called "American Pacificism" that has dictated the fate of this region, how it can be imagined, and how it can and should be secured.[27] Real estate in the forms of colonial outposts and military bases as well as the promised markets and resources of Asia are the stakes of past and con-tinued American interests in the area. Although it is not a uniquely U.S. invention, this mutual deployment of tourism and militarism has been managed successfully by the United States, which continues to navigate the "complex global/local dialectics of jet mass tourism and U.S. exoticism projected in the Pacific" alongside American military imagination, occu-pation, and U.S. interstate partnerships that produce the homosocial alli-ances and heteronormative romances of securing paradise.[28]

The United States was not the first or only colonial power to assert its hegemony in Hawai'i and the Philippines. However, its forays into extra-continental empire have enduringly defined these sites primarily as femi-nized tropics and subjected them to its masculinized modes of security. In contrast to the Philippines, held under Spanish colonial administration from the sixteenth to the nineteenth centuries, Hawai'i was a sovereign kingdom that was undergoing struggles for internal unification and also fighting off external attempts on its autonomy. Massive population de-clines in Hawai'i following the arrival of European explorers in the mid-1700s produced conditions for exploitation, dispossession, and cultural adaptation.[29] The arrival of American Calvinist missionaries in 1820 accelerated the erosion of the Kingdom of Hawai'i's political autonomy and cultural integrity, criminalizing Hawaiian cultural practices and imposing Western gendered norms of domestic behavior.[30] As an extension of this legal hastening of cultural death, the settler elite alienated Native Hawaiians from their land through legislative maneuvers that allowed foreign land ownership in Hawai'i by midcentury, which destroyed the foundations of Native political and economic self-determination.[31]

Where European empires had failed, an American economic oligarchy, in tandem with the rising American military, would succeed. Under the cover of a two-month tropical holiday, two high-ranking officers undertook a reconnaissance mission in 1873 that confirmed Hawai'i's desirability as a naval port.[32] Threatened by the resurgent nationalism of the monarchy and the Hawaiian people, an empowered plantation oligarchy (composed of missionary sons) and the U.S. Navy collaborated to virtually depose the monarchy by forcing the king to sign the 1887 Bayonet Constitution. This was followed swiftly by the revision and renewal of the original 1875 Reciprocity Treaty, which had allowed for the tariff-free importation of sugar to the United States. The territorial rights granted to the U.S. military—in what was essentially a land grant to Pearl Harbor—paralleled the political rights that white foreigners claimed for themselves even as the voting rights of Native men were rolled back. Mustering the military interests and muscle of the United States, and tying it to their capitalist interests, the foreign oligarchy styled themselves as men of modern republican rule, in contrast to the royal (and unmanly) excesses of King David Kalākaua. This maneuver was not a historical accident; rather, it was the culmination of decades of American longing for Pacific real estate and its strategic access to the markets of Asia, particularly China.[33] Securing American ascendancy in its imperial voyage across the Pacific and Asia, Hawai'i served as the American military's first foothold in the Pacific, which would have profound implications for the long-term sovereignty of both Hawai'i and the Philippines.

While Hawai'i struggled against the ambitions of its missionary-plantation oligarchy and the designs of the U.S. Navy, the Philippines had started on its long road to revolution against its Spanish colonizers. The Catholic Church had taken on the project of converting the indigenous peoples while Spanish colonial rule replaced the existing communal land system with feudal practices of land tenure, creating a land-owning elite on whom the majority of the landless rural population was dependent.[34]

By the late 1800s, tensions were at a boiling point in the Spanish colony: led by dispossessed and abused landless masses and an educated native elite, an armed anticolonial revolution had begun.[35] Eyeing the decline of the Spanish empire, and fueled by its own expansionist desires, the United States prepared for war against Spain's far-flung colonial outposts. Yellow journalism and jingoistic politicking successfully deployed anxieties about American manhood to prime a national public toward military intervention in Cuba.[36] The 1898 attack on the USS *Maine* in Cuba's Havana Harbor ignited war fever. Soon after, the United States declared war against Spain and sent invading armies to Cuba, Puerto Rico, and the Philippines. Effectively effacing the centuries of anti-Spanish rebellion by Filipino, Cuban, and Puerto Rican peoples, U.S. intervention in these territories ensured the continuation of empire, albeit under a different and more modern administration.

By the time the Spanish-American War broke out, the penultimate blow against Hawaiian sovereignty had already been struck. The 1893 overthrow of Queen Liliʻuokalani by a coalition of American business investors was secured by the tacit support of an American warship moored just off the coast of Oʻahu to protect "American interests." The outbreak of the war sealed the fate of Hawaiʻi, which had been resolutely protesting and resisting the "act of war" against its internationally recognized sovereignty.[37] As the host of the United States' main naval outpost in the Pacific, Hawaiʻi's military usefulness in the Pacific theater of what Ambassador John Hay called "a splendid little war" overrode any lingering ethical doubts about the illegality of the overthrow.

Once Hawaiʻi and the Philippines were pulled into the orbit of the United States, their modern fates became more interdependent. Having taken credit for dispatching the Spanish empire, the United States began its military occupation of the Philippine islands, much to the dismay of Filipino revolutionaries who had declared their independence from Spain prior to the end of hostilities.[38] The swift takeover of the Philippines illustrated the young American nation's political savvy and global ambitions as well as what would be an enduring impulse for unilateralism. Symbolically, the invading American fleet in Manila Bay included the USS *Boston*, the ship that had been instrumental in the overthrow of Hawaiʻi's monarchy just five years before.[39] When the Philippine-American War broke out, it also provided the perfect alibi to resolve the constitutionally vexed question of Hawaiʻi's status vis-à-vis the United States. Despite the considerable efforts of the Native Hawaiian people to resist both overthrow and annexation, shortly after the United States began hostilities against Spain, the protracted debates over Hawai'i's annexation were suspended when the United States annexed the islands without a popular referendum.[40] Inextricably tied together through the imperial military and commercial dreams of the United States in the region, Hawai'i and the Philippines would share linked fates as part of the American chain of islands: Hawai'i provided the perfect depot for American ships to refuel and take on supplies for what would be a protracted campaign of "pacification" in the Philippines, and the Philippines would send Filipino labor to the plantation economy of Hawai'i, further reinforcing the legitimacy of the plantation economy as the governing interest in the islands.

In this intense drive toward empire, the military was not the only colonial apparatus at work, although perhaps it wielded the most decisive power. Tourism as a cultural apparatus inspired and mobilized a deeply militarized desire for Hawai'i and the Philippines. Depicting the imperial encounter as the inevitable meeting of civilized people with the barbarians of the world, travelogues contrasted the tropics with the enlightened and industrialized West.[41] While these travel narratives ranged from outright racist portrayals to the more nostalgic romanticization of untouched and undiscovered premodern life, as a whole their production of the rest of the world as backward and in need of uplift served to justify the military project that would soon secure these territories as colonial outposts.[42] Indeed, the world of the soldier and that of the tourist were often one and the same, illuminating how the routes of travel were mapped out and shared by military and civilian alike. American travelers often doubled as early military reconnaissance. As I discuss in chapter 1, early travelers and embedded journalists often scouted just ahead of or alongside the military, writing about the adventure of being the first to penetrate into the hinterlands. Their early travel narratives and colonial fictions established the literary and visual terms that framed the tropical possessions of the United States as land to be claimed: this early tourist gaze, then, shared the inclination for ownership and control that defined military itineraries.[43] The masculine eye of military surveyors and travelers, their technologized mobilities, and their will to penetrate land they viewed as receptive to and in need of being claimed illuminate how the roots of tourism and militarism relied on a belief of the profound governability of the tropics. The 1898 annexation of Hawai'i, for example, recycled the military argument of protecting U.S. interests and applied it to the broader region through the deployment of these familiar gendered and racialized tropes. Queen Lili'uokalani fought a public relations and diplomatic struggle against an American press that portrayed her as a recalcitrant queen, a dictator, and a sorceress—especially gendered symbols of the Native Hawaiian people's incapability of self-rule.[44]

While debates raged in Congress over the colonial status of the Philippines, Hawai'i was further absorbed into U.S. circuits, and both sites were rapidly militarized. Investing in the development of Pearl Harbor and ceded Hawaiian lands, the United States began to establish a Pacific military garrison, initiating the first step toward the region's militarization.[45] In tandem with the ongoing brutality of the Philippine-American War, the Philippines islands were similarly militarized through an executive order that confiscated thousands of acres of land to establish air and naval bases.[46] As the influence of the United States grew in the region, it invested heavily in its Pacific military garrison, paving the way for increased military and civilian travel in these secured territories. In the years between World Wars I and II, the United States tripled the numbers of military personnel stationed in Hawai'i, and it further expanded its territorial and personnel presence in the Philippines.[47] This occupation of Hawai'i put in place a military regime that populated the islands with thousands of young, unattached men "needing" rest and recreation—Joe's predecessors.[48] Just as the United States viewed Hawai'i and the Philippines as feminized territories needing discipline and protection, so too did its soldiers expect eroticized relations with the people they disciplined and protected. Following the genre of travel narratives, the military enlisted familiar textual/sexual language and visual imagery of tropical paradise to lure soldiers to the perils of island tours of duty: it drew on "a picture straight from a prewar travel brochure," desires circulated in early twentieth-century hula tours on the continent, and, later, popular Hollywood films set in the tropics to recruit personnel.[49] These early military men, as proto–mass tourists, brought a particularly sexualized vision of the tropics-as-paradise into the American national consciousness. In Hawai'i and the Philippines, militarism jump-started the first tourist establishments on the islands: catering to military and colonial personnel, zones for rest and recreation cropped up, exploiting fantasies—if not always realities—of the exotic.[50]

Over the course of Hawai'i's Territorial Era (1898–1959), and the U.S.

administration of the Philippines (1898–1946), the close relationship between tourism and militarism was established. While the course of colonialism did not always run smoothly, and there were contradictions of vision and policy between the military and the settled white elite oligarchy in Hawai'i and the wave of civilian reformers that flooded the Philippines, their shared goal of imperialism eyed the benighted populations of the tropics as the ultimate target. Expanding the domestic—in its multiple senses—by exporting it and by enlarging the circle of colonial agents to include women, government administrators, missionaries, medical workers, teachers, engineers, and businesspeople, the colonial project undertook a slate of reform, hygiene, education, and economic projects *and* constituted the tourists of this early period.[51] The military secured the safety of the civilians as they undertook these itineraries of uplift, collaborating to smooth the path of occupation and colonial rule. Likewise, the U.S. military turned to the softer discourses and mechanisms of tourism to help mitigate the historical violence and reality of military occupation in the islands. For example, the military took on projects such as road building to rehabilitate its public relations, exchanging promises of constructive colonialism and mobility for its recent history of brutality and unfreedom. Even as they were increasingly militarized, Hawai'i and the Philippines were managed in a more "benevolent" fashion, reflecting the Progressive Era politics of the age, as well as a general belief in both the innocence of U.S. imperial motivations and its benign and modern brand of colonialism.[52]

However, though intertwining commercial and military desires led to the proliferation of military bastions of American-defined security in the region, it was not until after World War II and the subsequent Cold War that mass tourism emerged as a global force on par with militarism. Faced with the bold threat of an ambitious Japan and its vision of an Asian co-prosperity sphere that excluded Western influence, and spurred by the Japanese attack on Pearl Harbor in 1941, the United States entered into a protracted war against a competing imperial power. The war in the region comprised multiple engagements and fronts, animating place-names such as Pearl Harbor, Nanking, Midway, Bataan, Corregidor, Okinawa, Hiroshima, and Nagasaki with the grisly violence and sentimental power of war. Hawai'i (as the site of the first foreign attack on U.S. soil) and the Philippines (which hosted a series of spectacular and significant losses to and victories against the Japanese military) represented vital nodes of

U.S. military engagement during World War II. In the postwar restructuring and rebuilding of the region, they were also key locations of U.S. military occupation, as well as places where a reinvigorated and remade Japan established its postwar economic credentials as an ostensibly nonmilitary nation in partnership with the United States. The enduring narratives of masculine sacrifice and heroism of World War II constituted the framing narrative of these interstate relations.

Following World War II, the Philippines was granted independence, limping on to economic and political autonomy under the shadow of its former colonial master, and was subsequently marginalized from American popular consciousness. Unlike occupied and reconstructed Japan, the Philippines was not a centerpiece for American economic hegemony but was a showcase for official postwar decolonization. However, American bases remained firmly ensconced even after independence, as guaranteed through the 1947 Military Bases Agreement and Military Assistance Pact, and U.S. support for subsequent Filipino administrations remained necessary to political success. In contrast, the Territory of Hawai'i was named a state in 1959, substantiating a vision of Hawai'i as a Pacific economic hub and a bastion for American military strength in the 1960s. Signaling a shift in the racial politics of Hawai'i, a social and political revolution led by Japanese Americans pushed for statehood, further displacing Native Hawaiians from sovereignty in their own lands, and ushering in a long reign of Democratic machine politics.[53] Cold War militarization was accompanied by Cold War economic policy, and tourism played a vital part. With hot wars being waged in Korea and Vietnam—and escalating tensions with China—Hawai'i and the Philippines not only remained strongholds of American military might in the region and strategically important training grounds for Pacific troops, but also began aggressive tourism programs to boost their economies and images.

The democratization of travel in the post–World War II era— inaugurated, not coincidentally, by the militarization of Asia and the Pacific—deepened the ongoing collaboration between tourism and militarism. This legacy has durability: today, the military continues to be a significant "visitor" in the region. Following World War II, advances in technology, such as jet travel and traveler's checks, opened what was once mostly in the purview of the wealthy—travel to exotic destinations—to an increasingly middle-class clientele.[54] The territories of the Pacific, defended by the Allies, were transformed into new exotic frontier destinations, its rediscovery staged by the militarized geographies of war. During the Cold War, furnished with airstrips formerly used for refueling and repair and secured by the sacrifices of soldiers, these Pacific islands were poised for a new wave of invaders. Tourism in particular was a key export that displayed the benefits of capitalism and democracy during the Cold War era, a vehicle fit for disciplinary formations of knowledge production that accompanied the geopoliticking and hot wars of the Cold War.[55] The images produced by tourism had significant rhetorical influence when coupled with the sentimentality of Pearl Harbor, for instance, when Hawai'i campaigned for statehood.[56] In the context of the tensions in Asia and the Pacific, the Hawai'i of James Michener's imagination was a "paradise redeemed in Cold War terms," as was the Philippines, the newest decolonized nation-state on the block.[57] The Philippines, in turn, continued to be the U.S. military's "little brown brother," benefiting from U.S. military expenditures, as well as establishing its own fledgling visitor industry. The body of regulatory knowledge produced by tourism in Hawai'i and the Philippines helped to disavow colonial and World War II occupations and Cold War military interventions and to discredit the alternatives of active decolonization movements in these and other sites in the region.

In everyday terms, both U.S. military personnel and tourists are a familiar sight in both Hawai'i and the Philippines, and they are valued for the kinds of security they ostensibly symbolize as well as for the ways their mutually embracing forms of logic operate to affirm touristic hegemonies and regional militarization.[58] Today, the U.S. Pacific Fleet in Pearl Harbor, the world's largest naval command, stands guard over what Noel Kent has described as the new plantation society of tourism, which makes up just over 15–20 percent of Hawai'i's economy.[59] Likewise, the United States' 2007–2009 federal defense investment in this colonial outpost averaged $6.5 billion per year, contributing to 10–18 percent of the economy.[60] The Philippine economy, meanwhile, has historically struggled, posting slower growth than that of the Asian dragons, and today it shows a GNP barely twice that of Hawai'i's. Tourism, long touted as the panacea for developing economies, has lagged in the Philippines, despite efforts on the part of current and recent administrations at boosting the Philippines as a tourist economy.[61] Comparable Southeast Asian economies such as Vietnam post greater visitor numbers, yet the Philippines still touts tourism as one of its economic saviors. The U.S. military presence in the Philippines continues through Visiting Forces Agreements despite its official 1992 exit from Clark Air Base and Subic Bay Naval Facility, formerly two of the largest military bases in the region. Compared to what the Department of Defense spends in Hawaiʻi (as well as on Middle Eastern allies such as Israel and Egypt), official U.S. military aid to the Philippines is modest ($500 million from 2002 to 2012), yet it constitutes a significant military investment in East Asia and the Pacific.[62] Even with changes in military policy that call for greater flexibility of forces, the United States continues to oversee the region through a string of military bases: Guam is the most recent site of the kind of military buildup that promises to have massive ramifications for local and regional relations. With China passing Japan's surprisingly robust military spending (for its "defense" forces) in 2006, and with North Korea's emergence as a particularly troubling security issue for the United States, Asia and the Pacific have remained key areas for the United States to police.[63]

Trade, foreign capital, and U.S. "interests" remain the top reasons for such close protection: the region is a significant component of American economic health. Today, Asia-Pacific Economic (APEC) economies account for 60 percent of U.S. exports.[64] A military-industrial complex that has run rampant is another reason: since 2000, the global budget for military spending has increased 49 percent, an upward trend that benefited from post-9/11 militarization.[65] In the last few decades, the U.S. military budget has dwarfed its nearest competitors, constituting between 40–50 percent of global military spending, reaching $663 billion per annum in 2009.[66] The Pacific Command, which constitutes one-fifth of total U.S. military strength, consistently cites the economic importance of the region, as if to say that the increasingly bloated budget of the United States is necessary to the stability of this economically vital region.[67] More specifically, Asia and the Pacific represent key tourist economies that rely on the "protections" of the U.S. armed services. Tourism is a primary economic engine for the region, as well as the dominant gateway through which the region is imagined and understood. While Asia and the Pacific generate 8.4 percent of economic returns from tourism, they are not the standard-bearers of the tourism economy at large. However, collectively, Asia and the Pacific brought in international tourism receipts totaling $469 billion in 2011, and the region continues to emerge as a rising star of global tourism, with a projected growth rate of 4.9 percent in a sluggish economy, further illustrating the importance of tourism as a developmental strategy for states in Asia and the Pacific.[68] Within the region, APEC's member economies have been urged to use tourism as an instrument for developing countries due to its potential for generating jobs and income.[69] In partnership with the increasing visibility of tourism economies and cultures in the post-9/11 era, the region has also been increasingly militarized, though in more flexible ways that respond to the continuing security challenges of the region in an "era of persistent conflict" that "requires a strategy of persistent engagement."[70]

THE ARCHIVES OF PARADISE SECURED

I undertook the research for this project in part as a tourist in highly militarized and "touricized" (for lack of a more elegant term) spaces from 2000 to 2011. While also an ethnography of the everyday negotiations between tourists and hosts and their ramifications for national and international relations, in this inquiry I am more interested in how societies, in the ways they operate, prioritize the different logics and economies of tourism and militarism. I pay attention to the cultural artifacts and practices that are produced within the intersections of militarism and tourism. The archive of this project—ranging from more traditional literary texts, such as novels, poetry, guidebooks, and travel narratives; to visual texts, such as photographs and film; to constructed infrastructures, such as buildings, highways, and military bases; and to social experiences, such as tours, demonstrations, and interviews—attempts to capture the scope of sociocultural forms and meanings produced, sustained, and consumed in the places where militarism and tourism overlap.[71]

The sociocultural artifacts and practices examined in this book are contemporary. Yet while this is not a historical exploration of militarism-tourism assemblages in Hawai'i and the Philippines, it does attend to how specific historical moments generate different convergent formations of militarism and tourism. The organization of the book roughly follows U.S. war projects in Asia and the Pacific that are sutured to U.S. military-tourism practices: paired chapters discuss different sites and practices that deal primarily with the Philippine-American War, World War II, and the Vietnam War. Critically juxtaposing rather than comparing, the chapters elaborate upon the specific histories, actors, and apparatuses at work in the construction of military and touristic regimes, and how they are flexible and durable over time and space. This selection of social/cultural texts is by no means comprehensive, but it does illustrate the breadth and depth of collaboration between militarism and tourism.

Securing Paradise begins with a critical look at the sustaining gendered and racialized fictions of militarism and tourism within the larger historical context of American colonial domination. Chapter 1 reflects on the literary text as a key site of imperial representation as well as a location where feminist counterhegemonic theorizations about the relationship between tourism and militarism can take place. Opposing the masculine colonial fictions of traveling journalists during the Philippine-American War with the critical feminist fictions of Filipina and Native Hawaiian women during the late Cold War era, I highlight the invention of the tropics by the former and its contravention by the latter. Chapter 2 likewise draws connections between the early colonial era's progressive mission to the Cold War's programs of development and modernization by examining American road building in the Philippines during the earlier twentieth century and in Hawai'i during the late twentieth century as they shaped colonial and military modes of mobility, control, and surveillance. Both examples that I focus on here — Kennon Road in the northern region of the Philippines, built to create access to the colonial hill station of Baguio, and the modern H-3 Interstate, which connects two military bases through the Ko'olau Mountains on O'ahu — illustrate how the scenic highway is a modern regulatory apparatus that creates masculinized regimes of mobility and visuality (that is, ways of moving and seeing) in feminized occupied territories.

Continuing the exploration of other built texts and the structures of feeling they produce, the next two chapters focus on military bases as primary spaces where tourism and militarism interact. In chapter 3, I tie together Corregidor Island, the Bataan memorials, and the former Clark and Subic Bases in the Philippines in a circuit of military tourism that depends on an evolving notion of American liberation over the course of a century. In their updated incarnations as tourist destinations of World War II history and special economic zones, these sites are squarely positioned within Cold War and post–Cold War collaborations between the two nations, animating new fraternal alliances and relationships that rely on memories of American benevolence and liberation. Chapter 4 examines how the forms of tourism generated by the USS *Arizona* Memorial and its auxiliary sites produce an insistent narrative of innocence and sacrifice that is crucial to the continued military occupation of Hawai'i. Intertwined with this military/tourist pedagogy of preparedness and national security, a visit to the USS *Arizona* and its partner sites carries out a disappearance of historic U.S. military designs on Hawai'i. Steeped in nostalgic discourses of masculine heroic suffering and sacrifice, these public spaces tell stories of interracial and international military camaraderie in the throes of World War II while suspending histories of overthrow, segregation, disenfranchisement, and racial violence.

In the book's last two chapters, I look at two different technologies mobilized during the Vietnam War and the kinds of subjectivities and imaginations they enable today. These two chapters illustrate the increasingly slippery translations of military skills and technologies to tourism and back again. Chapter 5 examines the ubiquitous helicopter tours that are one of the most popular ways to take in the island landscape of Kaua'i. Negotiating the thin line between military violence and tourist pleasures, these helicopter tours enable reenactments of discovery narratives on feminized, indigenized terrains while forging an alternate ending to the masculine trauma of Vietnam. In contrast with the modern technology of helicopters, chapter 6 focuses on how an indigenous skill set was first militarized and then subsequently repackaged for tourists at the Subic Freeport's "jungle school." Masculinized notions of soldiering and touring are linked in this particular tour, as tourists play soldier and soldiers play native, shedding light on the ways in which indigenous masculinities are recruited into circuits of militarism and tourism.

My conclusion examines both the everyday and spectacular realities that result from how militarism and tourism intimately converge in Hawai'i and the Philippines, focusing on the assemblages of cultural life in the region after 9/11. While the landscape of the post–Cold War era, the increasing liberalization of the region under the influence of transnational capital, and even the global war on terror lack the drama of war that so deeply shaped the lives of those in Asia and the Pacific, both Hawai'i and the Philippines continue to have important roles in the constitution of American identity and power. The Philippines—as the first sponsor of Bush's war against terror in the post-9/11 era, continues to unofficially host American troops—and Hawai'i—as the home of the largest naval base in the Pacific—stand guard over this region as bulwarks against "antiterrorism" and the saber rattling of "rogue" states. Today, Hawai'i and the Philippines continue, with varying degrees of success, to promote themselves as tropical paradises and exemplify what it means to secure paradise in today's increasingly insecure world.

One

❋

MANIFEST DESTINATIONS
AND THE WORK OF
TROPICAL FICTIONS

Every society is known by the fictions that it keeps.
—CATHERINE STIMPSON, FOREWORD TO BEDERMAN, *MANLINESS AND CIVILIZATION*, XI

In a graphic torture scene in her successful 1988 novel *State of War*, Ninotchka Rosca conjures up a connection between the upsurge in literary and touristic consumption of the Philippines in the late twentieth century, and its long and complex history of domination by foreign militaries, economic policies, and politics. Set roughly during the Marcos regime in the Philippines (1965–86), which Rosca depicts as the latest episode of an undeclared and perpetual state of war, the novel weaves together the stories of three main characters whose genealogies represent the diverse archetypes of contemporary Philippine society. *State of War* unnervingly juxtaposes a dreamily textured and lushly tropical Philippines with a Philippines wracked by colonialism, corruption, and violence. Rosca's portrayal of the Philippines as a surreal, hazy tropics—bludgeoned and numbed by years of colonial violence—cannily uses an exploitative rhetoric of tourism to attract First World readers to a Third World spectacle. She perverts this language even as she deploys it, however, distorting these tropics while and by implicating the reader as a participant-consumer in a corrupt economic and political world order. Like James Clifford—who "hang[s] on to 'travel' as a term of cultural comparison precisely because of its historical 'taintedness,' its associations with gendered, racial bodies, class privilege, specific means of conveyance, beaten paths, agents, frontiers, documents, and the like"—Rosca embraces the taintedness and usefulness of travel as an enabling critical concept and method.[1] She refuses to dismiss the potency of the orientalizing rhetoric of tourism, infusing it instead with a historicity of its genealogy in colonialism: State of War wrestles with the dilemmas produced by the literary possibilities and tourist mobilities of the imperial moment and the economies of globalization.[2] It seduces the reader with its invocation of familiar and expected images and, in the same instance, exposes the terms of that seduction.

Written in verdant, almost lulling prose reminiscent of travelogues, State of War is punctuated with staccato bursts of brutality such as the torture of Anna Villaverde by the ironically named Colonel Urbano Amor:

> He turned her over to two soldiers who stripped her carefully, attached electrodes to her nipples, and proceeded to crank a field battery to life. The current of pain stenciled the meaning of error into her cells. Screaming, arching her back and head in a parody of passion, Anna could see the tiny letters on the canvas sheath of the generator. It was an important piece of equipment, blue seal as they would say, made in the U.S.A. A continent half a world away.[3]

Despite this torture, Anna—a young widow of a political activist and one of the novel's trio of protagonists—refuses to divulge the name of Guevarra, a guerrilla fighter and fellow prisoner who had escaped the political prison in which they were both held. Her stint in the prison—which parallels the wholesale tortures, kidnapping, executions and disappearances of the Marcos martial law administration—implicates the collusions between the Philippine state and its former colonial master—the United States—as one of the root causes of long-standing violence against the Filipino people. The dissonance between the novel's surreal tropical imagery and the matter-of-fact prose in this particular scene calls attention to the mutual partnerships and collusions at work in the production and consumption of the Philippines as paradise. Rosca implies that the dreamscape's pleasures could not exist without the discipline of a militarized state and, conversely, that the state of war is both alibi and guarantor of the Philippines as a literary-touristic fantasy.[4]

The scene of Anna's torture—and Rosca's novel, in general—walks the thin line of "spectacularizing" historical pain for aesthetic pleasure and of reifying a sexualized and racialized victimhood for the reader's discomfort *and* gratification: it is both bearing witness and pornographic. While the act of rape and torture haunts her novel, becoming the symbolic fulcrum upon which rebellion and revenge turn, embedding the presentation of those acts in a fictive tropical fantasy captures the dilemmas of the postcolonial writer whose work circulates mostly in the center of empire. Rosca's strategic narration of the savage tropics—using yet interrupting tropicalized imagery with explicit scenes of torture that are in themselves problematically spectacularized and consumed—performs multiple duties: it strips bare the violent discipline needed to secure paradise; it proposes a way to assemble an archive that at once reflects and critiques the conditions of postcolonialism; it advances a way to read this archive with attention to gender, the state, and power; and it grapples with the complicities of writing the tropics.

This chapter examines a double set of literary fictions that demonstrate how society-defining fictions—see the chapter epigraph—offer not so much conclusive evidence or clearly defined perspectives, but instead a set of critical questions about histories, archives, and methodologies. How do these fictions address the history of material and epistemological colonialisms that constitute the conditions of their existence? How do they, as Jenny Sharpe suggests, use fiction's license "to imagine events as they might have happened or in a way that history has failed to record"?[5] In what ways do these fictions constitute an archive that can address and illuminate how colonialism and postcolonialism operate? What other contingent, partial, and contradictory archives do these fictions suggest, and what modes of reading do they theorize for these provisional assemblages?

I use the term *manifest destination* in the chapter's title to encapsulate two kinds of work performed by the two sets of fictions that I have marshaled in this chapter. The first grouping of fictions this chapter attends to—those exemplified by Rosca's novel and Haunani-Kay Trask's poetry—presents a Cold War archive that understands the constructive impulse of a modern American global mode of governance to be an updated extension of mid-nineteenth-century Manifest Destiny. Writing from within the spaces brought into the orbit of the American Century, Rosca and Trask elaborate on the process of "manifesting"—that is, establishing—the world as a series of targets for the United States, both for its growing military power and the exportation of its model of political economy. In Hawai'i and the Philippines, manifesting destinations involve both the gendered and racialized justification and use of military force and the productive conversion of the tropics into eroticized commodities for the tourism industry. As the benevolent architect of this constructive global governance, the United States deploys both the carrot and the stick. The spectacular bombing of World War II in Hawai'i virtually guaranteed and justified the regarrisoning of the islands: during World War II and the Cold War, the U.S. military in Hawai'i expanded its land acquisitions, further eroding Native Hawaiian claims under the banner of security. The year 1947 marked the establishment of the new Pacific Command in Hawai'i, as well as the Military Bases Agreement that ensured continued U.S. occupation of military sites in the Philippines. The post–World War II era renewed the U.S. commitment to Asia and the Pacific in line with Cold War anxieties about Communist containment.[6] In the decades that followed World War II, the region was a primary theater for Cold War military posturing as well as violence: the Korean War midcentury emphasized Okinawa's strategic importance in the region, and the Vietnam War highlighted the vulnerability of the mightiest military in the world. With the invasion of Afghanistan in 1979 and the election of Ronald Reagan to presidential office in the following year, Asia and the Pacific continued to be important locations for Cold War performances, guaranteeing their continued militarization.[7] The concomitant ascendance of the tourism industry and mass "exoticization" of the American tropics, in turn, dictated the reception of narratives about the region as well as its commodification as a leisure destination. Rendering these archipelagos into paradises was not new, but a project that reached its apex in the Cold War era with the advent of jet travel and the general promotion of tourism as a quick fix for struggling economies yearning to breathe the free-trade air of the New World Order.

The critical fictions of Rosca and Trask work within and against the narrative constraints of tropicalization (which further legitimates and is further legitimated by the economies and cultures of tourism) to deliver a literary paradise with the jagged edges exposed.[8] Grappling precisely with what makes formations of American empire in the Pacific distinct and modern, Rosca and Trask trace the relations, logics, and practices at play in manifesting Hawai'i and the Philippines as destinations. In contrast to Rosca's and Trask's portrayals of compromised tropics, colonial-era journalists authored the tropics that we have come to expect as a set of destinations. These colonial fictions demonstrate the imaginative work of early fictions — that of making manifest, or obvious — the mission of American imperialism to uplift and properly develop the world's waste spaces. Like the first set of critical fictions, this collection of journalistic narratives addresses the history, archive, and method of empire but through a radically diametric, profoundly masculine perspective that has informed colonial fantasies of the tropics. Reading the second archive of fictions through the eyes of the first underscores the collusions of militarism and tourism as fundamental and specific to the manifestation of destinations by the United States.

THE ROMANCE OF SECURITY

Aimé Cesaire, theorizing the constructiveness of American empire in the years after World War II, points out how the drive to build — "The bulldozers! The massive investments of capital! The roads! The ports!" — marks the modern approach to imperialism that the United States exported to the world.[9] In erecting and gifting infrastructures of development, American imperialism in effect substitutes a narrative of benevolent paternalism for a history of expansion, dispossession, and genocide, a move akin to what Jodi Kim has described as Cold War projects of "gendered racial rehabilitation."[10] The moral force of American progressivism, which provided ideological cover and fuel for American expansion at the turn of the century, however, had long been in practice before the dawn of the Cold War, predating Césaire's predictions about the new nature of American imperialism as the "only domination from which one never recovers."[11] Building on the discourses of what Amy Kaplan has called "manifest domesticity" to ameliorate the violent reality of the U.S. colonial project at the turn of the century, Cold War formations of U.S. imperialism adapted to new configurations of capitalism, developing technologies, and updated forms of governance.[12] What Césaire depicts as the built fictions of modernization, the gift that the United States was holding out to the world, indicated the new "managerial" mode of governance that subordinated extraterritorial lands and peoples to American economic interests.[13]

My use of the term *manifest destinations*, however, not only emphasizes the constructive and productive facets of U.S. global policy, but also gestures to how the Cold War's use of death and pain draws from the tradition of Manifest Destiny's generative violence in the Anglo-American march across the continent. Rosca and Trask link and juxtapose Cold War American practices of death and pain to the United States' stated policy of life and liberty. While attentive to the ways in which American empire achieves its ends through a summons to modernity and progress, Rosca and Trask also grapple with its continued adherence to sheer, old-fashioned brutal force and how the two, in fact, are intimately linked tactics in a flexible imperial arsenal. Precisely because their critical fictions are traces of the unruly afterlives of long-running U.S. imperial occupations and interventions, Rosca and Trask are able to track the diverse exertions that manifest Hawai'i and the Philippines as the destinations of American military and economic desire. *State of War*, published after the Marcos regime was thrown out of the Philippines and written by a journalist and a human rights activist during that regime, captures both the Cold War complicities between U.S. and Philippine political elites, and the colonial historical trajectory that naturalizes these complicities. Rosca was a political prisoner of the Philippine state and an exile to the United States during the U.S.-supported Martial Law era and personifies the displaced postcolonial subject of these U.S.-Philippine collaborations. Haunani-Kay Trask, coming of age as a Native Hawaiian activist in a Hawai'i that had been framed as ineluctably American, faced the daunting tasks of writing against an established narrative of inevitable and beneficial American belonging and fighting the everyday and vexed battles championing indigenous rights against a state all too willing to erode Native sovereignty. Published in 2002, her poetry collection *Night Is a Sharkskin Drum* hones in on the cultural, economic, and political tragedies that were wrought by overthrow, annexation, and statehood in the islands. Taken together, Rosca's and Trask's narratives comprise an alternative formation of knowledge that illuminates Césaire's bulldozers, roads, and ports to be violent fictions of empire.

The potential contradictions between the destructive and constructive methods of manifesting destinations cohere through the romance of security. Relying on the gendered and sexualized romance of security, pain and death are transformed into a productive regime of modernization. Rosca's and Trask's feminist critiques track how the romance of security deploys gendered and sexualized modes and logics to contain the inconsistencies of U.S. global governance. Their interventions are twofold and interrelated. First, they attend to the seductive pull of security as a narrative that casts the United States as the masculine bestower of the gift of modernity (through apparatuses of technology and mobility such as bulldozers, roads, and ports). In turn, the romance of security-as-gift organizes the discourses through which the Philippines and Hawai'i have come to be understood as receptive, feminized tropics waiting to be acted upon and transformed. Attaching the project of manifest destination to the romance of security through auxiliary fictions of pacification, liberation, multiculturalism, and statehood, the fictions of Rosca and Trask break down how, today, it is nearly impossible to imagine these tropics as something other than destinations of leisure, of capital, or of some kind of humanitarian mission. Second, they contend that the romance of security is realized not only through the constructive scripts of U.S. Cold War modernization, but through the more intimate and often tragic encounters of colonial biopower, such as Anna's rape. Rosca and Trask highlight the distorted romances of security as the enabling conditions of modern American empire. For them, the manifold meanings of modern security operate with overlapping regimes of gendered and sexualized discipline, particularly through militarism and tourism. By naming rape and prostitution as the metaphors and corporeal materialities that describe the mutual circuits of tourism and militarism, Rosca and Trask unmask the romance of security as a sexualized relation of power.

In place of a romantic tropical scene, Rosca provides a rape and a rapist—an (ironically named) Amor, whose "love" violates in the name of security. To create a tropical paradise and make the Philippines safe for tourism—according to the prescriptive formulas imparted by the International Monetary Fund (IMF), the Asian Development Bank (ADB), and the World Bank—the Marcos regime carried out a reign of terror, militarizing Philippine society and criminalizing political dissent under the banner of martial law in order to attract foreign investment.[14] Rosca's portrayal of this relationship as rape has manifold dimensions. Col. Amor and his paramilitary thugs are the proxies for that machine that actually fuels Anna's sexual torture: the "made in the U.S.A." generator. On one level, the generator references the economic engine of American interests that drove a foreign policy rampant with intervention. On another level, it is also literal: the generator itself is the stuff of American (military-industrial) production (hence "made in the U.S.A.")—the surplus military paraphernalia that the United States shipped to its allies during the Cold War. As the source of the perverse desire behind the rapist figure of Amor, U.S. economic imperialism and its Cold War avatars of modernization and development are secured through the proxy war of Marcos's martial law regime. Held down and raped by Amor's soldiers, Anna-as-Philippines symbolizes the subordinate position of the Philippines vis-à-vis its American benefactor, a position established through colonialism and continued by "made in the U.S.A." debt and dependence.[15]

Anna's rape parallels the rape of the island of K—, a vicious process of penetration and extraction of value. It is no accident that *State of War* revolves around a tourist attraction: the Festival on the island of K—.[16] The majority of the novel is set during a bacchanalian celebration, where the critical scenes of political intrigue and attempted assassination take place. In preparation for a visit from the Commander (the fictional Marcos), the sadistic Col. Amor secures the island, infiltrating the carnival-like atmosphere with military troops. The Festival is the scene for two interlocking struggles. First, it is the site of violence—Amor's torture and blackmailing of two other political revolutionary protagonists. Second, the Festival demonstrates the potential for tourism to take over and commodify a local event: the military guards the economic elites who attend the Festival and plan the development of the island into a tourism resort where "half the town can go on with the Festival for the tourists" while the "other half" can be trained to "work in the hotels" (38). K—'s transformation from insular fiesta to international destination represents the conversion of the Philippine economy during the Marcos regime. By emphasizing the Festival as the central setting, Rosca recalls the 1973 birth of the Ministry of Tourism under the Marcos regime (a year after establishing Martial Law) as part of its bid to transform the Philippines into a transnational, capital-attracting New Society.[17] Under Marcos's martial law regime, political dissent was criminalized as a way to "clean up" the streets and bring in investment: with the new Ministry of Tourism running the show by 1973, visitors jumped up from 150,000 in 1971 to over one million in 1980.[18] This rise in tourism numbers was paralleled by a sustained spike in the incidences of extrajudicial killings, incarcerations, and torture.

For Rosca, the production of the Philippines-as-tropics is not only like a rape; it is a rape guaranteed by the penetrability of a feminized landscape to both capitalist exploitation and military occupation and the sexual sale and violation of Filipinos and Filipinas in a neoliberal market generated by U.S.-Philippine partnerships.[19] Rape is more than a metaphor for the exploitative penetration of the Philippine economy and polity by the IMF and World Bank structural adjustment policies, the deeply uneven Military Bases Agreement, and the increasing "prostitution" of the Philippines under the "socio-libidinal economy" established by the United States.[20] It is also a modus operandi of the garrison state established by U.S.-Philippine state collusions. Under the New Society inaugurated by U.S.-Philippine state of terror crafted under the Marcos administration—3,257 killed, 35,000 tortured, and 70,000 incarcerated—a domestic theater of seemingly random and overt brutality flourished, crushing political resistance and generating a politics of fear.[21] Rape was a common weapon in the arsenal of Amor's very real counterparts.[22]

Anna's rape and torture, with which this chapter began—especially Rosca's deliberate and perverse spectacularization of Anna's sexual violation—is a statement that goes beyond the brutal disciplining that produces "stability." It also suggests the wider complicities that generate alibis and deflect responsibility for this familiar and savage style of native-on-native governance. Anna's sustained abuse continues over "days, nights" and is exemplified by its sexual nature: the electrodes on her nipples and "the lieutenant with the smelly armpits who subjected her to odoriferous love for who knew how many times and for how long" (67). This graphic violation, even as it unfolds on the page, is also self-consciously manifested as a scene for literary consumption—interpellating, in real time, the tourist-as-voyeur into the economy of desire that relies on a stability secured through sexual torture. In other words, the reader's act of witnessing, of consuming Anna's pain in an act of leisure and pleasure, is itself a metaphor for tourism and its conditions of possibility. By spectacularizing Anna's rape as a fictional treat for the consumption of a global (mostly First World) readership, Rosca implicates literary desire as a kind of tourism and, by extension, identifies the consumers for whom this "pacification" is deemed necessary. In addition, by calling attention to the generator, Rosca also understands that the producers—the U.S. laborers whose work is so proudly emblazoned on the generator—are not innocent. They, too, produce work that operates in tension with those who labor elsewhere, such as the Filipinos who are understood to be the service workers of the hospitality industry depicted in *State of War*.

The novel chronicles the mutual work of militarism and tourism that at once reconstructs the island of K—, its culture, and its people into a tropical holiday. Manifesting the island of K— as a tourist destination, U.S.-Philippine economic, political, and military alliances are symbolically and materially secured through a familiar pattern of overturned sovereignty masquerading as global altruism. In other words, Anna's rape scene and its symbolic representation of the militarization of the modern Philippines under neoliberal governance faithfully follow an established American policy of dealing with Filipinos. Under Marcos, the specter of a "rebel-infested" countryside funneled American military assistance to the tune of hundreds of millions of dollars, transforming the Philippines into a garrison state, complete with 112 prison camps by 1984.[23] Rosca's description of Anna's rape-as-pacification is soon followed by an account of American forcible benevolent assimilation of the Philippines in 1898: its army "bred corpses: corpses in the streets, on rooftops, hanging from coconut trees—for by the glory of God the americanos dealt with the insurrection with great efficiency, torching villages and shoving two hundred fifty thousand corpses into mile-long graves, both men and women" (77). Referencing the Philippine-American War that broke out on the archipelago in 1898, Rosca's body count illustrates the "great efficiency" of technologies of the Progressive Era allied with the military training of veterans of the American Indian Wars sent on a new Pacific expedition. Anna's "made in the U.S.A." torture is not only powered by American generators. It is also styled after its former colonial master's strategies of pacification, illustrating the success by which ideologies such as "society must be defended" are taken up by native neocolonial administrators.[24]

By tying the torture of Anna to the atrocities of American colonial rule, Rosca insists on a deliberate and sustained connection between the United States and its former colony, especially as the depth and breadth of the violence has shifted to Filipino administrators and is increasingly distanced from American governance. The novel's dogged return to key moments of colonial and contemporary violence refuses the facile rearticulation of five decades of American colonialism to the crystal moment of post–World War II liberation. This is a deliberate thwarting move on Rosca's part: her deployment of tourist idiom and imagery in State of War grapples with how the promise of a modernizing economy and a tropics made available to the world confirms the hegemonic status of the American romantic narrative of security as far as how the Philippines is imagined, regardless of the body count attributable to U.S. military violence. Rosca identifies the dual and durable contiguous fictions of pacification and liberation as the narratives that elide and even transform the long-standing brutality of the colonial project in the islands into something resembling a romance of security. Bookending American colonial war and occupation of the Philippines, pacification (at the beginning) tempers a savage war of conquest by transforming it into a process of calming unruly peoples to render them receptive to civilization, and liberation (at the official end) supplants a vexed and contested colonial legacy with the enduring (and recurring) chronicles of rescue, deliverance, and independence. The substitution of pacification for genocide, the rehabilitation of pacification as a necessary evil, and the overshadowing of five decades of colonial rule by liberation recasts U.S. colonial policy as an aberration rather than the rule. The triumph of pacification and liberation as the structuring narratives of America's romance of security is apparent in the fact that for the most part, the dimensions of violence that the United States meted out in the Philippines are less imaginable than the Philippines as an exotic destination. Yet from 1898 to 1913, hundreds of thousands of Filipinos were killed in the U.S. pacification campaigns on the islands.[25] A century later, the Philippines is legible as a set of images: sun-drenched, palm-tree-ringed islands ready for exploration and enjoyment, the "Filipina smile" that beckons further discovery, the country's tragicomic political scene with its occasional bouts of Muslim extremist violence and mainstream political thuggery, and its vast, exported labor force.[26] In this context, the United States is a visitor, a liberator, an investor, and a security force that ostensibly helps bring stability to the country. It is decidedly not an army that razed the countryside a century earlier.

In *State of War*, Rosca illustrates how neoliberal governance resurrects these colonial fictions of Manifest Destiny through the martial disciplining of Anna and K— for the liberated economy of global consumption. In this updated romance of security, the redemptive rhetoric of tourism as a new liberation softens the brutal pacifications of U.S. and Philippine militarism. Rosca's prose echoes the dreamy idiom of the travelogue, just as the "islandness" of K— evokes tropical leisure, illuminating how the production of paradise—as safe and free (pacified and liberated)—redefines violence as productive. Generating instead, however, a counterromance of the tropics, Rosca knits together the icons of tourism (coconut trees, islands, the Filipina) with evidence of military violence (corpses, the equipment of torture, the soldiers) to show that these juxtapositions are not merely coincidences and aberrations of history, but rather intimate partners in a long-running violation of the country and its people. Thus the novel is never just about the personal lives of its three central characters as they navigate the challenges of a martial law state: it is also a larger indictment of the colonial violence that continues to limit their present political and social horizons.

In contrast to the Philippines's Cold War fate of decolonization (or, rather, neocolonialism), Hawai'i's was incorporation. This approach emphasized America's modern and liberal embrace of diversity and inclusion, including discourses of multiculturalism and statehood deployed to mitigate accusations of U.S. racial apartheid. As the more "successful" colonial project, avoiding the expense and violence of an armed insurgency, Hawai'i was an ideal Cold War showcase that touted the rewards of U.S.-style capitalism and military occupation. Its tourism industry displayed the profits of capitalism's conversion of plantation inequalities to consumer multiculturalism, while its inclusion in the union—granted as a form of acknowledgment for the exigencies and injuries of war— legitimated the murky and contested origins of American occupation. Although the United States did not carry out a war in Hawai'i, it perpetuated a giant land and political theft of breathtaking audacity: in 1898, with the mere stroke of a pen, the pending question of Hawai'i's sovereignty and the illegal overthrow of its monarchy were subsumed by American warmongering elsewhere. Half a century later, another war would provide cover for further dispossession. The smoking, sinking ship hulls that came to define Hawai'i's modern moment on December 7, 1941, were instrumental in recasting the less-than-noble U.S. history on the islands into a heroic narrative that would frame statehood as a just reward. As a territory then a state of the United States, Hawai'i's claim to independence became more historical and less legible. Today, it is almost impossible to conceive of Hawai'i as anything other than a U.S. state: the multiple protests of a dispossessed people are swept aside in the celebration of fifty years of statehood, images of a working multicultural paradise, the income brought in by Waikīkī's crowded beaches, the symbolic hospitality of the ubiquitous hula dancer, and the stalwart military stationed in the Pacific.

Celebrating Hawaiian statehood today disavows the illegitimacy of occupation and annexation and skips over the details of historical theft as inconsequential, instead promoting the familiar and tourist-friendly narrative of a multicultural paradise that is righteously protected by military sacrifice. Haunani-Kay Trask, a longtime activist-scholar who advocates for Native Hawaiian sovereignty, roots her poetry in indigenous genealogies in order to lay bare the shaky foundations of Hawai'i's image as a manifest destination. Against and alongside Rosca's violated tropics, Trask's Hawai'i is a paradise that on the surface has been more successfully incorporated into the United States but is nonetheless always in need of regulation. Where Rosca spotlighted the "made in the U.S.A." generator in a scene of torture, Trask describes a heroic parade of military equipment and personnel celebrated by tourists and locals alike. In place of a wrenching scene of torture, Trask describes an eerily ordered commemoration of World War II heroics on Hawaiian soil, animating how this martial history is integral to tourist fictions of paradise. Her poetry captures how the romance of security is based on an investment in multiculturalism that is contracted through martial fraternity and citizenship.

An entire section of her 2002 collection *Night Is a Sharkskin Drum* is devoted to how life in Hawai'i is shaped by the dominant partnership between militarism and tourism and, in particular, how that partnership operates to occlude Native claims to the land by bringing into relief a history more amenable to the romance of security. In the poem "Nostalgia: VJ Day," Trask links the U.S. military's occupation of Hawai'i to the successful fiftieth anniversary of the U.S. victory over Japan in World War II. Beginning with

A wounded morning
crippled by helicopters.
No bullet-proof skies
over our "Hawaiian Islands"
where presidents and
enemies dismember
this charmed Pacific

the poem hints at a longer history than the one so selectively recalled by the "faded uniform" of Japanese and Filipino regiments, whose inclusion in a national anniversary celebration operates to exclude Native Hawaiians on many levels.[27] Describing the spectacle of war commemoration as something that is injurious rather than therapeutic or celebratory, Trask indicts the ceremonial preservation of this history as essential to the continued militarization of the islands: a mis-remembering that becomes dismemberment. In other words, Trask argues that World War II operates on an exclusionary logic, belying the narrative of belonging that statehood and martial citizenship imply.

"Nostalgia: VJ Day" is an elaboration of how Cold War politics transformed the plantation-era ethnic and racial "problem" in Hawai'i into a multicultural paradise, a politics that for Trask is deftly wielded by the ascendance of the Japanese American–led Democratic party that came into power through the World War II heroics of Nisei men opting to fight in the war.[28] Bonded to the nation through their soldierly masculine sacrifice, the Filipino and Japanese American veterans in Trask's poem are the epitome of a deserving multiculturalism: they have become the protagonists in the romance of security. The martial alchemy that transmutes the base materials of plantation labor into heroic citizens, however, hinges on the subordination of indigenous sovereignty to the political model of the liberal democratic state. In other words, Asian laborers can become immigrant-citizens only by affirming the legitimacy of "our" Hawaiian Islands, rather than "their" Kingdom of Hawai'i. Singling out the Japanese American senator Daniel Inouye—"smugly/armless from the great war"—as the exemplar of martial citizenship and patriotism, Trask reveals the sentimental manipulation of World War II as the political gateway for Hawai'i's Asian settlers: by enlisting and fighting for "Old Glory" against Japan, Asians in Hawai'i were able to claim belonging.[29] Once marginalized and excluded from the American Dream, Japanese American and Filipino American veterans enter into the body politic through military fraternity. Just as their militarized heroics are put on display in Hawai'i's military-tourist circuits, so, too, are their plantation labor pasts recycled for the tourist industry, stepping in for Native Hawaiians on occasion and contributing to the narrative of commodified multiculturalism that further strips Native Hawaiians of sovereignty. As good multicultural citizen-soldiers, their patriotism seals the permanence of Hawai'i's relationship to the United States in 1959.

Statehood fictions and their patina of inevitability encourage the amnesia of overthrow and displace it with the romantic narratives of security, military tragedy, duty, and heroism. Trask ties the "wounded morning" of World War II commemoration to a Pacific "dismembered" by American theft and occupation because World War II was so instrumental to the final act in the century-long process of Native Hawaiian dispossession. With the collaboration of an Asian settler class newly empowered by the war, the fictions of statehood became fact, dismembering indigenous people from the 'aina (land). In the poem, Trask reverses this commemoration of VJ Day as an invasion of Hawai'i rather than as the victory over Japan it is meant to signify, where Asian settlers join forces (literally) with an occupying force to further remove Native Hawaiians from self-determination.[30] Statehood, in this case, was understood as a just reward for the suffering sustained by the islands and its peoples. Intertwined with these militarized narratives are the desires for Hawaiʻi's other attributes: its beautiful natural landscape, its climate, its multicultural paradise. Sheet music from the 1950s, when the Japanese American–led push to statehood was under way, illustrates the potency of statehood fictions as an elaboration of securing paradise:

> When God made Hawaii's islands,
> He blessed the U.S.A.
> He gave our states protection
> From many miles away.
> God gave Hawaiian moonlight
> Her beaches and her show'rs
> Her rainbows and her sunshine
> Her leis and all her flowers.
> [Chorus] Stand up! All Americans
> Make Hawaii a state
> With the Old Forty Eight."[31]

This potent and intimate relationship between military longing and travel fantasies resurfaced during the push for statehood, framing Hawaiʻi as a piece of property worthy of inclusion in the union. As the lyrics also demonstrate, Hawaiʻi's Americanness is linked to both modern military and touristic desires. Hawaiʻi real estate would provide a strategic military location as well as a real, live tropical fantasy. "God" and national Manifest Destiny, both apparently on fire for the United States at the turn of the twentieth century, had "blessed the U.S.A." with "protection" and "beaches"—the most beneficent combination of aloha—in its imperial Pacific voyage. The fact that Hawaiʻi had suffered a violation on behalf of the nation added to the argument for inevitable statehood, the desires of its indigenous peoples notwithstanding.

Today the most militarized state in the United States, Hawaiʻi also boasts one of its most successful tourist industries: Trask's poem "Nostalgia: VJ Day" points out that in fact militarism and tourism in Hawaiʻi have a symbiotic relationship. As Phyllis Turnbull and Kathleen Ferguson have observed, from "Honolulu International Airport sharing runways with Hickam Air Force Base; the Arizona Memorial and Punchbowl Cemetery serving as 'must see' tourist stops . . . interstate freeways connecting military bases . . . military vehicles competing with commuter traffic," tourism and militarism have come to be the modern-day framing narratives of the state of Hawai'i.[32] In the postwar era, particularly during the drive to statehood up until the present, the cultural economies of militarism and tourism were framed as beneficial rather than exploitative — especially in light of the visitor and war industry dollars they generated for the state of Hawai'i. Trask's poem meditates on how this commemorative moment becomes part of the islands' tropical scenery: the aircraft that patrol the skies over Waikīkī and Honolulu also penetrate into the tourist experience, as if to reassure that this "charmed Pacific" is, indeed, secured. Interrupting the sepia-toned war remembrances of old soldiers, they signal the legacy of modern militarization ensured by these veterans, and gesture to the ways in which military hardware become part of Hawai'i's land-, sky- and seascapes both physically and ideologically.

Trask ends "Nostalgia: VJ Day" with a haunting coda that locates the tourist sites of Waikīkī and Pearl Harbor (also an active military base) simultaneously within the orbit of U.S. militarism:

At Waikīkī and Pearl
Harbor, maneuvers
and air shows: jets,
carriers, even a black
"stealth bomber," modeled
by Star Trek. Ah!
the long-ago days
of real war, remembered
with tears,
when killing
was simple, and tall
young warriors went down
to bloodless death
in the noblest reaches
of empire: the United States of America.[33]

The spectacle of the military air show serves to remind tourists and residents alike of the history that counts when it comes to being able to live in and visit Hawai'i as a secured American paradise. The nostalgia over a war that the United States waged showcases the performance of a wounded masculinity deserving of inclusion in the "noblest reaches/of empire: the United States of America." Standing tall and proud, the nostalgic soldiers identify with America, but Trask shifts the frame and hints at a different war altogether, where siding with America meant siding against sovereign peoples in the "charmed pacific." Moving back and forth between a maudlin sentimental language deployed by commemoration and the sharper tone of critique and mockery, Trask's poetry points out the collusions between "remembering" the real warriors of World War II and forgetting that they are part of a long war that began even before 1941. At the same time, she concedes the ideological potency of the hardware paraded before the eyes of the soldiers (and the reader).

Her recital of the American military-industrial complex's arsenal attests to the militarized romance of security on the islands, where the maneuvers of stealth bombers and the procession of helicopters ostensibly secure the vulnerable "charmed Pacific" and protect its conversion (as well as the means of its conversion: the military) into a tourist spectacle. By juxtaposing the helicopters and bombers that also encroach into the (not-so) "charmed Pacific," Trask not only calls attention to the gendered relations between the military, tourism, and the islands, but also to their cooperation and collaboration in the process of securing paradise. In both these discourses, Hawai'i is constructed as passive—something to be visited, viewed, protected, bought, and conquered. Trask's theorization—both in academic and poetic forms—pays attention to these gendered relations and to the fact that under statehood, Hawai'i's fecund femininity is married to the discipline of a masculine military, sealing a union that in effect delegitimizes Native Hawaiian claims. Trask's poem envisions Hawai'i as the endpoint of the successful merging of military and touristic desires, where the military does not merely oversee the stability of a tourism economy but has become its central attraction.

"Dispossessions of Empire" theorizes the larger geopolitical "romance" that renders the islands into a feminized, penetrable territory: on the geopolitical stage, this exoticization of Hawai'i's islandness and culture fits into the romance of U.S. security in the region.[34] Identifying the multiple collusions that reduce Hawai'i to a tourist and military mecca, Trask uses prostitution on the one hand as a metaphor to critique Native and local cultural participation, and on the other as a critical term that illuminates the real libidinal complicities of securing paradise, linking interracial military cooperation to the commodification of Hawaiian women and land. Echoing and elaborating on her early academic work that framed tourism as akin to prostitution, the poem "Dispossessions of Empire" points out:

> Even prostitutes know
> their profession, but natives?
> The empire degrades
> through monetary exchange,
> leaving quaint Hawaiians
> dressing as "natives,"
> in drag for the 10 o'clock
> floor show, faking
> a singsong pidgin
> with the drunken crowd
> hoping for tips
> after the French kisses.
> . . . nothing amiss in the morass of Paradise.[35]

Leaving little room for the political ambiguities and refusals of performance, "Dispossessions of Empire" reveals the romance of tourism as a tawdry affair, an economic transaction that distorts the very meaning of aloha. The end result is the tragic compliance of the happy natives, who instead of planning revolution,

> . . . sit,
> observing the parade, or
> jump to join the passing
> fleet of noisy cars,
> waving at their destiny
> a musical good-bye,
> suffused with a sweet
> intention to smile
> and be happy.[36]

Trask's recourse to the metaphor of prostitution is meant to capture the conversion of the tropical into a commodity for profit where the performance of indigenous culture to entice visitors, and the collusion of an economic and political elite in the exploitation of feminized labor and landscapes, ultimately result in the exchange of a commoditized and alienated "aloha for cash." This exchange is meant to be marked by smiles and kisses, yet Trask points out how the tourist consumer freedoms rely on regimented performances ("the 10 o'clock" show) of commoditized culture ("faking") to demanding audiences ("the drunken crowd"). This "morass," rather than romance, relies on notions of consent—tourism epitomizes free market monetary exchange, after all. While taking to task Native Hawaiians who greet tourists with "French kisses" in exchange for "tips," Trask also unsettles the notion of consent by depicting hospitality as a profoundly exploitative and abusive relationship.[37] In the highly developed and secured state of Hawai'i, she suggests, the "happy" participation of Native Hawaiians "in drag" for visitor entertainment demonstrates how the spaces of tourism constrict movement and expression, reducing aloha to a commercial transaction. The VJ Day celebrations, the air shows that accompany them, the cultural drag shows and the shopping excursions of tourists that are tallied up in state coffers—all of these acts leave little room to envision alternative histories, economies, and futures. These alternatives are crowded out by the domination of tourism and militarism as the inevitable partnership that manifests Hawai'i as a destination.

In Trask's formulation of Native Hawaiians as prostitutes of culture, Asian settlers are recast as pimps rather than as military heroes who jointly participate in the further dispossession of Native Hawaiians. Ascendant Japanese American politicians' embrace of statehood and the massive influx of Cold War military funding were the rewards for offering the feminized landscape of Hawai'i for military and tourist occupation. That one of tourism's biggest clients on the islands is the newly flush and cosmopolitan Japanese is particularly ironic to Trask: what Pearl Harbor did not accomplish, tourism will. Under the peaceful, inclusive, and multicultural mantle of tourism's free trade economy, Japanese Americans in Hawai'i are transformed into the brokers of Native Hawaiian culture. The transformation of Hawai'i into a tourist marketplace masks the fact that tourism, just as surely as military occupation, reinforces a centuries-old process of theft. The invasive diplomacy of helicopter blades wounding the blue sky and air shows and bombers spiraling against the Pacific blue work in tandem with the troops of tourists with their constant show of cash to reduce the islands to a service economy and render sovereignty into an even more distant dream.

Earlier colonial fictions trace the historical roots and routes of manifest destination in Hawai'i and the Philippines in the fictions highlighted above. The "embedded" reporting of journalists traversing the Pacific in the early days of the Philippine-American War forms an archive of how the narratives of militarism and tourism coalesce through the project of empire. The overarching stories these journalists chronicle collectively about the inevitable absorption of the Philippines and Hawai'i's into American modernity form the foundation of the narratives that continue to be told about each place today. This detour into the colonial fictions of imperial journalism illuminates the early work of securing paradise as an unwieldy process that needed constant reinforcement even in its seemingly most successful moments, particularly when it came to how domestic anxieties over gender were exported and managed in America's new frontiers.[38]

Wars, as the newspaper magnate William Randolph Hearst knew well, generate circulation. Just as the Spanish-American War in 1898 was avidly reported in publications such as Hearst's *New York Journal* and *San Francisco Examiner* and, indeed, was partially conjured up through sensationalist journalism, the American imperial project in Asia and the Pacific likewise produced its own body of journalistic fictions.[39] These colonial fictions manifested the enabling imaginaries and desires for imperial ventures, deploying recognizable gendered and racialized taxonomies of peoples unfit for self-government, lands and resources inadequately managed, and heroic roles for white Americans to undertake.[40] Early journalists crafted narratives that further confirmed the rightness of the white man's burden. Sharing transportation and quarters with the pacifying army, these journalists reported from the point of view generated by traveling on military routes: they captured the global itinerary of the military through thick scene-by-scene descriptions and brought their readers back into the tropics through a textual tour of newly claimed territories. Transported to the tropics through the eyes of reporters, readers — regardless of gender — could assume the mobilities of the masculine explorer in which reporters styled themselves. In this way, domestic support for empire was nurtured through the romance of adventure and discovery: securing paradise had to do as much with these colonial fictions as it did with the arrival of troops and ships.

In particular, early embedded reporting illustrates the overlapping and interdependent workings of militaristic and touristic fantasies about the "new possessions" of the United States. The special correspondent Oscar King Davis, writing for the respected and politically conservative *New York Sun*, relates his journey aboard a military transport making its way to the Philippines during the tense transition from Spanish to American occupation. Traveling with the army that would occupy the Philippine Islands and essentially begin the Philippine-American War in February of 1899, Davis narrates the transpacific journey as a cruise. During a stop in Honolulu to refuel on its way to the Philippines, the tone of his reportage is that of a travel narrative.[41] Cruising into the waters of Honolulu, Davis combines travelogue with a patriotic voice that narrates his arrival as a voyage of discovery: "Land it is sure enough, and soon after luncheon the bold top of Diamond Head shows almost dead ahead. . . . We pull Diamond Head out of the faint mist, sharp and clean and beautiful. Beyond it there — see that — a great big, beautiful United States flag flying from the top of a tall, straight pole! Glorious old flag! Beautiful land!"[42] This moment of arrival emphasizes the expected embrace of islands that have essentially been made friendly to visitors (at least in Davis's version). Replicating the narratives of voyages of discovery inaugurated by Captain James Cook, Davis lays claim to Hawai'i and assumes the role of intrepid explorer. In contrast to how he and his companions "pull" the landscape out of the mist, the islands are perpetually in a state of waiting for discovery: his account describes the islands as full of "no one knows what delights" that await the exploration of its visitors.[43]

Inasmuch as he exclaims over its natural beauty and exotic offerings, Davis also underscores the Americanness of Hawai'i — from the first sighting of the "big, beautiful United States flag" to a careful explanation of the exact status of Hawai'i. Davis's Hawai'i is always being claimed: the American flag staunchly marks this territory the property of the United States. Putting to rest any anxiety or confusion his readers back home might have about Hawai'i, he assures them that while it is very different from their experience, it is, indeed, under U.S. administration: "Now we're in the channel. Honolulu lies just ahead there. See the flags! A perfect forest of poles, and the Stars and Stripes on every one! No, there are some Hawaiian flags there on the Government buildings — this is a foreign land, you know, if Americans do own and live in and rule it."[44] The short-lived Republic of Hawai'i — under the leadership of President Sanford B. Dole — had at this point been in power for five years, with the islands' uncertain status vis-à-vis the United States a result of domestic political maneuverings. Despite the continuing ambiguity and illegality of Hawai'i's status, Davis works to dispel his readers' doubts that this is, or shortly will be, America.

While Davis was on board to report a war in the Philippines, he was quick to erase any potential conflicts from the scene in Hawai'i, using touristic discourse to dispel the violence of a military mission on what is yet "foreign land." Reporting on the welcome laid out for the troops, he relates that "the men had the freedom of the city. They simply couldn't spend their money. Street cars were free and bicycles and horses were to be had for the simple signifying of the desire. The beach at Waikiki swarmed with soldiers."[45] In language perhaps more suited and familiar to Hawai'i's contemporary tourism industry, Davis describes the hospitality of the land and its people, erasing a very recent history of political overthrow and softening the hard reality of a traveling war machine. What he describes is a place that welcomed its occupiers, holding outdoor banquets on government grounds, demonstrating surfing and "hula-hula" to its visitors, and "crown[ing] them with flowers."[46] In portraying the soldiers as tourists, rather than as military figures en route to an imperial war, Davis narrates in the tradition of what Mary Louise Pratt has called "anti-conquest," a rhetorical style that disappears the instrumental role of tourist figures (and for that matter, embedded journalists) as imperial workers.[47] Softening the presence of military muscle by alluding to Hawai'i's ready welcome, Davis naturalizes hospitality by framing it as a gendered and sexualized relationship. At the same time, he extends the celebratory welcome of the ships to an already established military occupation of Hawai'i. Davis thus follows an insistent self-representation of American residents of Hawai'i as "welcome" to the islands despite the fact that in 1898 and 1899, when Davis was writing his articles, annexation was absolutely contested.[48]

Davis's narration essentially maps the outposts of American empire, allowing Americans to visualize the tropical possibilities that the U.S. military had secured for them. They are at once assured of its simultaneous difference and safety, and of the necessary mission of putting the Pacific under the influence of American power. In its Pacific tour, Davis's military transport passed by Guam on its way to Manila. While mostly a supply stop, Davis deftly inserts that "undoubtedly Guam would be a valuable possession for the United States. Its resources have never been touched; development of them has never been dreamed of. The climate about San Luis d'Apra and Agaña is delightful. It is almost better than Honolulu, and there are no mosquitoes."[49] Omitting any description of its native peoples, other than a fleeting mention of its attractive women, Davis assesses Guam as potential U.S. military real estate: "The islands can be made immensely valuable. The harbour of San Luis d'Apra can be made a magnificent coaling station at very slight expense. It is almost in the direct line between Honolulu and Manila, and the whole island is capable of the easiest and best defence."[50] Already eyeing Guam as U.S. property, and no doubt absorbing the opinions of his shipmates as they survey this Pacific territory, Davis describes it in terms of its particular geographic and strategic value as a military outpost, while also touching on its temperate climate and its wealth of natural resources just waiting to be exploited and explored. The violence and dispossession that this operation might entail, however, are first allayed by the familiar portrayal of these strategically useful territories as inadequately undeveloped and inhabited by, if not quite savages, certainly people who are not up to the task of civilization.

These overlapping techniques of using the reporter's perspective to relate a travel adventure, to disappear or render incompetent the natives of the land, and to highlight the land's natural resources and strategic importance prepare the reader for Davis's conclusion. Following the "real estate tour" of possible Pacific territories, Davis finally arrives in Manila, the final destination of this cruise. His description of the land around Cavite and Sangley Point (which would later become U.S. military bases) and his close attention to the political tensions that entailed Spain's surrender to the United States, rather than to the rebel Filipino army led by Emilio Aguinaldo, provide a foreshadowing of the U.S. takeover of these territories. Framing Aguinaldo as someone who "makes trouble" about Philippine autonomy, Davis dismisses him as a novice politician, someone to be brushed aside in the ineluctable march of the United States across the Pacific and certainly not someone who is capable of the complex political thinking necessary for governing a nation.[51] As little more than trouble-making savages, Aguinaldo and the rest of the Filipinos who had essentially waged a long-term, multifront guerrilla war against their Spanish colonizers, are disappeared as easily as the people of Hawai'i and Guam. Davis, instead, waxes poetic about the Philippine climate, finding, in its tropical breezes, a justification for empire. Following his description of the weather as "delightful" with "fresh, pleasant breezes and clear air," Davis then concludes that such a salubrious and lovely territory must inevitably become part of the American empire: "With Cuba, Porto Rico, the Hawaiian Islands and Guam ours, it seems as if the question of Imperialism, if it be so called, is already decided."[52] Describing at length the profound potential of the natural resources and labor of the Philippines, Davis obliquely argues that war is a small and ethical price to pay for properly developing these natural resources into real estate.

Other reporters and writers took on the monumental task of relaying the importance and duty of civilizing and improving the new U.S. territories. Another exemplar of this early archive, Trumbull White, illustrates the enormous amount of ideological labor it took to maintain empire. White, a well-known writer of the time whose extensive travels and experience as a war correspondent authorized his histories of "our new possessions," published his own observations of these new territories in book form, with the Philippine Islands, Puerto Rico, Cuba, and the Hawaiian Islands each occupying a volume in his series.[53] White's compendium of information was designed to demonstrate the moral rightness of American occupation and annexation of these territories, and to dispel any anxieties about the legality of U.S. interventions. To do this, he offers opinions that draw on familiar and useful racializations of Filipinos and Native Hawaiians as primitive savages who are unable to govern themselves. Dismissing both Filipino and Native Hawaiian resistance to U.S. colonialism as "complications with insurgents," White portrays these sustained, multifaceted, and sometimes violent struggles for self-determination as minor inconveniences wrongly fueled by "extraordinary perversions of history and fact, as well as bitter hostility to the party of civilization and progress in the islands."[54]

The bulk of White's guide to these territories, however, treats the islands as already American territory, and inevitably so, sidestepping any debate over the contradictions between U.S. foreign policy and its avowed republic origins, focusing on what the islands have to offer to the American global consumer. In writing about the Philippines, White focuses on the Spanish-American War and writes breezily about it as a tourist event: "When all the Americans who are here or who have been in the campaign in the Philippines reach home they will have carloads of souvenirs to show their friends. Nearly everybody is picking up little mementos of the war."[55] Ignoring the hostilities that would soon escalate into the

Philippine-American War and result in hundreds of thousands of Filipino deaths, White instead depicts the short and successful war against Spain as a tourist attraction, complete with souvenirs. In his account, the Philippine Islands are reduced to a series of travel narratives and tours for the potential American visitor. White intersperses his descriptions of Spain's long colonialism of the Philippines, Aguinaldo's "rebellion," and George Dewey's Battle of Manila Bay and occupation of Manila with photographs of natives, city scenes, and country delights, following the conventions of travelogues that distilled complex histories and peoples into "tourable" units. At the same time, he is careful to balance the successful civilizing project with an emphasis on the clear need for continued occupation. Even as he describes parts of the islands as "quite accessible as any Oriental city," he also points out that other parts—such as the southern region, which is populated by "dangerous Tulisanes"—are still untamed and characterized by "exceedingly unwholesomeness" that render them "far from attractive for the American traveler."[56] Constant policing, he implies, is a necessary element for enjoying the tropical resources and protecting the financial investments in the Philippines. Thus "tourability" is always tied to the security so ably produced by the U.S. military stationed in the Philippines.

In contrast, White's descriptions of Hawai'i situate the islands as much more securely American and celebrate its attractions as ineluctably made for tourism—an early instantiation of a manifested destination. Echoing a local publication's description of the islands as "the Paradise of the Pacific," White frames the American annexation to the islands as an added benefit for its status as a tropical destination: "The delights of island life in a perfect climate tempted men there for rest and pleasure." He goes on to claim that "there was nothing lacking that could appeal to the traveler. Then came changing conditions in island government that added the romance of history to the story of Hawaii."[57] Adding "the romance of history" to the ostensibly blank text of the timeless (and ahistorical) backdrop of the tropics and its people, the U.S.-engineered overthrow and annexation add touristic value to mere "rest and pleasure." White thus projects Hawai'i and its beneficial mix of American colonial administration, military security, and tropical climate as the ideal future of the Philippines, making a larger case for the benefits of U.S. occupation of its "possessions." The description of the Hawaiian islands that follows White's argument for colonialism further tropicalizes Hawai'i as a tourist destination just awaiting further discovery, as if to say that these scenes and resources are made accessible and safe under the aegis and guidance of American authority. For White, the proper harnessing of the islands' resources is a result of the masculine work of imperialism. As the war in the Philippines waged on, Hawaiʻi—as the other sizeable U.S. Pacific outpost, and one that took only the threat of military violence to secure—came to symbolize what the Philippines might someday become. The images of Hawaiʻi as a peaceful, stable outpost demonstrated what paradise could truly look like: exotic yet safe, different yet civilized, and, above all, hospitable to American improvement.

Davis and White, along with their contemporaries, produced Hawaiʻi and the Philippines as American tropics through their invocation of and embeddedness in early circuits of militarism and tourism. For them, securing paradise was a project that made sense when seen from the interdependent logics of tourism and its impulses of gendered exoticization and racialized discourses of uplift, and of militarism's unshakeable claims to security, liberation, and modernity. As authorities who used the technologies and rhetoric of tourism and militarism to produce their fictions of empire, Davis and White were among the cultural workers of empire, instrumental in both mitigating its violence and injustice, as well as relaying its benefits. Even as the fates of Hawaiʻi, Guam, and the Philippines were officially decided with the ratification of the Treaty of Paris in 1899, these colonial fictions continued to do the work of claiming these territories. They did so in the face of massive resistance on the part of the natives who found themselves partial subjects of an empire that was happy to take their lands but not exactly sure about what to do with its nonwhite peoples.[58] In the case of Rosca and Trask, the empire writes back.[59] Refracted through their critical feminist fictions, the colonial fictions of Davis and White are rendered into the imaginative labor of empire.

Rosca and Trask also propose an archive in partnership with the modes of reading and seeing produced in tourism's and militarism's mobilities and circuits. The scene of torture with which this chapter began and the commemoration ceremony witnessed by Trask and the travelogues of embedded reporting both suggest an interdisciplinary approach concerned with the visual and affective experience of tourism. Anna's body in pain, the generator that fuels her torture, helicopters, military bases, and performances of native culture—these are artifacts, infrastructures, and practices formed by the partnerships and processes that secure paradise.

Even as this chapter looked to the literary to theorize militarism's and tourism's crucial and productive work in manifesting destinations, the rest of the book extends its archive to objects, places, experiences, and people, keeping in mind that empire is not only textual, but tangible and heterogeneous. The following chapters examine how paradise is secured through a range of built forms—such as roads, warships, museums, and military bases—in tandem with more ephemeral experiences that generate affective and corporeal identifications—such as tours, flights, and performances. This is not to reduce material reality to narrative but to understand how stories are told through different modes and to acknowledge that both ideology and theory are produced, experienced, enacted, and felt in all sorts of different ways.

Two

SCENIC HIGHWAYS, MASCULINITY, MODERNITY, AND MOBILITY

It is said about the late Philippine dictator Ferdinand Marcos that "at least he built good roads." Modernization's foremost proponent in the Philippines, Marcos endorsed road building as the path to prosperity during his regime. Granting himself the title "Master Architect and Builder of the Nation," the savvy and charismatic leader undertook infrastructure development with the blessing of the United States and international banks. For Marcos, roads were a way to lay open the country's natural and cultural resources to international capital investment in the guise of tourism and other service-, export-, and extraction-driven industries.[1] Over the course of his administration, over 30,000 kilometers of roads were built to "link the diverse communities and islands and countryside into one national community and stable body politic."[2]

His ambitions to modernize the nation's infrastructure worked in tandem with his promotion of tourism as a way to generate quick returns for the massive loans incurred during his regime.[3] He was particularly quick to take advantage of the path to modernization advocated by international lending institutions, establishing the Philippine Department of Tourism during his administration to "realign efforts towards trade promotion and tourism development."[4] To assist the Department of Tourism, he charged the Philippine Tourism Authority with developing infrastructure, such as access roads to designated tourism zones, that would encourage a flow of visitors.[5] Among the projects built was an alternative highway to supplement the outdated Kennon Road, which had been constructed in the early U.S. colonial period. The aptly named Marcos Highway connected the Philippines' summer capital of Baguio to the existing main highway, opening up the mountain region to more travelers and democratizing the experience of leisure through modernization.

Whereas the previous chapter examined the romantic fictions of security, this chapter turns more fully to how these desires are made manifest in the built infrastructures of scenic highways. Roads—and the discourses and practices of mobility they engender—are critical to the workings of imperial modernity and the territorializations, deterritorializations, and reterritorializations of life under globalization.[6] In the Philippines and Hawai'i, scenic highways are instrumental to the history of these sites as American tropics—as places in need of pacification, management, discipline, and protection. Centering the means of transport so that they do not "slip out of the ethnographic [and critical] frame" links tourist freedoms and ways of seeing to military security and the benefits of the militarized neoliberal state.[7] The genealogies of scenic highways in these places are rooted in the needs and desires of the United States as a *modern* imperial power and, in particular, in the needs and desires of militarism and tourism as the means and ends to empire. As Césaire understood it, roads—scenic highways in particular—facilitate experiences, identifications, meanings, and desires that hew to the values of modernity, technology, capital, and the state.[8] Moving back and forth between historical and contemporary accounts and experiences of road building and road taking in the Philippines and Hawai'i—and using a range of materials including travel writing, testimonials, and guidebooks; state discourses on transportation, engineering, and security; expressions of political dissent; and the affective experience of mobility facilitated by the built roadway—this chapter tracks the tracks themselves. I look to roads in order to understand the imaginative forces, formations of knowledge, and material conditions that constitute mobility as a gauge of modernity.

Long since caricatured by his critics, Marcos is nonetheless useful because of the way he understood neoliberal governance, as a kind of mobility that was paradoxically generated by increased regulation, surveillance, and authoritarianism. Even as Marcos was touting road building as the path to building modern nations, his regime also tirelessly suppressed the rising opposition incurred by his vision of modernization. Assisted by his network of roads, Marcos extended his policing arm into the more remote regions of the Philippines, utilizing military violence against a populace he saw as precariously undisciplined—so backward and unruly as to be a danger to his New Society. His idealization of mobility as modernization did not merely rely on the exclusion of unfree subjects; it also produced and intensified the very conditions of exclusion and unfreedom for which his regime is known. Demonstrating that he was an apt pupil of U.S.-Philippine history and politics, Marcos's fixation on road building owed its genesis not only to the restructuring policies of international banks but also to U.S. colonial practices that first grasped the scenic highway as a dual technology of touristic voyeurism *and* militaristic surveillance.

PATHS TO PACIFICATION: ROAD BUILDING IN THE PHILIPPINES

In the sweltering summer months, the coastal city of Manila becomes a concrete prison of monsoon-wrought flooding made more miserable by the diesel fumes of gridlock. Those who have the means and the motivation to leave the city remove themselves to the mountains, following a long-established colonial exodus to cooler elevations. Today, a number of roads lead from Manila and other lowland locales into the mountain region, with Baguio City—the former American summer retreat—as the destination of choice for a vast majority of travelers. The trip from the capital by bus is the most popular way to get to Baguio, although now the large bus lines are shunted to the wider lanes of the more modern Aspiras (formerly Marcos) Highway instead of the older Kennon Road. Buses that travel on the Aspiras or Kennon roadways begin in the capital and work their way north before taking diverging mountain routes to Baguio City. They take passengers through the crowded and gritty maze of Manila, their large viewing windows transforming the city's conglomerate of slums, gated neighborhoods, and business districts into a strange kind of scenery. These buses lumber through narrow surface streets, joining the exodus out of the city, slowing down on occasion to pick up passengers. Manila and its traffic are loath to loosen their grip on the buses that jockey their way to the edge of the urban jungle, where finally, heading north on a four-lane road, traffic speeds up. Flat, green farmlands alternate with modern gas stations. Billboards occasionally line the road, casting shadows on shanties and unfinished subdivisions. Close to two hours after departure from the Manila bus station, the buses wind their way through the rice fields and lahar landscapes of Pampanga. The highway narrows into one lane, and the buses wind through a series of towns with yards, porches, steps, and doors abutting the road. The intimate spaces of everyday life pass by in a blur of diesel fumes. The buses share the road in perilous proximity with children walking back from school, pedicabs, and dogs. At La Union, where the buses take the turn to Baguio—a third road to the mountains—the Naguilian Road (which handles traffic from farther north) adds yet another route option. A short stint on the Mac-Arthur Highway in Binalonan brings the foothills of the Cordilleras into view. On the Aspiras Highway, the road is well-paved concrete, and the climb is smooth, offering panoramas of the countryside's patchwork of rice fields below. Along their journey to Baguio, as they continue to climb slowly in an ascending caravan, the buses pass makeshift roadside buildings and open shop fronts with displays of wood carvings.

Kennon Road, the original colonial scenic highway, has a smaller share of traffic, being narrower, much eroded, and prone to landslides in rainy weather—yet this somehow preserves its more exclusive, colonial feel. The roadway blasted through the Cordillera Mountains to ease transport for the summer citizens of the American colonial government is now mostly used by those tourists who are up for a harrowing six- to eight-hour bus adventure; students and residents who opt for travel on smaller, older, cheaper, and less comfortable buses; or those in private cars. Kennon Road does not offer vistas of the plains, cutting instead into the heart of the Cordilleras. The road generates a more intimate feeling, surrounded by mountains, with rivers churning below. Traffic is wedged into a narrow lane, and blind turns offer danger as well as breathtaking views of waterfalls, bridges, Twin Peaks, and the Bued River Gorge. As it makes its way from the mountains and ascends the famous hairpin curves leading up to Baguio, Kennon Road does not just provide additional thrills to the travel experience; it is part of the scenery. An observation deck at the upper part of Kennon Road overlooks this winding section of the road, and tourists can peer at the other cars making their way up the "zigzag."

As the proliferation of roads under the Marcos regime illustrates, what was once a road to a colonial summer retreat continues to provide a lasting American template for the Philippine path to modernization. When the U.S. colonial administration took over the Philippines in 1898, its insistence on road building was a crucial difference in governance. In the late 1800s, the Spanish friars in the Philippines had recognized the potential of roadways to undermine their power and authority and were wary of the consequences of easing commerce and communication between otherwise isolated towns and peoples. The Spanish metropole discouraged road building in its colony in order to slow the spread of anticolonial nationalism and facilitate distant governance by Spain.[9] In contrast, one of the first acts the Philippine Commission undertook upon becoming the new colonial legislative body was the appropriation of one million dollars for road construction, repair, and maintenance in the islands.[10] From the start, the United States understood roads as military infrastructure; as facilitators of communication, travel, and capitalist extraction; and as symbols and material evidence of the modern American style of governing.

This understanding was profoundly gendered. Roads provided evidence of how the American imperial project was distinct from a decrepit, feminized Spanish colonialism that was both corrupt and inefficient. Related to this conception, road building imposed distinctly masculine forms of discipline on Philippine lands and people deemed unruly, feminized, and backward: the adoption of a familiar gendered symbolic order that centered around the mobility of modern masculine adventurers in narratives such as those of Davis and of White in the previous chapter was reinforced by its translation to the militarization of the islands. Roads were meant to bring the islands under control by expediting troop movement "from the rendezvous to the extremities."[11] This mobility of disciplined male soldiers was intimately linked to a military presence that was to contain the landscape and the population, which was imagined by military leaders to be almost like a feminized body with "extremities" that posed unimaginable perils.

Framing roads as an infrastructure that would facilitate military discipline also overlapped with a shifting emphasis on a more benevolent strategy as narrated by the U.S. Congress—roads as a sign and means to a constructive colonialism. Defining roads as part of the civilizing project of the "white man's burden," the 1903 U.S. Congress agreed that "the road-maker fully as much as the school-teacher must be the evangelist of the Philippines."[12] Early American travelogues about the Philippines, which also doubled as military reconnaissance and natural resource scouting trips, reflected this ideology of roads as a precursor to modernity. Willis Bliss Wilcox's survey of the region of Luzon dreams up roads "yet unbuilt" for "stimulating production as well as . . . spreading information that will convince the native of the benefits of good government and encourage them in habits of thrift and industry."[13] Travelers like Wilcox, who also performed multiple duties as surveyors of the new territories, envisioned themselves as modern men who could take on the challenge of disciplining the tropics. Thus, even as the United States was appropriating large tracts of land for its military reservations and continuing an unofficial campaign of military repression in the islands (aided by roads), it also self-consciously pivoted to an imperialism that saw itself as benevolent. The narrative and purpose of road making expanded to accommodate this new strategy of domestication and civilization: road making showcased the roads as a product of a muscular metropole lifting up its little brown brother. It transformed the forces that had, just a few years earlier, razed the countryside according to the engineering needs of modern colonial governance.

Kennon Road, one of the first and arguably most infamous road projects by the United States in the Philippines, exemplifies how military and colonial touristic desires converged in the idea of mobility. Its construction and use embodied the joint operations of military and tourist mobilities and ways of seeing: it served colonial ends by featuring American modernity as a set of parallel values that prioritized surveillance and sightseeing, pacification and safety, penetration and access. Initially called the Benguet Road, Kennon Road projected an American fantasy of colonial power onto the landscape by transforming the previously impenetrable mountain region into scenery and an accessible destination.[14] It also served as a road to the colonial summer capital. Despite distinguishing itself from the fraternity of European colonial powers in Southeast Asia, the trappings of Old World colonialism such as hill stations — British India's Simla or Dutch Java's Buitenzorg and Bandung, for instance — remained potent touchstones for U.S. colonizers.[15] As American military occupation wore on, the economic and logistical practicalities of having a health resort for recuperating soldiers in the Philippines became evident, dovetailing with elite colonial desires. The Philippine summer capital of Baguio was built in the early 1900s as a convalescent sanitarium for colonial troops supposedly enervated by the tropical climate in the lowlands. It soon outpaced that function, becoming a primary vacation spot for colonial elites during the early twentieth century. Kennon Road was part of the same fantasy of imperial architecture and engineering, and it was built concurrently as the path to the colonial dream city.[16] From its inception during early American rule to its current incarnation as one of the nation's best-known and enduring scenic highways, Kennon Road—like Baguio City— embodied a modern, masculine infrastructure of control and discipline laid over the resistant wilderness.

Constructing Kennon Road is a story of American civil engineering forcing itself onto foreign terrains. Subduing and improving the rough country of the northern Philippines, road building recast a recent history of military violence into colonial productivity: this was *civilized* modern American colonialism. Yet as a showcase of modern American colonialism, Kennon Road was initially a disaster: instead of the technological advancements of American engineering forging roads where before there were none, building Kennon Road was a process characterized by the ineffective leadership of military men who had underestimated both the recalcitrance of the mountainous landscape and the manageability of the labor pool. Ultimately, however, the road was built, and the critiques about its cost and foolhardiness fell by the wayside. Today, Kennon Road's history encapsulates a colonial narrative of masculine persistence and triumph: it is named, after all, for the man who succeeded. In 1905—overcoming flooding, erosion, and landslides, and literally blasting and beating a road into the mountainside—the Army Corps of Engineers and its labor force of native and imported workers finally completed the Benguet Road, and Major Lyman Kennon drove a horse and buggy to Baguio.[17] Its opening coincided with the acceleration of Baguio's construction as a colonial city and the broader American penetration of the Cordillera region, militarily and touristically.

Though the lure of a colonial resort fueled this expensive, geologically ill-advised road project, the road was not just a means of access to a colonial fantasy. It was itself a site for the construction of social hierarchies and the exercise of colonial power that would translate in later years to a tourism economy. Even as Filipinos, too, were caught up in road building's new circuits of mobility as laborers, they were at the same time put in their proper place in the racial hierarchy of the islands. Trail construction forced thousands of Filipinos to work on road construction in lieu of a cash tax, marking which colonial bodies had to work under the new colonial regime and which bodies could afford to opt out.[18] Because of the conscripted nature of the work, Kennon found himself having difficulties with "supervising Oriental labor" and "the natives' persistent indifference

. . . to customary work ethics and material motivations," and so circumvented existing American immigration and labor laws by importing labor from Europe, South America, and Asia. This kind of labor recruitment from the region and abroad brought diverse and isolated groups of people in contact with each other, later an important factor in the rise of political regionalism and activism in the area.[19] But the existence of recruited labor also distinguished, in very visible ways, those people suitable for building the road and those people for whom the road was being built.

The class system enacted in road-building practices embodied the shift from imperial violence to the assimilation of colonial subjects into a new colonial and global economy typified by racial hierarchy and classification. At first, the argument of military necessity was an important counterbalance to the mainstream perception that Kennon Road and Baguio were elite indulgences, especially as the construction of Kennon Road took up a quarter of the total colonial budget. Insisting that the road's primary purpose was to "furnish the means of recuperating the army of the United States in these islands in the most economic method," Governor General William Taft explained that the road to Baguio was necessary to the very survival of colonial society.[20] With the shift from a colonial hegemony secured by military means to one that invited identification with colonial values, Kennon Road likewise became associated with the social and cultural opportunities opened up by American colonialism. The increasing use of the road by American and Filipino civilians alike further distanced the colonial project from its initial violence. Instead, Kennon Road facilitated an annual summer trek of the colonial government to the cooler uplands, creating an opportunity for Filipino elites to maneuver their way into spaces of power. Wealthy businessmen and prominent politicians—including Emilio Aguinaldo, one of the leaders of the Philippine Revolution against Spain and against the United States—were eventually lured to Baguio and all traveled on the new scenic highway.[21] Where once the Filipino elite had sided with a Filipino press critical of the expenses and vanities of Kennon Road and other colonial projects, they were now drawn to the notion of belonging offered by access to the summer capital. Only wealthy Filipinos and Americans could take Kennon Road to Baguio, making it—figuratively and literally—a road for the upwardly mobile of the American colony.[22]

Kennon Road inaugurated the journey to Baguio as a tourist itinerary. While early travel on the road was difficult and uncomfortable, it consolidated practices of sightseeing and notions of the picturesque that marked a particular mobility and modernity for those on holiday, secured by the ingenuity, persistence, and technology of the U.S. Army Corps of Engineers. During his stint as the commissioner of commerce and police, W. Cameron Forbes—an early booster of Baguio who would eventually become the governor general of the Philippines—describes a 1904 visit to a Kennon Road construction site: "The road, which from here passed through a mountain gorge, very picturesque to see, began to be the landing place for numerous waterfalls."[23] The journey on the serpentine mountain road, with its stunning vistas and breathtaking views of the mountains, became a central part of the transition from hot colonial capital to cool summer resort. The journey on the road itself was a transformative one: it produced identifications with U.S. colonial disciplining of the landscape. The views, it was made clear, came at a premium. Emphasizing the peril of the construction process, Forbes playfully narrates a near accident on the road as it was being forged into the mountain. He reminds his readers that their enjoyment of a vivid and striking view are made accessible through the hardships and dangers endured by colonial workers, positioning the heroic sacrifices and service of the Army Corps of Engineers and the colonial administration as the enabling conditions of tourist pleasure. Reminding the traveler of the costs of the road and the price of modern mobility, as well as the central role that the colonial government had in ensuring it, such narratives were akin to a colonial apologia. A central theme in travel writing about Kennon Road in the decades to follow, these stories of the price paid for the picturesque kept the benefits of U.S. colonial and military occupation firmly in view.[24]

Early twentieth-century travel writing about Kennon Road depicted the experience of its new tourist mobilities as a central element of the romance of empire. Travel publications focused on Kennon's dual attractions as a scenic highway and as an avenue for adventure and leisure specifically reserved for colonial elites. Transforming the Philippines from war zone to tourist destination, travel materials about Kennon Road and Baguio emphasized the ascending movement to the temperate mountains, away from the petty tropical squabbling of the colonial administration: "Gradually, as the traveler makes one bend of the famous Baguio Zigzag after another, the air grows cooler and cooler, while all around the vegetation changes from tropical to a temperate character."[25] Literally rising above the gritty realities of colonialism, the road was an escape route to a more remote and tranquil space for rejuvenation. As the traveler wound through the mountains north of Manila away from the cares of colonial administration, he could be reminded once again of the romance of empire: "The motor road to Baguio runs through wild, romantic scenery, climbing very steep, and zigzags like some great writhing snake up the mountain slope."[26] On this journey, the romance of empire has its proper male protagonist: the masculine traveler who embodies that understanding of the colonial mission as uplifting. A 1920s brochure featuring Kennon Road illustrates the transformative power of Kennon Road: on a fold-out photographic panorama (figure 2.1), two men are perched on one of Kennon Road's cliff-hugging curves, an automobile parked behind them on the one-lane road and a sheer rock cliff stretching upward. The man in front assumes the classic surveying pose, right foot resting on rubble, knee bent, surveying the vista before him, shading his eyes with his hand. The landscape stretches before and beneath him: he is at the same level as the clouds. In conveying a sense of dominion over the landscape, the pose constructs masculinity as tied to the ability to penetrate into previously inaccessible mountain regions and render these regions as sites from which to view scenery.

Framing Kennon Road in a tourist idiom recast a violent history of American colonialism into a narrative of tourist discovery: "When people started coming up the Kennon Road across the faces of dangerous cliffs and over hair-raising chasms, then up steep, sharp hairpin and horseshoe curves into the Baguio wonderland, enthusiasm replaced opposition."[27] The sinuous curves of Kennon Road became postcard fixtures (figure 2.2) that rendered the road and its surrounding landscape part of the tourist pilgrimage to Baguio. The initial purpose of road building, to facilitate military maneuvers and the speedy pacification of the islands, is here updated through the visual language of tourism—perilous cliffs and chasms replaced the military pacification of recalcitrant natives with the picturesque. The "opposition" to the colonial project is downgraded to a lack of foresight and enthusiasm about the benefits and pleasures of Kennon Road and Baguio City, occluding the reality of an armed insurgency that fought against an invading army. The road as tourist attraction becomes evidence of the conversion of the Philippines from combat zone to travel destination.

Tourism softened past and ongoing military violence not only by producing experiences and views of the scenic sublime, but also by tapping

FIGURE 2.1 An image from a foldout brochure about Kennon Road and Baguio, 1929. COURTESY OF THE JONATHAN BEST COLLECTION.

into the romance of discovery. Apart from bringing a contingent of health tourists seeking to recover at Baguio's sanitarium, Kennon Road opened up the previously inaccessible Cordilleras to tourists in search of the authentically indigenous, so to speak.[28] Filipinos from the Cordilleras, who at first had constituted a crucial part of Kennon's construction labor, now provided an attraction for sightseeing in the nascent tourism industry. In short, the road made Filipino mountain life into an ethnic bazaar, rendering people and place into exhibits.[29] Early travel writing and colonial administrative logs note how native bodies became an expected part of the scenic mountain itinerary. Characteristic of these searches for the

FIGURE 2.2 A Kennon Road postcard, 1928. COURTESY OF THE JACK TAYLOR COLLECTION, AMERICAN HISTORICAL COLLECTION, RIZAL LIBRARY, ATENEO DE MANILA UNIVERSITY.

authentic costumed native, an English travelogue written in the 1920s narrates how road-building projects permitted greater access to the so-called primitive: "The view over the mining district of Benguet was magnificent. . . . I left the main road and struck a delightful little colony of Igorot houses clinging to the edge of the mountain slope. They were of the most primitive type and picturesque in the extreme. A swarm of half-naked children[,] some of them carrying babies in slings on their backs, crowded around me and formed an interesting foreground to several photos which I took."[30] This tourist romance of contact was pedagogical: the tourist teaches native people their proper place as part of the scenery of an authentic travel experience. This English writer's freedom of movement secured by a history of U.S. militarism, he could envision the islands and their people through the lens of the picturesque. Subsequent accounts of travel on Kennon Road demonstrate how native people and places were made accessible for the consumption of the touristic gaze. A Japanese traveler, visiting in 1936 to commemorate his countrymen's participation in building Kennon Road, records his impressions in familiar tourist rhetoric: "The city is up so high that it is ever so cool, fresh and clean. . . . At the city market, I saw for the first time Igorot women in their native costumes."[31] Presaging the influx of non-American tourists, these early travelogues reflect the touristic desires and ways of seeing that were shaped by the Kennon Road's access.

These emergent tourist pleasures were sutured to Kennon Road's continuing function as a military thoroughfare, softening the brutality of continued military occupation and pacification. Despite the emerging romantic narrative of tourism, the realities of securing paradise meant that scenic highways also conveyed troops. The soldiers for whom Baguio was initially proposed had their own military reservation set aside for them from the first, and they were part of the colonial society fostered by early American administrators. Designed to house both convalescent military personnel and to give them a space for rest and recreation, Camp John Hay was built up with hospitals, dormitories, warehouses, and a gymnasium for the use of soldiers who were on active duty subjugating Filipinos throughout the archipelago.[32] Shortly, improvements in medicine shifted the use of Camp John Hay from recuperation to leisure: more recreation facilities were installed to adapt to the changing desires of the military, such as golf courses, a cinema, tennis courts, a pool, and other amenities. Rather than a sanitarium, Camp John Hay became a tourist destination for the off-duty soldier. More privileged tourists took advantage of the military base's leisure facilities, which in the 1920s and 1930s became more accessible to civilians. Thanks to its association with colonial leisure, and to the work laid out by the "one-man tour agency" of W. Cameron Forbes, by the 1920s and 1930s, Baguio was *the* place to be and had gained a reputation that paralleled other Southeast Asian colonial hill stations. Foreign tourists were drawn to its cosmopolitan spaces.[33] In 1916, visitors were double the local population of four thousand. Almost twenty-five years later, the number of visitors increased to 150,000 compared to a 24,000 resident population.[34] Tourist pleasures to be had in a military base were thus connected to the journey to Baguio, further effacing the military violence at the heart of the origins of Kennon Road and Baguio City.

In tandem with how tourist pleasures on Kennon Road mediated an increasing distance from historical and ongoing U.S. military violence, it also facilitated the mobilization of a self-policing populace. American soldiers were not the only ones to benefit from Kennon Road's gateway into the mountains. Baguio also became the new home to the Officer's School of the Philippine Constabulary in 1908, later renamed the Philippine Military Academy (PMA). The training ground for the neocolonial elite's military forces, the PMA would in later years be instrumental to the militarization of the Cordillera region. As road building by American authorities penetrated deeper into the Cordillera region, the central location of the

PMA was crucial for quick mobilizations into and infiltration of mountain region communities. When the PMA transferred from Manila to Baguio, Camp John Hay recruited Filipino men from the region into its own company of Philippine Scouts. Thus, even as Camp John Hay was transformed into more of a social center for U.S. soldiers, the initial vision of Baguio as an accessible site for military reinvigoration was fulfilled by the militarization of its native occupants, beginning a pattern of self-policing and native discipline that continues to this day. Kennon Road and other roads built into the remote regions of the Cordillera meant that a more diverse group of Filipino men could come together and be dispersed in the service of colonial security, completing the circle of colonial tutelage and further securing state and tourist mobilities as they penetrated into the mountains.

Kennon Road enabled a mobilization of bodies in the shifting social orders generated by an indigenization of the Philippines' policing force and a Cordilleran economy increasingly oriented toward tourism and other extractive industries. Interrupted only by the brief bombing and occupation by the Japanese military during World War II, the American character of Baguio—even after Philippine independence in 1946—was integral to its attraction as a destination. Between World War II and the 1979 signing of a Military Bases Agreement that placed Camp John Hay under a Filipino base commander, Baguio continued to attract domestic and Asian elites who were nostalgically yearning for the colonial romance of the mountain sanctuary. The return of affluent families to Baguio in the post-American era revived interest in the growing Filipino middle class to become part of the social scene.[35] The journey on Kennon Road was an authenticating centerpiece of the postwar tourism experience, facilitating, as it did, affective and corporeal relations that inscribed different bodies with different meanings. Scenic highways such as Kennon transformed Filipinos into tourist attractions defined by tradition and primitivism and in contrast to mobile, modern tourists. The network of roadways laid out during the U.S. colonial administration enjoyed a travel renaissance after World War II. The 1963 publication of *Islands of Pleasure*, one of the early modern guidebooks to the Philippines, noted the importance of the transportation infrastructure for tourist mobilities. While the author pronounces the highway system as "not first class," he still highlights the efficient bus systems established under early American colonial rule as the key to making the Philippines accessible for touristic pleasures. He reminisces that he "frequently travelled by bus in the provinces, for you get closer to the people that way and, besides, it is very inexpensive."[36] Just as Kennon had brought turn-of-the-century travelers closer to the authentic native, American roadways were once again facilitating intimate encounters between hosts and guests. A new generation was rediscovering Kennon Road as a nostalgic route to the past, ironically at the same time that the Philippines was undergoing another regimen of modernization. Under Marcos, while road networks were being modernized, a tourist economy selling the Philippines as an exotic destination meant that the mobilities on these roads did not extend to all subjects in the same ways.

Likewise, the resurgence of middle-class mass tourism revived Kennon Road's charms for a new tourist market and narrated the road experience in familiar terms. Travel writing about Baguio inevitably included descriptions of the actual journey and the feelings that the road engendered: "The second surprise came when I transferred from the train to a bus for the last steep climb through the mountains, zigzagging on a winding road that rose more than 3,900 feet in seven miles. The drive was exhilarating. Deep chasms dropped to a churning river below; old stone bridges spanned the gorge; the sound of waterfalls tumbling down the mountains permeated the fog-laden air."[37] Adopting the dramatic rhetoric of early travel narratives, mass tourism reactivated Kennon Road itself as part of the attraction of traveling to Baguio. This wonder over "the inaccessible made accessible" echoes early travel narratives that attributed the exceptionality of this experience to the conquest of nature by American technological modernity and superiority. The "twisting mountain road" continued to evoke admiration as an "engineering marvel" that carved out spectacular vistas from raw nature and made them available for visual pleasure.[38] Eliciting exhilaration from tourists, Kennon Road's ascent is significant not only because of the thrills of bodily risk that somehow confirm the authenticity of this journey to the mountain region, but also because these consumable embodied and affective pleasures repress other kinds of corporeal peril, such as military and paramilitary violence. The reemergence of Kennon Road as a tourist experience, after all, coincided with the rise of tourism under Marcos's New Society, which has been characterized as producing "a million kilometers of paved roads" at the expense of and as an alibi to its crimes against the Filipino people.[39] The modern embrace of Kennon Road as a scenic highway, finally, demonstrates the joys that come with the commodification of colonial and natural resources for a consumer market.

The natural elements over which American colonial technology initially triumphed and touristic fantasies extolled, however, have prevailed in the long term. While Kennon enjoyed a period of time when it was a highly open road, it has been closed off to all but light traffic since the earthquake that devastated Baguio in 1991, although this rule is often disregarded during the dry season by lighter, cheaper buses. The river that runs beside and below Kennon Road has risen meters above the old water level due to silting. The road continues to be eroded, as the area originally surveyed by the American colonial government was geologically incapable of sustaining a road.[40] Yet despite its questionable safety record and the competition from more modern roads such as the Aspiras Highway, Kennon Road remains a tourist attraction, providing one of the most scenic rides to Baguio. A majority of travel trade websites about Baguio highlight Kennon Road's "alternating steep rises, dips, and sharp turns, splendid waterfalls and lush vegetation."[41] Others offer warnings about the thrilling ride where tourists "will encounter sharp hairpin turns and blind curves . . . landslides . . . no guardrails . . . deep ravine[s] . . . and limited visibility."[42] It remains popular because it is still the fastest route from Manila, if not the safest. The element of danger, for some tourists, is also attractive: on Kennon, "you ride at your own risk as the road is very unpredictable."[43] As it had done earlier, the promise of bodily risk adds authenticity to the immersive feel of traveling on a colonial road. Careening around precipitous curves with nothing between car and the river below, negotiating the eroding realities of rubble and landslides, traveling on Kennon brings drivers and passengers closer to a sense of an unmediated "real" experience. For tourists taking the infamous bus trips, they get the thrill of hairpin turns at high speeds, as well as the opportunity to travel like most local folk who do not own private vehicles. They are being authentic and set themselves apart from the tourists who prefer a more cushioned ride—in chauffeured car or by plane. The mountains and the people seem more accessible and intimate this way—just as earlier travelers had pointed out.

Kennon Road continues to signal an escape to a place of colonial uplift, away from the humid tropics of colonial toil. From the gradual ascent that follows the path of the Bued River, to the twists and turns of its panoramas, Kennon's climb helps travelers and residents identify with the social and cultural uplift embedded in its narratives: it is escapism in more than one sense. A 1982 driving guide to Luzon concurs, connecting maps, sample itineraries, and driving etiquette for the adventurous traveler to a satisfaction in Americans' "less high-handed approach to the mountain peoples" that "open[ed] the area through road and trail building."[44] The drive up Kennon Road, though a short twenty-nine kilometers, remains popular because it continues to draw from a romantic colonial archive that frames American occupation in sentimental and nostalgic terms, eliding the brutal violence of imperial war. It keeps offering a worn but alluring alibi for historical colonialism, contributions now appreciable as tourist experiences and commodities as well as efficient postcolonial transportation.

Tourism in contemporary Baguio wrestles with the legacies of colonial and modern mobility. At the same time that tourism is a dominant frame for the region, the growth of the road network and the massive expansion of modern tourism have worn away the romance of colonial tourism. Baguio is now quite cosmopolitan and is a center for communication, development, education, and commerce. The roads that have brought tourists have also heralded rapid deforestation from indiscriminate logging; the stripping of land from copper and silver mining; pollution from diesel-fueled vehicles; and, for the residents of the mountain region, alcoholism, the spread of sexually transmitted diseases, and the swindling of villagers. The destructive changes facilitated by the roads, including increased policing and disenfranchisement during the Marcos regime, have also been met with Cordillera countermobilities. In line with a long-established practice of resisting Spanish invasion and incorporation, a broad coalitional movement of the Cordillera peoples fought the encroachments of extraction projects by the Marcos dictatorship in the mountain region. The resistance to the construction of a World Bank–funded dam on the Chico River that would have displaced thousands resulted in protracted military engagements and galvanized Filipinos in the area to join the rebel New People's Army against the regime's terror tactics.[45] The politicization of people in the region continues today, with indigenous political consciousness strategically playing to and rejecting the tourist gaze as Cordillerans continue to struggle with state interventions. Likewise, with the departure of the U.S. military from its Philippine bases in 1992, the faded military rationalizations for the construction of Baguio and Kennon Road were further removed and transmuted into the idiom of tourism. Camp John Hay—the old U.S. military base—was turned over to the Philippine government, which in turn leased it out for private development. Its former buildings, fields, and resources have now become tourist lodgings and amusements. Even the Philippine Military Academy, though actively training officers for the state's military, is open to tourists.

In the post-Marcos era, the region continues to be incorporated into the circuits of domestic and global tourism that the Philippine Department of Tourism continues to cultivate. Today, Kennon Road, like its more modern counterparts, operates as the gateway to even more remote upland areas, such as Banaue or Sagada, where the famed rice terraces and Igorot cultures offer more authentic mountain landscapes to fuel tourist fantasy.[46] In comparison, Kennon Road is bustling with the commercial transactions of tourism and the artifacts of everyday life for those who have settled near the road. Today's Kennon Road is further away from the colonial adventure-romance, though it still provides views and thrills: it is crowded with people trying to make a living. Small clusters of squatters have cropped up in the intervening years, left over from the mining interests that have devastated the land and moved on. Some squatter residents ply the occupants of buses and cars with snacks and drinks on stops on the way up to Baguio. Despite the increased cosmopolitanism and politicization of the people who live in the Cordillera region (eased in part by the road networks), the dominant script of tourism insists on their intelligibility as authentically indigenous, costumed, and performing. The buses and cars that travel on Kennon Road carry people who consume the authentic Philippines through both the real "thrills" of the colonial road, and the pleasures of authenticity as embodied by natives.

This last legacy of Kennon Road—its sightseeing incarnation—folds neatly into the desires of the Marcos administration to identify with the modern. Sightseeing, like all forms of sight, is an act of surveillance and power. Within touristic economies and cultures, sightseeing as a form of control and social practice ties the act of looking, and the ways that we are taught to look to the production of knowledge about native bodies, scenery, and a natural(ized) racial and national order. As a process and practice of knowledge production, sightseeing reinforces meanings about the proper places of and distance between tourist bodies and native bodies. As a tourist act, it is profoundly modern.[47] These tourist acts converge with military modes of observation that continue to police the

FIGURE 2.3 **The H-3 Interstate.** PHOTOGRAPH BY KENJI SAITO.

mountain today—assessing, cataloguing, reporting on unfamiliar terrains and unusual suspects—which are made possible by the intimacies produced by new mobilities.

MOBILITY AND ITS DISCONTENTS: THE HAWAI'I INTERSTATE

Whereas a road can provide intimate access to authentic embodiments as part of what it trafficks, O'ahu's H-3 would much rather that commuters, on this drive, overlook the Native bodies (and their ghosts) that haunt its concrete and asphalt thoroughfare. Snaking through a pristine valley on the leeward (south) side of O'ahu, tunneling though the dramatic Ko'olau range, and soaring over the windward (east) side with spectacular views of the coast on its mile-long aerial viaduct, the H-3 interstate offers one of the most breathtaking and dramatic drives in the United States (figure 2.3). Regardless of whether one is a resident commuter, soldier, or tourist, the corporeal, visual, and affective experience the H-3 was designed to deliver is transformative. The journey from Waikīkī to the windward side is the most dramatic, heightened by movement away from the tourist center and the gradual ascent on the elevated highway above Hālawa Valley. The highway passes over the preserve below, framing the lush tropical scenery. Climbing toward the Koʻolau, the mountain range closes in on both sides of the highway. Entering the lava rock tunnels dramatically cuts off the sensory pleasures of the landscape, which makes the wide panorama that greets drivers as they exit the tunnels that much more spectacular. Driving on the H-3 from Honolulu to the leeward side offers an experience akin to Kennon's elevating journey: it literally lifts commuters above and through the Koʻolau, floating them over the terrain and displaying the sheer rock faces on one side and the distant rugged coastline on the other. Traveling on this highway is a resolutely sublime experience: the panorama it presents to the viewer, along with the sense of soaring over the island, is meant to ennoble and uplift, to rise above everyday trivialities. In other words, the experience of H-3 is meant to inspire a transcendent physical, moral, intellectual, and metaphysical state removed from the everyday.

The H-3 operates as a visual technological prosthesis that amplifies the mobilities of modern sightseeing, yet it does so in a strangely disembodied and disembodying kind of way—particularly when considering a tourism industry that depends on the insistent, embodied tropicalization of the indigenous body as one of the sensual pleasures that makes Hawaiʻi tourism unique.[48] What follows is an exploration of how the scenic sublime in military, engineering, and tourist publications—using built text and corporeal, sensory experience—makes use of the indigenous while simultaneously rendering it culturally and politically invisible. What are the different stakes over space, history, and mobility that collide over the H-3's construction, and how does the H-3—as a technology of mobility and surveillance—produce ways of seeing and of not seeing on the vistas that it opens up? The mobilities produced by the H-3 Interstate regulate the touristic gaze, a way of looking that is also already profoundly shaped by the workings of the militarized state. Drawing attention to the "constructedness" of the H-3's scenic sublime demonstrates how certain gendered and racialized narratives and imaginations become more visible and urgent than others in an economy jointly dominated by tourism and the military.

In Hawaiʻi, as in the Philippines, the scenic highway cannot be detached from colonial and military histories. The modernization of roads in Hawaiʻi is linked to continental U.S. highway construction in the postwar era, but like many colonized economies, Hawaiʻi first systemically built roads to facilitate the extraction of capital. During its plantation heyday, imported plantation labor played a big part in the building and maintenance of access roads. When Hawai'i became a U.S. territory, it benefited from the road construction projects taken on by the military to ease military traffic around the islands as well as to continue to improve plantation access roads.[49] The Japanese bombing of Pearl Harbor led to the military conclusion that cross-island roads were needed in order to properly defend the territory—existing coastal roads were too easily shut down by enemy fire—and plans were made to create alternative and redundant routes to optimize military mobility.[50] The territory sought out defense funds to address this perceived threat, launching the modern road-building era in Hawai'i. The improvement of Hawai'i's older roads under the Federal-Aid Highway Act of 1959 was tied to its status as a new state in the Union, as well as to its strategic location "as the crossroads of the Pacific."[51]

As a modern scenic highway distinct from territory-era roads, the H-3 was born under the joint aegis of defense and tourism. One of the most costly and controversial stretches of road ever constructed in the United States, the H-3 Interstate was first conceived during the Cold War as part of the Eisenhower Interstate and Defense Highway System of 1960.[52] In part inaugurated by Hawai'i's statehood in 1959, the H-3 Interstate, which took thirty-seven years to complete, cost a total of $1.3 billion, one of the more hefty pork-barrel projects of its day.[53] Its primary function was to link the Pearl Harbor Naval Base and Hickam Air Force Base complexes on the leeward side of the island to Kaneohe Marine Corps Air Station on the windward side. Ninety percent of the funding for the bloated construction project came from federal funds because of its defense designation, courtesy of Hawai'i's savvy congressional delegates.[54] Supposedly, it was also planned in anticipation of Hawai'i's booming population and the development of new population centers farther from the expensive business center of Honolulu and its increasing traffic problems, but the selection of the route belies this rationale.[55] The H-3 was a military project, first and foremost. However, over the course of its construction, it also became a scenic highway. Hawai'i's emergent tourism economy was a crucial partner in recruiting existing highways into scenic itineraries for the influx of postwar visitors. In 1965 the Scenic Roads and Parkways Study by the State of Hawai'i's Department of Transportation linked the idea of traveling on improved, modern roadways to the activities and itineraries being generated by a burgeoning tourism industry.[56] Five years after the

highway system was chartered for military purposes, the institutionalization of the scenic highway also began. The Recreation Advisory Council,
a federal body created by the president, began to gather information for a
future national program of scenic roads and parkways: "A scenic highway
is a road having roadsides, or traversing areas, or relatively high aesthetic
or cultural value. Picnicking, parking, walking, camping and other recreational facilities may be built into the scenic corridor itself, or the highway may be pleasant access to such facilities."[57] Strategically planning for
industry growth, Hawai'i's Department of Transportation concurred that
"a well-planned scenic roads program will aid greatly in the implementa-
tion of Hawai'i's recreation program."[58] Hawai'i's natural beauty would
draw visitors to the "paradise of the Pacific," but a system of scenic (and
safe) modern drives would render the island's natural resources more ad-
vantageously accessible and "take one back to the peace and serenity of
old Hawai'i."[59] The ways in which the H-3's military origins were folded
into touristic logics suggest that highways are more than just convenient
infrastructure paving the way for efficient holidays and shorter workday
commutes: they are built evidence of the dominant scripts that narrate
Hawai'i.

It was precisely because the H-3 Interstate was at the heart of the politics of space, culture, sovereignty, and modernity that its construction,
like Kennon Road's, was characterized by contentiousness. Over the protracted and costly four decades that it took to complete the H-3, its one
consistent defining feature was the magnitude of opposition it engendered. Over its litigious, controversial, and much-politicized construction
process—which involved local, state, and federal officials; labor unions;
and environmental, antimilitary, and Native sovereignty groups—the H-3
inspired a variety of strategies and arguments from its supporters and de-
tractors. Many of Hawai'i's residents—Native Hawaiians and non-Natives
alike—understood the imposition of a military-driven pork-barrel project
as the latest battleground over representation, cultural ownership, and indigenous land rights on the islands. Beginning as it did in the year after
Hawai'i's dubious referendum on statehood was passed, the H-3's origins
were indelibly marked not only by Cold War geopolitics and Japanese
American political ascendance, but also by a long history of indigenous
dispossession and the resurgence of Native Hawaiian activism. The civil
rights and race power movements of the continental United States had
a counterpart in an increased political activism in Hawai'i that opposed

the mass evictions caused by development and tourism in the islands as well as the damage caused by militarization, tourism, and development. The long H-3 debacle represented another moment in a centuries-long process of dispossession and dislocation that was being actively contested on many fronts in the 1960s and 1970s. The fact that the H-3 took thirty-seven years to build is a testament to the resolve and success of the coalition of activists that fought against the highway's construction. Along its rough journey to completion, the H-3 was the subject of legal battles over environmental and cultural compliance that rerouted the initial plan several times.[60] Its main opponents, the "Stop H-3" coalition of environmental groups, served up a variety of obstacles ranging from lawsuits, to public hearing objections, sit-ins, and other demonstrations.[61] The discovery of historically significant indigenous sites on the planned route of the H-3 and the subsequent entrance of Native Hawaiian groups into the political fray enriched the opposition's legal case. The protestors' testimony before the U.S. Senate committee in 1986 framed the H-3 project within a political critique that centered indigenous sovereignty, to no avail.[62] That same year, President Ronald Reagan himself signed a waiver that essentially dismissed environmental and cultural concerns raised by the protestors, allowing halted construction to continue.[63]

One more obstacle would stand in the way of the H-3's completion in 1997: a public demonstration and occupation that brought into relief the gendered racial formations that generated the H-3 project. Led by five Native Hawaiian women, the physical occupation of Hālawa Valley began in 1993 as a protest against the Bishop Museum's dismissal of a consulting anthropologist who blew the whistle on the planned bulldozing of sacred sites in the valley to make way for the H-3. It ended up as a larger story about what, exactly, people on scenic highways could choose and refuse to see. In the process of the H-3's contested construction, this political action of the Native Hawaiian women was both late and brief by comparison. However, the emergent Native sovereignty movement's presence in the 1980s and 1990s catapulted it into the public eye and amplified what began as a spontaneous action into a long-term occupation that prioritized indigenous cosmology as the defining term of the latest anti-H-3 action. Even the environmentalist coalition had failed to seriously connect the question of historic indigenous dispossession to any question about land use in Hawai'i.[64] In contradistinction, the Native Hawaiian women who occupied the valley generated a very different vision of the space — suggesting alternative modernities and mobilities than those championed by the builders of the H-3. They insisted on a corporeally gendered language: referring to mystical occurrences, bodily occupation, community discussion, supportive networking, and communion with the land in ways that specifically identified these actions as Native feminine concerns. In short, they created a framework of intelligibility that forced people to encounter actual bodily and personal presences in the land through which the H-3 would pass, to think about the space as a part of a specific indigenous legacy, and to imagine indigenous connections to the land as alive and in the present. I focus here on their story because of the way that their indigenous stand against the built roadway understood and countered the state-marshaled abstracting discourses of mobility and modernity with alternative imaginings that have little place in paradise: stories, viewpoints, feelings of grief, antipathy, and ambiguity that are at once the product of historical violence, land theft, and sly legal maneuvers, and the constant resistance against them.

The women of Hālawa Valley took an indigenous stand against the roadway that understood and countered the state-marshaled abstracting discourses of mobility and modernity with an insistence on their embodied mobilities and modernities. Their occupation of the valley should not be understood as the opposition of immobility and mobility, or tradition and modernity, but rather as the generation of competing mobilities and modernities. The protestors, for instance, located themselves as cosmopolitan members of an expansive and linked Pacific community. Gladys Pualoa, sixty-four at the time, had just returned from Aotearoa (New Zealand) on a trip that she describes as opening up her "sensitivity to culture."[65] Her Pacific voyaging enabled her to more clearly identify the importance of understanding her Native Hawaiian heritage and link it to a larger indigenous world. Dawn Wasson, a friend of Pualoa's, had also been on this trip, which had similarly taught her about the systems of exchange between indigenous cultures and peoples in the Pacific. Further, the occupants hosted a number of pilgrims — from Hawai'i, the continent, and around the world — who acknowledged the sacredness of the site, mapping the valley as a node of mobility and exchange that was connected to others. This oceanic identification maps a long tradition of voyaging onto a contemporary consciousness, identifying these women as mobile subjects, and locating the Pacific islands in an itinerary of change and movement. In line with this theme, the women depicted their occupation of the valley as a journey. Upon their return to Hawai'i, they encountered the news about the firing of the whistle-blowing Bishop Museum anthropologist and decided to attend the protest. Pualoa and Wasson characterize themselves as never being activists, describing their occupation of the valley right after the protest as something that "just happened," yet they both describe a pull to "[take] what we had, [drive] into the valley, and [start] hiking in."[66] Hiking into the valley, rather than soaring over the promised landscape, Pualoa and Wasson practiced slower but more capacious alternative mobilities that they would use to counter the projected fast lane of the H-3.

Once in the valley, the women did stand their ground, refusing to move in the face of the H-3's army of construction. Instead, they staged a re-occupation, a move that dramatized an active habitation of and attachment to the land in contrast to the H-3's detachment. Even as their occupation garnered increasing publicity and attention from a resurgent sovereignty movement, the protestors insisted on bodies on the land as evidence of political commitment. Pualoa and Wasson did not necessarily identify as activists or as members of Native Hawaiian sovereignty groups, and they distanced themselves from the more established groups and individuals that constituted Hawai'i's diverse sovereignty movement. According to Wasson, "Everyone came with agendas. So we tell them, you sleep here first. . . . We were just simple people, not very astute about political maneuvers."[67] The publicity and the persistence of the occupation created an alternative community that was grounded in the everyday life of the valley—in the corporeally felt experience of being present on the land—and not necessarily in the political fluency of larger movements. The insistence on spending time in the valley was a strategic maneuver: it made Native Hawaiian everyday life visible, tangible, felt, and spatially and temporally present.

The occupation of the valley also created a public space for storytelling and dialogue where little had existed before: this was the very thing that the H-3 had hoped to silence with its promise of transcendent mobility. The women who occupied the valley understood their action as a counternarrative to the H-3's constructive fictions. As guides to increasing numbers of visitors who came to support the women and stay in the valley, Pualoa, Wasson, and their companions helped generate alternative imaginaries and itineraries for their visitors: "We would take people on tours," and they would "listen to our stories about living there" and about the "energies" and the "ley lines" that are part of the land.[68] Authorizing an indigenous genealogy of the land, the women identified their practices of habitation and storytelling as transformative: Pualoa recalls that "when we first went up, the sheriff wanted to arrest us, but they ended up being friends with us even when we were stern with his men. Later on, he brought his men up and their families to listen to our oration [about the valley]."[69]

The proliferation of ghost stories in Hālawa Valley is another testament to the lively and interactive practice of storytelling that the occupation engendered. Pualoa relates stories told by the construction workers and hunters who would see or even talk to apparitions in the valley. She recounts nonoccupant stories of a suddenly disappearing "big Hawaiian, sitting" on one of the machines, of apparitions, inexplicable battle noises, chants, and drumming, and of floating lights and other phenomena that did not have scientific explanations. The late Glen Grant, a local storyteller, describes freak accidents that caused deaths during the road construction, as well as accounts of "phantom hitchhikers," voices, and other ghostly apparitions that were related by activists, construction workers, engineers, and motorists.[70] These "chicken-skin" narratives do not merely provide thrills to the listener; they also describe the ways in which stories of the past resurface in the present to unsettle the consciousness.[71] The ghostly presences tracked by Pualoa, Wasson, and others represent historical and contemporary narratives elided by tourist fictions of Hawai'i. The way that these ghostly narratives crowd the present as living history is akin to Lilikalā Kame'eleihiwa's elaboration of indigenous history as something "in front" as a reference and accompaniment for living in the present time.[72] A particularly historical and located mode of knowing and seeing, these hauntings of Hālawa Valley were partnered and animated by the actual occupation of the space by living protestors.[73]

The occupation sustained a present and living space where Native Hawaiian land practices, narratives, and mobilities unsettled the commodified indigeneity — the marketed and alienable quality of being indigenous — of the Waikīkī tourist industry and the vast and passive landscape promised by the H-3's scenic vistas. Importantly, the occupiers did not position themselves against the construction of the highway, but rather as advocates for the land that the highway would cut through.[74] In order to do this, the occupation enlivened Native Hawaiian feminine genealogies located in the valley by tying them to the contemporary lives of indigenous women. The five women who formed the core kūpuna (elders) of the Hālawa Valley community were less troubled about halting the H-3's construction and more concerned with the integrity of the site through which the H-3 would be built, in particular the Hale O Papa, or women's heiau (sacred place), which was the crucial discovery of the Bishop Museum anthropologist. Their tactics of living in the valley, traversing its topography on a daily basis, conducting tours, and reestablishing a living narrative tradition of the land as actively used and part of an ongoing cultural practice were intended to animate indigenous genealogies by demonstrating them to be mobile and modern. The women's objections to the destructive route and the political machinations that tried to bury this feminine genealogy made their occupation a statement about the value of indigenous women's histories and practices. Pualoa describes the occupation as "hell yeah, a women's movement, still is," making sure that the gains of reoccupying the land extend to the present.[75] Their view of the land as a place for feminine indigenous practice and community offered a very different kind of understanding of gendered landscapes and Native women from those consumed in tourist itineraries. Rather than embodying the "soft primitivism" of the tropics, Pualoa, Wasson, and their companions insisted on the material presence, historical importance, and political significance of feminine indigenous genealogy that unsettled tourist fictions.[76]

Their tactics worked—to a degree. Today, thanks to their persistent efforts, the parts of Hālawa Valley that were found to contain cultural and historic sites have been set aside for Native Hawaiian use. The H-3 was finally completed in 1997 and was rerouted to avoid damaging the sites. However, the overdetermined rhetoric of the touristic and engineering sublime that proliferated after the H-3's completion indicates that its abstracting hegemony needed a great deal of narrative support. While nothing quells dissent quite like the fait accompli of a built, immovable highway—particularly one that is regularly used—the H-3 continues to exist as a vexed site for many residents, in no small part because its sheer bulk and its vaunted sublimity are constant reminders of yet another attempt to overwrite history. Its construction process—particularly the questionable burial (or reburial) of evidence regarding the H-3's bulldozing of sacred indigenous sites—necessitated an avalanche of fictions in order to once again lay to rest intractable Native claims. In shoring up discourses of the scenic sublime, the state—which triumphantly completed the H-3's construction—legitimated military and tourist logics, which in turn rendered indigenous claims as both hysterical and historical.

In the aftermath of the occupation and the decades-long resistance to its construction, the practices and narratives of indigenous mobilities and modernities that these kūpuna lived out and told for months on end were absorbed by the H-3's completion. When it was finished, the state's strategic deployment of discourses of environmentalism, cultural sensitivity, and a technologically achieved sublime deflected the H-3's history of contention and dissent: then-governor Ben Cayetano claimed that "the H-3 was planned and engineered to preserve and protect the environment through which it passes."[77] Prominent patriarchs of the Democratic Party machine who had secured the funding and pushed construction—including Senator Daniel Inouye, who had fixated on the H-3 as his legacy to the state—positioned themselves as the rational, modern leaders of a unique, multicultural Pacific state of which Native Hawaiians were a small part. This rhetorical maneuver of appealing to an abstract Hawai'i citizenry was played out in the way environmental concerns were suddenly touted as the concern of a general public. In contrast, Native Hawaiians were represented as a special interest group whose concerns the state nonetheless generously accommodated. In carefully calibrated language, the state acknowledged the cultural importance of Hālawa Valley, placing repeated emphasis on its responsiveness and sensitivity to the protests: "The route was altered twice to avoid sites considered culturally significant by some Hawaiians."[78] Publicity literature produced by the Hawai'i Department of Transportation and its advocates argued that the freeway "had to be rerouted several times" in order to avoid "historic agricultural terraces and specific Hālawa Valley sites considered culturally significant by some native Hawaiians."[79] The repetition of "some" as a qualifier to Hawaiians balances the state's continuing lip service to being sensitive to Native Hawaiians with its desire to appease *and* isolate this politically significant and increasingly vocal community.

Even as it identified Native Hawaiians as a disproportionately vocal group, the state positioned itself as the most effective arbiter of Native Hawaiian culture, which it framed as firmly archaeological. A paternalistic language reminiscent of colonial benevolence dominates the state-sponsored literature on the H-3, which actually credits the H-3 project as the impetus for the "discovery" of these previously forgotten sites.[80]

According to a report produced by the Hawai'i Department of Transportation, "An often overlooked benefit of the H-3 project is the wealth of archaeological knowledge uncovered. . . . Recognizing the possibility of unearthing artifacts of the ancient Hawaiians, HDOT hired archaeological experts . . . to find, survey, and study archaeological sites. After the most important areas were identified, H-3's alignment was designed to avoid any adverse impacts. . . . A Bishop Museum archaeologist declared that the H-3 process saved these priceless sites from private development."[81] The report describes the court battle history further, careful to describe the opposition as "a small group of opponents."[82] In the official published records, as well as in the professional journals, narratives of modern technical know-how paired with cultural sensitivity rewrote the long battle waged by the diverse protest coalition into a story of a careful and responsive state. Further, by placing Native Hawaiians in archaeological time, Native Hawaiians are dismissed—even disappeared—from the story of their own sites, their sustained protest against the H-3 smoothed over by a narrative of benevolent discovery and sensitive multiculturalism. The paternal state's concessions to "a small group of opponents" further isolated Native Hawaiians, rendering them antimodern. It separated them from the otherwise multicultural paradise of the state, infantilizing them as a cultural special interest group to be placated even as the rest of Hawai'i moves on.

This rewriting of the H-3's history parallels the U.S. colonial administration's triumphant narrative about Kennon Road. The transportation and tourism agencies of the state publicized the H-3's completion as the victory of modernity, engineering technology, and democracy. Building the H-3 allows access to a "stunning" experience of the land, making this identification with the transcendent democratically available: "Indeed, without the freeway, no one—except for the few who had the ability to hike the rugged terrain—would have had an opportunity to see this scenery."[83] The "small group" of "some" Native Hawaiians is reduced to insignificance next to the feat of engineering and modern design that supposedly serves the *rest* of the "citizens of Hawai'i" by giving them an uplifting experience of mobility.[84] The H-3 was increasingly and consistently identified as a roadway that inspired feelings of the scenic sublime. Persisting against the "mountain of obstacles," its designers and builders are finally "heroic," producing a "highway that celebrates and preserves its lush natural surroundings."[85] This epic masculine achievement outlines a gendered understanding of technological discipline dealt upon the literal and figurative mountain of obstacles understood as irrational, feminine, and nonmodern. Finally disciplined by the completion of the interstate, the narrative continues, the natural surroundings of the tropics are showcased as a picturesque landscape, to be equally experienced and seen by everyone, uncluttered by the trivialities of historical occupation, overthrow, and colonialism. The languages and "techno-logics" of tourism, military efficiency, and modern engineering are instrumental to the H-3's production as a site where tourists and residents can access an experience that exceeds and transcends the particularity of Native Hawaiians. This discourse of the technological sublime is politically indispensable to the state because it abstracts the material conditions of the H-3's production, making land once again alienable from indigenous life.

In the postconstruction celebration, the tourism and transportation agencies of the beleaguered state government chose to underline the H-3's benefits to *everyone*, particularly the state's tourism industry. Binding engineering virtuosity to the touristic sublime, these discourses further bypass Native Hawaiian claims to the land, rendering them unmodern and invisible in a new global landscape. The H-3's viaducts, avenues, and tunnels that cut over, across, and through the landscape were enlisted in state narratives that aligned with the ideas of mobility ascribed to the modern subjects of tourism.

Soaring over and through the island to get to an idea of "old Hawai'i," uplifted by the panoramic vistas, and swept away by the concrete and steel sublime of its flying viaduct, people who take this highway cannot help but *feel* liberated from the earth. The structure and design of the road elicit a nostalgic desire for an "old Hawai'i" that is divorced from actual Native Hawaiians. It does not engender an identification with the Native Hawaiian women who are literally going about life in the valley below; rather, it produces subjects who desire the perfect, abstracting mobility of the road that ascends into and above the land. In this move, while referencing tourism, the state excises the usual object of the tourist gaze: the Native Hawaiian. What former governor Cayetano hailed as a "drive into the future" both helps the tourist escape from the crowds of Waikīkī to an unpopulated "old Hawai'i" free of Native Hawaiians and their messy histories, and enacts a transcendence of history and the present, away from the unsettling aspects of a secured paradise.[86] Driving on the H-3 thus conjures that ultimate tourist fantasy—a claimable Hawai'i—because it is a Hawai'i alienated from Native Hawaiians. In contrast to the way that Kennon Road embraced the intimacies of Native embodiment, the H-3 represses and denies that upon which it simultaneously capitalizes and relies. By invoking the European romantic vista through modern mobility's production of Hawai'i-as-landscape, the H-3 experience of tourist disembodiment overcomes the spectral counterclaims of indigenous subjectivity, history, and nationhood. This experience — captured best by the notion of the scenic sublime invoked by state transportation and tourism agencies — operates through abstraction, leaving behind contentious and inconvenient histories and bodies that would otherwise be roadblocks to securing paradise.

Just as tourism infused the dominant script of the H-3 in the late twentieth century, what was disavowed during the litigious and combative construction of the highway reemerged as the original author of the road: the military. Although military security logics had initially spurred the construction of the H-3 through massive federal appropriations, and even though its presence was understood to be the trigger for the entire H-3 project, the military lay low during the long construction process. After the road's completion, the more controversial aspects of the militarily driven project and process were initially elided through a surfeit of tourist narratives about its democratized benefits. Once the highway was deemed a success, however, narratives about the advantages of military engineering and a militarized state economy were validated and reinforced. These articulations are so ingrained that even some of the protestors concur: "We never would have seen that valley without the military."[87] That military-sponsored technology allows democratic access to this dramatic, transcendental experience is crucial. Indeed, the engineering innovation cited by the state was more aggressively linked to military modernity. Emphasizing the H-3's engineering design reinserted a consciousness of how the militarization of Hawai'i benefits and informs the construction of the interstate, deflecting critiques of Hawai'i's extensive military occupation. The speed and almost-flightlike feelings of travel that it manufactures not only distance its users further from the more distressing relations of paradise but also detach violence from the military project of securing paradise. In the end, the H-3's conversion into a tourist attraction transforms the military-as-occupant into a beneficial guest that continues to contribute to the hard, constructive work of securing Hawai'i as a modern, multicultural paradise.

This chapter has explored roadways as a mobile stage where the tensions and contradictions produced in and by security states play out. In the Philippines, roadways—by presenting material evidence of civilization and modernization—represent a benevolent paternalism that paves over the violence of colonial conquest and neoliberal governance. Although the scenic highway in the Philippines emphasized tourist modernity and mobility through an act of sightseeing that holds the indigenous hostage to the tourist gaze, Hawai'i's scenic interstate bypasses the vexed politics of overthrow and occupation with its abstraction of the indigenous. A joint project of a state economy dependent on tourism and militarism, the H-3 showcases a strategy that references the idea of the indigenous without actually seriously considering Native Hawaiians as real political subjects.

The same structures of mobility, however, also offer a means to trouble, blur, and contest the interlinked logics of a tourist-military state. That is, scenic highways at once conceal *and* invoke histories that were once writ large, carved into the land, and blasted into the mountains. These inconvenient histories, phantoms of modernity's violence that might otherwise chafe at the edges of a well-earned holiday, are not always easily dismissed. Highways built to ease military traffic or facilitate tourist access provide more efficient means of communication and organization and serve as public sites of protest. In the Philippines as in Hawai'i, scenic highways have the potential to become a theater, a conduit, a social space where the contradictions of tourism and militarism emerge and remain unresolved. These alternative modernities, existing outside but alongside the hegemonies of the scenic sublime and tourist-military mobilities, offer tales of flattened earth, displaced populations, corruption, and coercion. They have a dangerous potential for trouble, inviting links to an already-unsettled present. In fact, they might remind the tourist that his or her ability to get around, to have access to a sublime vista, to penetrate a hidden interior, or save on precious time—each benefit is contingent on another's historical or immediate unfreedom.

Illustrating the contradictions of modernity and mobility, today, the Philippine state has taken up the mantle of Marcos's fixation on road building to further ease the traffic of resources and labor in the Philippines. Recently, the Subic-Clark toll road hailed the emergence of a new industrial region outside Manila, connecting the former American military bases at Angeles and Pampanga in Luzon. Largely funded by the Japan Bank for International Cooperation to help develop investment infrastructure, its main goal is to facilitate traffic flow between the two special economic zones into which the American military territories have been converted. This direct linking of the two former bases, along with the Luisita Park in Tarlac and the Bataan Technology Park, creates a "new economic growth corridor" outside Metro Manila.[88] This modern highway produces subjects that identify with the fast-tracked, globalized mobility of the freeport, reducing the region to nodes of investment possibilities and tourism opportunities. Yet at some point, the road ends, and its users must then contend with the places linked by these highways. The next chapter explores one such circuit produced and connected by these roads—the former bases that have been transformed into freeports—as part of a neocolonial tourism-military complex that updates historical infrastructures of domination to contemporary modes of governance.

Three

✻

NEOLIBERATION AND
U.S.-PHILIPPINES
CIRCUITS OF SACRIFICE
AND GRATITUDE

When the embedded colonial journalist Oscar King Davis sailed into Philippine waters in 1898, his acquisitive eye was already surveying the real estate at Cavite and Sangley Point as part of American territory. Soon after the U.S. Navy dispatched Spain in the very short Battle of Manila Bay, it set up shop in these two sites, took over Spanish military installations, and created more of its own. Today, the landscape of Luzon reflects the expanded cartography of these first colonial military outposts: the former military bases are now networked by the road system created during the colonial and postwar eras. Whereas the previous chapter showed how the uses of highway systems shift over time to accommodate different configurations of militarism and tourism, this chapter and the next look to how regimes of tourism update the spaces and structures of militarism. Moving from the modern scenic highway to the stops along the way, I linger at destinations created by the convergence of tourism and militarism, considering World War II sites that today operate as tourist attractions.

Here, I focus on tourism in the hallowed grounds of American World War II valor and sacrifice in the Philippines: Corregidor Island and the Bataan peninsula. Corregidor, an island fortress in Manila Bay, was initially established as a military zone by the Spanish empire and then later transferred to the United States after the War of 1898, when the United States effectively took over the colonial reins of the archipelago. Corregidor achieved international renown during World War II, when General Douglas MacArthur used it as the Allied headquarters before the fall of Bataan to the north and the subsequent loss of the island to Japanese invaders in May 1942. Bataan, its partner site in military history and cultural memory, is infamous as the penultimate stand of a decimated American military in the Philippines and the site of the Bataan Death March. Within a month of Bataan's surrender, Corregidor followed suit. Recognizing the power of the sentimental—particularly the emotional appeal of returning to rescue the fallen Corregidor—MacArthur staged a high-risk and dramatic operation to retake Corregidor as one of the first moves to return the Philippines to Allied command.[1] As the theater of the MacArthur-led Allied effort to retake the Philippines and the rest of the Pacific in 1945, Corregidor along with Bataan are evocative of American World War II martial heroics and perpetually reinscribe the familiar story of U.S.-Filipino fraternity and fellowship through mutual suffering, sacrifice, and triumphant liberation. These potent narratives frame Corregidor and Bataan as sites of military tourism today.

In contrast, Subic Bay and Clark are names that are tainted by the illicit sexual economies and violence produced in sites of military occupation rather than the heroic narratives associated with Corregidor and Bataan. In Olongapo, the United States took what had been a Spanish arsenal and repair facility and expanded it into the Subic Bay Naval Base, one of the largest in Asia. Clark Air Field in Angeles was established soon after the U.S. occupation of the islands and grew to be a sizeable American overseas installation. Though both bases played important roles during World War II, they also became infamous bywords for licentiousness for their off-base "entertainment" economies and patterns of military sexual violence.[2] In 1991, the Philippine Senate, in a burst of nationalist fervor, rejected an extension of the Military Bases Agreement that had essentially outlined a contract for the U.S. military occupation of its former colonial bases since Philippine independence.[3] Since the departure of the U.S. military, Subic Bay and Clark have been transformed into special economic zones under public-private partnerships and now operate as commercial and tourist hubs for the neoliberalizing economy of the Philippines. Despite their reincarnation as modern centers of commerce and tourism and their new role as potential engines of the Philippine economy, Subic Bay and Clark grapple with the seamy reputations they had earned as former American playgrounds.[4] Because they symbolized the high price of U.S. friendship, the former Subic Bay Naval Base and Clark Air Field have never attained the reputation of innocence, sacrifice, and valor connected with Corregidor and Bataan.

Rather than understand Corregidor and Bataan as separate and distinct from the militarization of Subic Bay and Clark, this chapter connects the suffering and bravery of Corregidor's and Bataan's martial masculinity to the ignominy and infamy of Subic Bay and Clark. When the United States military departed, the reterritorialization of Subic Bay and Clark into Philippine freeports ameliorated the stigma of U.S.-style occupation in these sites, signaling a shift in the modalities of American militarism in the Philippines.[5] The renovation of Subic and Clark as the new economic hopes for the islands hinges on the success of Corregidor and Bataan as tourist shrines to heroic American military action. The World War II narrative arc of sacrifice to liberation in Corregidor and Bataan animates the transformation of Subic Bay and Clark into liberators of the Philippine economy. In this maneuver, the long history of U.S. imperialism, military violence, and occupation is remade into a narrative of fraternal benevolence and generosity, and the altered strategy on the part of the United States of flexible militarization in the Philippines is recast more firmly as a state-to-state partnership in the interests of security and stability.

Tourism in Corregidor and Bataan, with their intense narratives of masculine sacrifice and valor, generates an alibi for the unfreedoms and relations of brutal domination secured by continued U.S.-Philippine collusions.[6] In the absence of formal American military occupation today, rendering Corregidor and Bataan tourable is a militarized maneuver that places Subic Bay, Clark, and the Philippines itself within the ever-expanding borders of U.S. territorialism. Indeed, this ostensibly "post-bases" era has seen broader U.S.-Philippine military cooperation than ever before, with U.S. economic investments tied to the security relationship long established by the 1951 U.S.-Philippines Mutual Defense Treaty. In 1998, the Visiting Forces Agreement (VFA), a bilateral agreement between the United States and the Philippines, allowed the U.S. military to have access to Philippine ports for fueling, repairs, supplies, and rest and recreation, in effect continuing the military relations between the two nations. Under the VFA, the United States has made ship visits to Philippine ports and conducted combined military exercises with Philippine forces, most recently targeting Muslim Mindanao. In many ways, while Clark and Subic Bay have become sites of neoliberal economic policy, other parts of the Philippines—such as the southern region of Mindanao—have been territorialized as American military outposts and combat zones. The framing and consumption of touristic narratives of American rescue and liberation in Corregidor and Bataan are crucial to the enterprise of legitimizing broader relations between military and tourism endeavors in the Philippines' struggling neoliberalizing economy. The continuously "visiting" U.S. military, in this framework, serves as a guarantor of political and economic stability, as well as a potential customer for the goods and services of a properly stable Philippines.

FROM LIBERATION TO NEOLIBERATION

In 2003, Richard Gordon—then the Philippines' secretary of tourism, former mayor of Olongapo City (which hosts Subic Bay), and past chair of the Subic Bay Metropolitan Authority that was charged with the base's transition to a freeport economy—announced a plan to produce tourists out of soldiers in order to stimulate the country's beleaguered tourism industry. His strategy: to recruit American soldiers who were already "visiting" the Philippines under the aegis of the VFA as more active and conscious tourists. Hoping to tap into existing nostalgia for former playgrounds and to reinvigorate the tourist market for the still-struggling freeports, Gordon's proposal included an invitation to American servicemen who had been previously quartered in Subic Bay Naval Base and Clark Air Field to return to their old haunts for a reunion. With this plan, Gordon sought to conjure tourism practices that would draw from the sentimental journey of remembrance and gratitude instilled by a history of U.S. military occupation in the Philippines. Coupled to evocative place-names such as Corregidor and Bataan, Subic Bay and Clark take on new meaning in a political and economic order that embraces the logics and methods of neoliberalism. Gordon's call for Americans to undertake a new kind of military tour in the Philippines updates the story of securing paradise and casts tourism as the new savior for a postcolonial economy by reactivating and reinforcing earlier narratives of courageous alliances under duress, fusing them to a modern capitalist partnership.

Gordon's stewardship of the former American military reservation at Subic Bay, particularly his call for American soldiers to revisit their old stomping grounds, needs to be contextualized within a doubled narrative of American liberation that frames militarized sites. The first narrative is steeped in World War II Allied sacrifice as emblematized by Corregidor and Bataan. The alchemy of intense sentimentality associated with the chronicle of Corregidor's valiant but futile stand and Bataan's suffering prisoners converts a colonial history into a tale of liberation. The fiftieth anniversary of the fall of Corregidor also happened to take place (not by design) during the same year that the United States was forced to leave its military base territories in the Philippines. On this auspicious occasion, the U.S. ambassador to the Philippines, Frank G. Wisner, retold the drama of the American soldiers who defended Corregidor against Japanese military invasion:

> Fifty years ago the whole world watched the drama unfolding here with intense interest. We must also remember how it was that day and the sacrifices that were made. Most of all we must remember why those sacrifices were necessary and what we must do to ensure they never have to be made again. . . . We must always remember that freedom does not come cheap. We must remain eternally vigilant and not let our defenses deteriorate as Americans did during the Inter-war years. . . . The Pacific region is prosperous [today]. The seeds of democracy have been planted and taken root. . . . A strong and cooperative defense remains a key to peace. The United States and the Philippines must remain together and vigilant. Although Americans are removing our bases from Philippine soil, and the American flag that once flew so proudly over Corregidor and elsewhere in this country will come down for good later this year, our partnership in peace and prosperity can and must remain. The form will change, but the goals and spirit of cooperation need not change.[7]

Describing the sacrifices made in the name of freedom, Wisner credits the United States, in cooperation with the Philippines, for the success of democracy and capitalism in the Pacific. In this account, the 1947 Military Bases Agreement was a way for both nations to secure a continued U.S. military presence in the Pacific theater after the United States granted Philippine independence — an added reward for loyalty during the vicissitudes of war. This militarized pact of brotherhood and occupation, sealed with the blood of war and resistance, was a product of "long-standing fraternal collaborations" between Filipino and American ruling classes.[8]

While briefly acknowledging the imminent American departure from the Philippines, Wisner's insistent return to the language of continued partnership is wrought through his use of nostalgic imagery to describe Corregidor's last stand. He bids farewell to the Philippines in the same moment that he lays claim to the perpetual stakes of the United States in the region.

His speech capped half a century's worth of similar opinions from visiting U.S. senators and other dignitaries that effectively inscribe World War II heroics as the dominant narrative of U.S.-Philippines relations. In 1943, shortly after the fall of Bataan, Congressman Stanley Fish exhorted Americans to remember Bataan "as we did the Alamo in the Mexican War [and] the *Maine* in the Spanish War," locating Bataan (and Corregidor) within the tradition and mythos of American freedom fighting.[9] U.S. Senator Frank Moss, while visiting Corregidor on the occasion of the twenty-first anniversary of Pearl Harbor almost thirty years prior to Wisner's speech, further cemented World War II sacrifice as the formative connection between the two nations, declaring that "Corregidor is physical proof of the bond between our two countries."[10] Wisner's sentiments in 1992, marking as they did the departure of American troops from the Philippines, follows this long tradition of claiming territorial rights through the purchase of American blood.[11] This sense of entitlement to the Philippines and its people, continually justified by the sacrifices of American soldiers, has persisted in sentimental form even after the departure of American troops from the bases. Renewed and reinvigorated at key intervals by Wisner and his predecessors, the strength and endurance of mutual suffering coupled with MacArthur's liberation narrative permeates Corregidor and Bataan as sites of Allied memory making. Thus, even with the official departure of American troops in 1992, Wisner was still able to remind Filipinos and Americans alike of American stakes and feelings of ownership in the region by strategically giving his speech on the island of Corregidor and wrapping it in the mantle of military sacrifice and valor.[12]

While the story of liberation was rooted in the commemoration of World War II, the second liberation narrative, what I call *neoliberation*, is tied less to a historical moment than to a political and economic relationship that began in earnest during the Cold War. By the time the U.S. military departed the Philippines in 1992, American neoliberal economic policies had already profoundly damaged the Philippines. Washington edicts — taking the shape of World Bank, Asian Development Bank (ADB), and International Monetary Fund (IMF) structural adjustment policies — were familiar to the debt-ridden Philippine economy. During the Marcos era, the country's indebtedness averaged an increase of 27 percent every year, compounded by debt-service charges on World Bank and ADB bailout loans. In 1984, in exchange for more IMF loans to further develop its economy, the Marcos government agreed to devalue the peso, liberalize trade restrictions, and raise interest rates, policies that harshly affected the economy and the lives of Filipinos.[13] The discourse of neoliberation inverts the brutality of these policies by reinscribing them in narratives of liberation. The "return" of the base properties to the Philippines became evidence of American generosity: the bases' subsequent transformation and use as special economic zones neatly fit the narrative of neoliberation as a leg up, courtesy of Uncle Sam. The Yankees who had been urged to go home were now the benefactors of modern infrastructure that would enable the national economy to emerge from its malaise. Neoliberation, however, would have no potency without the first story of World War II liberation.[14]

As the chair of the commission that oversaw the conversion of the former base into a special economic zone and later as the secretary of tourism, Gordon manipulated this narrative of American neoliberation, melding it inextricably with a story of Philippine economic independence and autonomy while simultaneously incorporating it into his own political story. In Gordon's model of a secured market for tourism, colonial ideologies of travel and militarism are neatly folded into gendered and racialized neocolonial economies of desire and transnational structures of world policing. His investments in neoliberation were reflected in his own self-fashioning as a public politician. Having long championed the continued development of the Subic Bay economy during his stint as mayor of Olongapo and leader of Subic Bay's freeport transition team, Gordon embodied a heteropatriarchal statesmanship that framed the formal removal of the bases as a moral victory for the people of the Philippines, even as he oversaw its return to the former structures of economic dependence that characterized it during U.S. occupation. Gordon's long-running and deep identification with Olongapo and Subic Bay helped him to cast himself in the role of the new Filipino, a visionary disciplinarian, who — with the help of his American allies — would clean up the Philippine economy and shape up its people. His tough love approach to managing the city and the transition of the base to a freeport economy made Gordon infamous.[15] While literally criminalizing laziness and stupidity in his "fiefdom," Gordon also rallied tens of thousands of volunteers who worked without pay to guard the Subic Bay facilities after the U.S. Navy's departure, and to eventually staff its conversion to a freeport.[16] His mixed-race Filipino American ancestry and American military roots contributed to his charismatic public persona, imbuing him with the kind of frontier hybrid masculinity necessary in the backward and corrupt badlands of the American empire.[17]

The neoliberation narrative also served to mask the eventual return of U.S. troops to Philippine soil. By 2003, when Gordon made his announcement to recruit American soldiers as tourists to the ostensibly legitimate tourism economies of Subic Bay, American soldiers were already touring the Philippines as part of the military invitation extended by the VFA. Even more noteworthy, this reoccupation—under the aegis of mutual training exercises—becomes decipherable and desirable through a rearticulation of the doubled rescue narrative. Instead of liberation from Japanese invaders, the VFA ostensibly guaranteed increased security against the Muslim extremist Abu Sayyaf Group, an argument that had increased traction after the events of 9/11. The VFA thus continued to support the Philippines' goal to secure a stable political climate for capital investment, ensuring the viability of neoliberation through mutual military cooperation. Gordon's strategy practiced a statecraft that produced the post-1992 military formations between the United States and the Philippines as a good liberation, one that is necessarily guaranteed by a continuing U.S. military presence. He effectively tapped into the still-dominant Allied rhetoric of Corregidor and Bataan, which—not coincidentally—he also aggressively promoted as new destinations through the Department of Tourism. Indeed, his proposal to produce Subic Bay and Clark for a new, improved touring soldier-subject was timed in anticipation of President George W. Bush's 2003 visit to the Philippines. The intent was to secure further cooperation for the United States and the Philippines' armed relations against terror and to guarantee a future in which the American military continued to occupy and tour the Philippines. On the national and global stage, Gordon's dream of a Philippines laid open for a soldier-tourist reinvasion disguises in the vestments of neoliberal economic modernity what is essentially a militarized, colonial fantasy, casting the United States in the role of liberator, again and again.

The hybrid soldier-tourist subjects conjured in Gordon's complicit fantasy are the exemplars of the privileged subject of modernity: the masculine, Euro-American traveler who is at once a symbol and arbiter of state power and violence.[18] These tourist subjects invoked in Gordon's plan to drum up business operate as a fetish to conceal those conditions that make their presence possible: the tourist sites that they are imagined to inhabit are places of past and present violence and occupation. For many people whose livelihoods continue to revolve around these militarized economies, such tourist-friendly manipulations of history enhance the contrast between the rhetoric of uplift and cooperation and the realities of often-violent survival.[19] Gordon's disingenuous call to recruit tourists from the ranks of American soldiers elided the robust state-sponsored sex tourism trade that flourished before the U.S. military's official withdrawal in 1992 and that still exists today under the VFA.[20] Emphasizing instead the "legitimate" types of tourism that the special economic zones are attempting to get off the ground, Gordon's strategy sanitized the present-day product of what Cynthia Enloe notes as the collusion of "Philippine nationalism, land reform and demilitarization" in the region.[21] As noted earlier, however, characterizing the post-1992 era as one of demilitarization is premature and misleading. Instead, under Gordon, the Philippine Department of Tourism has actively produced a state narrative of military tours disarticulated from the seamier history of American military occupation even as such histories continue to structure these tours in the contemporary Philippine context.[22]

CONSTRUCTING AN ALLIED FRATERNITY: HEROICS AS ATTRACTIONS

Steeped in nostalgic discourses of heroic suffering, sacrifice and valor, Corregidor and Bataan take on new life within tourist circuits. Like Bataan, which lies just north of it, Corregidor Island is saturated with these potent narratives, which lend themselves to forms of tourism that emphasize pilgrimage to historical military sites. In these intensely patriotic places, monuments that portray the homosocial bonds of men at war and the mutual suffering and interracial camaraderie of American, Filipino, and other soldiers temporarily suspend histories of segregation, disenfranchisement, complicity, and sustained racial and gendered violence. Instead, tourists who come to Corregidor and Bataan feel grief, shame, awe, and euphoria. Finally, and perhaps most significantly, they feel gratitude not only for the pain that American soldiers suffered on their behalf, but also for the return and rescue of these soldiers in the face of this experience of pain. In these sites, visitors pay their respects to the dead, take part in an overdetermined ritual of remembering, and are "touched" by sacrifice as they follow in the footsteps and explore the haunts of the brave, injured and dead. The selective and layered construction of memory and nation that tourists encounter in Corregidor's museum and assemblage of monuments, for example, carefully crafts a nostalgic and heroic space that produces a grateful tourist subject and an even more grateful host nation. The military-tourism scenes in Corregidor and Bataan perform a kind of ideological labor — contributing to what Neferti Tadiar has called the "fantasy-production" of dominant transnational imaginings about the Philippines.[23] Such imperial imaginaries and the labor they perform locate the Philippines squarely within the political and economic reach of Washington, D.C., returning the islands once more to the fold of American colonial influence. To this end, touring Corregidor and Bataan simultaneously reinforces American colonial and neocolonial geographies — an act supported by both the U.S. and Philippine states.[24]

The infamous Allied losses at Corregidor and Bataan highlighted the continued anxieties over the uncertain corporeal inclusion of the Philippines in the United States and Filipinos into the American body politic, and the understanding that the bonds of war could be parleyed into citizen rights. This ambiguity was politically useful. Almost immediately after Corregidor and Bataan fell, Filipinos in the United States used this loss as evidence of their worthiness and belonging within American society through shared heroic war narratives. During the Cold War, the U.S. state wielded this flexible narrative to extend its territoriality by reminding the Philippines of World War II alliances. Indeed the potent symbolism of Corregidor and Bataan was immediately recognized: calls for Corregidor and Bataan to be enshrined as war memorials began almost immediately after their consecutive surrenders. In 1943, an American aircraft carrier was named after Bataan to symbolize that Bataan was "now an enduring monument to civilization, a symbol of freedom lost, a battleground where Americans and Filipinos sealed with blood a lasting friendship and gave expression to the supreme determination of . . . two peoples to fight together until the enemy is crushed and lost freedom is regained."[25] In Hawai'i that same year, Filipino workers in the navy planned to build a Corregidor Hall to commemorate the last stand of the Philippines. This geographical tie between Pearl Harbor, Corregidor, and Bataan served to reinstate the Filipino within the heart of American cultural consciousness even as it was also deployed by Filipinos in the United States to address issues of prejudice and racism. The enemy's wounding and killing of American and Filipino soldiers spurned somewhat contradictory, yet strategic, critiques of racism and exclusion as well as petitions for belonging. The exiled Colonel Carlos P. Romulo exhorted Americans in California and Arizona to "take them into your hearts!" and "stop discriminating against the Filipinos in their midst" because of their demonstrated brotherhood with Americans.[26] Even the noted writer Carlos Bulosan urged the United States to take on a naturalization campaign for Filipinos based on the "recognition of our heroic stand in Bataan and our sincere cooperation with the United States in defense of democracy."[27] Paralleling the successful campaign of other "aliens ineligible for citizenship" who earned citizenship through soldiering, Filipinos in the United States—with their peculiar legal status—urged Americans to translate war alliances to national ties. In the face of uncertainty as to the war's outcome, the use of Corregidor and Bataan—to remind the United States of its obligations—was crucial to the production of cultural memory on the part of anxious Filipinos in the United States.

Following the war, the campaign for the memorialization of Corregidor escalated, bolstered by the Philippines' key role in a Communist-threatened Asia. This time, the U.S. state took the reins to produce state-sanctioned commemorations that would best deploy the intensely affective sites at Corregidor and Bataan to its advantage. While the Military Bases Agreement guaranteed the United States a long-term foothold in the Philippines, memorializing Corregidor and Bataan as reminders of heroic cooperation cemented a relationship through informal as well as formal means. The Corregidor-Bataan National Shrines Commission was created in 1954 as a joint project between the Philippines and the United States and was dedicated by then-congressman Ferdinand Marcos. However, it was not until 1962—on the anniversary of the attack on Pearl Harbor—that this "joint national crusade" found momentum, when visiting American senators Frank Church and Gale McGee recruited the liberation narrative of Corregidor into a broader anti-Communist cultural campaign. They suggested that "in restoring this rocky fortress and transforming it into a place of re-dedication and reflection for all the peoples of the Free World," Corregidor would become "symbolic of the partnership principle whereby each member of the Free World coalition underlines its determination to come to the assistance of any member threatened by communist aggression."[28] Extending its symbolic power past the story of rescue against Japanese invaders, Church and McGee play on the theme of mutual assistance against a new enemy, essentially translating the North Atlantic Treaty Organization's terms to Asia through more unofficial means. Two years later, the Corregidor-Bataan Memorial Commission explained the selection of the site over that of Guadalcanal, Midway, Iwo Jima, and Okinawa due to "its proximity to Manila, one of the largest cities of the Western Pacific and . . . , accessib[ility] to thousands of tourists."[29]

Corregidor's emergence as a tourist site during the Cold War points beyond its symbolic importance to the Philippines' international value as an anti-Communist regime in Asia and the Pacific.[30] The development of international tourism was a part of Washington's multipronged efforts to retain allies, bolster historical partnerships through cultural and economic ties, and spread its own doctrine of capitalist democracy and consumerism in the region.[31] During this period, the Philippines was hugely important to U.S. interests in the region, particularly as a "stronghold of Cold War 'security'" and as a recipient of surplus military goods.[32] Showcasing the story of U.S. economic and political support by making the story of Corregidor available to the wider audiences of tourism recruited heritage tourism in the service of nationalism, the state, and anti-Communist discourses.

Marcos, who worked with the United States to contain Communism in Asia, and who was one of the founders of the Association of Southeast Asian Nations (ASEAN), a regional group committed to fighting the spread of Communism, was well aware of the power of martial heroics.[33] When he campaigned for president in 1966, his skillful fabrication of a World War II heroic persona propelled him to victory. Two years later, he presided over the dedication of the Pacific War Memorial on Corregidor, which was built with U.S. congressional appropriations: this maneuver of recruiting old memories of triumphant militarism and new relations of U.S.-Philippine cooperation helped to smooth over critiques of his authoritarianism.[34] As "America's Boy" in Asia, Marcos headed a regime that mirrored the lopsided cultural, economic, political, and military relations between the United States and the Philippines during the Cold War years yet resonated with the theme of brotherhood and partnership laid out by the narratives about Corregidor and Bataan.[35] Marcos's dedication of the memorial captured the multifaceted foundations of his regime: continued

U.S. economic and political backing linked to vigilant military cooperation and an increasingly militarized Philippine state. Four years after dedi-
cating the Pacific War Memorial, Marcos instituted martial law, following
it with the opening of the Ministry of Tourism in the Philippines. Promising to guarantee safety in paradise, Marcos's military state secured increased investment in tourist infrastructure as well as promised safety for
the tourist class. In this early period, Marcos installed the Death March
road markers and the Mount Samat memorial in Bataan, cementing the
narratives of World War II cooperation as an ideological cornerstone of
his administration. This militarized tourism strategy both deploys historically masculine modes of travel, and puts into play discourses of "making
the world safe for tourism" even as tourism has not always made the world
itself safer for everyone, especially in the military-tourist zones of the
Philippines.[36]

The memorializations of Corregidor Island and Bataan as battle sites
are inseparable from the national and international circuits of Allied war
memories that insist on the primacy of stories of Filipino and American
brotherhood-through-suffering. From World War II to the Cold War, the
Philippines operates under what Vicente Diaz has called the "liberation"
mode of remembering, which casts American military occupation and
economic hegemony in the same heroic light, rather than as a "second invasion."[37] By emphasizing this fraternity of war as the official public narrative of U.S.-Philippine relations, the masculine heroics of World War II
replace American colonialism in the Philippines as *the* formative emotional bond between the Philippines and the United States. Corregidor
and Bataan thus play crucial roles in this tenuous neoliberation of the
Philippine-American "special relationship": they embody exactly those
narratives of rescue and brotherhood and of American honor in fulfilling
heroic promises to its colony. From the side of Philippine national memory, Corregidor and Bataan are exemplars of the "special relationship" between Filipinos and Americans. Marcos's presidency, the mythology he
wove about himself as a World War II hero in Bataan, and his politics of
economic and military dependency on continued American support exemplify the ideological power behind these Allied war memories. Today,
with the unceasing military collaboration between the Philippines and
the United States and the Philippines' continuing reliance on American
economic aid, the image of Allied suffering, victory, and triumph through
sacrifice plays out in the recurring patterns of U.S.-Philippine statesman-

ship. Corregidor and Bataan thus serve multiple ends, instilling World War II narratives of liberation within shifting international relations and new modes of governance.

With the embarrassment of the U.S.-sponsored Marcos dictatorship and the receding threat of the Cold War, the symbolic power of Corregidor and Bataan needed to be renewed. Despite the early start on the memorialization of Corregidor Island, it was not until 1986, under the administration of Corazon Aquino, that it was turned over to the Department of Tourism, which then funded the tourist infrastructure, development, repairs, hotel construction, and piers that have transitioned Corregidor to a tourist attraction targeted at domestic and international tourists. In 1987, the Corregidor Foundation, a private, nonprofit civic organization led by retired Philippine military officers and American expatriates, and housed in the Department of Tourism, took on the mission of "balancing" tourism with history.[38] In 1987, the foundation commissioned an architect to produce a five-year development plan to convert Corregidor's existing infrastructure into a tourist destination: since 1992, the plan has been self-sustaining. During Richard Gordon's 2001–4 term as secretary of tourism, the Department of Tourism aggressively promoted Corregidor as a national attraction in line with his vision of creating a network of island destinations. The campaign was successful: Corregidor is now regularly promoted as a site of historical interest by official and unofficial tourism publications and agencies. Today, it is best known for its role as the last stand of the American military in the Philippines, as well as the staging ground of the Allied powers' retaking of the Pacific against the Japanese Imperial Army. Promoted by the state for its historical heritage, Corregidor is often profiled in various publications addressed to the tourist, such as in-flight magazines, tourist brochures, websites, and mainstream newspapers. According to these materials, Corregidor is the "hero island," which must be visited "especially [by] the young, so they will be able to appreciate the sacrifices of their parents and grandparents in defense of the freedom they take for granted today."[39] It is the "island fortress," synonymous with "Dunkirk and the Alamo," whose dramatic and horrific stories are relived again and again.[40] It is, as the Philippine Department of Tourism unironically calls it, the "Island of Valor, Peace and International Understanding."

Despite the passing of the World War II generation, Corregidor remains a popular site, primarily because its ideological message has been so successfully translated to serve continuing U.S.-Philippine relations. The island hosts daily tours led by a company that has a virtual monopoly over tourist traffic to Corregidor. The full all-day tour includes boat transportation to the island, trolley transportation with an accompanying guide, lunch, and a light show: this runs a hefty two thousand pesos (forty-six U.S. dollars) per person, which is exorbitant by Filipino standards.[41] As a result, the tour targets a certain class of visitors, mostly attracting foreigners, of whom a majority are American tourists or expatriates, along with some Japanese veterans and overseas Filipinos. Filipino families come here when the only other transportation option, a tour costing five hundred pesos, reaches a minimum of sixty-five people. Similarly, students who see Corregidor do so on school-sponsored field trips and usually hail from private schools, not the overburdened and undersupported public school system. Very few World War II survivors are left, but active servicemen, including veterans from other, more recent military actions, continue to tour Corregidor. For these new tourists, Corregidor continues to generate identifications and meanings that are inevitably shaped by narratives of liberation and neoliberation.

TOURING HERO ISLAND

The tour itself consists of a round-trip ferry ride from Manila that takes forty-five minutes to an hour each way, a morning tour of half the island, lunch, and an afternoon tour of the other half of the island. The itineraries of various tour groups can be quite different, depending on the guide, but all cover the essential elements of a tour of the island's massive (and photogenic) gun batteries, ruins of military barracks, and stops at the Pacific War Memorial, Japanese Friendship Garden, Filipino Heroes Memorial, Malinta Tunnel, and the gift shops. With its unapologetic paean to American bravery and grit, the tour is tailored to fit the demographic of foreigners and domestic tourists, as well as Balikbayan Filipinos visiting from abroad. Depending on the number of tourists on any given day, the tour breaks into several groups who cover the sights and sites in varying orders to avoid overcrowding. This management of the tourists also extends to a flexibility of narrative. Good guides tailor their tour to their group, addressing the perceived interests of each group, which are assumed based upon the nationality or language of its members.

The customization of tours indicates that tourism operates to generate and manage different sets of expectations and experiences, though this does not necessarily lead to "new opportunities for remembering" that provide critical insight about nationalism and the politics of war memorialization.[42] The executive director of the Corregidor Foundation characterizes the Japanese tour as more positive, emphasizing more ambivalence about war atrocities, and highlighting the contributions that Japan has made to the Philippines in the post–World War II era. To address American tourists who "tend to glorify their role" as soldiers and liberators, guides focus on more hegemonic Allied narratives of suffering, rescue, and liberation. All the guides I interviewed were quick to point out that the narrative of the tour as well as the history of the island itself are most attractive to American tourists: one guide points out that "you have to consider that Corregidor is part of American history."[43] Filipinos, because of their historic role as the "support group," tend to feel marginalized in a national tour that seems to be geared more toward Americans than Filipinos.[44] Most guides have developed a system for gauging their groups. One guide characterizes Americans, Australians, and British tourists as being "very serious" and more interested in history while Balikbayan and local Filipinos "want to have fun and do picture-taking" like the Japanese and Koreans.[45] Another guide describes Balikbayan Filipinos as wanting *masaya* (enjoyment), and Filipinos as tourists who "don't want history. They want to go to the beach. They take pictures and make you a photographer."[46] While one set of tourists may feel more affinity for the Allied history of Corregidor, and another will look to the island as more of a getaway from the pollution and crowds of Manila, both sets of tourists nonetheless experience and enjoy a space that has been shaped by the story of liberation. For these tourists who feel marginalized by an American-dominated Corregidor story, Corregidor's historical attractions are props for their identities as consumers of leisure and cultural capital. Thus, even as Corregidor's history is secondary to their tour, their own enjoyment of their tourist identities on Corregidor rests on a tour narrative of liberation secured by U.S.-Philippine military, economic, and political partnerships.

Despite the existence of alternative tour narratives that result from the guides' tourist management, the production of Corregidor as a visitor attraction depends on nostalgic accounts of masculine suffering and heroism that play up the almost messianic roles of General Douglas MacArthur and the American "liberation forces" during World War II. On this tiny island, stories of American valor are laid on with a heavy hand. The imaginative architecture of this journey, in the end, limits the amount of flexibility that the guides have when addressing different groups of tourists. Those who choose to take the Corregidor Island tour are treated to the same prearrival experience, which prepares them for their tourist encounters on the island. The journey to the island is the first part of the tour's architecture. The tour is bookended with video documentaries that run on both the outgoing and return legs of the ferry trip, setting the mood and expectations for the tourist experience. Over the course of four years of my intermittent fieldwork in Corregidor, the onboard entertainment has become more tourist savvy. Most recently, a well-produced video greets tourists as they embark, in an excellent imitation of the Travel Channel genre. Attempting to expand the kinds of tourisms available at Corregidor, the video rehearses the different tour packages that are being developed for tourists, highlighting adventure tours, team-building itineraries, and even honeymoon packages. When all the passengers are seated, a recorded prayer and emergency information about the catamaran interrupts the video. As the tour departs, the screens proceed to show the next chapter of the Corregidor tour video, including a "then" and "now" segment that contrasts archival photographs with present-day images of the island, accompanied with audio narration of what a visit to "the Rock" will entail for the visiting tourist.

Half an hour into this video, lulled by the hum of engine noise, the rhythmic rise and fall of the catamaran on the waves, some tourists nap. Others talk with their companions, only occasionally paying attention to the next video, a 2000 television documentary titled *Fortress of Courage*. The film's dramatic voice-over and soaring score get a little more audience attention. *Fortress of Courage* has become standard fare for the Corregidor ferry trip: it previews the liberation narrative that the tourists will hear again and again on the actual tour. The narrator declares that Corregidor and Bataan were the last American stands in the Philippines against "Asia's greatest war machine" during the dog days of World War II. Recapping the events after General MacArthur's abandonment and during twenty-six days of bombing, *Fortress of Courage* mourns "the Rock's" surrender by General Jonathan Wainwright. MacArthur's oft-repeated and media-savvy mantra "I shall return" theatrically structures the ultimate American comeback. "Like a spider to ensnare its prey," the film thrillingly narrates, the "tightening of the web" heralded the "liberation of Luzon" and the retaking of lost Pacific territories. MacArthur's return to the island to "pay tribute" to Corregidor caps the narrative of eventual dogged survival, ingenuity, and triumph. At the end of the film, the American flag is raised on Corregidor once more. This sets the scene for the tourist to "retake" the island, where both the tourist and the destination have been secured by the military sacrifice of American soldiers.

Time permitting, the documentary is followed by a short informal lecture given by one of the guides. This lecture covers a broad history of the island before American occupation and some coverage of the Spanish-American and Philippine-American Wars to give context to the American takeover of the island. On one trip, the guide calls the latter the "Philippine insurrection" while on another the lecture emphasized the "raw deal" the Philippines received after the Spanish-American War, leaving room for alternate perspectives on this history. The lecture provides a deeper historical context for Corregidor in the framework of global relations, but it also works to set up the tour experience itself, which focuses on American occupation, defense, and liberation. After what has been at least an hour of video and lecture presentations on Corregidor history and present-day tourist experience, the ferry finally arrives at its destination. As the small island comes into view outside the windows and the engines are cut, the lecturer reviews the logistics of disembarking and the passengers stir in anticipation of arrival.

A cannon on the dock greets tourists as they exit the ferry to a military march. The tourists board reproductions of the trolleys that once crisscrossed the island during its American military administration, an ideal vehicle for viewing the island. A gigantic statue of MacArthur presides over the dock area. Once the tourists choose their trolleys, their tour begins. Each tour guide, in perfect English (except for the occasional guides who attempt some Japanese phrases for Japanese tourists), starts with an early history of Corregidor, mentioning the island's designation as a U.S. military reservation in 1902 and its fortification with guns, batteries, and magazines between 1904 and 1922. The obsession with military facts and figures, such as gun size and type of ordnance, is a major — even a fetishized — component of the tour.

The whole island is an overt tribute to Filipino and American symbols of triumph, heroism, and brotherhood, arranged in different sets of parks or monuments. On Topside — so-called because it is the highest elevation on the tadpole-shaped island — and Middleside are the structures that made up the former nerve center of military operations. Topside and Middleside also house the war monuments, gun batteries, and ruins that make up the heart of the Corregidor tour. The story of a long-standing, tested, and enduring Allied fraternity is the keystone to the basic daylong tour taken by the vast majority of visitors, tying these various sites into a coherent experience. Whisked through a relentless array of monuments, ruins, and other sights, tourists understand that Corregidor's importance is showcased by its "dramatic past," which is once again conjured up for the tourist to experience as an "eternal witness to the valiant heroism and chilling horrors of war."[47]

Corregidor's monumental and affective architecture evokes the narrative of American valor and the supporting role of Filipino friendship and bravery, tapping into gendered and racialized notions of heroism. The masculine perspective of the soldier dominates the island, generating a mode of "fantasy-production" that revolves around the melodrama of suffering masculinity and the story of sacrifice.[48] The Pacific War Memorial, finished in 1968, is emblematic of this story.[49] Built to commemorate fallen American and Filipino soldiers who fought in World War II, the memorial works as a grave marker, reminding tourists that Corregidor Island remains a mass grave. Its stark white dome was designed with a circular hole at the top to allow a shaft of sunlight to illuminate the marble slab below it every May 6, commemorating the fall of Corregidor. Tellingly, Ferdinand Marcos dedicated the memorial with these words:

> From this day on, this new edifice on Corregidor will also be a monument of peace. The men whose memory we honor with this memorial fought to make peace, if not possible, an enduring condition of human life. We who now behold it, do so as the living beneficiaries of their sacrifices. We look at this monument with eyes used to the spectacles of a peaceful life; the bright and soaring quality of its architecture symbolizes for us the heights of human achievement that we can reach, not in war but peace.[50]

As "beneficiaries" of a peace secured by violence and sacrifice, Marcos was reminding Filipinos and Americans alike—for his sake and the sake of his U.S. backers—to be thankful for the peaceful life secured by suffering and death. His 1968 address continues to resonate in Corregidor's new touristic incarnation. Producing a national memory of militarized security, even as it simultaneously evokes peace, the Pacific War Memorial links masculine sacrifice with the continued sacrifice of a benevolent American protector. Thus the "spectacles" of the tourist gaze are adjusted

to see only the theatrical narrative of liberation, not the calculated malevolence of colonialism and neocolonialism.

Beyond the memorial, a wide concrete walkway leads to a massive steel
sculpture of the eternal flame, mounted on a deck that also provides a view
of the ocean and the Bataan peninsula in the distance. On either side of
the walkways are marble panels listing the narrative of World War II, from
the "Defense of Hawaii" to "Philippine Liberation." This is an American
historiography of the Pacific Wars.[51] These panels praise the "Philippine
Resistance Movement" for its "repeated blows against the armies of the
invaders in a heroic fight for the cause of freedom." Yet the overwhelming
message is that liberation was largely an American act—to narrate it any
other way would untether the drive for "liberation" from "America." Following the walkway's narrative arc from attack to victory, tourists arrive
at the viewing deck. The sculpture of the eternal flame at the end of the
walkway encourages contemplation of the long and arduous retaking of
the Pacific by American troops, and the price they paid with their lives to
secure Corregidor and the Philippines. It is both a solemn and celebratory
moment: tourists pose for photographs in front of the flame, with Bataan
in the background.

The Pacific War Memorial Museum completes the trio of memorial
structures juxtaposed in this site. The museum sits next to the war memorial and is a more compact version of the island itself, with smaller guns
guarding the entrance, and dog tags, badges, broken crockery, and utensils
miniaturizing and making more personal the narrative told by memorials and ruins outside. Tourists walk slowly through the glass cases, sifting
through the prosaic articles of military routine on the island. The museum displays the stuff of everyday life, animating the guides' somewhat
dry dates-and-figures account with personal and human-scale relics. A
display of the artifacts from the last Thanksgiving meal before the war—
including serving ware and a menu—personalizes life on Corregidor as
distinctly American. Importantly, this holiday celebration also domesti-
cates the space in another way by emphasizing the habits of home that
soldiers carried with them abroad. The tableaus and scenes evoked by the
displays belie the inherent violence of soldierhood. Instead the museum
produces military occupation as innocent, small, and banal by framing the
everyday routine of young men on duty as if they were merely going about
performing the everyday tasks of family life—chores, meals, leisure activities.[52] Even the photographs that capture the more heroic poses, such

as cleaning guns and parading, are somehow folded into the larger fantasy of prewar innocence that covers the walls—that of young men in bunks, joking around, working together. The soldiers are young for the most part, just boys far away from home. The attack of the Japanese military into this nostalgically remembered colonial occupation violently interrupts the feeling of the everydayness that the museum otherwise constructs.

On one of the museum's photograph-lined walls, a particular snapshot exemplifies the shifting meanings of liberation negotiated by Corregidor. This oversize color photograph, taken in 1994, stands out against the black-and-white photographs of preinvasion Corregidor. In it, smiling former presidents of the United States and the Philippines (Bill Clinton and Fidel Ramos, respectively) pose with each other during a tour of the island—heads of state as prototourists. The image is a tourist souvenir, distilling in visual terms a long history of travel and relations of security underpinning neoliberal partnerships. In the photograph, the smiling faces of Clinton and Ramos imply that present-day freedoms—including the privileges of travel—hinge on the dramatic heroism of Corregidor's dead men and, by extension, the continuing vigilance of mutually supportive militaries in the Pacific. Paired with the black-and-white photographs of American paratroopers retaking the island in a daring air attack, the almost casual photograph of Clinton and Ramos completes the arc of Corregidor's narrative. As brothers-in-arms, Clinton and Ramos watchfully preside over the neoliberal legacies of U.S. colonialism in the Philippines. This frozen moment captures a quick stopover that Bill Clinton made to Manila en route to the APEC summit in Indonesia that year. Two years after that, APEC was held in Subic Bay, where mansions had been constructed to host the heads of state and whose new status as a freeport was the ultimate symbol of the Washington consensus. Today, after the 1997 Asian crisis demonstrated the failed vision of neoliberal globalization, the photograph of Clinton and Ramos illuminates the steadfastness of a U.S.-Philippine partnership that continues to deregulate and privatize the Philippine economy in the name of freedom and in the face of the repeated failures of neoliberal governance.

The Pacific War Memorial's triptych of memorial, eternal flame, and museum promotes the enduring results of mutual collaboration between the United States and the Philippines—a collaboration that in this version of the story dates its origins to World War II. Actively generating a sanitized history woven around these martial narratives, the memorial appeals to a new generation of tourists who are further removed from World War II memory, less attached to World War II history than to acts of tourism in general. At the museum, tourists have an opportunity to reflect in silence on the militarized itinerary they have experienced on their tour thus far. While they may not actively identify with "our boys," in the act of touring they are made aware of the protections extended to them by the sacrifice of American and Filipino soldiers. Consuming historical narratives and sites that are not part of their own personal experience, such tourists nevertheless are invited to appreciate the legacies of the historical narrative depicted in such tours. Whether they actively grasp the historical-touristic narratives seriously, reject them altogether, or merely use the ruins and guns as backdrops to their own tourist snapshots, the liberation narrative figures centrally in their experience.

The aptly named Filipino-American Friendship Park emulates a similar affective investment in brotherly love. This memorial park is dominated by a statue of Filipino and American soldiers assisting each other on the Bataan Death March (figure 3.1) and bordered by markers that record the different battalions that fought during the war. A familiar figure of interracial fraternity, the larger-than-life sculpture embodies the emotional and ideological weight of Corregidor as a war monument. With its realistic depiction of suffering and its idealistic portrayal of interracial brotherhood, the monument captures camaraderie under pressure: a transcendent theme of empathic humanity, shared suffering, and lasting friendship. The plaque at the base states, "In these hallowed surroundings where heroes sleep may their ashes scatter with the wind and live in the hearts of those who were left behind. They died for freedom's right and in heaven's sight. Theirs was a noble cause." The photograph of Fidel Ramos and Bill Clinton resonates with and updates this message of martial brotherhood, providing a model of cooperation built from the bonds of suffering—the contemporary embodiment of "freedom's right." As beneficiaries of the first liberation, one brought about by the mutual aid depicted by the statue, Ramos and Clinton reenact the scene and sentiment of the enduring "special relationship" between the United States and the Philippines in a setting most appropriate to the character of that relationship.

There are other stops on the tour—such as the Japanese Garden of Peace, or the Filipino Heroes Memorial—that offer potential sites of historical remembrance that are not so tightly tethered to a World War II

FIGURE 3.1
The Brothers in
Arms sculpture,
Corregidor.
PHOTOGRAPH BY
THE AUTHOR.

narrative. Yet by virtue of their location on Corregidor and the island's dominant themes of memorialization, these alternative memorializations are nonetheless pulled into the dominant orbit of sacrifice and brotherhood in the service of nationalism and liberation. The Japanese Garden of Peace was funded by a private group based in Japan and is meant as a place of reflection for Japanese war veterans and their families. Featuring a large stone Buddha and reflecting pool along with other Japanese shrines, markers, memorabilia, and weaponry, it is an incongruous part of the tour, lying outside of the triumphant liberation narrative and calling attention to Japanese military history in Corregidor. For some of the steadily decreasing numbers of World War II Allied survivors, this peace garden is a contested place, where the "enemy" has been granted space and recognition. However, for an increasing number of tourists who have less of a personal or emotional investment in Corregidor's Allied narrative, the Garden of Peace may symbolize the new relations between Japan, the United States, and the Philippines, thereby effectively eliding the history of imperial competition between the United States and Japan that launched the war. A few might also note, however, how these updated "friendships" in the form of aids and loans have rearticulated Philippine-Japan relations by transforming the enemy into an neoliberal ally. The garden, in this sense, contributes to smoothing over the intensely affective tours of Corregidor by offering alternative interpretations of the past and present.

Corregidor's obsession with World War II overrides the early U.S. imperial history that put "the Rock" in American hands. Likewise, the narratives of sacrifice and liberation are limited to an American tradition. The Filipino Heroes Memorial, which depicts revolutionary movements in the Philippines dating from the Battle of Mactan in 1521 (where Ferdinand Magellan was killed) to the People Power Revolution in 1986, is another such site that is potentially unsettling but is inevitably recruited into the American version of Corregidor history. A large square dominated by a statue of a farmer-soldier fighting for his country's freedom, the message of this memorial emphasizes the heroic action taken by ordinary Filipinos who were forced to respond to tyranny. The murals that border the walls of the square favor a teleology of revolutionary action that begins with Western contact and ends with the overthrow of the Marcos dictatorship. Yet what is strangely absent, particularly in light of its historical significance, is the Philippine-American War. This absence recurs in other sites on the island, where — despite its overmonumentalization — there is no mention of the war that marked the beginning of United States imperialism in the Philippines.[53] If an imperfect recollection of the past is a key element in the production of heritage destinations, Corregidor's World War II ghosts successfully sanitize the realities of war and remove its "savage malevolence."[54] Producing Corregidor as a tourist site allows for narratives and histories of valor and brotherhood, yet leaves little room for remembering the legacies and material realities of imperial military occupation in an overseas colony.

The glaring lacuna at the Filipino Heroes Memorial and the provenance of the early fortifications constitute shadow narratives that are subsumed by Corregidor's feature story. The biggest and most unusual photographic opportunities on the tour are the gun batteries (figure 3.2) and barrack ruins that still bear the marks of World War II. As tourist attractions, these massive guns represent the last stand of the United States on Filipino soil.

FIGURE 3.2
Gun batteries as
tourist attractions.
PHOTOGRAPH BY
THE AUTHOR.

However, the batteries on which people climb and pose are named after
American officers who fought in the Philippine-American war — a detail
that is not included in any tour guide's talk. Tourists consuming the narrative of World War II liberation can easily overlook these potentially sub-
versive ironies recalling an earlier imperial war, because the romance of
World War II liberation is more compelling, and because little exists on
the tour to make these other narratives legible to their tourist experience.
As the trolleys circle around the island, tourists see the old barracks, their
bombed-out ruins overgrown with vines and populated with the ghosts of
young innocent men sleeping in their quarters, walking the hallways, and
joking around with comrades. The tour narrative focuses on American soldiers, not on the stewards and servants who attended them, and certainly
not on the racial segregation that kept Filipino and American troops and
their families in separate quarters and schools on the island.

In the ideal itinerary, the tour capstone is a visit to the light-and-sound show installed in the Malinta Tunnel. Originally an arsenal and underground hospital used heavily during the Japanese military's bombing of the island, the tunnel is now the stage for the story of American and Filipino resistance. In the dark, sealed tunnel, tourists are prompted by guiding lights to move down the main tunnel in concert with the audio narration of the attack on Corregidor. The sound effects of bombs echo in the dark chamber, and a fog machine reproduces the smoke and haze of exploded ordnance. Tucked into the lateral tunnels, life-sized dioramas re-create scenes from the bombing. The dramatic, if static, display summarizes the history lesson that the tourists have heard all day, immersing them in the aural, visual, and embodied experience of war. The climax of this didactic light-and-sound show drives the point home: in the sudden darkness at the end of the story of Corregidor, a spotlight shines on the flagpole standing opposite the entrance to the tunnel with a Philippine flag waving at the top. The tourists stop and stand still for the Filipino national anthem, reenacting the American "return" of Corregidor to the Philippines as the resolution to the historical drama to which they have been witness. Today, Malinta Tunnel is blown up again and again as part of a touristic itinerary of remembrance and gratitude. It repeats the narrative of sacrifice to which visitors have been subject all day on the tour, which ultimately ends in the return of Corregidor to its rightful owners by the loyal and noble sacrifice of American troops. The sheer repetition of this narrative in memorial after memorial over the course of the day does not end at Malinta Tunnel. On the boat ride on the way home, tourists watch Douglas MacArthur's *I Shall Return* video biography, which returns over and over again to sacrifices made and the obligatory gratitude for this gift of freedom.

BATAAN'S SUFFERING SUBLIME

In comparison to the overly monumentalized Corregidor, Bataan is a minimalist mapping of Allied suffering at the hands of the Japanese Army. The Bataan peninsula, with its gray profile guarding Corregidor from the north, haunts the tour of Corregidor in more than one way. Visible from the island, it is the point of reference for other tours of American valor. Bataan's history is intimately intertwined with Corregidor's: the fate of one military stronghold would affect the other. Less accessible as a touristic site than Corregidor's compact and regulable "islandness," Bataan's claim to fame is the Bataan Death March, the grueling 184-kilometer jungle-and-road trek that American and Filipino prisoners of war were forced to undergo after the fall of Bataan.

Compared to the surfeit of memorials on Corregidor, and belying its greater infamy, Bataan is less ready and friendly for tourists, as well as less containable. There are few organized tours here, and any visitors who decide to come must arrange their own itineraries. The kilometer road markers that the Marcos administration put up in 1964 have long since been vandalized or stolen, and the recent move to replace the missing markers is going slowly (see figure 3.3 for a replaced one). Under the auspices of the Filipino-American Memorial Endowment—an organization that works with the American Chamber of Commerce, U.S. expatriates, and Filipino allies to promote U.S.-Filipino historical and contemporary relations—the kilometer markers are steadily reappearing. Individually sponsored by private organizations, former and current soldiers, and others, these obelisk markers are small and unobtrusive. Standing alone, marking long stretches of road, and interrupted by the occasional World War II monument, they do not constitute an easy or compelling tourist attraction, and few tourists come here. Those that do are small groups of soldiers, families of survivors, or history buffs on tours that specialize in history and war.[55] The most tourable site that people can visit is the Dambana ng Kagitingan (Cross of Valor) memorial, built during the Marcos regime, which houses a museum similar to Corregidor's, with marble panels depicting scenes of soldierly bravery and sacrifice.

The memorial, a ninety-five-meter-high cross made of concrete and steel and erected atop Mount Samat in Pilar, Bataan, is unequivocally a symbol of sacrifice. Another Marcos project in Filipino-American Cold War statesmanship, the Dambana ng Kagitingan memorial is inevitably autobiographical because Marcos staged his heroic World War II narrative in Bataan. Claiming to have been a guerrilla fighter and a one-man army against the Japanese military in the Battle of Bataan, he assumed a mantle of suffering and heroism that catapulted him to the presidency.[56] In the months leading up to his declaration of martial law in 1972, Marcos and his media machine increasingly stage-managed his heroism on Bataan as a way to remind Filipinos of the sacrifices he had made. An October 3, 1971, feature in the *Sunday Times Magazine* describes a "young lieutenant" who had "pledged to put up a cross on Mount Samat in memory of his fallen comrades." The writer goes on to describe this dramatic moment:

FIGURE 3.3
The Bataan Death
March Memorial
marker. PHOTOGRAPH
BY MIGUEL LLORA.

"As he always does at every opportunity, he re-traced the uphill, winding road leading to the shrine to spend a few minutes with the men whose blood was shed on those slopes in the hell of the last days of Bataan."[57] The following year, on the thirtieth anniversary of Bataan Day, Marcos once again inserted his heroism into this larger historical narrative, while also describing a pilgrimage that could be turned into a tourist site. The commemorative program marking the occasion features a photograph of Marcos gazing reflectively over a now peaceful countryside, a pose mimicked today by tourists who look out from the cross.[58]

This structure, which visitors can climb, offers extensive views of the Bataan peninsula from the viewing gallery on the arms of the cross. From this position, tourists can survey the landscape stretching out beneath and beyond: it is easy to imagine the war playing out on the backdrop. Using *the* archetype of Christian masculine sacrifice, the memorial allows visitors to visualize what was made possible by the deaths of American and Filipino soldiers. Over the backdrop of Bataan scenery, one can imagine the already-familiar narratives of suffering, survival, and brotherhood occurring over the landscape. From the cross, the route of the Bataan Death March seems impossibly long, and the view—while panoramic and striking—is saturated with the weight of sacrifice. Simultaneously evoking a landscape of war and sacrifice, as well as enabling a tourist gaze structured by the "spectacles of a peaceful life," the vista from the cross performs double duty. The pleasures of this panoramic sublime coexist in productive tension with a profound identification with suffering, producing not guilt but gratitude for the tourist freedoms enjoyed by the viewer.

In their entirety, these encompassing narratives of Bataan and Corregidor—with their icons of the wounded, tortured soldier, and the brave and stoic general, the bombed-out magazines and batteries, the lone markers on a busy road—elicit gratitude for the sacrifice entailed in liberation by what is now known as "the greatest generation."[59] This chapter's emphasis on the centrality of the sentimental, ostensibly former, American militarism in these sites serves to link the symbolic guardianship of the Philippines' "Big White Brother" to the neoliberal ideologies that underpin the emergence of tourism as the economic savior of the neocolonial world. By providing spaces where public memorialization of heroic military action takes place, Corregidor and Bataan gesture toward the necessary centrality of state-sponsored and condoned militarism even as the market has eroded the state's other public functions. In other words, what tourists tour in Corregidor is not *just* a historical site. It is a story about continuing American-Philippine relations that casts contemporary American-style neoliberal policy in the familiar role of hero—neoliberation. The imaginative labor that Corregidor and Bataan perform as tourist sites is thus inseparable from the exploitation of material labor at the nearby freeport zones in Clark and Subic Bay. These military bases reconfigured as tourist commercial hubs rearticulate colonial discourses of uplift, modernity, progress, and salvation in their militarized, privatized borders, much in the same way that narratives of liberation are circulated and consumed on Corregidor and Bataan. Yet the heroic Allied narrative continues not only to structure these commemorative sites but also to obscure the contradictions between the World War II American-rescue account and American political and economic manipulation that arose during the U.S.-sponsored Marcos years and that continue today.

At Clark and Subic Bay Freeports, former American military reservations have now transitioned with some struggle and hard work on the part of Philippine government officials, former antibase activists, and global capital into legitimate centers of business and pleasure. These conversions of military infrastructure have extended to other sites also formerly controlled by the United States. For example, the back of a brochure about the different types of military tourism possible in Bataan offers an alternative—a tour of Bataan's "rise to economic development and progress." This tour visits the first export processing zone, built under the Marcos regime in 1969 as part of his World Bank/IMF-engineered economic policy.[60] Today, the zone is a tourist destination, showcasing a different kind of partnership between the Philippines and the United States. Subic Bay and Clark, decades later, would follow the same path, with Subic Bay being the ultimate showcase of neoliberation at the 1996 APEC summit. In tourism as well as other industries in these export processing zones, jobs are provided, "service" learns its place, skills are imparted, and the infrastructure left behind by the benevolent giant serves to continually uplift the struggling "Little Brown Brother." It could not be otherwise according to the liberation narratives of Bataan and Corregidor. Yet even in their ostensible return to the Filipino people, these former military lands constitute another node of neocolonial domination, a theme I explore more fully in chapter 6.

Today—in between the repetitions of praise to the loyal, steadfast soldier, and the loyal, steadfast military occupier—other narratives of militarism and tourism lie in wait. The Critical Filipino and Filipina Studies Collective (CFFSC), among other progressive and activist groups—Bayan, Anakpawis, and GABRIELA, for instance—points out that the intertwined logics of capital and militarism have served to rationalize the contemporary surge in the systematic killings of progressive Filipino and Filipina activists as "terrorists" by Philippine paramilitary forces trained by U.S. troops. According to these organizations, this war against the Filipino people is not an aberration; rather, it is part of a long-running strategy necessary to colonial and neocolonial economies.[61] The targeted remilitarization of the islands works in tandem with neoliberation: the suppression of dissent is masked by the animated corpse of the World War II sacrificial soldier in order to create "new sites of investment and profit and new opportunities for the aggrandizement of unlimited power and wealth for the few."[62] Thus the tourist narrative of the wounded, brave soldier pushing on, dying, or returning becomes a tourism that celebrates the aftermath of that sacrifice (the imposition of neoliberal policies) while also functioning as a guarantor and an alibi for the continued intimacies between militarism, the state, and capital today. Tourism, in this instance, ties itself to an act of gratitude—appreciation for what soldiers gave up, what foreign militaries contributed to, and what is secured today in these unique contact zones.

Inviting soldiers to officially become tourists, as Gordon did, further extends the welcome mat to an otherwise illegitimate occupying force. By tying militarism to tourism more securely, a modified yet familiar narrative of benevolence and protection emerges. In this new narrative, different memories of tourism-militarism are highlighted, such as those of Gordon's ostensibly new soldier-tourist, the epitome of the modern mobile subject. Under the VFA, this new soldier-tourist subject is the ultimate protected subject: at the cost of the Philippine government's sovereignty, American soldiers committing crimes in the Philippines are not under the jurisdiction of local laws. As the new "rescuer"—providing not only tourist dollars for a struggling Philippine economy, but also a protective force to guarantee "stability"—the soldier-tourist becomes a new privileged subject of both states. Tragically, the potency of such masculinized narratives of military suffering also submerges contemporary moments of gendered and racialized violence committed against Filipinas, who register most keenly the collateral damage of these new military maneuvers. Against this backdrop of military-tourist modernity, the "incidental" stories of base-related sexual violence become footnotes.

These Filipina narratives—those that interrupt the protector narrative in particularly gendered and racialized ways—become, in effect, the new (yet familiar) refrain of sacrifice of the Philippine nation. A long-running collaboration between "masculinity, combat and sex" structures the ways in which Gordon's soldier-tourist continues to be the privileged subject of these neoliberated economies.[63] In November 2005, six off-duty American servicemen who were acting like tourists (in a karaoke bar) in the Subic Bay Freeport allegedly raped a young Filipina woman. The six men were in the Philippines taking part in U.S.-Filipino "counterterrorist" training.[64] By no means was this an isolated incident: in 1992, investigations of fifty-two cases of rape and of physical and sexual abuse were suspended when the United States officially returned the base territories to the Philippines.[65] While a debate soon followed in the Philippine legislature and in the media regarding the police custody of the men and jurisdiction over the crime, the Armed Forces of the Philippines were quick to announce that the rape case would not have any impact on the continuing joint military exercises.[66] Although one of the soldiers was found guilty in criminal court, his freedom was secured by the U.S. Pacific Command's threat to cancel joint military exercises and humanitarian activities in the Philippines. Ninotchka Rosca, whose rape scene in *State of War* begins this book, commented on the outcome of the case, tying the permissibility of raping Filipina women to a state that allows it.[67] The key role that base tourism—as the fifth most important source of revenue for the Philippines—plays in the economic big picture essentially leaves Filipina women vulnerable: the incidental violence that military tourism produces has near-diplomatic immunity. With base tourisms transformed into freeport tourisms, and U.S. military occupation reconfigured under the VFA, these patterns of near–state sanctioned violence remain unchecked.[68]

Tourist and military masculinities bolster each other in the joint exercise of controlling bodies and narratives that interrupt the nostalgic World War II memory of rescue and liberation that continues to inform these neoliberated, militarized spaces today. At stake, then, in the project of the making of transnational memories in which military tourism takes part is a gendered project of complicit patriarchies. Brought together in collusion by the silencing of these other narratives of violent military tourism, these state patriarchies produce a vision of a modernity founded on past brotherly cooperation that is guaranteed by the continuing vigilance over the violable bodies of Filipina women. To tour the footprints of the American military today necessarily rehearses the acts of gratitude produced through tourist narratives of neoliberation and allows for the rewriting or disappearance of stories of brutal domination, as the next chapter's meditation on the Pearl Harbor military-tourism complex further demonstrates. These attitudes of neoliberationist thanksgiving—as demonstrated in the tourisms of Corregidor and Bataan—are particularly resonant in the contemporary moment, as U.S. militarization in the post-9/11 era rearticulates colonial geographies through ideologies of security, stability, and the "freedom to travel." Military tours function in this moment as a vehicle of imperfect memory, making possible the continuation of gendered nationalism and militarized societies, and the promise of violent futures.

Four

❋

REMEMBERING PEARL HARBOR, REINFORCING VIGILANCE

Whereas tourism takes up militarism in explicit ways in the Philippines, in Hawai'i, the image of the islands as a tropical paradise occludes while also making possible the U.S. military occupation of the state. Belying the Hawai'i Visitors Bureau's campaigns to produce Hawai'i as an exotic place gifted with tropical climate and fauna and served by a multicultural and hospitable population, the state's most popular tourist attraction is a military site—the USS *Arizona* Memorial—which is located in Pearl Harbor, the largest naval base in the Pacific Ocean and the active headquarters of the U.S. Pacific Command. This sunken memorial to the sailors trapped and killed in the *Arizona* following the attack on Pearl Harbor draws nearly two million visitors a year. How is it that this memorial to death and war trumps all other attractions that O'ahu has to offer? Rather than understand the commodification of Hawai'i as tropics and the USS *Arizona* Memorial's commemoration of World War II as opposing impulses, I argue that they are mutually constitutive. The business of tourism benefits from the high drama of war: the war economy of the United States means that war-related attractions such as those at Pearl Harbor stay in demand.[1] Likewise, the U.S. military benefits from the blurring between public relations and tourism that occurs in sites that feature war memorialization and that generate public appreciation and support as well as federal funding for the robust presence of the U.S. military in Hawai‘i.[2] The towering military and cultural presence of Pearl Harbor helps rationalize and secure 22.4 percent of O‘ahu's land for the military.[3]

More significantly, beyond these benefits, the Pearl Harbor military-tourism complex recruits the pleasures of tourism to retract American histories of imperialism, illegal overthrow, and ongoing occupation and to enlist civilians into U.S. circuits and logics of security. Tourism in Hawai‘i inhibits the understanding of Hawai‘i as a contested and occupied site. It deflects the history of how U.S. geopolitical desires for Pearl Harbor prompted the navy's threat of force during the 1893 overthrow of Queen Lili‘uokalani and provided subsequent motivation for the continued denial of petitions for the return of sovereignty to the Kingdom of Hawai‘i. The tourisms of war at Pearl Harbor—with their glorification of American cultures of war and specifically World War II's dramatic story—help visitors justify, desire, and identify with the militarization of Hawai‘i, Asia, and the Pacific region while averting their gaze from the fact that Hawai‘i was, and is, contested territory. In the previous chapter, the circuit of neoliberation illustrated by Corregidor, Bataan, Subic, and Clark highlighted the links between colonial logics of militarism and liberation and contemporary neoliberal governance and ideologies of security. This chapter explores how the relationship between tourism and militarism in Hawai‘i manages potential moments of danger, violence, and contestation by recruiting them into a specifically American narrative of the Good War. As in the Philippines, the memorialization of World War II plays a key role in this process: Pearl Harbor's hallowed place in U.S. historiographies of World War II is further secured by the ways its narratives of sacrifice and heroics operate to lend a mantle of righteousness to contemporary U.S. militarism in the region.[4] By making hypervisible the histories of war violence, reinforcing familiar narratives of innocence and sacrifice, underscoring ideologies of multiculturalism and statehood, and crafting moments of intense sensory and affective identification with a defining moment of war, the tours that "remember Pearl Harbor" undertake the important cultural labor of recruiting sympathy for U.S. visions of security and for the measures the United States must take to achieve them. The acts of touring—roaming the grounds of the memorial, listening to the audio tours, watching a film, riding on a boat to see the memorial, paying homage to the names of the dead displayed throughout the site— not only are acts that encourage the consumption of a particular version of American history by linking security to pleasure, but also are acts that elicit tourist identifications with particular national narratives and versions of patriotism.[5]

Military bases and tropical tourist paradises would not seem to occupy the same universe, but in Hawai'i they are inextricably linked, illustrating that securing paradise is an ongoing project, and one achieved through the mutual workings of tourism and militarism. Indeed, the massive yet largely accepted presence of the military in Hawai'i demonstrates that there is much more than a historical tour — or opportunities to remember and mourn — at stake in examining the USS *Arizona* Memorial and the Pearl Harbor military-tourism complex. The biggest and most visible representative of the 161 military installations in Hawai'i, Pearl Harbor is powerfully symbolic of national sacrifice and service. Constituting *the* hub of military tourism in Hawai'i, the Pearl Harbor military-tourism complex, anchored by the USS *Arizona* Memorial, naturalizes and makes desirable the military's massive economic and physical presence in Hawai'i. Pearl Harbor's vaunted history of World War II combines with and mitigates the implicit dangers of an active military installation, and the incongruity of a heavily militarized tropics. Substituting a history that frames the U.S. military as hero rather than occupier, the Pearl Harbor military-tourism complex — now a part of a much larger Valor in the Pacific National Monument — transforms the potential menace of military weaponry, personnel, and space into a benign and even inspiring destination for pleasurable tourist activity.[6]

The sheer array of military equipment on display for tourists demonstrates the *efforts* of securing paradise. Nestled alongside the *Arizona* Memorial is the USS *Bowfin*, a submarine-turned-hands-on museum, where tourists can clamber aboard the docked submarine, explore its inner workings, and play with its guns. In the adjacent USS *Bowfin* Park, the concrete walkways are lined with Tomahawk torpedoes, and Polaris submarine–launched ballistic missiles tower over tourists by way of monuments. The USS *Missouri* (a battleship where the Japanese signed their surrender at the end of World War II), the Pacific Aviation Museum, and the USS *Oklahoma* Memorial (for a ship that suffered the second-highest number of casualties during the Pearl Harbor attacks) complete the World War II narrative of the forced entry of the United States and its decisive concluding role in the war.[7] Visitors to the Pearl Harbor complex consume a familiar and seductive story that begins with nostalgic innocence, gets interrupted by treachery and violence, and ends with sacrifice and triumph over adversity. As one of the most important sites of Allied defeat and dogged struggle toward victory during World War II, Pearl Harbor—like Corregidor—is largely a metonym for this broader narrative arc. While the familiar story of military sacrifice is the primary register of tourism at Pearl Harbor, what becomes apparent through the massing of military machinery and machinery for hands-on experience is the labor it takes to shape a national myth that is instrumental to Hawaiian dispossession.

COMMEMORATING DECEMBER 7, 1941

Touring the complex achieves a crucial threefold purpose. First, it underscores the imagery of Pearl Harbor as a historic war zone, a place where *American* innocence was ambushed in a haze of smoke, debris, and sinking ships. This moment effectively and convincingly locates Hawai'i within an American World War II temporal and spatial frame: images of a sinking and smoking USS *Arizona* published in national newspapers galvanized the American public. Americans leapt to protect and avenge a physically far-off and culturally dissonant territory as definitely American, which lent itself to the incontrovertibility of present-day U.S. military rights to this place. Just as importantly, while the narrative arc of the Pearl Harbor military-tourism complex tour began with the catastrophic bombing that launched the United States into the Pacific war, it ended with the victorious resolution of that war. The USS *Missouri* brackets this triumphant arc of U.S. World War II commemoration and provides a tour of the muscular hardware that contributed to American victory, reinforcing the message of resolve, victory, and vigilance. This U.S.-centric narrative of World War II—typical of National Park Service interpretations—sutures the USS *Arizona* Memorial to its auxiliary Pearl Harbor sites and extends to the overall massive U.S. military presence in Hawai'i, Asia, and the Pacific, demonstrating the cultural, social, and ideological labor of colonial strategies in Hawai'i that work to replace violence with innocence, occupation, and land theft with service and sacrifice.

Second, in contrast to the Philippines, where World War II narratives and their rearticulations under the conditions of globalization assert heroic histories in place of past brutality in order to promote a neoliberal vision of the future, in Hawai'i, the fetishization of December 7 overwrites January 17, 1893—the day that the Kingdom of Hawai'i was overthrown by an alliance of U.S. businessmen backed by a U.S. warship—as *the* day that Hawai'i was attacked. Framing Pearl Harbor as a place of violently and tragically betrayed American innocence additionally obscures any instances of America's own acts of treachery. Indigenous claims to sovereignty, and to Pearl Harbor in particular, are thus rendered unintelligible in this space.[8] The iconicity of December 7 further reinforces the rationales for continuing military "protection" and security in the Pacific: remembering Pearl Harbor bolsters a "never again" emotional response as well as a lingering conviction to continue to secure this strategic terrain as American territory. That "date which will live in infamy" anchors the version of World War II history commemorated in Pearl Harbor within an American periodization and historiography of the war as well as an American vision of the present and future. This dedication to December 7 is reflected in the inclusion of additional attractions to the original USS *Arizona* Memorial: the USS *Bowfin* Submarine Museum and Park was opened to the public in 1981, followed by the "museumization" of the decommissioned USS *Missouri* in 1998; the opening of the Pacific Aviation Museum on December 7, 2006; and the dedication of the USS *Oklahoma* Memorial on December 7, 2007.[9] At these linked auxiliary sites, December 7, 1941, is relived over and over again, and the story of World War II American valor is tailored to visitors as a discrete unit, consumable in one visit as part of a Hawai'i holiday itinerary.[10] With this repetition and Pearl Harbor's arrangement of World War II attractions, the "Good War" and its seeming moral clarity about the mandate of the United States to defend the world from the encroachments of Japanese military imperialism and the horrors of Nazi fascism emerge as the dominant ideological register of the Pearl Harbor complex. Every day, for a sizeable domestic and international audience, the repeated injunction to remember Pearl Harbor cements World War II as the defining historical claim to this place: "Valor in the Pacific" effectively dispels Native histories and Native claims to the land and their government and sutures the far-flung islands more securely to linked sites in Alaska and California, which are part of the National Park Service's mapping of World War II American territoriality.

The third key effect of the Pearl Harbor tours is that they allow for the business of an active military base and the business of tourism to overlap in pleasurable ways. The institutionalization of the hegemonic narrative of soldierly sacrifice and military success at the USS *Arizona* Memorial and the overall Pearl Harbor complex illustrates the successful and potent strategy of mixing an economy of death with that of pleasure.[11] The emotionally and viscerally powerful narratives of war, the carnage of the attack, and the vulnerability and devastation of the American military, nation, and family—these generate the ingredients of a satisfying melodrama that is eventually resolved by the resilience of the American people. Suffused with sentimental narratives of family and nation—and the sacrifices needed to secure their survival and prosperity—the tourist sites at Pearl Harbor operate through the registers of nostalgia, anguish, mourning, fear, love, and exultation. The narrative of loss is transmuted into a storyline about sacrifice, illustrated by dogged military men, brave women, and technological might. Even though tourists experience grief and sadness during their visits, such emotions are crucially part of, and not contradictory to, tourist pleasure. Tourists identify with a beleaguered but eventually triumphant national masculinity and are rewarded with a satisfying (if emotionally wrenching) resolution.[12] They are touring these sites because America won, after all. In Pearl Harbor's military-tourism complex, proof positive of the triumph of democracy and freedom lies in the tourists' robust presence, performing a public and collective ritual of consumption—an act that defines contemporary participation in social life. Because they are on a tropical holiday that is secured by American military presence in the Pacific, tourists can tie the pleasures of touring to the sacrifices of the military in an act of pilgrimage.[13] Invited to emotionally identify with the American narrative of World War II, tourists become part of the American family through the technologies of affect with which Pearl Harbor's military-tourism complex is armed and, in turn, are integral to its continued militarization. The recent renovations to turn the complex into part of the Valor in the Pacific monument have essentially made the entire complex more visitor friendly, further underscoring the military's interests in the public relations effectiveness of tourism and its effective partnership with the National Park Service, and framing consumer pleasures of tourism as a right guaranteed by military vigilance. Indeed, even as the numbers of living veterans of World War II decrease daily, the numbers of visitors have steadily increased over the years, testifying to the successful marriage of militarism and tourism in this particular site and the continued relevance and effectiveness of the Pearl Harbor military-tourism experience for generations that do not, themselves, remember the war.

The much-touted renovations to the USS *Arizona* Memorial's visitor center, which debuted in 2011, showcase, on the one hand, the emphasized reterritorialization of Hawai'i as part of U.S. World War II commemorative geographies and, on the other hand, updated amenities, modern architecture, attention to visitor comfort and enjoyment, are added efficiency and access to auxiliary Pearl Harbor military-tourist sites such as the USS *Missouri*. Most importantly, they display an inclusive and nuanced multicultural narrative aimed at twenty-first-century sensibilities.[14] These physical and discursive accommodations, however, illuminate how militarism and tourism can adjust to and operate within liberal logics of race, nationality, and consumer freedom even as these logics are also recruited in the service of Native Hawaiian dispossession. In other words, the different modes of inclusion and welcome that operate in the new center are not far removed from the old. The professionalized consideration of tourist physical comforts and ease of use, a gentler narrative that absolves Japanese civilian-tourists from blame and invites them as innocent consumers of this space, and an expansive national narrative that includes Japanese American masculine martial heroics as well as local civilian losses — all of these modes operate just as well, if not more effectively, to obliquely build a case for U.S. occupation.

Upon arriving at the renovated Pearl Harbor complex, tourists encounter a space that has been specifically designed with them in mind. The site's expansive layout regulates tourist traffic more efficiently than did the older and smaller visitor center, and tourists enjoy an easy-to-navigate experience from the very first. As they walk from the parking lot to the memorial complex, they join the traffic of other tourists who are hoping to procure the limited number of free tickets to visit the USS *Arizona* Memorial. The capacious entry beckons the visitor, and just beyond it, a ticket booth with several lanes efficiently handles arriving guests. At this booth, tourists can request tickets for the *Arizona* experience, which indicates a reserved time for the film and includes ferry transport to the memorial in Pearl Harbor. Tourists can also purchase individual or bundled tickets for tours on the USS *Bowfin*, the USS *Missouri*, and the Pacific Aviation Museum, the latter two of which are served by free shuttles. The design of this entryway encourages an orderly flow and a feeling of choice and freedom: tourists can choose which sites to explore,

FIGURE 4.1 The grounds of the USS *Arizona* Memorial visitor center. PHOTOGRAPH BY THE AUTHOR.

the order in which they choose to explore the available sites, and how much time to spend at different points.

While waiting for their allotted time slots for the *Arizona* memorial, tourists are invited to explore the grounds that encompass both the *Arizona* and *Bowfin* memorials. The welcoming and open design of the renovated visitor center is echoed in the manicured grounds intersected by smoothly paved, meandering walkways (figure 4.1). Many visitors immediately take leisurely walks around the grounds. The clear signage and interpretive panels unobtrusively introduce tourists to the tragic national history in the space, and these prompt people to move along to consider different points along the paths. Palm and pandanus trees provide shade and wave in the ocean breeze, providing important contrast to the concrete and steel buildings and equipment in Pearl Harbor just beyond. The architecture for the whole park is cohesive yet open, with the modern lines of the visitor center's buildings effectively framing the backdrop of the harbor, coastline, and island. In contrast to the old visitor center, the outdoors is a more active partner in producing the new center's mood and message, balancing the tropical landscape with a message of freedom tempered by somber reflection.

The new visitor center registers the political and sociocultural shifts in Hawai'i through an expansion of the racial, gender, and national representations in the visitor center, exceeding the architectural, landscaping, and visitor management concerns. The original visitor center, because of its racially exclusive narrative of sacrifice, generated critique from the diverse population of Hawai'i as well as from white American tourists and veterans who found the presence of Japanese tourists and a Japanese point of view in a site they felt was essentially American to be baffling or offensive.[15] The visitor center as it exists today manages these tensions with an eye to a host space that markets its multiculturalism as a unique attraction. Aimed at an increasingly more diverse American visitor demographic, the largely Japanese American social and political leadership of the islands, and a military that has become more racially and ethnically diverse, as well as Japanese mainstays of tourism in Hawai'i, the most noticeable changes have been inclusion and attention to more diverse perspectives and experiences of the war. In particular, the renovated center pays meticulous attention to a multicultural narrative of December 7, 1941, responding not only to the emergence of revisionist historiographies of the war but also to the multicultural rhetoric of Hawai'i's tourist paradise. However, while the visitor center has included more diversity in its storytelling by recruiting the recollections of a wider range of people, the overall story itself has not changed. If anything, the embrace of a multicultural narrative of sacrifice reflects the ascendance of Asian settlers in Hawai'i and the increasing dependence of the islands on foreign exchange and their mutual roles in the further alienation of Native lands from Native hands.

At the visitor center, two adjacent museums divide between them the story of December 7, 1941. One sets the historical context for the attack — the larger global historical, political, and economic forces that produced the conditions for war. The other museum — connected to the first by an open passageway — focuses on the day of the attack and its immediate aftermath. Both exhibits effectively alternate between large-scale history and more personalized stories, using historical artifacts and images to transport the visitor to the historical period of the war. Tourists wander in and take in the museums' displays at their own pace, though they can opt to pay for an audio tour that provides more narrative detail about the histories of World War II. They pause at different stations, stopping to read captions on maps and enlarged period photographs, watch and listen to television footage and audio recordings that generate a sense of immersion in the early 1940s, and observe artifacts of war and soldiering in glass cases.

While December 7 remains the dominant narrative for both museums, the story of multiculturalism has also been promoted as a significant thread that expands the affirming narrative of sacrifice to a wider membership. Entering the first museum, whose exhibit narrates *The Road to War*, tourists are immediately greeted by an image that sets the tone for how the museums might challenge a national history of this specific moment that has largely been imagined as white and male. A photographic collage of faces representing the diverse race, ethnic, and gender identities of the people who lived and worked in the base industries and on the island—including civilians—insists on a multicultural framework from the first. The successful integration of multiple perspectives in this museum's exhibit, however, does not necessarily challenge the largely white, male, and military national historiography of this moment (which was, for the most part, the organizing narrative of the original museum), but merely adds local color to it. The white history of American military occupation, its increased militarization of the islands, and the civilian elite's social and political hegemony are instead recast as parts of a larger multicultural undertaking and thus, implicitly, as consensual. Juxtaposed with the displays and photographs of military defense projects that fortified Hawai'i in anticipation of Asian military aggression, the photographs of Asian settlers in Hawai'i during the time leading up to the attack operate as visual shorthands for the tolerant and inclusive protections of the islands by the United States, belying the racialized social and political hierarchies that structured Hawai'i and the United States during this period.[16] In contrast to the American model of military protection, the story of imperial expansion is borne solely by Japan, which is framed as an aggressive and ambitious colonial power. However, even with its identification of Japan as an overreaching military aggressor, the multicultural narrative of *The Road to War* museum operates on an international level to recuperate Japanese civilians as innocent bystanders. Rather than casting the Japanese in general as villains, the museum carefully delineates between the imperial ambitions of the Japanese military junta and the innocence of Japanese civilians. While noteworthy in its sensitivity, by placing the burden of imperial guilt squarely on Japan's military, the display also navigates the tensions that might arise from this space, considering that

Japanese tourists today make up a significant number of visitors to the museum and bring in consistently high tourist receipts. By invoking a selective international multiculturalism that targets Japanese military imperial expansion, this particular part of the display serves both to absolve an important tourist market, and to further redirect critiques of imperialism at the Japanese military, and not the U.S. military, a discussion I will return to below.

Most tourists take in the museums in chronological order: following the historical buildup provided in *The Road to War* exhibit, they move on to the second museum, which focuses on the attack itself. *The Attack* exhibit is straightforward and immersive — the sights and sounds of the day predominate in the museum's re-creation of December 7, 1941. At the entrance to the second museum building, a color mural of Oʻahu's profile — as seen from the perspective of low-flying attack planes — curves around a wall leading into the interior of the museum. A reproduction of a Japanese Zero fighter plane is suspended over the entryway, and the scene of war is set through audio effects of zooming planes on approach, engines straining, and the quietly menacing splash of bombs being dropped into the water. Across the entryway, "Tora Tora Tora," the Japanese code for an achieved surprise attack, is starkly lettered on an otherwise blank wall. Inside, among displays of the infamous failed radar station, a U.S.-sunk Japanese midget submarine, and a Japanese torpedo, a small viewing room regularly shows a dramatic short film that uses documentary footage and computer-generated images of the aerial attack to capture the short, purposeful, and successful design of the Japanese attack. While the film begins with the surprise attack and enumerates the massive losses in visual form, it also ends with a "fighting back" narrative that nicely sets up the Pearl Harbor auxiliary sites.

However, what is noteworthy in the second museum is not its compelling presentation of the attack, but rather its further inscription of multicultural narratives into the story of December 7, 1941. Perhaps because of its intense affective structure, this exhibit and the way it affirms the heroic injuries incurred in war operate as a crucial moment for claims of multicultural inclusion. Artifacts that were transferred to this new exhibit from the old museum, which produced "our boys" as young white soldiers, are now evidence of multiculturalism rather than racial segregation. Photographs of sailors greeted by hula dancers, purchasing souvenirs, and enjoying the tropics drive home the pleasures of militarism in the tropics while images of young men in sports teams and a varsity let-ter adorning a sweater on display fabricate imaginations about carefree American youth. Juxtaposed next to evidence of Asian settler militariza-tion and civilian sacrifice, these artifacts confirm the diverse stakeholders of this place. Aside from the prominent presence of the story of the all-Japanese-American 442nd regiment's undeniable bravery and sacrifice, claims to martial belonging through civilian multicultural narratives of loss and hardship expand the affective circle of December 7 beyond the military. For example, in the museum, viewing stations include the stories of local civilians recounting the everyday textures of a martial law state, the routine of working at the shipyards, or how curfews worked, ensur-ing that their experiences of the war are added to soldierly narratives. Yet these local stories do not so much interrupt, but enrich and strengthen, the existing national historiography of the time before the attack. By enu-merating the specific ways that their lives were entwined with the domi-nant military history of Pearl Harbor, these civilians' testimonials insist on the extension of the familiar narrative of sacrifice to their own ex-periences and add further credence to the way that Pearl Harbor's mili-tary history supersedes Native Hawaiian history. Claiming this multicul-tural narrative of sacrifice, along with highlighting its particularly local flavor, also reflects the way that for Hawai'i's many residents of Asian ancestry—in particular Japanese Americans who avoided internment in Hawai'i—World War II created a martial pathway to heroism and citizen-ship (realized through statehood). The stories of civilian life under mar-tial law dominate the museum's exit, implying that for Hawai'i's diverse citizenry today, 1941 is the defining moment of national belonging.

These stories of Asian settler inclusion to what had been, until the re-cent renovations, a white military narrative of innocence and injury, de-ploy multiculturalism as an official state narrative that operates to further occlude Native Hawaiian presence, genealogy, and sovereignty. In con-trast to the affective and detailed architecture of both old and new visi-tor centers and their careful and nostalgic narrations of December 7, the consistent marginalization and near-absence of Native Hawaiian genealo-gies indicate an unwillingness to grapple with Hawaiian history as a "mo-ment of danger" that could potentially unravel U.S. claims to the islands.[17] In the original museum, Native Hawaiians were disappeared by virtue of their framing as prehistoric—before the modern life of Pearl Harbor. Taking up an entire wall in the museum, the military narrative of Pearl

Harbor's origins avoided the details of colonial conquest and illustrated the emptiness of premilitary Puʻuloa by displaying a lone sepia panoramic photograph of the landscape with two palm trees in the foreground. The original display presented the intervening years between the establishment of "American interests" in Pearl Harbor, the subsequent military reconnaissance trips of the mid-nineteenth century, and the negotiation of the 1887 Reciprocity Treaty that gave the United States unprecedented "limited rights to Pearl Harbor"—essentially portraying the overthrow of the Hawaiian kingdom and the construction of the naval base soon after annexation as merely milestones on an inevitable march of progress and modernity courtesy of the United States. Working from the Reciprocity Treaty of 1887 as the true beginning of Pearl Harbor, a treaty wrested from a weakened but sovereign monarchy, the display swiftly brushed aside the story of the illegal overthrow and established the American military presence as the result of a lawful and inevitable annexation: "Actual construction of the naval base was delayed until after Hawaiʻi was annexed by the United States. In 1908, Congress approved funding, and soon afterward work crews began dredging a channel through the coral reef barrier at the harbor's entrance. Three years later, construction commenced on the Marine barracks." The wall panels, with their deliberate omissions of American occupation, offered no disruption to American mythmaking in the Pacific.

In the updated visitor center, the political force and narrative of multiculturalism do not merely fail to extend to indigenous history; they depend on its exclusion and absence. Between the two museum buildings, an open breezeway connects *The Road to War* to *The Attack*. In this transitional space, an unobtrusive series of images accompanied by a small interpretive panel constitute the story of sovereign Hawaiʻi. Symbolically semitransparent, a series of images from the archives of premilitary Pearl Harbor have been printed on thin metal screens, whose surfaces have been punched through to create a pixilated and aged effect. On the side of the path, a concrete sitting area encourages visitors to stop and rest— with their backs to the display. Unlike the meticulously planned interactive exhibits housed within the two museums, this seating area is not meant to draw attention to itself or encourage close, sustained engagement with the presented information. Designed to literally marginalize indigenous history, this pathway puts Native history in a period external to *the* narrative of Pearl Harbor, and as incidental to the broader arc

FIGURE 4.2 **The overthrow of the Hawaiian kingdom in the margins.** PHOTOGRAPH BY THE AUTHOR.

of United States national myth.[18] The narrative on the panels and flip-books—for those tourists who bother to read them—gives an abridged account of how Hawai'i, particularly Pu'uloa, was seen as militarily strategic for the "expanding American empire." This brief mention of U.S. imperial military desire is soon deflected by the familiar story of the Reciprocity Treaty, which—instead of being explained as a step toward dispossession—is used as a legal alibi for occupying and militarizing the harbor. A treaty, after all, implies the consent of two parties. In contrast, the display downplays the overthrow and the dubious legality of annexation. The panels narrate the overthrow in passive voice—"The kingdom of Hawaii was overthrown in 1893" (figure 4.2)—only after which (however questionable it was) the United States finally annexed the islands. The last of the interpretive panels in this series explains the "massive defense spending" that then inaugurated the territory's annexation into the United States and signaled the kind of investment that justified continued occupation. Such familiar rationales for the militarization of Hawai'i are implicitly framed as an improvement from the "tight economic control of the plantations."

This creative revisionism of American imperial history in Hawai'i works in tandem with the multicultural theme in the renovated *Arizona* Memorial narrative. Just a few feet across this easily overlooked display, a small "island" bordered by similar concrete seating holds partner panels printed with vintage images of life in Hawai'i during the 1930s and 1940s. In this same island, a small, little-viewed interpretive panel tells the story of the Kanaka Maoli, including a brief story of the encroachment and loss of land and water access that has reduced their numbers to only 15 percent of the population by 1940. There is little explanation of the factors that caused this loss of land and water access in the first place. The focus on the disappearing native in the 1930s and 1940s underscores a perception of Kanaka Maoli as unable to survive in the rapidly changing conditions on the islands, especially when contrasted with Asian settlers who were thriving: multicultural modernity, it seems, did not agree with indigenous Hawaiians. A quote from a Native community leader stands out momentarily: "It is not that the ships and armed soldiers themselves are menacing, so much as the sense that they belong to this place and we do not." This potentially revealing and critical statement, however, is folded into the overall story in this seating area, which is ultimately a narrative of how Hawai'i became a multicultural society, "a home to many peoples."

The physical marginalization of Kanaka Maoli claims to the land is further reinforced in historiographic form through the war-centric storytelling of the museums, a framework that renders Native Hawaiian historiography unintelligible. In the first building, two maps illustrate the "prehistory" of the attack, exemplifying the ideological work of historical museumization in a site as charged as a military base on occupied territory. A map of Asia and the Pacific — color-coded to indicate different territories and colonial possessions of Japan, the United States, and Europe on the eve of World War II — drives home the point that the Japanese empire was growing steadily in the 1930s; the map outlines the changes from year to year, the slow and menacing bleed of color taking over more cartographic space. Indeed, the selective periodization of the map, which includes dates earlier than the purported 1937 starting dates for Japan but not the United States, leaves out the U.S. imperial maneuvers that had already secured both the Philippines and Hawai'i: the map identifies only Japan as an expanding empire. A second map, farther inside the first building, illustrates O'ahu's militarization. Implicitly framed as a response to Japanese expansion, this map offers a defensive alibi for the island's fortification, rather than explaining it as a long-running American policy. In contrast to the story of Japan's military run amok, American militarization of Hawai'i is not explained as an imperial act, despite the fact that Hawai'i was a sovereign kingdom. This continued disavowal of empire and occupation parallels the soldierly innocence on display in the museum, and it further legitimates the overall narrative of sacrifice created by the Pearl Harbor military-industrial complex.[19] Lending texture and contrast to the map's illustration of the steady and ominous growth of Japan's territorial reach in Asia, the interior displays focus on domestic American politics through newsreels and floor-to-ceiling photographic panels of familiar images from the 1930s. A relic from the original visitor center—a glass display case representing a soldier's life in Hawai'i with a fringed souvenir pillow cover, handwritten letters and photographs—preserves the iconicity of young white men as innocent bystanders dragged into a war produced by Japanese aggression, rather than as armed agents of U.S. imperialism and occupation.

Yet, of course, imperial desire is foundational to Pearl Harbor's existence. Although Hawai'i's geographic location in the center of the Pacific was instrumental to American expansionist plans in the region—by 1814, the first U.S. warship had arrived in Honolulu, making it a regular stop on their Pacific cruises—Pearl Harbor was the central object of that desire. A permanent rotation of warships had begun by 1867, establishing a regular American military presence and beginning the slow naturalization of the U.S. military occupation of the islands.[20] Secretary of War William W. Belknap sanctioned a secret reconnaissance mission for Generals John Schofield and B. S. Alexander under cover of a tropical vacation, beginning a promising partnership between military and touristic desires and practices and the capitalist developments in the region that would soon come to define American "interests."[21] These early military reports-cum-travel narratives salivate over the possibilities that Pearl Harbor offered the navy: the secretary of the navy urged a more permanent arrangement to guarantee the control of the harbor's military potential for providing "perfect security."[22] Shortly after, the first Reciprocity Treaty (1875), which eliminated the tariffs on U.S. importation of Hawaiian goods, primarily sugar, and on Hawai'i's importation of U.S. goods, was negotiated. When the official treaty was renegotiated and signed in 1887, Lili'uokalani noted in her diary, "Today a day of importance in Hawaiian history. King signed a lease of Pearl River to United States for eight years to get R. Treaty. It should not have been done."[23] The treaty was the beginning of the official U.S. military occupation of the islands: A few years later, the USS *Boston* stood by in the waters of Honolulu as the overthrow of Queen Liliʻuokalani was carried out by a consortium of American businessmen led by Sanford B. Dole.[24] Claiming to be "under orders to protect American citizens and their property," the navy supported the "revolution" by securing the new independent republic of Hawaiʻi under American military protection.[25] Today, while this early foundational moment of securing paradise for "American interests" appears in bastardized form in the peripheral breezeway panels, for the most part it is unintelligible in the narratives of the USS *Arizona* Memorial, which insists both on American innocence *and* sacrifice. Regardless of the glimpses of this shadow narrative that might filter through, the museums' emphasis on December 7, 1941, eclipses one kind of historical violence with another. Further, its renewed focus on making this story more multiculturally inclusive legitimizes the sacrifice narrative by inviting more people to identify with its transformative martial romance. In the end, the story of a spectacular national injury that pushed an unwilling and innocent people into war is far more compelling and inspiring than a story of geopolitical intrigue, military intimidation, and overthrow.

RESILIENCE OF INNOCENCE AND SACRIFICE

The museums' exhibits exist in productive tension with the centerpiece of the memorial—the actual visit to the sunken *Arizona*, an experience that has for the most part remained consistent over the years. The rusting hull's silent outline under the waters of Pearl Harbor is understood to be beyond the visitor center's revisionist narratives that sometimes generate debate and conflict. Regardless of what tourists are doing in the visitor center, when their assigned time for the visit to the USS *Arizona* arrives, they line up in front of the theater to partake in this signature experience. Before they are allowed to embark on the navy-operated launches that take visitors to the memorial, tourists are first required to watch a film that exhorts them to remember Pearl Harbor and to meditate on the unimaginable loss suffered on "that day."[26] For the most part, the racial-national tensions of the film are successfully subsumed by the inclusive call to remember the dead that ends the film's narration and interpellates the tourists as part of the abstracted injured American family.[27] At the conclusion of the film, the lights go on in the small theater, and the audience is finally herded on to the waiting navy launch.

FIGURE 4.3 The USS *Arizona* Memorial. PHOTOGRAPH BY EVAN ANDERSON.

By the time the launch approaches the memorial, the summary effect
of the visitor center has already set the emotional register of the experience. The launch docks and the tourists disembark, silently entering the
memorial. The memorial itself is an unassuming white structure (figure
4.3), spanning over but not touching the width of the sunken battleship
Arizona, which lies in the shallow waters of the harbor. Its design showcases the *Arizona's* sunken hulk not only as a symbol but also as evidence
of American innocence and sacrifice: the clean white structure, with its
simple, utilitarian lines, stands guard over the *Arizona's* dead, officiating
a narrative of sacrifice and heroism. Designed to emphasize "an open
and soaring effect" that would allow for a "serene and noncoercive atmosphere for contemplation," the structure reflects the architect's view of
the United States as a pacifistic nation that would nonetheless rise from
its injuries.[28] Yet viewing the memorial from its deck, particularly after
having walked around in the visitor center's museums, gift shop, lawn,
and theater—all of which are located in a massive war complex—is far
from a neutral experience. Conditioned by narratives of heroism and sacrifice, and covert stories of lost innocence, the act of viewing is suffused
with nostalgia and longing, especially as the memorial is essentially sus-

pended over a mass grave.[29] When visitors contemplate the *Arizona*'s 1,177 dead in alphabetical, democratic order in the separate shrine room at one end of the memorial, they are already engaged in the act of remembering this moment of death and national injury. The presentation of the names of the dead in alphabetical order further occludes the racial hierarchies that existed in the military in 1941: everyone is equal in death just as all the tourists have equal access to the Pearl Harbor complex. Having been asked to behave solemnly and with respect, visitors spend their time on the memorial in a quiet and somber fashion; they look over the list of names of the dead carved into the far end of the memorial and contemplate the underwater wreckage. But because it is also a tourist attraction, people take photographs and lean over the railings where the visible parts of the ship project. They study the oil that leaks from the hull and stare at the rusted outline of the ship as it rests in the shallow waters of the harbor. After about ten minutes, they are called back to the launch to return to the visitor center.

The memorial's consistently large draw as a tomb has twofold significance in that it lies outside the touristic imagery associated with Hawai'i and is located squarely within the operational base of the U.S. Pacific Command. The incongruity between grave, island, and base is resolved by the work of the memorial's visitor center. Stitching together the potentially contentious identities of the memorial, the visitor center has adapted over time to the changing values and beliefs of its different stakeholders, but the one thing that has remained consistent is the memorial's focus on sacrifice. Like Corregidor and Bataan, the sunken battleship's path to memorialization was driven by the ideological forces of the Cold War: a memorial would both honor the fallen of Pearl Harbor and the Pacific War theater, and remind Americans not to waste the sacrifice of young innocent white men with lack of preparedness, flagging vigilance, and impotence of political will. This sacrifice messaging was tethered to the campaign for statehood in the 1950s. Presciently, the memorial's boosters—local business and social elites, Japanese American war veterans, and national-level politicians—linked the pedagogical and affective power of the memorial to the economic and political potentials of tourism as an ambassadorial vehicle for U.S. values.[30] Poised on the cusp of statehood and the tourism boom, this strategy married Hawai'i's historical military sites to a vision of a future dominated by both industries.[31] The sacrifice of young American men doing the work of securing the region on behalf of the nation, the civilian and military sacrifices of December 7, 1941, the sacrifice of innocent youth rising to the challenge of war, and the continuing sacrifice of present-day enlisted men and women—these repetitions on a theme frame the deaths of 1941 as the blood price of American freedom.[32] Sacrifice generated big tourist numbers. The memorial, which opened in 1962, became a focal point for Hawai'i's tourist itineraries. The memorial was initially run by the navy, but its management then transferred to the National Park Service in 1980 after it registered phenomenal numbers and called for a greater need for professional visitor management. As an icon of a nation violated, the *Arizona*'s sacrifice-themed memorialization sanitizes a troubled history that existed before the "Remember Pearl Harbor!" rallying war cry became the dominant narrative of Hawai'i for most Americans. Its "clean, pristine white concrete and marble" distances tourists from the messy details of war, "death and disaster," as well as the history of illegal occupation and dispossession of Hawai'i made possible through American military might.[33]

In the end, the *Arizona* Memorial's success as a tourist draw hinges on its ability to link the privilege and freedom of travel with the innocence and sacrifice of the military. Today, nearly two million people a year visit the memorial for a variety of reasons: to pay tribute, to satisfy curiosity, to learn about family or national history, or to cross another must-do off their list. Some make it a point to stop at the memorial during their regular visits to the islands, making repeated trips there over time.[34] The visitors are diverse, from local residents, military personnel, and their families; international tourists from Asia (primarily Japanese and Korean) and Europe (who consist of almost a third of the total number); and tourists from the continental United States. Regardless of their diverse backgrounds and motivations, these visitors are invited to identify with the idea of lost innocence and sacrifice, and to experience this identification in partnership with their freedom to travel and consume the secured tropical landscape of Hawai'i. Looking out from the beautifully and simply landscaped grounds of the visitor center, these tourists can scan the area where the December 7 attacks took place. The span of the horizon invites them to imagine themselves as part of the attack, to superimpose their archive of cinematic and photographic images of the attack on Pearl Harbor on the horizon, and to identify with the trauma and historical drama that unfolded that day. From there, tourists can also see that Pearl Harbor remains an active military base: "visitors standing on the lawn of the visitor center looking across the harbor take in a panorama of modern weaponry and naval power that must signify, for some, the moral of military preparedness long associated with the story of Pearl Harbor."[35] Often, there are large ships like aircraft carriers docked within sight of the memorial. Unlike the picturesque vista from the cross at Mt. Samat in Bataan, the military landscape surveyed from the lawn of the visitor center displays the active work (and sacrifice) of vigilant soldiery as an integral element of tourist scenery. Indeed, in the act of touring Pearl Harbor, tourists see themselves as taking part in the larger mission of vigilance substantiated by the events of December 7: visiting the site reinforces the fact of American occupation and corroborates the continuing ethics of securing paradise. This act, importantly, does not necessarily alienate the 30 percent of visitors who are not Americans. Rather, it invites all tourists to identify with, if not as, subjects of a mythic American global family defined by freedom, good intentions, and democracy.[36] As they circulate through the visitor center, tourists consume an actively managed historical narrative that rests heavily on portraits of innocent whiteness (then), and multicultural paradise (now), as well as the evasion of unsettling narratives of the space they are inhabiting. The durability of the Pearl Harbor narrative continues to do effective work precisely because it is implicitly tied to American freedoms and the tourists' way of life *and* their ability to tour on American land secured by the gripping story of American innocence, heroism, and exceptionalism.

PEARL HARBOR AS A MILITARY THEME PARK

The Pearl Harbor military-tourism complex succeeds because it manages the difficult balancing act of emphasizing serious historical and emotional content with the expectations of tourism in a tropical place. Without the draw of a mass grave, the *Arizona* Memorial's auxiliary sites depend on the pleasures of military machinery and hardware and a satisfying resolution to war. At the USS *Bowfin*, the USS *Missouri*, and the Pacific Aviation Museum, the narrative of sacrifice is completed and extended as something entertaining: tourists consume stories of sacrifice, resilience, technological might, and, ultimately, victory. The modes of tourism in these sites fit more neatly into familiar tourist practices of going to museums and theme parks while evoking an experience of war beyond the *Arizona* Memorial's more passive narratives of innocence and sacrifice. As such, they perform fewer ideological acrobatics. Unlike the USS *Arizona* and USS *Oklahoma*, whose decaying hulk or sheer absence marks tragic moments of sacrifice, the USS *Bowfin* and USS *Missouri* in particular are available for hands-on experiences that allow tourists to "play" at being soldiers. These decommissioned ships invite tourists to enter into the world of a working sailor, circa World War II (and later, in the case of the *Missouri*) and to imagine themselves as part of an ongoing war effort. Tourists who pay to see the *Bowfin* and *Missouri* up close get a chance to interact with authentic military apparatus, further intensifying the interactive experience of the *Arizona* Memorial's visitor center.

Viewable from the grounds of the *Arizona* Memorial's visitor center, the USS *Bowfin* mostly offers a photo opportunity with World War II hardware, supplementing the more sober experience of the *Arizona* Memorial. The *Bowfin*'s small park — formerly separate from the *Arizona* Memorial's grounds — is now connected, and tourists can venture directly into the park's walkway display of Poseidon missiles, Tomahawk torpedoes, and other massive ordnance. This theme of treating military machinery as props for a tourist experience is epitomized by the ways in which the *Bowfin* and *Missouri* have been transformed into large sets for tourist education, imagination, and play. In what has become standard practice at many tourist attractions in Hawai'i and elsewhere, a private company has been subcontracted to take group or solo photographs with the submarine or the ship as backdrop. After their tour, tourists have the choice to purchase this photograph, which is imposed on a World War II–era newsletter, complete with period advertisements. The caption, which is positioned underneath the bold headline "War! Oahu Under Attack," claims that tourists (who are pictured) "Help Out When Needed," tying tourist identities to willing, continued support of a military under duress.

In contrast with the experience of the *Arizona* Memorial, which emphasizes the theme of "sacrifice in death," the *Bowfin*'s tour produces an active identification with "sacrifice in *life*." For the tourists who pay the admission fee and who can then venture past the park into the submarine itself, the tour of the *Bowfin* is a close-quarters experience of life in a submarine. Following the cues on a rented audio tour or going it alone, tourists descend into the interior of the ship, which has been converted into a museum, and track the paths of ghostly sailors. Despite the fact that the USS *Bowfin* Submarine Museum and Park has a public memorial honoring the fifty-two submarines sunk and over thirty-five hundred submariners who lost their lives in World War II, death is not the structuring narrative

FIGURE 4.4 The USS *Bowfin*. PHOTOGRAPH BY THE AUTHOR.

of this attraction. Rather, the visitors who take part in the tour actively imagine the lives of the sailors who lived in the close quarters of war-time submarine vessels. While tourists never forget that they are basically clambering around the insides of a large weapon, the absence of any kind of visceral violence, or scenes of destruction, such as at the *Arizona*, makes the tour more about the day-to-day travails of operating this machinery and the kinds of perils that sailors experienced as it slipped through the cold, dark waters of war. This kind of life on the edge — a life whose hori-zon has been severely curtailed by the necessities of war — is what tourists read in the stifling confines of the USS *Bowfin*. Imagining the young men operating this submarine on war patrol is an act of feeling and embodying their sacrifice in life.

Touring the USS *Bowfin* makes a powerful impression, most of it due to the ability of the tourist to enter, touch, and roam the submarine (figure 4.4). Inside the submarine's metal skin, tourists experience the claustro-phobic embrace of a war machine and identify with the absent sailors who operated it. Stepping on the submarine, laying hands on its hard-ware, climbing up and down ladders, and stooping to get through its small doors, tourists can literally feel the physical closeness of the ship and of each other. Held close in the warren-like spaces of the ship, tourists feel what it might have been like to live for extended periods in perilous ocean depths, isolated from the sun and life on shore. They do not have to work hard to imagine the stuffy smells or the strange muffled noises of being underwater. They are forced to assume the posture of a submariner while they wince at the sight of the tiny, cramped bunks where sailors slept and wonder at the constricted spaces where they cooked, ate, and relieved themselves. Moving slowly around the submarine's exposed pipes, protruding parts, and other hazards, tourists carefully navigate the everyday routes of sailors at work. As the tour progresses, tourists begin to physically take on the poses of these sailors, to maneuver around the obstacles that were second nature to those that lived in this environment.

The messy reality of death is elided, ironically, by focusing on the submarine's weaponry as points of tourist interest rather than equipment meant to cause mass and calculated destruction. For the tourists on the *Bowfin*, its decommissioned and museum status are evidence of its success. Submarines were effective in the maritime war against Japan, taking down over half of Japanese shipping, disrupting its supply lines, and rescuing downed pilots. As an exhibit of a war apparatus that survived intact until the end of the war and helped in the overall war effort—unlike the *Arizona* or the *Oklahoma*, which never left the harbor—the *Bowfin* does not remind tourists of actual deaths of American soldiers, even as it caused the deaths of enemy combatants and stymied their war efforts. Anesthetizing the deaths of real people, the *Bowfin*'s website tallies up its casualties through tonnage rather than lives: thirty-nine Japanese merchant ships and four Japanese military ships (a total of 67,882 tons sunk).[37] Its success and survival elicit perhaps more positive and even playful responses from tourists. The *Bowfin*'s weapons cache is displayed in the torpedo bay as a compelling point of interest. Tourists peer out from the periscope and seat themselves in the control room. After the tour of the dark interior of the hull, they finally climb the ladder to the conning tower and emerge onto the deck. Here they enjoy the warm sun on their faces and also get a chance to "play" on the massive guns, posing for pictures and enjoying the end of their short submarine tour. The physical movement of the *Bowfin*'s tour epitomizes the cumulative narrative arc of the Pearl Harbor sites— descent into peril, stoic resolve in the face of unrelenting danger, and, finally, the emergence into triumph, victory and freedom—all the while excising the blood and gore of war.

The *Missouri* anchors the story of sacrifice (in death and in life) begun at the *Arizona* and continued at the *Bowfin*. The tourists who take in the Pearl Harbor complex's entire experience usually end with a tour of the *Missouri* because it provides the victorious resolution to World War II. Docked in Ford Island, the battleship enjoys the professional tourist management of a former Polynesian Adventure Tours president who has worked to successfully incorporate the "Mighty Mo"—as it is often referred to—into the Pearl Harbor military-tourism experience. The *Missouri* attracts over four hundred thousand tourists a year, making it one of the most visited paid attractions in Hawai'i, allowing it to be self-sustaining, a rare occurrence for a museum.[38] This popularity, despite its not-inconsiderable entrance fee of twenty dollars (with additional fees for different kinds of tours), attests to the success of this venture and to the draw of a battleship as hands-on museum.[39] The USS *Missouri* Memorial Association, which aims to "create and maintain a fitting memorial to the people and historic events reflecting our nation's legacy of duty, honor, strength, resolve and sacrifice," produces a unique touring experience that dovetails with the somber atmosphere at the *Arizona* and *Oklahoma* memorials and that merges seamlessly with the tourist experience and continued dominance of the military in Hawai'i. Most importantly, as the ship that embodies the overwhelming power of American military might and its results, the Mighty Mo offers the last ingredient of the Pearl Harbor military tours: fun. Victory defines the *Missouri* tourist experience. Punctuating the overall Pearl Harbor narrative of sacrifice and resolve, the Mighty Mo represents the end of the war and the triumph of one of the most efficient military-industrial complexes the world has ever seen.

Approaching the *Missouri* from the shuttle's drop-off point, tourists are struck by the sheer immensity of this battleship and are reminded of how the superior strength of the U.S. military was a deciding factor of the war. As both the tour guides and the memorial's website are fond of pointing out, the *Missouri*, standing on end, is 332 feet taller than the Washington monument, 279 feet longer than the *Arizona*, and 5 feet longer than the *Titanic*.[40] Going aboard the Mighty Mo, tourists enter a metal giant of shipbuilding and are able to roam its massive and complex structure. Compared to the *Bowfin*'s cramped spaces, the *Missouri* embodies American-sized technology. Most tourists only get to explore a fraction of the Mighty Mo, but even what is commonly available to those who pay only the basic admission fee can take hours to explore. Tourists can chose to tour the ship at their own pace, join tours escorted by veterans or "patriotic citizens and volunteers," take a behind-the-scenes "explorer tour" of the ship's batteries, or select from an array of different audio tours. For youth groups and special interest groups, the *Missouri* even offers overnight Encampment Tours, which allow participants to experience "life aboard a U.S. Navy vessel" complete with dog tags and bunk lodging.[41] Actively walking around the ship, climbing up and down the steep ladders that enlisted men until recently used, making their way around the ship's mess, the officers' quarters, and even the control room used most recently in the Persian Gulf incursion, tourists can imagine the ship alive with soldiers at work and at war. The *Missouri*'s size communicates the feeling that this is an impregnable fortress, that life on this ship is passed routinely but is also highly disciplined, and that overwhelming military and technological modernity was and is the defining characteristic of the U.S. military.

Due to the size of the ship, no two tours are alike; moreover, tourists (even those on guided tours) can stray from the script and the recommended route. However, the tours all share three important elements: an appreciation of the Mighty Mo's massive size, admiration for its military firepower, and acknowledgment of its historic significance. As the guide leads his or her group of visitors around the different parts of the battleship, part of the narrative that tourists hear is the war pedigree of the *Missouri*, emphasizing the key role that the ship played in the last battles of World War II. Because it took three years to complete, the *Missouri* did not steam into Pearl Harbor and the Pacific War until Christmas Eve, 1944. When it did finally enter the war, the Mighty Mo took on duties that included the firebombing of Tokyo and the battles of Iwo Jima and Okinawa. As the flagship of the Pacific Third Fleet during the last month of the war between the United States and Japan, the *Missouri* ensured its place in history when it was chosen as the site of Japan's surrender to the Allied Forces. Anchoring the U.S.-centric history of World War II as narrated by the Pearl Harbor military complex, the Mighty Mo is material proof of the inspiring resilience and technological superiority of the U.S. military that propelled it to victory in the face of initial tragedy. Its post–World War II cruises represent the continuing military vigilance necessary in the Cold War era. Even as it fought in the Korean War and the Persian Gulf (after its initial decommissioning and extensive modernization), the Mighty Mo's association with World War II history was solidified when it sailed into

FIGURE 4.5 The "Mighty Mo" and her guns. PHOTOGRAPH BY EVAN ANDERSON.

Pearl Harbor as part of the fiftieth commemoration of the Pearl Harbor attack.[42]

   This ship, with its ability to kill and destroy at a distance, embodies war at a remove, away from the sweat, blood, and carnage of vulnerable foot soldiers in combat. As an efficient killing machine, it recalls — oddly enough — not the visceral realities of war and death but a sanitized and abstract vision of violence even more detached that than of the *Bowfin*'s. The Mighty Mo's massive guns, with their contained violence and austere silhouettes, are what the tourists have come to see (figure 4.5). This is sheer military muscle on display: nine defining sixteen-inch guns with gun barrels weighing 116 tons each, which are capable of shooting shells weighing 2,700 pounds a distance of twenty-three miles in fifty seconds with "pinpoint accuracy."[43] The guides relate these statistics with relish. The guns tower over the deck, their shadows looming over the tourists who stroll below. Protected by thick steel armor and targeted by what was the most advanced computer system of its kind at the time of its construction, the USS *Missouri*'s guns embody the invincibility of industry harnessed by the militarized state. These unimaginable numbers and the kind of abstracted violence they have wreaked in past military conflicts confer an aura of invincibility and awe on the Mighty Mo. Its huge guns, with their inconceivable power, represent that vision of America with a big stick, acting as the world's peacekeeper, going where needed to use necessary force. Posing against this evidence of uncontestable firepower, tourists take photographs of their holidays as secured by military technology and removed from the grisly human details of war.

As a tourist attraction, the *Missouri* represents that triumphant resolution to a grim, expansive, and protracted war. When tourists take photographs of themselves against the backdrop of its guns and massive hulk, they record not only the invincibility of the U.S. military-industrial complex, but also the anticipated and celebrated results of American might: assured victory. The historic moment of World War II victory hosted by the ship, much like her guns, defines the Mighty Mo's appeal as a tourist attraction. On this site, the United States and Japan ended a three-and-a-half-year bloody war in a decisive fashion, with a clear victor. The lives lost and disrupted and the lives and livelihoods destroyed during the course of the war are made much more acceptable with an uncontested resolution such as the one the Mighty Mo represents. This is war at its cleanest and most orderly, free of moral ambiguities, and as such it represents an uncomplicated, tourist-friendly narrative.

From the upper deck of the *Missouri*, the guns point inland toward O'ahu in an eerie replication of the *Boston*'s 1893 posture. Tourists who roam the deck have an expansive view of Pearl Harbor—including the *Arizona* Memorial in the distance and the active workings of the base itself—as well as the jagged silhouette of O'ahu further beyond—the implicit territorial target of U.S. military protections. The positioning of the *Missouri* in the shallow waters of Pearl Harbor also reproduces, for tourists, the view of land from the deck of a boat, reenacting a familiar trope of arrival, discovery, and conquest. Their view from their location on the *Missouri* positions tourists as the privileged consumers of Hawai'i's tropical landscapes and multicultural offerings and as the modern agents that help legitimate Hawai'i's status as a playground for both tourists *and* the military.

MILITARY PLAYGROUNDS

On February 9, 2001, the U.S. Navy nabbed international headlines when one of its nuclear submarines, the *Greeneville*, rammed into the Japanese fishing vessel *Ehime Maru* ten miles off the coast of O'ahu, sinking it and killing four high school students, two teachers, and three crew members. While the *Ehime Maru* was on its way back to Japan after its crew had rested and shopped in Hawai‘i, the *Greeneville* was giving a tour of American military hardware in the waters off Diamond Head to sixteen VIP civilians, some of who were sitting at "nonessential" controls at the time of the accident.[44] Prior to the media exposure, it was not common public knowledge that the U.S. Navy played tour guide for civilians in so crude a manner. However, in the two years preceding the accident, the Pacific Fleet had organized nearly four hundred such cruises for almost twenty thousand civilian guests.[45] Indeed, the outcry of outrage and astonishment following the incident belied the fact that tourism and the military on Hawai‘i had long been intimate bedfellows and that in Hawai‘i, the most popular tourist experience was essentially an extension of the Distinguished Visitors Program concept to all comers.

At the Pearl Harbor complex, the narratives of security and democracy far outstrip occasional military accidents, which, tragic as they may be, are after all to be expected as the small price to pay—the collateral damage—for continued global security. While the *Ehime Maru* tragedy was buried finally and most conclusively as an aberration in a larger story of sacrifice, the incident brought into stark if fleeting relief the ideological contortions that naturalize the long-standing relationship between militarism and tourism in Hawai‘i. It served as a reminder that Hawai‘i remains a territory under duress and that the forces of tourism and militarism work together to conceal a lingering history of violence behind the image of a secured paradise.[46] Precisely because militarism inevitably produces collateral damage, and more recently because of the reputation of the United States for unilateral military action, military-tourist sites such as those at Pearl Harbor are valuable pieces of ideological real estate. The distillation of World War II into a stop on a tourist itinerary obscures the actual enabling conditions and relations that make Hawai‘i a tourable space: Pearl Harbor as tourist attraction works to secure continuing military occupation just as surely as Pearl Harbor the military installation does. In the specific case of the Pearl Harbor military-tourism complex, compared with other modern war memorial sites in the United States and worldwide, touring war and death is, on the one hand, about remembering history or people and, on the other, about reenactments of sacrifice as an implied price already paid for entitlements to the Pacific. The losses of the *Ehime Maru* are understood to pale against these larger sacrifices.

While long-standing and ongoing resentment against the military in Hawai'i does exist, the ideological work of the Pearl Harbor military-tourism complex actively and constantly works to defuse the collateral damage of military occupation by thickening the affective ties produced by World War II military sacrificial stories. World War II's bloody martial history is a crucial ingredient in the military's "Plumeria and Steel" relations with the state: the "freedom we enjoy" and the security that "makes Hawai'i a better place to live" rest on the sacrifice, cooperation, and gratitude of this "partnership in aloha."[47] Thus tourism becomes a way to appreciate, along with military prowess and protection, the generosity of U.S. troops who serve in support of the Asia-Pacific region. Within these touristic circuits, the military adopts poses of service and sacrifice, eliciting and obliging one of gratitude from tourist-citizens: blood has already been paid for this experience. In the intimate collusions of the military and tourism industries, it is a short distance from December 7 narratives of soldierly sacrifice and valor to contemporary claims of benevolence, protection, and possession. By highlighting World War II narratives at the expense of other histories, the Pearl Harbor complex generates a commonsense understanding of the heroic and beneficial role of the military. The ideological work performed by Pearl Harbor military-tourism sites shows the contemporary resonance of a World War II narrative and its applicability and resurrection in moments of contemporary crises from 9/11 to saber rattling by the North Koreans—further driving home Hawai'i's crucial symbolic and material role in the upkeep of U.S. military domination in the region.

Lastly, Pearl Harbor's ideological value enables the further territorialization of Hawai'i into military property in the present day. What should not be lost in how the constant and almost seamless merging of tourism and militarism in Hawai'i has rendered the islands into tourist playgrounds is how this partnership operates to produce the islands as a place where American soldiers play at war, with tragic consequences. Not only did the *Ehime Maru* incident illuminate the continuing intimacies between tourism and militarism; it was made possible precisely because the oceans around Hawai'i have long been forced to host cruising ships on war exercises and other military maneuvers. Whereas the Pearl Harbor sites generate identifications and desires in line with the U.S. military's continued occupation of the islands, the stationary exhibits of the *Bowfin* and *Missouri* do not quite capture the remarkable mobility and activity of the U.S. military in Hawaiʻi, and its habits of seeing the islands and its re-sources as absolutely available for military use. The next chapter further elaborates on the use of the islands as targets in the service of American empire, a condition that is partially secured by the work done at Pearl Harbor.

Five

THE MACHINE IN THE GARDEN

Helicopter Airmobilities,
Aerial Fields of Vision, and
Surrogate Tropics

The opening sequence of the much-beloved 1980s television series *Magnum, P.I.* begins with an establishing shot of a Hughes 500D helicopter dramatically diving to just above the surface of a churning blue ocean, accompanied by a driving, upbeat theme song. The next quick cut tracks the helicopter coasting just offshore from Waikīkī's array of hotels with the mountains of Oʻahu silhouetted in the distance. Interspersed with footage of the lead actor Tom Selleck and the rest of the show's cast are more helicopter-centered scenes: a view from above of the aircraft hugging a rocky coastline, a tracking shot of another piece of Hawaiʻi coast from the vantage point of a helicopter, and a close-up of the cockpit with Theodore "T. C." Calvin, the pilot, at the controls, while another character takes surveillance photographs. The presence of the helicopter, both onscreen and off, as much as the array of tropical signs—green foliage, blue skies, exotic flora, bikinied women, a multicultural supporting cast, aloha shirts, and beaches—authenticates both the geographic and temporal setting of the show.

More significantly, the helicopter as filmic prop and as film technology establishes a visual and logical narrative that links Hawaiʻi's tropics to the Vietnam War: it signals the successful transfer of militarized skills, mobilities, visual regimes, and modes of discipline to the islands' tourist economy. T. C.'s ability to translate his experience as a combat helicopter pilot in Vietnam to Island Hoppers, his own tourist sightseeing business, is historically accurate: helicopter tourism in Hawaiʻi, as elsewhere in the United States, was first established during the war and took off in its aftermath. Many of the pilots who flocked to the aerial sightseeing business were veterans who were familiar with the civilian variations of military helicopters that began to flood the commercial market following Vietnam.[1] T. C.'s story reflects the broader logics of the show, which follows the adventures of Thomas Sullivan Magnum IV (Selleck) and his three close friends—all of whom are military veterans—on Oʻahu as they transition their military skills into the private sector in the post–Vietnam War era.[2] Although the Vietnam War is a recurring theme in the show, the show's main characters are portrayed as capable and morally upstanding citizens whose military experiences enhance rather than damage their identities. In particular, the show's convergence of military technologies and visual regimes with those of tourism's was a crucial element of Magnum, P.I.'s therapeutic neoliberal message.

The award-winning series, which had a high viewership and ran for eight seasons, played a significant role in not only rehabilitating the image of Vietnam veterans but also establishing Hawaiʻi as a familiar (if exotic) domestic locale for this rehabilitation. It provided the entrepreneurial opportunities that showcased Magnum and company's myriad skills and resilient characters.[3] Following on the heels of the long-running police drama Hawaii Five-O (1968–80), which was also shot on location in Honolulu and throughout the islands, Magnum, P.I. understood Hawaiʻi as a place to be protected, policed, and consumed.[4] From the views afforded by T. C.'s helicopter, Oʻahu's topography was both an ideal landscape for exploration by sightseeing tourists and a place that needed the visual policing best supplied by ex-military professionals and militarized equipment. The postwar reconversion of helicopter technology and military skills operated in tandem and in tension with several other historical developments in the post-Vietnam era, most importantly the increased tourism marketing of Hawaiʻi and a growing, sometimes contradictory visual archive of helicopters and helicoptering produced by news media, television, and film, to which Magnum, P.I. contributed.

This chapter examines the ideological work performed by emergence of the helicopter tour in Hawaiʻi in the post–Vietnam War era. Following Paul Virilio's genealogy of the interlocked technologies of industrial film and military surveillance, I argue that the helicopter tours that developed in Hawai'i further extend the fused "functions of the weapon and the eye" from battlefield to landscapes of tourism.[5] The helicopter tour as it operates in Hawai'i collapses the distance between military and tourist visual logics and ideologies. While seemingly benign, this civilian application of helicopter technology is inseparable from the helicopter's roots in military warfare because, as Caren Kaplan has argued, the mobility of airpower "is always violently conceived and executed."[6] Promising the ultimate kind of accessibility, helicopters in the age of modern tourism generate mobilities, fields of vision, and structures of feeling that produce landscapes for tourist pleasure but are also profoundly interconnected with past and present military violence. Regardless of the helicopter's myriad present-day uses, its origins and continuing development are tied to the research and development projects of a war economy subsidized by the U.S. military and to its weaponization in U.S. war making. Binding the helicopter tour to the "helicopter war" in Vietnam as well as to U.S. military interventions and projects in Hawai'i and elsewhere, this chapter traces the ease of exchange and translatability or, to use a military term, the *interoperability* of technologies, visual systems, and logics of tourism and militarism upon which helicopter tours rely.[7]

Just as a helicopter tour is never just a helicopter tour, neither are the islands they fix in their sights just islands.[8] Both are products of processes deeply imbricated in colonial and military domination; in this case, they are also formed specifically through the mutually implicated logics of aerial perception, "targetability," and consumption. While the *Magnum, P.I.* opening credits reference O'ahu as the site of the emergent visual regimes of helicopter sightseeing, Kaua'i was and is actually the most popular island to tour by helicopter. Tropical islandness is fungible to a degree, but Kaua'i's identity as the "Garden Isle" was solidified by the marketing strategies of Hawai'i's tourism economy in the 1960s and 1970s, which began to differentiate between different island experiences. While neighbor islands also showed off their tropical landscape through helicopter tours, Kaua'i's smaller, compact landmass and geographic and biological diversity made it eminently tourable by air. Its success as an island best seen by helicopter, however, is just as significantly traceable to the Vietnam War—and not only for the surplus equipment and pilots that the war produced. The emergence of helicopter tourism in Kaua'i works because its particularly lush tropical landscape offers an alternative to the jungle battlefields of Vietnam. Contra Leo Marx's American pastoralism — which looked to the "idyll" interrupted by the intrusion of industrialization as a formative cultural consciousness of the American mind — the machine in this garden affords a movement toward, and not away from, a romanticized natural setting.[9] The most popular one-hour tour around the island presents tourists with the expected tropical fantasy — one that is welcoming and tacitly secured by a successful American project of militarization.

The tour's aerial experience, with the panoramas it offers of Kaua'i's landscape and the technologized pleasures and thrills of the helicopter's swift and responsive maneuvering, presents a substitute to a national visual and affective archive of helicoptering recalled by the nightmare of Vietnam, replacing images and filmic footage of downed helicopters with a more immediate, personal memory of a tropics without the trauma.[10] This particular machine, in this particular garden, mediates the Marxian tensions embodied by Vietnam, where the "recurrent image of the machine's sudden entrance into the landscape" were amplified to nightmarish proportions and ultimately played up not just the tensions between the natural idyll and industrialization but also the contradictions between the myth of American exceptionalism and the brutal clarity of empire.[11] Helicopter tours present a harmonious resolution in place of this national trauma. Instead of a perilous jungle harboring hostile enemies, Kaua'i's "garden" gestures to a hospitable, domestic, feminine Pacific best approached and appreciated through technology. Like *Magnum, P.I.*'s rehabilitation of Vietnam War soldiers, skills, and technologies, the success of the helicopter tour — particularly on the island of Kaua'i — is due to the tour's reimagination of an alternative and pacific ending to the spectacular imperial failure of the United States in Vietnam.

The slippages between war and tourism for helicopter technologies and tropical topographies are the conditions of possibility for Kaua'i's tours; at the same time, these slippages also haunt the tours, reminding the tourist that Kaua'i's islandness is produced jointly by the gendered logics and technologies of visuality and mobility. Indeed, the successful interoperability of helicopter tours in military and tourist systems depends on their common application of masculinized technological prostheses of mobility and surveillance to feminized landscapes (produced either as touristic objects of visual pleasure or as targets needing discipline and punishment). During the Cold War, Hawai'i—Kaua'i in particular—operated as surrogate tropics for Vietnam by way of providing a rehearsal ground for military bombing campaigns. This was nothing new—the United States had used Hawai'i as a training ground to prepare for tropical warfare, most notably prior to and during World War II. The Cold War's conflicts—and in particular, the Vietnam War—escalated and intensified this practice. Like the Philippines, as I discuss in the next chapter, Hawai'i stood in for Vietnam: its rainforests, oceans, airspace, and islands were subject to military exercises and bombings that prepared troops for the Southeast Asian theater of war. In other words, Kaua'i's present-day touristic island-ness was generated in large part through its past militarization as a proxy Vietnam: its feminized landscape—both as fantasy tour destination and target tropics—operates through the same logics of interoperability ascribable to helicopter technology, mobility, and visuality.

Today, Kaua'i's tourability as the "Garden Island" simultaneously depends on and draws away from this historical articulation with Vietnam. In contrast to the overdetermined historical tours of World War II valor explored in the previous chapter, helicopter tours in Kaua'i operate in greater tension with overt military association to produce tourist pleasures, primarily because the war they inevitably reference is one that the United States lost. Vietnam and other wars must be absent, or nearly so, for Kaua'i's helicopter tours to succeed in producing the Garden Island as such, and yet they haunt, rather than just activate, the island's tropicalization. Particularly in Kaua'i, these tours take place in and reference territories that have been profoundly shaped by the violence of U.S. militarism, and they draw on military technologies that have secured, and continue to secure, these territories or territories like them. Further, this Kaua'i generated by helicopter tourability not only operates as a surrogate tropics, where a rewriting of the Vietnam narrative can be repeatedly experienced and confirmed, but also as an imaginative node where the Cold War militarization and continued, present-day occupation of Hawai'i can be sublimated. In other words, the pleasures of helicopter tours are deeply entangled in historical and ongoing processes of dispossession, occupation, and extermination on the islands and in the "elsewheres" of U.S. military interventions. Such experiences, located as they are in lands that have been historically occupied by the U.S. military, overwhelmingly visualized through a racialized and gendered topographical imagination, and connected in intimate and tragic ways to other American tropics, are never innocent.

To articulate tourism to militarism and to trace the interchangeability of tropical places, this chapter's itinerary is necessarily indirect. First, a detour to the Vietnam War establishes the historical roots and routes of the helicopter war and the ambiguous mobilities and visual archives that helicopter technologies produced. Second, a stop in Kaua'i tracks the emergence and development of helicopter tourism and closely examines how tour narratives and experiences craft an averted tourist gaze that rehabilitates the surplus technologies, war memories, and personnel of the Vietnam War and more recent U.S. military interventions. In its production of Kaua'i as a tourable island, the helicopter tour restores U.S. ideologies of security and simultaneously generates alibis for past and present militarization on Kaua'i and at other sites in Hawai'i. Finally, the chapter makes multiple stops at key sites of military occupations that were, and are, at odds with and camouflaged by the image of the so-called Garden Island.

THE HELICOPTER WAR AND ITS VISUAL ARCHIVE

It's been a helicopter war all along. And the strange, ungainly, unlovable craft have reached the peak of being needed and the peak of being vulnerable at the same moment. Everyone who has flown over combat zones in VN in a helicopter knows the heart-stopping feeling you get when you have to go below 2,000 feet. Well the men going in and out of Laos rarely get a chance to fly that high.

— Reasoner, "During the Viet Nam War"

In a 1971 news commentary for the American Broadcasting Corporation, the journalist Harry Reasoner elaborates on the particular terrors of the Vietnam War's helicopter troops and their unique proximity and exposure to the dangers of combat. By the time Reasoner pointed out the perils of a war technology that was supposed to win the war, media coverage had shifted to reflect increasingly negative public opinions about the war.[12] Contrary to conventional wisdom about the antiwar character of the first "living-room" or "television" war, routine press coverage was far from gory or graphic. Early reporting was positive, with a battlefield roundup approximating World War II reportage; a Washington, D.C., policy story; and a film report from the field. The self-immolating monk; the slaughtered villagers of My Lai; the American soldier on patrol, under fire, wounded, or dead; the napalmed girl with her clothes burned off her body—these iconic and brutal images that define Vietnam's visual and affective archive today were the exceptions to the rule of television and photojournalism reportage. Fewer than a quarter of Vietnam field reports depicted images of the dead or wounded.[13] In this context, Reasoner's assessment of the vulnerabilities of helicopters mirrored the public's disillusion about the quagmire of Vietnam and paralleled a growing kind of reporting that occasionally invaded the domestic space of both living room and nation with televisual and photographic images and opinions that emphasized the interminable feel of the war and its rising human costs.

Reasoner's news commentary about the "strange, ungainly, unlovable" helicopter was all the more disquieting for its recasting of American technological superiority as fragile rather than invincible. The Vietnam War was intended to be a showcase of the expanded American military-industrial complex, and early press coverage dutifully documented the massive array of the latest war technologies and American soldiers' specialized skills in handling such weapons. Superpower technology—from aircraft carriers, fighter planes, and even the uniform and armaments of the soldier—became as much a part of Vietnam War reporting as the devastated livelihoods and landscapes of the Southeast Asian peninsula. The recurring appearance of military technology in the visual documentation of the war was made possible by embedding journalists in order to allow them the same kind of mobilities and visualities the military had. Among the most indelible of journalistic images was the helicopter. Before the iconic footage of overloaded American CH-46 helicopters airlifting evacuees from the rooftop of a building in Saigon stood in for the Vietnam quagmire and the ultimate failure of U.S. political and military intervention in the region, helicopters had become omnipresent in news footage and photographs of Vietnam as well as in the skies of Indochina itself.[14] In Associated Press photographs and network television news, the familiar and regular presence of helicopters came to symbolize the new cavalry of modern war making, providing cover fire and reinforcement for ground troops. Particularly against enemies characterized and feminized as Indians, the helicopter represented a technologized, hypermasculine prosthesis for the soldier-as-cowboy in the new frontier West of Vietnam.[15]

Indeed, the Vietnam War was *the* helicopter war: the military's needs defined and accelerated the development of helicopter technology during the war to make the helicopter a formidable game-changer.[16] From the CIA's infamous covert passenger and cargo airline, Air America, to the early years of President John F. Kennedy's administration, helicopters were a key presence in the buildup of weaponry and advisers that preceded the decision to send the first major combat troops in 1965.[17] To aid in navigating and penetrating the inhospitable terrain of South Vietnam, which included mountain ranges and jungles in the northern and central parts and river deltas in the southern region, two helicopter companies were dispatched in 1961, comprising thirty-two helicopters and four hundred men.[18] By 1965, both U.S. war production and personnel training were responding to the increasing demand for new helicopters and pilots.[19] Helicopters had first seen military duty in World War II and were used regularly in the Korean War, where the "new war horses" changed the face of war with their ability to bring weapons, supplies, and reinforcements to the battlefield, but the Vietnam War regularized the use of helicopters in combat.[20] The "Huey" was, in essence, the child of the Vietnam War: these ubiquitous Bell UH-1A helicopters were the product of an army design competition in 1964 that had in mind the mobilities needed for war maneuvers—reconnaissance, troop carrying and extraction, search-and-destroy missions, and medical evacuations. By the time the Gulf of Tonkin Resolution in 1964 gave President Lyndon B. Johnson the power to carry out an undeclared (and already ongoing) war against North Vietnam, American military helicopters were a regular presence in the war effort. Mobile air warfare, the defining advantage and characteristic of American military engagement in Vietnam, was hailed as the key to a decisive U.S. victory.[21] As the commander of the U.S. forces in Vietnam, General William Westmoreland said, "Our tactics in Vietnam were based on massive use of helicopters. . . . We might as well have asked: 'What would General Patton have done without his tanks?'"[22]

Coming of age under the media spotlight cast on the Vietnam War, the helicopter became part of the experience of the war, not only for the soldiers, guerrillas, civilians, and reporters who came into direct contact with it, but also for Americans at home. Associated Press photographs of helicopter gunships and television news footage of choppers in action reinforced the iconicity of the helicopter as a symbol of the Western augmentation of the soldiering body through technology that was optimized for war in the Southeast Asian landscape. Images of helicopter companies accompanying and assisting ground troops framed them as technologized workhorses that would take on the burdens of troop and equipment transport, provide aerial platforms for command and strategy, spread defoliant, and deliver cover fire. The contrast with Vietnamese guerrillas could not be more stark. As the war wore on, and as the tone and perspectives of press coverage shifted, the representation of helicopters also became more ambiguously charged and more akin to Reasoner's tone. Part of this shift was due to the penetration of enemy territory that helicopters enabled, which in turn was increasingly and more closely documented by embedded journalists, who covered the war on the front lines and often hitched rides on helicopters. The helicopter's flight, with its elevated perspective above the tree line and its swift access to enemy territory, constituted a mobilized way of seeing that transported the viewer unsettlingly close to the war. Unlike fixed-wing aircraft — such as the fighter planes that bombed Northern Vietnam's landscape in Operation Rolling Thunder — helicopters were slower but more nimble, able to move in all directions, hover, and land and take off in tight spaces. At the same time, their ability to penetrate enemy territory also meant greater use and exposure to hostile troops.

Even as the fields of vision made possible by helicopter flight produced the bird's-eye view of weaponized mobility and put Vietnam and its people in its crosshairs, the images that came out of helicopter flight also produced a feeling of immersion for the viewers at home that was not always in line with the ideological needs of warfare. For one, it put journalists at the front lines, enabling them to capture images that were not always in the interest of the U.S. state. In the case of Henri Huet, a star photographer from the Associated Press's Saigon Bureau, helicopter mobilities helped expose "Vietnam's agonies — soldiers in sodden misery, peasants terrorized" and the unrelenting menace and despair of the war.[23] One of his 1966 photographs — taken from the ground and depicting the shadowed outline of an American soldier killed in action in the jungle as he is lifted up into an evacuation helicopter — illuminates the ambiguity of war with its exposure of the intimate moments of death. The soldier's body dangles midair just below the hovering helicopter. The sky is a stark white against the corpse and the machine, and thin stalks of bamboo crisscross the background, slightly blurred by the force of the helicopter's rotors. In this moment, the helicopter is not a weapon or a means of escape, but a hearse.

The tactical disadvantages of flying low-level missions (to mitigate the disadvantages of being louder than ground combat troops and guerrillas) resulted in five thousand crashes (both accidentally or due to enemy fire), killing 2,197 pilots and 2,718 crew.[24] This susceptibility to crashing was documented by journalists, further reinforcing the "ungainly" image of downed helicopters and negating the assumption of invincible, superior American military technology with visual proof of its fatal vulnerability. A well-placed explosive could down a helicopter, especially at low altitudes. Faced with this new technology, North Vietnamese troops had exchanged anticolonial insurgent strategies with Algerian forces who were fighting against their French colonizers and, by 1961, had started radio broadcasting instructions on taking down helicopters. Journalists in the field recorded the resulting crashes, documenting in stark terms the vanquishing of the U.S. military Goliath with the inferior firepower of the North Vietnamese Army.[25] In a 1966 photograph, the Pulitzer Prize–winning photojournalist Horst Faas, who also worked for the Associated Press, suspends the moment just before a Marine CH-46 Sea Knight helicopter crashed after being hit by enemy fire, capturing the last, unimaginable seconds before the deaths of thirteen men aboard. In Faas's photograph, the helicopter is a silhouette of smoking metal spiraling inevitably to the ground while soldiers on the ground look on, paralleling and standing in proxy for the helpless viewers at home.

As the war continued, the ways in which embedded journalism increasingly captured the intimate vulnerabilities of superpower technology were also amplified. The most shocking occasions were journalist deaths on the battleground, which, in turn, became news. The 1971 helicopter crash fatalities of four leading war correspondents covering a U.S.-led attack into Laos blurred the boundaries between civilian and soldier, further reducing the distance between reporters in Vietnam and Americans at home.[26] Rather than the distance of the "growing derealization of military engagement" described by Virilio to be the product of militarized optics, the weaponization of helicopters generated visual proximities that rendered not only Vietnam and Vietnamese people as targets, but American soldiers and civilians as well.[27]

Because Vietnam's helicopter war is linked to the signal and singular defeat of the modern U.S. military, helicopter visualities and mobilities are inseparable from the ignobility and trauma of the war, ambiguities that have carried over to the post-Vietnam era. Most tellingly, the last twenty hours of the U.S. presence in Saigon is documentable in helicopter imagery and lore. Photographs of civilians climbing a ladder to a rooftop to enter a waiting Huey, accounts of evacuating helicopters retreating under barrages of fire, reports of helicopter crashes on U.S. carrier decks in the South China Sea, and images of helicopters having to be pushed overboard ship decks to make room for massive numbers of evacuees capture the desperate last hours of the United States in Vietnam and the failure of a long, costly, and unpopular war.[28] In the nearly four decades since the end of the Vietnam War, this lingering feeling of vulnerability, exposure, and defeat informs the visual archive of the helicopter.

Adding to the press coverage produced during the latter years of the war, post-Vietnam film and television entrenched helicopters as visual shorthands for the physical and psychological textures of the war, linking helicopters to war trauma long after the war ended.[29] Television was slow to add to this archive. During the war, only the dark sitcom M*A*S*H— set in the Korean War but inevitably an allegory of Vietnam—tackled the subject material of the war. Airing weekly for eleven seasons, the popular series depicted life in a mobile surgical unit. From the first frame of the opening credits, viewers are prompted to confuse the temporal and spatial frame of the show and locate it instead in the synchronous conflict in Southeast Asia. As the haunting instrumental theme starts, the camera moves from the back of a nurse's head to the mountains where she is looking and zooms in on two helicopters in the distance. The title appears superimposed on a sustained eye-level shot of the two helicopters in flight, and a circling aerial view of the medical unit buildings (clearly shot from a helicopter) combine to establish the frontline location of the show. The last scenes of the opening sequence are frantic: quick cuts that feature rescue helicopters in action bringing in the wounded. Throughout the forty-five-second sequence, the unrelenting sound of helicopter rotors generates a feeling of urgency. In M*A*S*H, the helicopter was a key presence as a filmic prop, on the one hand, and as a technology that re-created the ambiguous mobilities and visualities of the war, on the other.[30] The sound and sight of the rotor blades, the profiles of the aircraft, the dizzying feeling of "airmobility" recorded by onboard cameras, the uncanny shifts in perspective — these specific sensory encounters communicated the particular traumas of the Korean–as–Vietnam War to audiences.

In contrast to television's more politic use of helicopters to recall the ambiguities and vulnerabilities of war, Hollywood films were more forceful in linking helicopters to death and destruction. Although Hollywood also had a hesitant start with Vietnam War films, once it got going, cinematic productions that focused on Vietnam proliferated and veered into darker territory. Helicopters took a starring role in the films as props that authenticated the combat scene and—to replicate airmobilities for audiences—served as mounts for cameras. In 1978, *The Deer Hunter* was the first commercially successful film in a decade to take on the raw realities of war, breaking from John Wayne's ideologically anti-Communist *The Green Berets* (1968) to take a critical and controversial stance on the Vietnam War. Its portrayal of working-class men ruined and disillusioned—driven to suicide even as they survived the nightmare of Vietnam—established an approach that did not shy away from gritty realities. The helicopter scenes are unequivocally brutal: the film makes clear that the helicopter is not a vehicle for rescue or victory, but for immersion in the tropical hell jungle of Southeast Asia. The film's Vietnam War section begins, for instance, with a scene in which U.S. helicopters are napalming a Vietnamese village. Another unit of helicopters drops off soldiers in the middle of a combat zone, where they are taken captive and tortured. When they escape, a helicopter accidentally comes across them but can only take one of the three protagonists aboard, symbolizing in the starkest terms the inadequacies of supposedly superior technology and the inability of the United States to fully rescue its troops from the nightmare of war. In *The Deer Hunter*, as in films that followed—such as Francis Ford Coppola's *Apocalypse Now* (1979), Oliver Stone's Vietnam War trilogy, and Stanley Kubrick's *Full Metal Jacket* (1987)—helicopters came to represent the psychological and physical damage of war.[31] These films feature helicopters cruising through the tropical jungle, hovering over innocuous-looking but treacherous terrain, and taking their human cargo deep into the heart of peril. Shots from the interior of the helicopter bring along the viewer to experience the precarious mobility of the soldier—the near-out-of-control handling of helicopters under fire—and allow for the alignment of perspectives along the sightline of guns onboard as they target the enemy with bullets, missiles, and incendiaries. The contrast between the deadly machinery and the rolling green landscape below is a stock visual convention: this should be paradise, but it is not. In this hell, helicopters are far from invincible and are often themselves targets. These films drive home the truism that *"war is cinema and cinema is war."*[32]

Even with the Vietnam War long over and only a memory for younger generations, the ways that helicopter fields of vision inhabit popular culture through globalized news coverage, television, and film continue to recycle these postwar images to reference a conflict that the U.S. military behemoth did not win. Loss is only one part of the trauma: as John Carlos Rowe points out, "What is finally unrepresentable is the immorality of our conduct in Vietnam."[33] Vietnam's spectacular failure converges with the helicopter's. The Vietnam War as the "helicopter war" haunts the helicopter's diverse applications today, especially in modern combat. Most recently, in Iraq and Afghanistan, the helicopter experience has proved that the technological advantages it offers are offset by its vulnerabilities: the war reportage includes notable helicopter disasters.[34] More recent films extend and exploit this feeling: the helicopter's mobilities and visualities are integral to representing the feeling of war. Such feelings are not always triumphant; more often than not, both films and news footage note the unsettled terrain of modern war. Ridley Scott's *Black Hawk Down* (2001) replicates the vulnerability and violence of helicopter technology in its portrayal of a downed helicopter crew's fate in Somalia. Shot down by rocket-propelled grenades, the film's helicopters crash in the city, which is transformed into a war zone that the surviving crew must navigate on the ground. Supporting snipers who are dropped in by helicopter are killed when Somali forces overrun the site. For contemporary film and news media, helicopters operate as death traps or vehicles that insert people into disaster. Even the successful assassination of Osama bin Laden in Afghanistan was accompanied by a side story of a crash of one of the mission's radar-evading helicopters, which had almost derailed the whole operation.[35] Long after the United States abandoned its helicopter war in the tropics, the haunting images of the helicopter at work and in trouble extend to new territories and new projects of empire.

HOW TO PACIFY AN ISLAND: SEEING KAUA'I FROM A HELICOPTER

Kaua'i's airspace is crowded with helicopters. Their silhouettes are a familiar sight, circling the island in a well-worn flight path, accompanied by the whirring hum of rotor blades. "Flightseeing," as helicopter brochures state, is the "only way" to truly encounter the hidden gems of the Garden Island. These tours have become commonplace because of the island's largely untouched, verdant interior and because the geological spectacles of the Na Pali coast and the Waimea Canyon—its signature features—are inaccessible to wheeled vehicular traffic or even the most intrepid of hikers, despite the prominent appearance of these features in tourist publications. If any island was made for helicopter viewing, it is Kauaʻi. With its incredible topographical diversity packed into a small geographical area, a typical fifty- to sixty-minute tour efficiently takes in the highlights.[36] From the air, one can discover the ostensibly authentic, natural Kauaʻi. Guaranteeing an "ultimate eco-tourism adventure," "outstanding sweeping views," and a "thrilling experience," helicopter tours allow tourists to "safely explore Kauai's remote wilderness areas and coastlines" and reach the "70% of Kauai [that] is inaccessible."[37] For the Americans, Europeans, and Australians who make up the majority of the tours' clientele, the ubiquitous, roughly hour-long helicopter ride is one of the most popular ways to take in the island's breathtaking topography and is a signature attraction of Kauaʻi tourism.[38] Today, visitors to Kauaʻi are most likely to take a helicopter or plane tour than on any of the other islands.[39] Prior to Hurricane ʻIniki in 1992, which wreaked its destruction primarily on Kauaʻi, the island boasted the highest number of helicopters (thirty) amongst its neighbors, with another fifty or so spread out between Oʻahu, Maui, and Hawaiʻi.[40] In the 1980s, its helicopter tours accounted for 50 percent of the traffic at Lihue's airport, triggering a "gold rush" for independent operators, along with traffic, noise, and safety complaints.[41] Today, the dozen or so helicopter tour companies on the island contend with rising operating costs and the saturation of the market, but a recently completed multimillion-dollar helipad makes clear that the business of helicopter touring remains important in island planning.[42] From its modest beginnings in the late 1960s, with Jack Harter's one-helicopter operation, to the more than one hundred thousand flight hours per year now logged by helicopter tours, seeing Kauaʻi "on a higher level" remains the signature way to experience the island.[43]

In contrast to the Vietnam War's visual archive of a vulnerable empire, the images and experiences produced by Kauaʻi's helicopter tours draw on familiar habits of framing Hawaiʻi through the lens of hospitality. Viewed from the helicopter, Kauaʻi is not enemy territory but a landscape of pleasure and discovery. Kauaʻi tourism, which exploded at the tail end of the Vietnam War, telescoped a long, primarily European and American settler tradition of selectively generating and combining ideologies of civilization, multiculturalism, and environmentalism into the production of Kauaʻi as the "Garden Island" destination.[44] Fixing Kauaʻi in their sights, helicopter tours operate in much the same way, condensing the tourist industry's narratives about Kaua'i to generate and reinforce the idea of Kaua'i as a tourable, viewable, and discoverable island commodity. Producing Kaua'i's islandness relies on the gendered equivalence of tropical land to feminized space, something to be tamed and made productive through masculine ways of seeing and knowing, desire and action.[45] Paradise is a woman, as demonstrated by travel narratives of Hawai'i.[46] "Above all," as Haunani-Kay Trask has wryly put it, "Hawai'i is a 'she'" in all her "magical allure."[47] The tourism industry produces this feminized "magical allure" by playing up the island's dramatic and inaccessible topography, suggesting that only the most intrepid can fully explore and appreciate its raw natural and seductive powers. Resorting to tropes of masculine adventure and conquest, the visitor's bureau produces Kaua'i as a mysterious and spectacular fantasy landscape that is untamed yet provocatively inviting discovery.

Kaua'i's tourable islandness becomes discernible through the temporal and spatial narratives deployed by its tourism industry. Located twenty minutes by air from O'ahu, the island of Kaua'i is the northernmost of the Hawaiian islands, as well as its oldest at six million years. While Native Hawaiian genealogies of the island are sometimes invoked in discourses of tourism, for the most part a focus on the indigenous or even a commodified Polynesian culture is not the dominant theme in the marketing of Kaua'i. In stark contrast to the contemporary material reality of tourist developments that dot Kaua'i's coastlines, the sixty-seven thousand residents who make their home on the island and work in the tourist industry, the highways (and traffic) that circle its perimeter, and the military base on its western shore, Kaua'i is insistently described as natural, uninhabited, and ancient. According to the county of Kaua'i website, "The tropical paradise of Kauai basks amidst the sparkling blue waters of the Pacific ocean. . . . Formed some six million years ago, the island . . . is the oldest . . . of the main Hawaiian islands" and is characterized by "the quiet majesty of the island's lush tropical setting and extraordinary natural heritage."[48] While — like Maui, O'ahu, Moloka'i, Lāna'i, and the Big Island of Hawai'i — Kaua'i has its share of tropical beaches, its tourist niche is based on its "geographic diversity," "colorful flora," and geologic prehistory.[49] Rising out of the Pacific Ocean in an impressive display of impenetrable green vegetation and implacable black rock, Kaua'i lives up to its Edenic marketing, gesturing to a long natural history ready for modern tourists to discover and navigate. Here, on this ancient landscape, tourists can ostensibly encounter "a primal piece of paradise"—a spatial and temporal otherness truly apart from the tropical island experience as typified by the Waikīkī package tour or by other neighbor islands.[50]

Casting Kaua'i in geologic time and space operates on several levels. First, it reinforces the tourism industry's coordinated production of Kaua'i as a unique island destination outside of the usual menu of package tourism. Contrary to the projected image of its untouched terrain, Kaua'i is also modern and developed. In contradistinction, the concerted mediations of the tourist industry produce an image of Kaua'i as a spatial and temporal frontier, as exemplified by Kaua'i's Department of Tourism: "In the island's more than 5-million-year lifespan no one has ever seriously questioned the supremacy of the natural forces that dictate the patterns of life here. And just as nature is left to its own devices, so, within reason, are the diverse cultures that populate the island."[51] Second, framing the island in geological time and space emphasizes prehistory over the present. In the Department of Tourism's narrative, Kaua'i—as geologically ancient terrain—is the host: in the face of the vastness of geological time, humankind is only an insignificant part of history. This discursive maneuver proposes an updated *terra nullius* framework, rendering all claims to the land equal. Under geological time, the "diverse cultures" who have managed to "populate" the island and the indigenous peoples who have left "relics of ancient Hawaiian civilization" are as much visitors to the land as tourists.[52]

Third, and relatedly, this emphasis on geological time operates to pacify alternative and contentious claims to Hawai'i and annuls political framings of Hawai'i as a long-occupied and militarized territory. The tourism industry relegates Native Hawaiians to being scenery—at best, a former civilization whose cultural legacy can still be appreciated through the pleasures of tourism. While over 18 percent of local residents are Native Hawaiian and work in the tourism industry—as tour guides; hotel, restaurant, and retail service workers; and entertainers—for the most part, tourist engagements with Native Hawaiians end there.[53] Parlaying its indigenous population and its settler histories into heritage tourism, a former mayor of Kaua'i describes the island's allure as "steeped in the traditions and cultural heritage of the ancient Hawaiians."[54] Intimately linked with the denial of contemporaneity to Native Hawaiians, the emphasis on geologic history also effaces living or more recent history, which helps drive home the point that Kaua'i is a tourable, and not a troubled, island.[55] According to Will Squyres, the owner of an established Kaua'i helicopter tour company, "In Kalalau, several hundred Hawaiians lived much like their ancestors—worshipping their gods, catching the brightly colored fish from the ocean, eating the fruits and vegetables that grew wild, and raising taro in terraced fields in the floor of the valley. . . . When I spot the remains of the taro terraces from the air and see the taro that now grows wild along the streams, I realize that there really was a Garden of Eden after all."[56] This relegation of Native Hawaiians to the past is critical to the success of helicopter tours: the emphasis on geologic time and space writes over Vietnam time and its Cold War remilitarization of the islands.

Working within the tourism industry's framing of Kaua'i's islandness, the helicopter tours deftly navigate the tensions between modern technology and the promise of the ancient. There is little irony in showcasing the helicopter as the means by which proximity to Kaua'i's essential topographic self can be achieved: as the Jack Harter Helicopter tours claim, they are "so advanced they will take you back in time."[57] In Kaua'i, the helicopter as time machine affords a fantasy of "leav[ing] civilization behind," despite the fact that modern technology enables tourists to hover over the tropical canopy and weave in and out of geological history.[58] While sitting comfortably in a helicopter customized for sightseeing, tourists consume a double thrill: the helicopter ride and an opportunity for time travel. Modern technology is the key to this experience of geologic time; it returns the modern subject to the pastoral, augmenting rather than fragmenting this ideal.[59]

Helicopters also help produce geologic time through their increased use in the island's film industry, which coincided with their arrival in the early 1960s as vehicles for aerial touring. By this time, Hawai'i was already an exotic but recognizable site that Americans primarily encountered through World War II films and *South Pacific* cinematic tropicalizations.[60] These Cold War–era films, which coincided with the advent of mass tourism in the islands, celebrated Hawai'i's positioning as a U.S. territory and state, a new consumer destination and a space secured by a newly vigilant military, remaking a Hawai'i that had been an international battlefield into a Cold War showcase for multicultural society, capitalist freedoms, and militarized governance.[61] As mentioned earlier, television shows of the 1960s–80s—such as *Hawaii Five-O*, *Fantasy Island*, and *Magnum, P.I.*—familiarized viewers with America's tropics, teaching them how to frame the islands as an exotic, but secured, part of the United States.

The use of helicopters in filming generated an archive of aerial perspectives and panoramas that profoundly shaped the tourist gaze. When Jack Harter—one of the pioneers of the helicopter tour industry in Kaua'i—arrived in 1962, he saw the *South Pacific*–like setting of Kaua'i as being ideal for aerial tourism.[62] By the early 1980s, Kaua'i's helicopter tour was a specific draw for tourists, with six companies competing for business on the island.[63] With the tourism boom in Hawai'i after the Vietnam War came a more careful and delineated marketing of the islands. The Big Island of Hawai'i became known for its volcano, Maui for its tropical beaches, and Kaua'i for its dramatic geology and lush vegetation. Working with the strategic differentiation of the islands to optimize tourist consumption, the emergent helicopter tourism industry took advantage of an updated television archive that portrayed Kaua'i as otherworldly and a place out of time. In contrast to the large body of Vietnam War films that also emerged during this time, some of them shot in the Philippines, Kaua'i's filmography framed the island as a site for adventures and thrills that were located far from the when and where of war. Blockbuster adventure films have been shot on location on the island. Two Steven Spielberg films—*Raiders of the Lost Ark* (1981), which filmed its main character escaping from decidedly unfriendly natives along one of Kaua'i's rivers, and Kaua'i's most cited film credit to date, which is *Jurassic Park* (1993)—have introduced the lures of "ancient" Kaua'i to contemporary global audiences. Tourism and film had a symbiotic relationship, drawing from each other to generate a common visual grammar of Kaua'i's pristine islandness. The sweeping filmic panoramas and location shots that feature Kaua'i's unique geological formations and tropical vegetation (and shot from many of the helicopters that offer the tours) are interchangeable with the images that Kaua'i tourism uses to market the island. For instance, both Spielberg films concur with the tourism industry's production of Kaua'i as out of place and time by using the island to suggest the untouched jungle where savage tribesmen remain undiscovered (*Raiders*) or a prehistoric park where dinosaurs roam (*Jurassic Park*). In further reinscribing Kaua'i as that otherworldly and "othertimely" place, films about the island operate as a preview and a reference for the actual tour, confirming tour narratives that imagine Kaua'i in the past tense.

Kaua'i's helicopter-aided film archive—in tandem with the actual flight experience and tour narration—produces the feeling of "leaving civilization behind." Helicopter airmobilities conjure a different sense of time through the motion of flight, the new types of sensory knowledge it generates, and the types of filmic knowledge it references. Tim Blackmore, writing about the postmodern battle-space produced by the detachment of helicopter technology from the earth, suggests that the effect of a "dizzying flow of time" is the primary result of the machine's speed and maneuverability.[64] Under the conditions of tourism in Kaua'i, however, time stops and reverses. This return to a geologic past is an effect of the visual narrative and corporeal experience created by the mobility provided by the tour. Bookended by the commercial transaction of paying for the flights, getting to the helipad, and listening to safety, embarkation, and debarkation instructions, the tour's aerial itinerary traces a departure from (and an eventual return to) civilization. While the preparation and the wait for the helicopter are activities that are very entrenched in the economic transactions of tourist time, once the passengers are strapped into the aircraft and welcomed aboard, time begins to slow. Music is piped into the noise-canceling headphones, which mitigates the rotor's volume: the tour's musical soundtrack replaces the adrenaline and anxiety-inducing whirr of the rotor blades with recognizable and familiar tunes that are often easily associated with movies or television shows, providing powerful resonance with the production of a cinematic mode of experience.[65] The helicopter imperceptibly lifts into the air, dips its nose slightly as it skims over the ground, and gradually climbs higher as it moves forward. The feeling of takeoff is different from the sheer power and speed of an airplane. It is more subtle, akin to floating with purpose and direction. This moment of detachment from the earth generates the alternative temporality and spatiality of the tour. The ground recedes, the helipad growing smaller in the distance. The airport and the roads around it fade back, and passengers switch their perspectives outward toward the horizon to alleviate vertigo and to realign their visual habits to the helicopter's mobility. Yet the feeling and the view are not altogether unfamiliar; passengers have "seen" these aerial perspectives in film and television before.

The narration by the pilot has an arc that parallels the spatiotemporal itinerary of leaving civilization behind and entering the unchanging interior and inaccessible islandness of Kaua'i.[66] As the helicopter distances itself from the helipad, the pilot-as-guide points out the golf courses, bay, marina, and cruise ships. The altitude of the helicopter begins to level off, and as it advances toward the Hoary Head Mountain Range, the pilot mentions that the river feeds into the fishponds that Hawai'i's legendary original inhabitants, the Menehune, supposedly cultivated "over 2,000 years ago, before the Polynesians" and which operated as the set for a scene in *Raiders of the Lost Ark*. There are some other signs of civilization below, such as a ranch and a former sugar plantation town converted for tourists, but the helicopter is decidedly moving away from developed parts of the island. The sun glitters momentarily through the viewing windows. The helicopter hovers alongside Manawaiopuna Falls, otherwise known as the "*Jurassic* Falls," circling around so passengers on both sides can have a turn at seeing the water cascading down the rock face. In a bit of metacommentary, the pilot describes the waterfall as the place where the *Jurassic Park* helicopter drops off the film's main characters to start the action of the movie. For those tourists who have seen or heard of the film, it is not difficult to superimpose a filmic memory over the aerial panorama now in front of them. The act of renaming Manawaiopuna and reframing it within a cinematic lens helps make the exotic familiar: it updates a cartographic technique of colonialism.

Once past the "*Jurassic* Falls," the helicopter tour ventures deeper into the interior. The helicopter descends a little, putting passengers on the same level as the rock faces of the mountains, the narrow streams of water cascading down, and the shadowed crevasses that texture the landscape. The pilot reiterates the age of the island, mentioning that Kaua'i's age — in comparison to that of the other islands — is what makes possible its erosion-carved topography. The helicopter floats over the massive rock formations that make up the mountain range and swoops toward the center of the island toward Mount Wai'ale'ale, where wisps of clouds veil the top. A bit further on, Waimea Canyon, with its surprisingly semiarid landscape, comes into view. As the helicopter drifts by the ridges that tower above the canyon, tourists are prompted to note how the rock striations are evidence of the island's age. "Each layer," the pilot intones, "was made by a separate volcanic eruption" over the course of millions of years, then sculpted by 300,000 years of erosion. The helicopter coasts over the Kalalau ridges, dramatically rounding the side of a tall cliff to showcase the Na Pali coast. The pilot states half-jokingly, "If you are afraid of heights, don't look down."

Remote, unpopulated, difficult to access, and undeveloped, the Na Pali coast is one of the most photographed parts of Kauaʻi, with its jagged ridges rising as high as four thousand feet above sea level and plunging dramatically to the sea. The hanging valleys between the razorlike ridges end abruptly at cliff's edge, with small hidden beaches and waterfalls adding to its image of a rugged, isolated, and inaccessible place. This site—above all others—is the centerpiece of the tour and emphasizes the access and mobility that the helicopter makes possible. Here, the corporeal sense of drifting over space and the new panoramas that are made accessible by the helicopter augment the feeling of being outside of time. With the Pacific Ocean stretching out to the horizon on the left, and the spectacular cliff faces on the right, the helicopter feels insignificantly small. The helicopter's ability to hover allows its passengers to see a site from multiple perspectives: from a distance, and slightly above; on approach; and hovering alongside. This mobile and visual mastery adds to the exhilaration produced by the scenery and the filmic sensation of the tour. These vantage points are not something that passengers could replicate without technology, and they recall the aerial footage of establishing shots in films like *Jurassic Park*. The passengers' experience of the helicopter's airmobilities and maneuverability parallels the feeling of motion captured by footage filmed on helicopters. For the helicopter tourist, the Na Pali coast is a majestic wilderness (see figure 5.1) but is ultimately successfully navigable by and open to man. As the helicopter departs from the Na Pali coast, it slowly heads back toward "civilization," passing over the town of Hāʻena and the tourist center of Princeville before pausing at Wailua Falls, which was featured in the TV show *Fantasy Island*.[67] Approaching Lihue, the pilot's narration begins to describe the scenery below, which includes a river tour and lūʻau and, more prosaically, road traffic and the Hilton Beach resort. As the helicopter lands, it has fully entered back into the present.

By further fusing the visual regimes of tourism and film, tourists are encouraged to imagine themselves as partners in the production of this at once exotic and yet familiar experience of the tropics. For example, tourists can insert themselves into their own tour film: for an additional fee, most helicopter touring companies are happy to film the actual ride. Other companies sell preproduced film of the tour complete with soundtrack and narration for tourists to take home as souvenirs. Judging from the admittedly selective litany of praise in tour company websites and brochures, the helicopter tour is a highlight of Kauaʻi's tourist itinerary:

FIGURE 5.1
A view of the Na Pali coast from a helicopter. PHOTOGRAPH BY THE AUTHOR.

the professionalism and personalities of the pilot guides, the breathtaking scenery, the thrill of the helicopter ride, and the ability to access the inaccessible are common themes. Replacing the wounded tropics of Vietnam with a different filmic archive, the helicopter tour creates a new adventure distanced from military disaster. The thrill of the ride is both generated and tempered by an association with the danger and uncertainty of technological failure, but this cinematic adventure is decidedly not a Vietnam film or reportage of more recent Middle East helicopter encounters. These helicopter mobilities are adventures that might flirt with an unfamiliar mode of transport. They are certainly not part of a "war we could not have considered without helicopters," in which soldiers as proxies for Americans were "being shot at more often and more accurately."[68] Instead, the perspective of the tour allows the mobile tourist subject to be "above it all" and, in the space of an hour, to imagine an island unpopulated by its contemporary inhabitants and liberated from the ongoing conflicts borne of past dispossession.

Although the helicopter's association with the Vietnam War has most relevance to older generations that more immediately experienced it, younger generations of tourists also continue to contend with the Vietnam War's cultural legacy and with the way this historical failure trickles into contemporary wars wrought by the United States. However, the present-day incarnation of the helicopter tour is quite distanced from its pioneering days, when associations with the helicopter war were more immediate. Early helicopter tours—with their veteran pilots still translating their military flying skills into tourism and the Vietnam War's wounds fresh in popular memory—had to work alongside and against active associations of the helicopter with war trauma and Kaua'i's Vietnam-like vegetation. In the 1980s, when the market was most saturated, tour companies would try to outdo each other, sometimes by offering a more thrilling ride: these military-trained pilots who "fl[ew] as civilian pilots, [did] things that are only acceptable in combat training. It's more spectacular and thrilling to fly close to the ground at a high rate of speed, but it's also very dangerous."[69] While selling thrills for tourists on holiday was effective marketing, it created crowded conditions and flying styles that *Sunset Magazine* and the *Los Angeles Times* likened as belonging in a "war zone." The rash of helicopter crashes that resulted from lack of regulation was a little too closely associated with the helicopter war, and Kaua'i helicopter tours came under attack.

The flying styles of veteran pilots had to be adjusted for the tour industry, which was also becoming more family oriented. Today, the work of time and the successful domestication of the helicopter tour through Federal Aviation Administration (FAA) regulations have made helicopter tours in the tropics into family-friendly adventures. The tour manages any potential unsettling associations with the Vietnam War and contemporary military helicoptering by countering images of military vulnerability with narratives of military experience and discipline. While pilot ranks are still filled with veterans from the military because it remains one of the few affordable ways to earn the flight time needed for licenses, many of them hail from conflicts after Vietnam. Referencing the masculine technological expertise of military training, tourist brochures and individual company advertisements do not hesitate to inform and reassure their passengers that many of the pilots are veterans with "flying experience over similar terrain."[70] As one company boasts, "Only the very best pilots fly for Blue Hawaiian. All are high-time experts, and most are military trained, decorated veterans."[71] Safari Helicopters uses the military biography of its owner, a former pilot in the U.S. Navy who also flew civilian missions for Air America, to assure potential clients about the flight experience and integrity of the company.[72] Instead of the cowboy/cavalry mythology of the combat helicopter pilot, we have certified, awarded, and safe veterans, and, implicitly, a secured tropics.

The increased regulation of helicopters as the tours themselves have become more popular over the years contributes to this feeling of domesticated technology. Restrictions on minimum altitude that came as a result of the dramatic increase in helicopter tour companies on the island mitigated the open-market frontier competition that crowded Kaua'i's skies in the 1980s and early 1990s. In contrast to the feeling and practice of "freedom of flight" that characterized early helicoptering on the islands, when tourists could fulfill their *South Pacific* fantasies through spontaneous landings at secluded beaches and waterfalls, tours today are much more regulated and generic, optimized both for safety and consumer satisfaction.[73] In 1994, FAA safety regulations, resentment against the invasion of tourists, and residential noise complaints together changed the quality of the helicopter tour from a more individualized, rugged experience during which pilots customized the tour to tailor to the more adventurous. Prior to 1994, helicopters could fly much closer to the tree line and hover in close proximity to waterfalls, as well as land and take off in inaccessible and remote areas. Although various companies have chafed at these altitude restrictions, the overall experience of a higher flight mimics the familiar filmic "God's-eye" view, and moves further away from the tree-skimming proximity of combat helicoptering. Today's tours are much more regulated with an eye to marketing and preserving "the vision of a peaceful tropical paradise" that had been endangered by the rising numbers of helicopter tour companies.[74] There are the occasional companies that will fly with the doors off, but for the most part, helicopter tour companies have yielded to safety concerns and marketing to vacationing families. The more recent spate of helicopter crashes in Kaua'i during the mid-2000s have added to startling statistics of 107 accidents and 98 deaths between 1988 and 1995 on Kaua'i.[75] Coupled with intermittent accident reportage of military helicopters—some of them with crew based and trained in Hawai'i—stationed in the Middle East, these stories and images of helicopter crashes link the dangers of tourism to military disaster and represent potentially harmful associations for its market. As one online commentary puts it: "Kauai must be the most dangerous for helicopter tours on Earth, aside from Baghdad. Alas, it's also one of the best places on Earth for a helicopter ride."[76] As a result, helicopter tour companies have taken pains to promote their safety records as a way to insulate themselves from associations with traumatic helicopter memories. While occasionally marred by crashes and fatalities, helicopter tours on Kaua'i work hard to produce a fantasy of the tropics as safe, discoverable, claimable, welcoming, and pacific. Their emphasis on militarized "safety" through experience, rather than on cowboy masculinity, is an assurance of the systematic and modern management transferred from military training.

As I have argued in previous chapters, remembering that these tours are underpinned by the technologies and practices of colonialism and militarism means understanding that desires to "get closer to nature" and away from civilization are made possible by a sedimented history of violence and are in themselves symptoms of other kinds of desires. The helicopter was part of a colonial mass fantasy and was made possible and desirable by a burgeoning war economy. Harnessing and domesticating surplus military technology and personnel, the helicopter tour in Kaua'i generates a new sense of islandness through tourism's fields of vision, transforming Kaua'i into a welcoming paradise ready for the pleasures of viewing, knowing, and claiming. As Safari Helicopters claim, these are "*your* waterfalls, *your* rainbows, *your* canyons, *your* Pali, and *your* tropical rainforests."[77]

SURROGATE TROPICS: PROXY WARS IN PARADISE

Locating Kaua'i at the liminal edge of empire, one of its more popular tourist publications claims that "though Kauai is in the United States, it's still not in America."[78] The geologic uniqueness of the island, its tropical vegetation and climate—so prized by its tourism industry—are the markers of its commodifiable exoticism and evidence that Kaua'i is not in "America" (as defined by a continental cultural idea). Yet its tourable islandness, which places it outside the geography and culture of "America," is also what places it firmly within the orbit of the United States. The ability of tourists to claim its waterfalls, rainbows, canyons, cliffs, and rainforests illuminates the way that Kaua'i's islandness not only mitigates the commercialization of tourism but also camouflages the dispossessions and violence of militarism in Hawaiʻi. Kauaʻi's location "in the United States," is, after all, contingent on the military occupation and illegal takeover of the Hawaiian Kingdom. This liminal location is what enables Kauaʻi to stand in as a surrogate tropics and rehabilitate the traumatic narrative of Vietnam, but it is also, crucially, what makes it and other islands in Hawaiʻi ideal for military use.

Domesticating the new fields of vision made possible by the helicopter, tourism and its aerial regimes obscure the fact that tourable islands are also targetable islands. Caren Kaplan and Raegan Kelly expose the military foundations of aerial visuality, tracing emergent modes of perception in Europe to nationalist and imperial histories. As they suggest, the seeming transparency of the view from above generates social relations and cultural politics of sight that render certain people and places targetable.[79] Hovering over the landscape, Kauaʻi helicopter tours enable a field of vision that deflects the gaze away from the violence of militarism in Kauaʻi, offering instead a pacified and consumable islandness secured by the military. This process of securing paradise, as the last section showed, is never portrayed as an ongoing, contested, and violent project: it is a fait accompli that is both desired and beneficial. However, securing paradise historically also involved the use of Kauaʻi and other islands as surrogate combat zones for U.S. military conflicts in the Asia/Pacific region.

By the time the helicopter had been made practical as a mass-produced piece of military machinery, Hawaiʻi had long been a U.S. territory. World War II and the experience of Cold War proxy battles had already underscored the importance of the islands as a training ground for the Pacific garrison of the United States. Its location "in the United States" but "not in America" made it ideal for military occupation and use. Just as Kauaʻi became a surrogate tropics that rehabilitated Cold War–era anxieties through the regimes of tourism, the islands of the state of Hawaiʻi likewise became surrogate tropics for actual battle training. The logics and technologies that rendered Kauaʻi's tropics tourable were also instrumental in making other islands into nontourable targets. The interchangeability of islands—and their ostensible hospitality to these new operations—drew from the same gendered and racialized colonial ideologies about the tropics that understood them to be always waiting to be acted upon and made productive and useful. In Hawaiʻi, Oʻahu's Mākua Valley and the island of Kahoʻolawe are exemplars of how the U.S. military generates islandness for military purposes. There is no smoking gun that ties civilian helicopter tours to the ways that these places have become military targets. However, the colonial logic of the fungibility of islands, the material preparations of U.S. military warfare and occupation, and the interoperability of militarism and tourism point to how the helicopter's violent imperial airmobilities frame islands through the sight of a gun.

On Oʻahu, Mākua Valley, an area near Kaʻena Point in Waiʻenae, the "amphitheater-like mountains surrounding the valleys," home to "rare and endangered plants," was taken over for military training exercises during World War II. Here, public land was transformed into an area where "gun emplacements, fortifications and coast defenses" were installed for the "protection of the Territory of Hawaiʻi."[80] By the end of the war, the U.S. Army had used 6,600 acres of land in Mākua Valley for "intensive training," returning only part of what it had confiscated under martial law. In 1964, in the midst of the Vietnam War, President Lyndon B. Johnson resolved the back-and-forth disagreements between the state and the U.S. military over Mākua Valley's land tenure through an executive order that reserved over three thousand acres in Mākua Valley for military-training purposes.[81] Since its takeover, Mākua Valley has become a utilitarian military training ground that can stand in for future targets of the U.S. military.

Just as the first helicopter tours were getting off the ground in Kauaʻi, Mākua Valley was hosting an entirely different kind of visitor. Mākua Valley's aerial targetability—the way that its tropical territory operated as a surrogate for Vietnam—made it prime real estate for the U.S. military, which was embroiled in a long war in Southeast Asia. Situated far from the tourist center of Waikīkī, Mākua Valley was essentially an island unto itself. This land was profoundly important for Vietnam's helicopter war, as documented in a cultural history report requisitioned by the army: it hosted training including "troop maneuvers, the firing of rockets from helicopters in training actions, and the disposal of old ammunition" in order to simulate "actual war-time activities."[82] Gunnery training in the valley was rehearsal for Vietnam: "they fire rockets and machine guns from the helicopter while in flight at 5,000 feet above the ground, and over fire at 50 feet."[83] Testing out the maneuverability of the machine on terrains similar to what they would encounter, the U.S. military conducted dry runs on already-occupied territory to project and imagine its occupation of new ones. The new fields of vision produced by the helicopter war were thus also rehearsed on the surrogate tropics of Mākua Valley, bringing the space of Hawai'i into focus through this visual regime. This imaginative and violent process of target making has been reinforced over the years as Mākua Valley has continually hosted trainings for new combatants. Today, Mākua Valley, with its ideal "complex terrain," holds live-fire training exercises for the Stryker Brigade including, once again, the use of helicopters in war maneuvers and the training of new pilots.[84] These ongoing war games are not just about testing the state of readiness of the U.S. military; they are rehearsals that produce violent imaginings on occupied territory, to be projected outward through military intervention. Regardless of the new kinds of terrain of current U.S. wars, the continuing targetability of Mākua Valley tutors troops in how to see and pacify other "islands," collapsing, as Virilio suggests, the *function of the weapon* with *the function of the eye*.[85]

The ultimate example of island targetability, however, is undeniably Kaho'olawe. In line with the use of atolls and islands in Asia and the Pacific region during World War II and its long aftermath, Kaho'olawe functioned as America's very own practice target range. Once known as "Bomb Island," in contrast to Kaua'i's "Garden Island" moniker, Kaho'olawe is today still recovering from long decades of military devastation. Like Mākua Valley, the island was taken over by the U.S. military through martial law at the outset of World War II, ending existing ranching activities. The Korean War made its mark on Kaho'olawe, as targets and mock airfields were built on the island to simulate the battleground for air-dropped bombs and strafing runs.[86] Later, as a substitute tropics for Vietnam, Kaho'olawe's conversion from island to target made it an ideal host of live ammunition training and ordnance tests.[87] With the transfer of the island from the navy to the air force, the island was increasingly viewed and targeted by air. The only "major U.S. live-bombing target in this part of the Pacific," use of Kaho'olawe grew in the early 1960s "because of the increased activity in Southeast Asia."[88] By 1967, it was a "testing and training range for the air war over Vietnam," hosting simulations of nuclear blasts and home to "the only Naval gunfire qualification range between the West Coast and Vietnam."[89]

While on occasion U.S. soldiers enjoyed the island's beaches—"There's a good beach at Smuggler's Cove, and there are some fine spots for swimming and skin diving, which the sailors enjoyed on their off hours"— for the most part, the military insisted that Kaho'olawe was both a "very rugged and barren piece of land" that was also a place for pilots to "get the full effect of what a real bomb feels like when it is dropped."[90] The military, in other words, was making an otherwise unproductive island useful (while making what had been a productive island barren).[91] Complaints of disturbance from neighboring islands against the bombing exercises were not enough to halt operations.[92] The navy made clear that Kahoʻolawe was key to national security as a place the military could "evaluate their personnel, planes and weapons . . . immediately before shoving off for Vietnam . . . like a final practice before the big game."[93] The least Maui could do, in other words, was to appreciate the sacrifice of the troops and note that their peaceful, tranquil, and beautiful islandness was secured by the military.

After the Vietnam War, Kahoʻolawe continued to be used for bombing exercises, but like Mākua Valley it became a lightning rod for antimilitary and sovereignty activists.[94] The shift in imagination took touristic terms at first: "Kahoolawe may some day become a recreation area, but for now this island is 45 square miles of military scrap metal, goats, desolation and death."[95] Proposals were floated for a county park, or a "'South Sea' island park with low-rise hotels" in the midst of lawsuits to halt bombing and clean up the island.[96] It took until 1990 for antibombing activists to succeed and President George W. Bush to issue an order to stop use of the island as a weapons range. Today, the state of Hawaiʻi has appointed the Kahoʻolawe Island Reserve Commission to manage the restoration of the land, which is now in trust for a "future Native Hawaiian sovereign entity."[97] For these reasons, Kahoʻolawe's islandness remains outside the dominant tourist narrative that frames Hawaiʻi. Just as the decades-long devastation of this neighbor island is unimaginable during something like a Kauaʻi helicopter tour, so too is the end result of the activism that resulted in the return of Kahoʻolawe to Native Hawaiians. The profound symbolism and reality of a reclaimed territory, the central presence of a politicized and contemporary Native Hawaiian people, and the kind of revolutionary imagination that the *return* of territory puts in play are at odds with the narratives of tourism and militarism in Hawaiʻi, as exemplified by Kauaʻi's helicopter tour narratives. Kahoʻolawe is no longer at the crosshairs of an approaching bomber, rendered into a target. Neither is it an island for tourist consumption. Instead, its islandness conjures a different kind of imagination rooted in the care of the land. Kahoʻolawe is today being rehabilitated and restored for the "perpetuation of Native Hawaiian customs, beliefs and practices"—acknowledging both the historic stewards of the land, as well as their contemporary agency.[98]

TARGET KAUAʻI

Along with its tourability as a natural Eden, Kauaʻi itself is also a key point of U.S. militarization. Compared to Oʻahu, where over one-fifth of the land is militarized, Kauaʻi can lay claim to its "Garden Island" title partially because of the comparably light footprint left by the military. To begin with, Kauaʻi was not as important in terms of military strategy until the development of airplanes and was spared military occupation until the 1920s, when airfields were first established. In 1939, the Works Progress Administration started to construct a more permanent army airfield at Barking Sands. As early as World War II, Kauaʻi's terrain was eyed for the way it replicated potential theaters of war in the region; the war effort converted parts of Kauaʻi into jungle warfare training facilities for thousands of Army troops to be deployed in the Pacific.[99] The Cold War and the expansion of the military-industrial complex left its mark on the islands. On Barking Sands, the modest militarization of the air force was transferred and transformed into a navy state-of-the-art weapons testing and training range system now known as the Pacific Missile Range Facility (PMRF). Located on the western shore of the island, the PMRF—with its supporting sites at Makaha Ridge and Kokeʻe State Park—tracks the vast ocean range of the Pacific Ocean, standing sentinel over the territory underwater, on the surface, and in the sky.

Today's helicopter tours do not engage with the island's past and present militarism. Despite the impressive technological array at Barking Sands, the path of the helicopter tour does not take tourists into military territory—military airspace is sacrosanct—and the narration on the tour rarely mentions Barking Sands. While the PMRF is the most palpable example of U.S. occupation, taking up, as it does, a big slice of the western shore of the island, its relative absence or significance in the everyday realities of the tourist demonstrates the profound success of both the tourist industry's marketing of the island as a tropical garden and the U.S. military's preference (in this case) to maintain a low-profile image. For the most part, Kauaʻi's interoperability as a proxy paradise not only overrides the militarization of neighbor island territories, but also strategically downplays its own historic and contemporary status as an outpost of the U.S. military. This tactical elision of militarism helps regulate the de-

CHAPTER FIVE

sires that the helicopter tours generate: rehabilitating a national memory of military defeat into successful pacification and ineluctable, silent-but-stalwart military service and protection.

However, the terrain and tropical foliage viewed from the helicopter are not as virgin and impenetrable as they would seem. The temporal and spatial narratives woven by the helicopter tours emerged hand in hand with the U.S. military's eyeing the island for war. In other words, Kaua'i itself has historically stepped in for Vietnam, even as its helicopter tours rehabilitate and even evade that particular memory. During the Vietnam War, over twenty-one million liters worth of the dioxin-based herbicide Agent Orange were sprayed in Vietnam, successfully defoliating natural guerrilla cover, as well as contaminating its soil and causing birth defects, cancer, and other types of illness long after the war.[100] This aerial attack on Vietnam was coordinated through planes and helicopters alike. In the mid-1960s, Kaua'i was one of the sites in the United States that hosted testing for herbicides.[101] The lush vegetation that today constitutes the garden of the Garden Island was the target for research experiments on the usefulness of different combinations of chemical defoliant, among them Agent Orange, conducted by the University of Hawai'i and the U.S. Army.[102]

The 1960s aerial application of the herbicides in Kaua'i was meant to both test the effectiveness of the chemicals and rehearse its planned method of application in wartime. Kaua'i's "dense, nearly impenetrable" vegetation and its challenging terrain offered an alibi for the systemic and large-scale spraying of swathes of land: the potential military application was obscured in language emphasizing how cleared jungle would "contribute significantly to strengthening the economy of the State" through its conversion for "recreational use," grazing, and agriculture.[103] It also justified the aerial application of the chemicals. In the 1968 report "Defoliation of Tropical Jungle Vegetation in Hawaii," a one-year experiment discharged a variety of "rapid defoliants" by air over "dense tropical and sub-tropical areas" to aid in the "conversion of impenetrable jungle to productive grasslands," citing the difficulty of accessing the test-site terrain by foot or vehicular traffic.[104] The use of light aircraft to disseminate the herbicides was as crucial a part of the experiment design as were the chemicals used. As the conclusion of the report states, "Information gained from this investigation may aid in the development of an economically sound jungle clearance program throughout the tropics."[105] The ability of airplanes (and, in actual practice in Vietnam, helicopters) to accurately dump chemicals over specific parts of jungled terrain was also at stake: the Agent Orange experiments were practicing the effectiveness of aerial application as much as the "kill" degree and duration of the defoliants. The role of the civilian airline contracted by the University of Hawai'i's Department of Agronomy was being paralleled by U.S. pilots and aircraft in Vietnam. By this time, Operation Ranch Hand—as the aerial chemical defoliation of South Vietnam's jungles and mangrove forests was called—had already been in operation for a few years.[106] The U.S. military-sponsored experiments in Kaua'i were testing out new chemical combinations to further optimize defoliation.

The mobilities and visual regimes produced by helicopter tours today replicate these Vietnam-era forms of logic and practices. Tourism, in particular the sightseeing pleasures derived from the island as tourable and scenic, converts "impenetrable" and "dense" jungle into a desirable commodity. In tandem with these convergent logics of productivity, the production of Kaua'i as a tourable island depends on the same operation of the visual practiced by the Agent Orange experiments. Just as the tourist pleasures of truly knowing the island derive from the bird's-eye view of the helicopter, so too did military knowledge fix the island in its sights as a target. The 1968 report that was essentially a feasibility study for the destruction of Vietnam's jungles illuminates the aerial perspective's importance to the operability of the modern military. The report includes photographs of the experiments and its results, among them, the preliminary bird's-eye view of the test sites. The aerial photographs of the Wailua Game Refuge and Hanahanapuni sites look like standard images taken from a touring aircraft, depicting the contoured landscape, lush vegetation, and even occasional wispy clouds. On each photograph, three areas are marked out by white quadrilateral shapes, indicating the target areas for the airplane's cargo. Rendering the landscape into a series of target areas, this collaboration between university and military fixed Kaua'i through a lens that understood it to be an expendable surrogate for Vietnam. Eyeing Kaua'i as a target, planes were guided by personnel from the Kaua'i Agriculture Research Station, sprayed their toxic chemicals on their targets, and left.[107] In stark contrast to the ecotourism claims of most helicopter companies, this historical detail illustrates that nature on Kaua'i has long been under attack by destructive military technologies. Today that initial aerial perspective has been widened and turned outward: the PMRF at Barking Sands expands the surveillance and targeting of Kaua'i to the region at large.

This chapter has explored how the pleasures of touring draw on military technologies while, at the same time, attempt to dispel the traumas and vulnerabilities of imperial overreach. The visual regimes produced by tourism and by militarized modes of knowledge production and weapons testing demonstrate the interoperability of these systems, and the ways in which they render tropics as surrogate sites of domination, occupation, *and* pleasure. Even as the memory of Vietnam fades with passing generations, its indelible imprint continues to inform the practice of military warfare elsewhere in the world, making Kaua'i's targetable islandness continually relevant as long as U.S. military occupations and interventions need both reinforcement and forgetting. The next chapter also examines another Vietnam-era legacy of war "technology." Whereas, in Hawai'i the United States used the helicopter's mobilities and visualities for military and later touristic ends, in the Philippines, the United States drew on indigenous practices to shore up its ground combat troops' survivability and success in Vietnam. This variable use of different "technologies"—from traditional to cutting edge—highlights the flexibility of U.S. military tactics, as well as their convertibility to tourism regimes in times of relative peace.

Six

PLAYING SOLDIER AND GOING NATIVE IN SUBIC FREEPORT'S JUNGLE TOUR

The Cold War era, and in particular the Vietnam War, generated new militarized subjects and militarized indigenous knowledge in the Philippines. As a prominent U.S. ally in the Asia-Pacific region, the newly independent Philippine nation positioned itself as a long-term partner in the fight against Communism and renewed its commitment to host massive military bases, most of which had been installed in the northern region of Luzon during the U.S. colonial administration. This partnership was mutually beneficial: the decades following World War II were particularly troubled ones for the Philippine state, which struggled to suppress a robust peasant movement fomented by anemic land reform efforts. The U.S. military and political interests in stifling dangerously class-based dissent formed the core of the Cold War martial fraternity between the United States and the Philippines, which showcased the Philippines as a democratic and capitalist state in the region. Modernizing its military bases in the Philippines as well as the Philippine military's equipment and training, the U.S. military reinforced the new Philippine garrison state's goal to suppress political dissent through force of arms. However, what the ensuing protracted struggle made clear was that technological modernization did not guarantee victory. As the previous chapter illustrated, the trouble with Vietnam was that it refused to conform to the logic of technological dominance, thus assailing the hegemony of the U.S. military-industrial complex. Yet the Vietnam War and other instantiations of U.S. military domination also demonstrated the U.S. military's flexibility regarding the use, exploitation, and weaponization of indigenous knowledge and technologies for the purpose of war. During this period, the U.S. military rediscovered and remilitarized indigenous people in the Philippines in order to study their jungle survival skills and produce soldiers better able to withstand the guerrilla war in Vietnam. Recruiting men from the indigenous Aeta group to share their expertise, the military administration at the Subic Bay Naval Base established a "jungle school" within its reservation in order to efficiently transfer this training to its troops. In other words, the U.S. military "went native" in order to become better soldiers.

This chapter examines the Jungle Environment and Survival Training (JEST) tourist destination in the Subic Freeport after American occupation. In the early 1990s, after the withdrawal of U.S. troops from the Philippines, the former Subic Bay Naval Base facilities were converted into a commercial and tourism center for foreign investors, international tourists, and cosmopolitan Filipinos. The public-private partnership that currently manages the properties of the former military base were savvy in marketing the JEST camp as an ecotourism attraction, in line with emerging tourism trends. Today, the rainforest that had once been a staging ground for soldier training now hosts jungle skills demonstrations, hikes, and overnight camping trips for ecotourists. The same men who served as jungle survival trainers for the American military—teaching American soldiers how to build traps, fires, and weapons, and find food, water, and shelter in hostile jungle territory in preparation for their Vietnam deployments—now work as guides for the JEST camp and host domestic and international tourists who frequent Subic Freeport's myriad attractions. The camp—a clearing in the jungled hills of Subic Freeport—has been expanded and renovated but retains the basic layout of demonstration spaces and surrounding audience seating from its military days. A rudimentary barracks now houses the Aeta guides. With its location and history, its contemporary incarnation as a tourist hub and its personnel, the camp captures the convergent desires of being an ecotourist and playing soldier within the militarized landscape of the Philippines.

This almost seamless transition of militarized skills into the tourism trade demonstrates how cultures of military occupation and war continue to thrive even in the supposed absence of the U.S. military. It also emphasizes the ways in which indigenous peoples and practices are recruited into the circuits of militarism and tourism, a development that has profound stakes in the growing militarization and policing of indigenous people and places globally.[1] Indeed, the fact that they are now tour guides illuminates how Filipino peoples have been successfully incorporated as participants in this New World Order that is not so different from the old. Tourist experiences such as those offered at the JEST camp are meant to produce subjects who learn a curriculum and consume an experience that draw on sanitized histories of U.S. military pacification and occupation, masculine fantasies of Hollywood war narratives, romanticized ideas of warrior indigeneity, and innate knowledge of the natural world. Also integral to the experience are neoliberal values that understand militarism as necessary to the whole enterprise. While these lessons are not perfectly transmitted or received, they are nonetheless derived from Vietnam-era U.S. military desires and crafted with contemporary investments in neoliberal governance and continuing U.S. military and political partnerships at their core.

As tourist commodities, the experiences offered at the JEST camp situate the freedom to travel and consume squarely within the confines of a former military base, paralleling the ideological projects of Pearl Harbor. The JEST experience illustrates the ideological maneuvers that connect the pleasures of tourism and playing soldier to a neoliberal economic order supported by a Philippine garrison state and the increasingly flexible but no less efficient practices of U.S. militarism in Asia and the Pacific. At the same time, even as the U.S. military has since given over control of its bases to the Philippine state, the JEST camp provides tangible evidence of the legacies of U.S.-Philippine state collaborations, and the Philippine state's continuing partnerships with U.S. military desires and activities in the region. The stakes are illustrated by the fact that long after the U.S. military left the base, the jungle school that it established still offers survival training to the Philippine National Police and U.S. soldiers alongside its menu of tourist packages. In this particular example of the natural resources and landscapes of the global South stepping in as the new frontier territory of sustainable tourism, what stands out are militarism's profoundly entrenched yet responsive cultural and material regimes, and tourism's agility and adaptability to these regimes.

PEDAGOGIES OF ECOTOURISM: NEOLIBERAL AND MILITARY FANTASIES

"So you want to be a weekend Rambo?"

—Roberto Reyes, "Rainforest Trek in Subic," *Mabuhay Magazine* (1993): 31

This invitation to be a "weekend Rambo" appeared in a Philippine Airlines in-flight magazine feature article about the new attractions available in the emerging tourist hub at the former Subic Bay Naval Base. Inviting tourists to fulfill Hollywood-inspired jungle survival fantasies, the travel narrative focuses on the offerings at the newly opened JEST camp. The author describes a trek into one of the last virgin tropical rainforests in the Philippines, using language and imagery designed to appeal to a developing consciousness about the value of the natural environment and its allied consumer practices. His outline of the stripped-down, basic survival techniques that are taught by indigenous guides is followed by an account of overnight camping in virgin tropical rainforest—an experience of truly "roughing it" without food, shelter, or water. For him, the JEST camp is the perfect setting for the Rambo-inclined thrill seeker: its pristine jungle remains protected by the new Subic administration, and its staff—indigenous men from nearby Aeta settlements—are old hands at showing their skills to strangers.[2]

While invoking Rambo seems antithetical to ecotourism values—the U.S. military is consistently cast as a destroyer of ecology—his primal masculinity lends itself to a militarized fantasy of dominating and being at home in raw nature. Even if the invitation to become a "weekend Rambo" was nothing more than a rhetorical flourish or a marketing device, it is no accident that ecotourism desires readily filter through the action-hero avatar of Sylvester Stallone's military maverick. The Rambo conjured up by this ecotourist narrative does not draw from the David Morrell antiwar novel of a Vietnam veteran gone rogue, but from the filmic, muscular Stallone: a man reduced to his most basic and primitive survival skills who can out-native the natives of Vietnam and other global South regimes.[3] Rambo's rogue element—his story is entrenched in and critical of militarism and modernity—flavors ecotourism's parallel desires to escape the concrete jungle and reject the alienating trappings of civilization, but the travel narrative does not make use of this critical potential. Rather than generating ideological contradictions, being a weekend Rambo resolves the tensions between the perceived values of ecotourism and militarism. Rambo—camouflaged by mud and dirt, using what he can find for weaponry and survival, and distilled to his shirtless, muscled body—is the ultimate image of masculine survival. He is the archetype of the modern ecotourist.[4]

However, lest the references to Rambo go too far, the author makes clear that playing native at JEST is a modern activity, not a rejection of civilization or modernity or even militarism (as in the first Rambo film). It is a temporary break from routine to rejuvenate modern masculinity.[5] Indulging in a tour package of traditional indigenous hunting and cooking, medicinal and survival techniques, and tramping around an unspoiled forest setting, the ecotourist also self-consciously participates in an activity associated with cosmopolitan travel, sustainable ecopolitics, and multicultural values. Moreover, that such an activity takes place within the massive territorial expanse of a former military reservation a few hours north of Manila—with its full array of tourist amenities such as hotels, restaurants, and shopping—means that playing Rambo, while allowing tourists to get in touch with primal and primitive masculinities, is not a disavowal of modern life but rather an endorsement of the types of modern habits and ways of life brought about by neoliberal governance, which itself is made possible by military-secured stability and infrastructures.

The emergence of JEST as a new tourist destination in the Philippines also signaled the timely convergence between the ascendance of ecotourism as the latest travel trend and the acceleration of neoliberal economic processes brought about by the conversion of the U.S. military bases. One national Philippine newspaper headline describing how "former US Marine instructors [were] now instructing tourists" called attention to the new regime's successful overhaul of the former military economy for properly capitalist purposes.[6] The "instruction" of the Aeta tour guides was also a lesson for Filipino consumers—that Subic Freeport was open for their business. The anxiety over the U.S. military's exit and fate of the base economies that had come to depend on them was thus allayed: the tutelage of the state demonstrated that even marginalized indigenous people could assume capitalist habits; that Filipinos once again had access to their territory; and, more importantly, that the state—with the close partnership of the private sector—was an authoritative and competent manager of the resources left behind by the U.S. military. Under the guise of ecotourism, the Subic Freeport could serve overlapping desires and constituencies: the spectacularized modes of tourism, global consumer culture, the rise of sustainability discourse and politics, and environmentalism and "nature" writ large.

The theme of resource stewardship links both military logics and neoliberal values. Part of the effectiveness of U.S. colonial and military administration in the Philippines lay in the assumption that its modern and efficient methods and institutions were superior to anything the natives could produce. Projects administered by the U.S. government, such as the military reservations, were understood to be under the best kind of stewardship for the land. When the military prevented logging at Subic, thereby protecting the rainforest, that too was seen as the judicious preservation of disappearing resources. Under the private administration of the newly public and national resources at Subic, this adoption of the familiar narrative of stewardship is essential to the perceived success of Filipino modern management. The continuing preservation of the protected natural resources—in particular the forest and the Aeta peoples— for new tourism regimes demonstrates not only that Philippine neoliberal management can successfully govern this space, but that it also shares the same values of sustainability and preservation as the previous military administration. Indeed, what makes the JEST tourist experience so effective is its unique, strategic, and opportune packaging of these values alongside the commodification of indigenous traditions and American martial histories for the emerging ecotourism market.

Ecotourism—in the absence of the neoliberal state—is cast as the manager and protector of the natural environment and, by extension, indigenous people. However, tourism at Subic hardly fulfills the ideals of ecotourism: while it strategically deploys green rhetoric, it does not conform to the moralistic standards of tourism sustainability (which is not itself unusual in the ecotourism market). The use of ecotourism idioms illustrates the industry's ability to co-opt new trends. In the 1990s, the modern tourist looked to the backward Third World as the site of his "'new style' holiday," his gaze encouraged by the restructuring policies imposed on "developing countries" by the World Bank and the International Monetary Fund (IMF).[7] Rehabilitating its crisis-ridden, violent image, the Third World's embrace of ecotourism was a way to appease both First World environmentalism, the demands of transnational capital, and ever-changing tourism trends. As the "passport to development," the phenomenal growth of tourism has contributed to the conversion of the Third World from undesirable real estate to the new green space of the tourism sublime.[8] In its new role as the nature reserve of biological (including human) and geological diversity, the Third World has become the modern wilderness for the First World. Its proper management and use, then, become concerns for the global citizen, blurring national and local boundaries and sovereignties through the rule of a universalized idea of the environment.[9] This progressive, efficient management under the new regimes of sustainability and environmentalism is a racialized and gendered mode of control that casts the Third World as a resource in need of regulation, and the tourist—armed with his (or her) environmental ethics—as its protector-consumer, updating earlier phases of colonization that were similarly enacted through resource management and the deprivation of rights.[10] In this case, the articulation of ecotourism and so-called sustainable development ideologies represents a "complex alliance of transnational firms, national financial strategies, and local elites which perpetuate discourses of the subaltern and natural other who is in need of science, technology, productivity, narratives of participation and restoration," echoing U.S. military narratives of occupation and colonial ideologies of civilizing.[11] At JEST, ecotourism as such operates through the contradictory construction of the wilderness as a modern concept—the consumption of Rambo-esque indigenous fantasies in a preserved jungle guarantees the tourist's modernity and ethical superiority.

The desire to be a weekend Rambo, under these circumstances, manages the tensions between a lethal, primal masculinity and a modern, expert authority. In the publicity materials produced by the Subic Freeport, as well as articles on tourism in print and on the Internet, potential tourists were being educated as proper consumers of this distinctive experience in decidedly gendered and racialized terms. At JEST, this shift from soldier to tourist economies and cultures operated through a masculine register, with the figure of the indigenous man accommodating flexible fantasies of primitivism from jungle warrior to champion of sustainability.[12] Aeta indigenous masculinities translated a symbolic and material economy that had been defined by the tough masculinities of U.S. soldiering to one defined by the management and preservation model authorized by a neoliberal Philippine state. The consistent presence of the Aeta men—as military instructors, then as tourist guides—marks the gradations of masculine primitivism contained and managed by the promises of ecotourism in this particular space.

The flexible uses of indigenous bodies are also part of the instruction transmitted by the Aeta guides. The Philippine Airlines article was satisfied with the Rambo-as-Stallone icon, but the fact that Aeta instructors teach tourists how to connect with the wilderness through their primal selves corresponds (even if only coincidentally) with the little-remembered fact of Rambo's indigenous ancestry. That Rambo is part Navajo and embodies primitive jungle masculinity is, by design, intelligible: Native people are understood to have a natural connection to nature.[13] His Special Forces training, the experience of capture and captivity at the hands of North Vietnamese forces, and his return to the jungle are details that mark Rambo as the optimized composite of indigenous ability and modern military training.[14] While accessing Rambo through Aeta instruction conflates different indigenous people, it points to a long-standing pattern that links the ideologies underpinning ecotourism to militarism: the concurrent use and dependence on indigenous people and knowledge while also desiring their absence or annihilation.

"USING INDIANS TO CATCH INDIANS"

Playing Rambo makes absolute sense at Subic: Rambo epitomizes JEST's ecotourist fantasies; furthermore, he gestures to the long history of U.S. military history in this space. Rambo's story goes beyond the truncated narrative of a U.S. military base that was handed over to the Philippines: it alludes to deeper and more sustained connections between the United States and the tropical landscapes it has colonized. The fictional Rambo's defining Vietnam experience was enabled by the real military support provided from Subic Bay Naval Base and other military bases in the Philippines, Okinawa, and Guam, which were all products of the systematic militarization of the region. Rambo's story also illuminates the role of the Philippines as a central accomplice to this particular U.S. foreign policy in a way that is not often made clear. The origins of the JEST camp at Subic Freeport—where tourists get to play Rambo—illuminate the fictional Rambo's very real Vietnam War encounters.

The story of Rambo's real counterpart, however, began much earlier than the U.S.-Philippine partnership during the Vietnam War. The use of indigenous people in combat has its historical roots in colonial military strategy. In its initial military "pacification" campaigns of the Philippines in 1898, and in its subsequent colonial occupation and administration, the United States was already exporting practices and patterns that had become familiar in its nineteenth-century subjugation of Native peoples on the continent. Employing Native peoples against each other, the U.S. military had a successful record of militarizing indigenous warriors. Indian scouts were used by both British and American sides in the War of 1812, and against Seminoles during the 1830s and 1840s. The "Indian killer" himself, Andrew Jackson, relied on Cherokee allies to slaughter the Creeks.[15] By the century's end, the Indian Wars and Indian Removal Act policies had radically reduced the numbers and the territories of indigenous people in the United States.[16]

Not coincidentally, the weaponization of indigenous men also emerged hand in hand with a rudimentary ethic of environmental preservation and stewardship. Theodore Roosevelt, America's proto-Rambo, went native to play cowboy and went to war and on safari to recuperate and rehabilitate an embattled American manhood via the primitive bodies of Africans and indigenous peoples.[17] Writing on the Indian Wars, Roosevelt defended the necessity of war against "savages" to defend American civilization by preserving the vast land reserves of the West as the necessary training grounds for white supremacy: "The *rude, fierce settler who drives the savage from the land lays all civilized mankind under a debt to him.*"[18] Roosevelt's "rude, fierce settler," in eliminating savages, takes up the stewardship of the land. It is no surprise that the era's chief imperialist was himself one of its most vocal conservationists, placing large tracts of Indian territory under the administration of the U.S. government. Setting aside these lands for the purposes of conservation *and* tourism encouraged a domestic reinvention of the traveler as naturalist and laid the groundwork for the ecological argument as an alibi for removal and genocide.[19]

The twentieth century would see the personnel, weaponry, ideologies, and institutions of Indian removal relocated to its Pacific territories with the outbreak of the Spanish-American War.[20] Once the continental United States had been secured, veterans of the American Indian Wars volunteered for service in the Spanish-American War, then the Philippine-American War, bringing with them the techniques and ideologies they had used against indigenous peoples in the United States.[21] When the Philippine-American War broke out in 1898, racist epithets such as "nigger," "gugu," and "squaw" reflected how American soldiers navigated the new racial terrains of the archipelago.[22] As expected, the United States likened rebel Filipinos (in particular) to "bandits, 'chifs,' and 'hostiles' of a tribe comparable to the Sioux and the Seminole," ideologically facilitating the genocide in the archipelago though familiar racist taxonomies.[23] This understanding of American racial warfare was shared by both parties: the insurgent Philippine Republic government had promised to "repeat the North American Indian warfare" should the United States not honor their pledge to withdraw once the Spanish were routed.[24]

Military overreach, however, meant that the U.S. military had to recruit the help of "new Indians" in its pacification campaigns. The U.S. war against Filipino insurgents was an uneven affair: the Philippines' diverse geography and ethnic divisions, the localized governance of Filipino people under Spanish colonial administration, existing enmity between different Filipino ethnic groups, and the ongoing insurgency made "pacification" a largely ad hoc and multitactical project involving a range of violence, the garrisoning of towns, public punishment, torture, threats, and coercion to achieve its aims.[25] In their military pacification of the Philippines, U.S. forces were stymied by the tropical heat and humidity, unfamiliar terrain, and disease.[26] The U.S. military was also massively outnumbered: to control nearly eight million Filipinos, it had an average rifle strength of twenty-six thousand men, inadequate for dealing with the guerrilla warfare tactics of the insurgent Philippine Republic.[27] Once the Spanish had given over control of the Philippines to the United States, military logistical dilemmas forced the Americans to resort to auxiliary Filipino assistance to establish a military and colonial dominance on the islands. In 1899, General Elwell Otis, a veteran of the American Indian Wars, employed Filipino troops recruited from Luzon to police Manila as "good Indians" while American soldiers fought elsewhere in the archipelago.[28] In the middle of 1899, when the insurgent leader Emilio Aguinaldo switched to guerrilla warfare, the U.S. military returned to tried-and-true methods from the continental Indian Wars: "us[ing] Indians to catch Indians."[29] The most infamous of these native recruits were from the town of Macabebe, in Pampanga Province—an ethnic group long loyal to Spain and hostile to Tagalogs and the Philippine Republic.[30] Their success was attributed to their expertise in the local landscape and language: "The indigenous scouts were able to survive with minimal supplies and rations, and they were able to transit the jungle quickly by using their sharp *bolo* knives to cut trails, and their narrow boats, known as *bancas*, to navigate the many streams and rivers."[31] This tactic of "irregular" warfare proved to be so successful that more native troops were organized, trained, and used in combat against the Filipino rebels. By 1900, native auxiliaries were crucial in garrisoning towns in central Luzon and Bicolandia and were routinely joining the U.S. Army into the mountains to hunt for revolutionaries.[32]

The Native Scouts, as they were known, was initially a motley crew of Filipinos from different ethnic and language groups, including some recruits from indigenous strongholds in the mountain regions of Luzon.[33] Drawing mostly from central Luzon—in the Pampangan and Ilocano speaking areas—and less from the potentially treacherous Tagalog-speaking population, the Native Scouts epitomized the U.S. strategy of "fomenting and attempting to direct race war between specific Philippine tribes."[34] As the violence of pacification and resistance escalated, the Native Scouts—eventually fifteen thousand of them—became a key source of support for the U.S. Army.[35] Because the insurrection continued after the official surrender of Aguinaldo in 1901, and had turned to the use of guerrilla tactics, the U.S. military switched to harsher methods, "going native" to respond to the tactics of rebel warfare. Ostensibly reduced to barbaric practices in order to battle unmanly and dishonorable savages, the U.S. military razed the countryside, resulting in mass devastation, such as the reduction of the island of Samar into a "howling wilderness" in order to plant the seed of civilization.[36] In the early years of the twentieth century, the U.S. military found itself drawn into a long-running pacification campaign stretching the length of the archipelago, but especially in the southern Muslim region, where it lasted for the next decade. The Native Scouts were so useful that they were sent—under the supervision of American officers—to suppress the Muslim Moro rebels in the southern region of Mindanao when the U.S. military was otherwise occupied with World War I.[37] In concert with the deployment of Filipino auxiliaries throughout the archipelago, the U.S. administration also encouraged the self-policing of indigenous peoples. In the early years of occupation, the "non-Christian tribes"—the new classification for indigenous Filipinos in Luzon and Mindanao—were placed under the "protection" of the U.S. colonial state, presumably against the incursions and race hatred of Christian Filipinos but mostly to protect the rich natural resources of their regions for colonial extraction.[38] Local native scout troops were formed in these regions, inviting "non-Christian tribes" to take part in the project of self-policing and setting an early precedent for the fortification of a garrison state. Establishing the Mountain Province was part of an administrative production of indigenous people as protected subjects, which inculcated new loyalties to the American colonial administration, holding in reserve the threat of an "upland" army against the possible insurrection of "lowland" Filipinos.[39] This early tutelage in self-policing and U.S. military authority and loyalty would continue throughout the colonial era.

The twentieth century reveals the initially inconsistent investment of the U.S. military in developing the Philippines as a modern armed fortress, reflecting to some degree the ambivalence that it felt toward its native troops: the specter of armed natives never sat easy. Insofar as the militarization of an indigenous army was critical to the success of the empire, however, the installation of Filipinos as part of an American military occupational force was a tolerable intimacy.[40] Once the Philippines was firmly under American military and administrative control, Filipino participation in self-policing and self-defense became more commonly accepted, paralleling Filipino elites' consent to and membership in colonial administration. U.S. military reforms in the early part of the century, as well as the necessary growth of the military to accommodate the increasingly global reach of U.S. interests, led to the establishment of the Colonial Army system in the Philippines.[41] While the Philippine Scouts continued to function as a small, capable, and reliable local force, the United States did not build a large native militia in the Philippines in the interwar years.[42] In this undecided landscape of militarism, space for indigenous Filipinos was limited. At one point, the pictorial transition from a barely dressed savage to a uniformed scout had been an index of the success of the U.S. colonial project.[43] The push to modernize and expand—and the threat of an ascendant Japan—meant a departure from the usefulness of indigenous skills in warfare. At best, indigenous men served as menial labor around military garrisons. Even with the proven use of guerrilla skills during the Japanese occupation, for the U.S. military and the Philippine colony indigenous peoples were anachronisms in a modern military. After World War II, the kind of Filipino soldiery rooted in indigenous knowledge of terrain and environment became marginal to the operational strength and efficiency of the military bases, as the modernization of military technology became the joint project of the U.S.-Philippine military partnership. The Philippines began to train its own troops with the assistance and modeling of U.S. military institutions such as West Point and the Naval Academy, distancing itself from the guerrilla methods of the Philippine-American War and emphasizing modern and disciplined soldiering patterned after American armed services.

Yet despite this programmatic move to modernize on a massive scale, a Cold War military partnership that was directed against domestic subversives reserved and often resorted to the tactic of "using Indians to fight Indians." The counterinsurgency warfare against peasants in the Philippines flourished alongside and complemented the military's drive to modernize. In the postwar era, the reinvigorated collaboration between a landlord-dominated Philippine government and the U.S. military forces in the region once again turned its attention to the problem of the tenant farmer class.[44] Noting the near-collapse of the new Republic of the Philippines government against a new broad-based peasant movement, and taking into account the rising Communist movement in the Philippines, the U.S. military stepped in with money, equipment, and training to put down the rebellion. In tandem with the Philippines' signing of the bases agreement in 1947, U.S.-assisted counterinsurgency interventions in the 1960s and 1970s signaled the remilitarization of the islands and the joint U.S.-Philippine war against the Philippine poor. Rather than invest vast amounts of capital and weaponry into "low intensity conflicts," small teams or agents were sent into remote locations to train with and assist U.S.-friendly indigenous forces and governments.[45] The Philippine Military Academy trained its graduates in counterinsurgency techniques that encouraged the localization of its agents and the participation of local groups in order to better infiltrate the territories where the New People's Army drew its support. Some of the members of this counterinsurgency strategy were from the marginalized Aeta/Negrito tribes and were fittingly called the "Black Army."[46] Yet even when militarizing indigenous peoples to hunt down enemies of the state, the Philippine and U.S. militaries—much less the Philippine state—never considered indigenous peoples as full, modern citizens.

At the same time that it was recruiting indigenous peoples in its counterinsurgency efforts, the military collaboration between the U.S. and Philippine states operated to displace and dispossess indigenous groups, following a familiar historical pattern. After the Military Bases Agreement was signed in 1947, the U.S. military took over massive areas of land, including the ancestral lands of Aeta groups. Clark Air Base in Pampanga Province and Subic Bay Naval Base in Zambales Province—totaling over one hundred sixty thousand hectares of forest and marine territories — enclosed the former hunting grounds of the Aeta people who had lived in the area. Pushed into the mountains, the Aeta people were prohibited from entering their land, and even their mountain retreat was eventually declared part of the air base territory.[47] These conditions of dislocation, alienation, and impoverishment, while making them potentially sympathetic to the insurgent movement, also made them vulnerable to recruiting by Philippine paramilitary personnel looking for ways to employ indigenous peoples in their counterinsurgency efforts.[48] This tension between the usefulness of militarizing indigenous people to suppress Filipino peasant dissent and the disenfranchisement and dispossession of Aeta groups makes sense only when we understand the disposable value of indigenous peoples in the overall project of empire.

Even as the United States and the Philippines insisted on a definitive portrayal of indigenous people as out of time and place, the domestic counterinsurgency project and, more spectacularly, the Vietnam War made indigenous Filipinos militarily relevant once again. Because the "Viet Cong simply melted into the jungles," they were impossible to fight despite the considerable weapons advantage of the United States.[49] "Primitive" skills often trumped modern weaponry. Alongside the recruitment of Southeast Asian peoples into their counterinsurgency efforts, the United States military also looked to indigenous people in the territories it had already pacified to bolster its war effort. The Philippines, presaging its cinematic role as a proxy setting for Hollywood interpretations of America's Vietnam experience, was brought more firmly into the orbit of American military involvement in Southeast Asia as a proxy Vietnam.[50] Rambo was about to be born.

THE JUNGLE SCHOOL

With its tropical rainforests and friendly natives, the existing military reservation at Subic Bay was already a natural training ground to prepare for jungle warfare. In the early 1960s, as it took its first steps into the Southeast Asian peninsula, the American military began to recruit local Aeta men as instructors once it became clear that overdependence on modern weaponry was a disadvantage in Vietnam-style combat. When it seemed that the ability to find potable water became as important a military skill as the ability to pilot a fighter plane, Aeta men were called on to share the subsistence, tracking, hunting, scavenging, and forest skills upon which their own continued survival depended. Lunesto Bulatao, a descendant of one of the founders of the jungle school and a JEST guide himself, remembers that stories of pilots being shot down over the jungles of Vietnam drove home the urgency of setting up a system for training American soldiers in the basics of jungle survival. Graciano Duero was one of those original instructors. In 1962, he stated, "Naghahanap sila ng mga Negritos" (The U.S. military was looking for Negritos [another name by which Aeta people are called]).[51] By this time, Aeta people found that — coupled with migration of others into their territories and their exodus from lands claimed by the U.S. military bases — the land tracts that once belonged to them had radically shrunk to the land surrounding Mount Pinatubo. They had settled on the outskirts, and even served as forest surveyors and service personnel at the military reservation's yacht club, golf course and club, and restaurants.[52] Salvador Dimain remembers that his relatives were employed as security guards at the base by the Negrito Security Guard Agency, providing labor for outsourced jobs.[53] Initially, Bulatao states, there was no pay, only military rations. The Aeta people essentially "volunteered" to work this way for a year, before the navy started to pay them.[54] By 1965, the jungle school had become formalized and Aeta men had once again been enlisted into the ranks of the U.S. military, their indigenous "primitive" skills weaponized for war. Kept in the ranks of a menial reserve labor force and held in close proximity to the base, Aeta people transitioned their skills once again to American military desires.

With the establishment of the jungle school in the forested hills of Subic, the Philippines became a substitute tropical terrain for the U.S. military, enabling its soldiers to practice survival techniques before engaging in the actual realities of war. Like Hawai'i, the Philippines' securely militarized terrain operated as a staging ground to imagine and rehearse the militarization of yet another tropics. Thousands of American soldiers are estimated to have gone through the curriculum presented by the jungle school. Bulatao states, "Barko ng barko pumunta dito. Yun ang pinapadala sa Vietnam" (Ship after ship came here. Those were the ones sent to Vietnam).[55] Duero, who did not officially join the jungle school roster until 1972 but had conducted ad hoc instruction as needed, describes the soldiers he taught as coming from various U.S. military service branches: "halo-halo sa Navy, Marines, Air Force."[56] Monico Dimain, who was not officially on the regular payroll until 1992, remembers how during the 1960s he worked sometimes as a "guide sa gubat" (forest guide) for

Marines.[57] At times when the numbers of American soldiers who needed training exceeded the capabilities of the regular roster of survival guides, he was fetched from the village to help out. Salvador Dimain remembers that he "went to the base and was hired as a survival guide. They liked me and said I was good because I '. . . . aroused the interest of the student.' I was a guide for two years, and then an instructor until the base closed."[58] As U.S. combat troops were sent to Vietnam in greater numbers, more and more Aeta instructors were once again brought into the orbit of the U.S. military.

The curriculum for the jungle survival school was based on the skills that Aeta people cultivated to eke out a living in the reduced natural resources they had at hand, including lessons on "evasion, and how to escape and live in enemy territory."[59] Duero describes teaching soldiers specifically how to track in the jungle, how to navigate at night without flashlights, and how to camouflage their presence. He demonstrates how he taught soldiers how to step in the same footprints to hide their numbers, and how to back-walk to trick the enemy. These skills are traditional skills—"ginamit kung kailangan, for enemy only" (used when needed). Duero explains how jungle school trainers taught American soldiers how to construct traps using arrows and tripwires, how to understand the jungle's natural warning systems, and how to use bamboo to create a makeshift alarm system.[60] As Salvador Dimain corroborates: "They only hired Aytas because we knew our jungle well." For example, Dimain and his Aeta cohort shared "a process that makes a poisonous potato edible" along with "fishing in the wild, food gathering, sleeping securely, how to start a fire using bamboo."[61] Drilling their charges, Duero states that their goal was the moment of "kakagisnan" (realization or awakening) that "all you need is a knife to survive."[62]

The jungle school curriculum—of turning to natives to fight a war against other natives—was reflected in developments in the larger military policy regarding the war. As the Vietnam War dragged on, the Nixon Doctrine described the military strategy that would relegate the burden of fighting the war to its allies while the United States ostensibly transitioned to an advisory capacity. Militarizing the minority populations of the Southeast Asian peninsula, the U.S. military continued to fight a covert war against natives using natives, pulling in substitute bodies as U.S. combat troops withdrew. United States Special Forces, for instance, were deployed in more strategic ways, "embedding with their host-nation counterparts, speaking the hosts' languages, and using the hosts' equipment" in exchange for learning tactical skills specific to the host's terrain, such as jungle warfare.[63] Thus even as the Vietnam War officially wound down for the United States, the value of skills indigenous to the local terrain of war remained unquestionably pivotal for the U.S. military, which continued to have a high demand for its jungle school instructors. For Juan "Johnny" Denito, the transition from being a yard boy and a shoeshine boy for Americans stationed at Subic occurred during this period. In 1972, while occasionally employed in menial service jobs, he also accompanied his father into the mountains and the forest, learning the skills that would later be translated into an official position with the jungle school. He states that "taga-bundok ako. Andoon na yung skill. Kinagisnan" (I'm from the mountains. That's where the skill comes from. From birth [literally "awakening"]). He was able to join the jungle school's roster officially in 1979, when one of the original instructors retired.[64] By 1979, then, the jungle school had been institutionalized to the point of having interviews for its potential employees, even as the Vietnam War was officially over. Julio "July" Denito, Johnny's younger brother, likewise joined the jungle school roster late. He, too, was a shoeshine boy for the U.S. Navy, but in 1986, he began to train not so much in Aeta forest techniques but in how to present them. He was tested in front of a panel of current instructors and navy personnel after a two-week apprenticeship.[65] This institutionalization of the jungle school, complete with an interview and apprenticeship process and a board constituted by military and proven Aeta instructors, illustrates its continuing importance to the training of American soldiers.

In light of the rediscovered value of indigenous jungle survival skills to the adjusted military strategy of the United States, the jungle survival school continued to have a healthy enrollment. The elder Denito notes that, even after the Vietnam War, many soldiers continued to come for training. He mentions that they were always amazed by what they learned and that he encountered many pilots who were doing the training in the event of being shot down in enemy territory: "handa sila sa gubat" (they would be skillful in the forest).[66] In the post-Vietnam era, Alfred Viernes remembers, the 1980s was the "American time"; he describes working (and being able to depend on) back-to-back shifts: the military was highly efficient about scheduling its trainings and bringing its troops. At one time, he estimates five hundred soldiers as divided among seven guides.

The military also regularly returned for refresher courses.[67] Monico Dimain claims that in the mid-1980s, when the American soldiers entered the "survival" modules of their training, the guides would take them on overnight stays in the forest of one to two nights. Each guide was assigned twenty to thirty students on average, and taught their pupils the basic skills, including finding edible ferns and plant shoots, catching and eating snails and frogs, and using the forest herbs and medicinal plants for first aid.[68] Jungle Environment and Survival Training guides give variable estimates of having trained 100,000 to 250,000 soldiers (some of them repeats) since the jungle camp's inception.[69] In partnership with the expansion and modernization of U.S. military bases in the Philippines and globally during this time, a continuing investment in low-technology survival training was essential to the kinds of wars being fought in the global South. This intimate and symbiotic relationship between immense and advanced firepower courtesy of the U.S.-military-industrial complex and the decidedly low-technology approach of jungle survival training was working out to be an ideal and routine partnership.

In the early 1990s, the U.S. military pulled out of its Philippines bases, its departure ushered out by the eruption of Mount Pinatubo and the natural disaster in its wake. Johnny Denito remembers how things changed with the volcanic eruption. He was camping with soldiers on June 12, 1991, when they saw the "cauliflower cloud" and were sent home right away. A few days later, the major eruption took place, and the U.S. Navy evacuated. Denito states that he and some others chose to return to the jungle camp headquarters and survived on ready-to-eat military rations, because the volcanic ash raining down made cooking difficult and foraging and hunting impossible.[70] Despite the immense scope of this natural tragedy, and the loss of life, homes, and livelihood it entailed, some members of the jungle school stayed to guard the facilities and the forest against looters: "nagbantay ng gubat, ng facilities. Ginagardiya namin lahat" (We watched the forest, the facilities. We guarded everything).[71] For Viernes, it was a sense of ownership and protection of land and legacy that the Aeta guides considered theirs, for future generations, as well as watchfulness over a livelihood given to them by the U.S. military. Salvador Dimain suggests that the Aeta guides who stayed did so because they valued the forest as a survival resource and because of their loyalties to the U.S. and Philippine militaries: "Noong nagsara ang base tinanong ako ni Col. Bada: 'Pare, could you help me to patrol the jungle to protect the forest?' Ang motto naming noon ay 'to protect and preserve to prosper,' kaya binabantayan namin ang gubat" (When the base closed, Col. Bada asked me, "Brother, could you help me to patrol the jungle to protect the forest?" Our motto then was "to protect and preserve to prosper," so we watched the forest).[72] Johnny Denito remembers that on November 1992, the United States pulled out completely, although April 1992 was the jungle's school's last month: "pina-alis kami" (they were asked to leave) with severance pay, and they all went home.[73] Bulatao calls this the "malungkot" (sad) time. By 1992, he notes, "wala nang Amerikano dito" (there were no more Americans here) and thus no work, so he like others returned to Zambales with a modest severance pay package.[74] Mang Eking Bulatao, the original founder, who at that point had worked for over thirty years for the U.S. Navy, was fast tracked for immigration and settled near Camp Pendleton in southern California.

Without exception, all the remaining jungle school guides remember the "American time" warmly. When asked to describe the U.S. administration of the base, Duero states: "Sa 'kano kasi, malaki ang itulong nila dito. Inaalaga nila kami, pati ang mga kahoy. Mga gamit nila, matitibay" (The Americans contributed a lot here. They took care of us, and also the forest. Their equipment is durable). He points out the buildings that are the legacy of the military such as the navy squadron dormitory (Building 8636) and JEST's barracks (Building 8086). Duero goes on to say, "Iba sila magpatrabaho—stricto sila" (They operated differently when it came to work—strict), admiring the discipline. He recalls that the soldiers also shared Meals Ready to Eat and rations with them, which made a big impression on many JEST guides.[75] It is clear that the U.S. military occupation of these bases, regardless of the contested nature of the land they occupied, is a cause for nostalgia for the JEST crew. This yearning for the pre-Pinatubo time of American military authority is partially attributable to the U.S. departure coinciding with the destruction of Pinatubo, and the particularly heavy burden that the Pinatubo-area Aeta settlements carried in the aftermath of both. However, the Aeta men of the JEST camp also remember Americans fondly because, during the American administration of the bases, the Aeta group was accorded a status that had not been historically theirs: respect for their indigenous knowledge of the place and the protection of environmental resources from logging and poaching, as well as value and admiration for their indigenous survival skills. Regardless of how Aeta peoples had been pushed from their ancestral lands by the installation of the military bases, for them the U.S. military did more to protect their natural resources and provide a regular and dependable living than the Filipino state has to date. Today, as guides to weekend Rambos or to tourists who are curious about the local cultures, the Aeta guides acquire authority and a continuing livelihood through the former militarization of their indigeneity—that is, their cultural legacies, identity, and knowledge as indigenous people—but it is nowhere as prestigious a status nor as dependable a living as their occupations as jungle survival instructors.

When the U.S. military left, the lands they had occupied once again became contested property: this time, the Philippine state assumed control of these territories. In the postbase era, the IMF and World Bank have dominated the course of Philippine development, and indigenous ancestral lands have essentially come under the dominion of government-private corporation partnerships that ignore the ancestral land claims of many indigenous groups. Even with the more recent Indigenous People's Rights Act of 1997, protections and enforcement of indigenous rights are at the whim of a compromised and corrupt state process. The volcanic debris that had swept out the U.S. military has had the long-term effects of making the affected lands ideal for agriculture but also more desirable to others. The various Aeta groups who had already been forced to settle outside of their former territories, and who had been evacuated and resettled by government agencies after the Pinatubo disaster, are for the most part taken into minimal consideration in the decision-making process regarding the fate of the former base territories. Today, several Aeta groups have put forward claims to the land against mutual management by government and corporate agents, arguing that government rehabilitation efforts and corporate development are mere "showcase projects" that have proceeded "without consultation" or consent of Aeta peoples, relegating them, once again, to being wards of the state.[76] Against this ongoing and seemingly uphill battle, the JEST project represents one of the few ways one small Aeta group has managed to carve out a semblance of independence in a changing economy.

JUNGLE ENVIRONMENT SURVIVAL TRAINING

Upon the devastation of Subic Bay in the aftermath of the Mount Pinatubo eruption and the subsequent departure of the U.S. military with the nonrenewal of the bases treaty, the Aeta trainers found themselves without a livelihood. Richard Gordon, who became the administrator of Subic Bay Metropolitan Authority after his stint as the mayor, assisted in converting the jungle school into an ecotourism destination. He spearheaded the transformation of the former U.S. military training center into a destination that capitalized on not only local indigenous Aeta culture but also American military history. Johnny Denito remembers that even in its early days, "May bumibisita na rin" (there were already visitors) as Gordon had already begun to promote the jungle school as a tourist attraction. Sealing these new tourist transactions, Denito recollects that these first tourists gave monetary tips that helped the Aeta people make it through the lean times following Pinatubo's eruption. Under Gordon's supervision, Denito maintains, the jungle school instructors once again started to receive payment in 1993 for "security" services while they began to transition their skills to the tourism trade.[77] With this maneuver, Gordon replaced militarism with neoliberalism as the new face of fraternal cooperation.

Today, the immense military territory that made up the former base has been converted wholesale into a freeport, where transnational investment is welcomed with minimum bureaucracy and regulation. While the United States "returned" the base to the Philippines, little has changed in the geography of Subic other than the clear signs of its privatization: the airport hangars are painted with FedEx logos, factories and shops occupy buildings previously used as mess halls, and the golf course is now open to tourists. Old barracks for military personnel house management personnel for a Korean ship-building company or Filipino seamen who are training for overseas labor. The former checkpoints and borders between the freeport and Olongapo City instead delineate Subic Freeport's new designation as a zone where capital reigns supreme. As a haven for an intensified neoliberal economy, Subic Freeport brings in international investors who have taken advantage of the modern infrastructure established by the U.S. military, as well as domestic and international tourists wanting to holiday in the leisure centers that have cropped up around former military recreation centers such as beach resorts, golf, casino hotels, duty-free shopping, or even a safari tour. Filipinos are welcome as long as they provide the cheap labor that attracts foreign investment or become tourists who identify with a cosmopolitan leisure class.

In Subic Freeport's massive and very modern territory, the comparatively tiny JEST camp stands out because of its unique emphasis on the

FIGURE 6.1 The view of the Subic Freeport and harbor from the JEST camp. PHOTOGRAPH BY THE AUTHOR.

indigenous traditions of the Aeta people and their singular transactions with the U.S. military. The tourists who choose to visit the JEST camp are motivated by at least one of two things: the Aeta men's demonstration of jungle survival skills and the fact that these jungle survival skills were previously taught to the U.S. military. The first reason is related to a desire for some kind of indigenous authenticity on exhibit, the second by a wish to identify with the prior American inhabitants of the freeport. Over the course of their visit, the ecotourism packaging of the JEST experience and the location of the JEST camp in a territory that still holds many of the markers of its previous tenant make it difficult to disentangle the twinned histories of indigeneity and militarism. Located at the edge of the forested hills of Subic, the JEST camp is farther away from more central attractions (figure 6.1). The camp boasts several views that remind tourists that this is a former military territory: standing at its overlooks, tourists can see an airport with several runways and the immense harbor where cargo and military ships are often docked. In the camp, the visual markers of the partnership between the Aeta men and U.S. military are everywhere: the military fatigues comfortably worn by the guides and the big crest resembling military insignia painted on one of the small barracks-like buildings with the names of the jungle school guides written inside it. For its current visitors, the existence of the JEST tour is often met by amazement—even by those from nearby Olongapo. Much of the uniqueness and newness of this tourism activity stems from the security that the U.S. military placed around the base. Julio Denito states that "bawal talaga ang civilian" (civilians were restricted access) during the U.S. occupation—the survival skills of the Aeta people were, in a sense, classified military information.[78] As a tourist attraction, the locale holds this added cachet.

Today, about two hundred to three hundred tourists a week—mostly Filipinos, but also international—come to JEST, validating it as a dependable tourist destination.[79] There is no typical tourist that comes to JEST: the Aeta guides note that their clientele hail from various places and backgrounds, such as Japanese, Chinese, European, American and Filipino, with a recent notable increase in Koreans. Increasingly, the camp has become a common stop for school field trips. In line with the instructional figure of the Aeta man, Filipino students come to learn about Aeta culture through the same displays that they offer to tourists. Men and women, old and young, domestic and foreign—the JEST camp takes on all paying customers. The common denominator that links them together is the most popular offering at the camp. Belying the Philippine Airlines "Rambo" article, most of the tourists who come to JEST take in the half-hour "mini" jungle survival demonstration, then explore the rest of the scenery around the camp. Some take a short guided hike lasting one to three hours, with only a few indulging in the more adventurous and arduous immersion experience of camping overnight in sites with no running water; hiking on trails overgrown with thick vines, ferns, and bamboo; and "going native" to find and cook food.

The experience of the mini jungle demonstration shapes the impression of the jungle survival attraction for the majority of tourists. There is, as many of the guides call it, a "standard operating procedure" that they use for this demonstration.[80] After paying for admission, tourists enter the camp and are greeted by a guide, usually dressed in a T-shirt emblazoned with "Jungle Environment Survival Training" across the front, camouflage fatigues, and combat boots or rubber slippers. Depending on the size of the tour group, the guide leads them to an appropriate sized demonstration area with seating and welcomes them. The demonstration is essentially the same, differing only due to personal touches based on the individual personalities of the small staff of jungle survival trainers, and

PLAYING SOLDIER, GOING NATIVE

203

small adjustments regarding the size of the audience. The guides handle all comers—who can range from large student field trips to small groups of tourists—with poise and humor: they have taught under much stricter regulations and for more exacting audiences. The Aeta guides have converted an exhibit style produced for the military gaze to one tailored for the tourist gaze. In the end, it does not matter that the tourists are quite different from each other. Like soldiers who are disciplined to function as a unit, tourists are treated to a standardized instruction. The demonstration's instruction goes both ways by teaching tourists to consume an experience and teaching Aeta people to produce a commodity for tourist consumption.

The guide stands in the middle of the clearing, surrounded by tourists seated at benches. If there is an overflow audience, they find makeshift seats or stand on the outskirts. After welcoming the visitors to the jungle camp—in clear, if occasionally halting, English, peppered with dependable joking asides—the guide demonstrates the jungle skills that the tourists have come to observe. First, he shows them how to find water without a clear water source. Using a sharp bolo (machete) that hangs from a rope around his waist, the guide skillfully slashes at a piece of creeping ground bamboo which has been previously harvested and stored for the day's demonstrations. Whittling one end to a sharp point, he shows the audience the clear water that oozes out, and then invites them to try it. Some audience members volunteer, and he tips the bamboo into their mouths, letting the water trickle down. They comment on how clean it tastes, and sometimes the guide will add that the U.S. military had the bamboo water tested and had confirmed that it was pure and had beneficial nutrients. Next, he shows them how to make cups for drinking, as well as utensils and "plates" for eating whatever animals one manages to find in the jungle. As he models how to make a cup from bamboo segments, he jokes that American soldiers had a hard time using the thin bamboo cups, playing up the stereotype that white Americans have long noses. He modifies the design of the cup, slicing off a piece of the rim to show the audience how the guides accommodated these elongated proboscises. As he moves on to making plates and utensils, he continues to make fun of American soldiers, this time focusing on their fastidiousness: "Nahirapan silang magkamayan" (They had a hard time eating with their hands). He fashions a spoon from a long piece of bamboo with a pointed "fork" for picking up meat and vegetables at the other end. During the demonstration, these

constant references to the U.S. military, even as an object of comedy, are subtle reminders to the audience that the demonstration they are seeing had its origins in American military necessity. Using them drives home the point that the Aeta guides closely associated with Subic's previous inhabitants. The guide hands out the sample cups and utensils as souvenirs.

The mini jungle demonstration is well designed and nicely paced. It ends with a dramatic finale—an exhibition of how to start a fire "without matches or lighters." The guide carefully outlines each step for his audience: "You have to find the right kind of bamboo. It has to be dry." He shows them an array of different bamboo samples, chooses one, and deftly carves out a bamboo contraption that works through friction (figure 6.2). He scrapes small curls of kindling from the bamboo, positions it in the inside curve of a piece of halved bamboo, and starts to rub another piece against it. There is a momentary skepticism about how this might work, but within seconds, he produces smoke, then fire. The audience gasps in admiration and applauds. The guide holds up the bamboo containing the fire for tourists and poses for photographs. "Now you can cook," he says, and shows the audience how to set up the other parts of the bamboo as makeshift "pots" to cook rice and whatever food has been foraged or hunted. Sometimes the guide will mention that the soldiers had to do this all on their own while navigating the jungle in order to "graduate." Sometimes the fire-making exhibition ends with tourists posing with the guides for photographs. The demonstration, while reminding tourists of the past lives of the guides and the knowledge they are consuming, never veers from its upbeat tone. It asks tourists to identify with the triumphant and successful acquisition of these unique skills, not with the conditions that required them for survival.

To wind down, the demonstration once again veers toward the lighter side, with the guide showing the audience "Tarzan's vine" so that, even in the jungle, one can maintain civilized standards of hygiene. He mashes a piece of gnarled brown vine and produces some suds for the audience to try, adding some water from the creeping bamboo. There is some back-and-forth joking with the guide and the audience. After about twenty minutes or so, the demonstration is over, and the audience disperses to explore the rest of the camp's attractions, which include an aviary, a "spiderworld" exhibit, a souvenir display, and a viewing deck over the bay and runways. The guide will sometimes make a pitch about going on a short hike into the woods to deepen tourists' knowledge. If they are not on a fixed itinerary, and are wearing appropriate clothing, some will take the guides up on this offer, which will cost a bit more.

On the one- to three-hour hike, tourists apply mosquito repellent, adjust their hiking boots, and follow the guide, who walks them through the camp and straight into the jungle. Bolo in hand, he hacks through the thicket of vines and giant fern fronds, making a fresh path through the foliage. He recounts, as he hikes deeper into the woods, that American soldiers had a hard time sneaking up on their Aeta instructors: again and again, they would be discovered. Finally, when one of the officers asked why this was the case, the Aeta instructor told him that it was because of the telltale smell of mosquito repellent. The story is told humorously but is yet another reminder of the intimacy that the U.S. military shared with its jungle school instructors. Five or so minutes into the hike, the guide chops down a small sapling, peeling off its rough outer layers to reveal the

FIGURE 6.3 **On the jungle mini tour.** PHOTOGRAPH BY THE AUTHOR.

tender, pale flesh beneath (figure 6.3). The hikers sample it. He tells them, "You can find food in the jungle if you know where to look." Munching on their snacks, the hikers follow him farther into the forest, which has become increasingly untamed. Here and there, a tree stump sticks out, and he identifies them as trees he used to show the edible part to another hiking group a few days before. He leads the hikers to a plant, showing them its unique leaf patterns. It is a medicinal plant, and he crushes the leaves to release its juices and applies the mash to his arm to show that it is a topical remedy. "This is jungle medicine," he points out, "good for wounds, fever, infection." The trek into the jungle essentially displays those plants that cannot be easily incorporated into the mini jungle demonstration. He shows the hikers where to find the creeping bamboo and what it looks like on the jungle floor, he shows them how to identify dry bamboo when it is come across in upright bamboo groves, and he decorates the hikers with adhesive leaves from a plant, "as natural camouflage." At the end of the hike, he fashions rain hats from large heart-shaped leaves for sun and rain protection; everyone then begins the hike back to the camp.

JEST fits right into the new neoliberal regime: the instructiveness of

Aeta masculinities attests to the ways that the conversion from military economies to special economic zones relies on the availability of certain marked bodies of labor and the reterritorialization of a military jungle into an ecotourist wilderness. The knowledge that the guides share during the mini jungle demonstrations, as well as on the hikes, is basic and a key part of the military's jungle school curriculum. One of the JEST guides makes clear that "yung tinuturo namin ngayon, yun ang tinuturo namin noon" (that which we teach now, we taught then). In other words, there is a clear overlap between the skills that have become tourist attractions and the skills that the military needed.[81] Also clear in the demonstrations at the camp and in the jungle is how the pedagogy of the new tourism regime has taken root in Aeta culture. Aeta stakes lie not only in perpetuating jungle survival skills but also in adapting these skills to a new economy. The adaptability of the Aeta people to the new regime was, in fact, the showcase for Subic Freeport's successful conversion. According to the same *Philippine Star* article that touted the Aeta men instructing a new set of tourist-subjects, after the military's departure "depriv[ed] the Negritos and 40,000 other Filipinos of their livelihood," the Philippine state and its corporate development partners stepped in to "convert the base into a freeport and tourism center" that "enables the forest-dwelling Negritos to maintain their ancient way of life."[82] Two years later, the JEST guides officially became employees of the Freeport Services Corporation—which was subsidized by the Subic Bay Metropolitan Authority—and worked as waged "tourism" employees. The message was that neoliberal governance presented a benevolent attention to indigeneity and sustainability, as shown by the conversion of Aeta men from military trainers to tourism guides. Juan Denito describes this fortuitous discovery: "Napapasaya namin, parang magik" (We were able to make [the tourists] happy, like magic).[83] This "alchemy" was swift and profitable. By 1994, Subic's transition to a tourism economy was complete, and the tours that are now in place had been established. The transformation of the jungle school into the JEST tourist destination had immediate results, gesturing to the seamless connection made possible by the Aeta guides' labor and the commodification of their culture for tourism.

The rhetoric that frames the Aeta men as exemplary subjects of neoliberalism's human side fails to acknowledge that this particular Aeta population is exceptional in this regard. The ancestral lands around Pinatubo to which various Aeta groups have laid claim remain contested. Private corporations have partnered with the state to develop the lands and infra-structures that had formerly been enclosed in the base borders, continu-ing to ignore Aeta claims. At the neighboring Clark Freeport (the former Air Force Base), Aeta groups see the Clark Development Corporation's designs to develop the infrastructure as antithetical to their interests and claims, and have been contesting the planned conversion of certain areas into tourism sites, fearing that these incursions will mean continuing or permanent loss of their independence.[84] In their scattered areas of re-settlement, the Aeta community as a whole has had to cope with rapid changes and state interventions that do not address their unique commu-nity practices. For the group at JEST, however, the articulation of indige-nous masculinities and subsistence skills to military needs and ideolo-gies of stewardship smoothed the transition from militarism to tourism. Otherwise marginalized in Philippine culture and society, and largely unprotected by the state, the JEST guides have found that as consent-ing waged employees of the Subic management, they are recognized as subjects by a neoliberal state and its corporate partners. There are re-wards for this. The income earned by the JEST school goes a long way to support the two thousand Aeta people near Subic with a steady source of income. Today, the JEST guides view their new occupation of training tourists with a pragmatic eye. Juan Denito states of their new wage em-ployment: "Naka-survive at naka-aral ng anak" (It is enough to survive and send the kids to school).[85]

NEW RAMBOS

The Jungle Environment and Survival Training's showcase of militarized indigenous culture goes beyond merely illuminating the transition from one regime to another; it highlights the continued and intimate links be-tween military violence and tourist pleasure in the contemporary Philip-pines. The convergence of tourism and militarism in this instance needs to be understood within both the broader framework of U.S. militarism's increased flexibility and efficiency, as well as tourism's pivotal role as a neoliberal poster child for the developing world. Rather than happen-stance, these links are absolutely critical to the neocolonial economy of the Philippine and U.S. states. The fantasy of playing Rambo illuminates one of these links: the success and draw of the JEST camp are intimately wrapped up with the fact that tourists experience both an authentic in-digenous display and a piece of actual U.S. military training. Playing at being natural warriors, tourists at the JEST camp get to play soldier *and* go native, so to speak: they embody both the global muscle of U.S. military masculinity and a local indigenous masculinity that has been recast through a cosmopolitan ecotourism narrative.

The value placed by the U.S. military on indigenous knowledge plays into the ways that the ecotourism industry—as the neoliberal heir to the military—finds proper uses and value for indigenous knowledge, optimizing and commodifying it for consumption. The JEST camp's amenability to shifting its focus from teaching soldiers to teaching tourists means that it can be positioned as beneficently continuing to employ local Aeta peoples in a struggling, transitioning economy, just as the U.S. military did. It is an ideal attraction—low-impact, needing minimal infrastructure, and able to take advantage of a cheap labor pool—with the added value of the lip service it pays to sustainability and indigenous conservation. Under the benevolent watch of the neoliberal order, the guides can retool their skills and transform themselves into new kinds of subjects for a kind of world where they can ostensibly actively participate and be included.

Yet the substitution of tourism for the military economy is indicative not of a transition from U.S. military occupation to a Philippine-managed civilian project, but of an updated collaborative regime defined by flexible militarization and neoliberal policies. Although the U.S. military no longer occupies the massive reservations it once did in the Philippines, it continues to have a dominant presence in the Philippines and elsewhere, shifting its tactics to "use forces" who are of "a similar character" to their targeted enemy.[86] Military tactics scholars and historians trace this changing battlefield from conventional warfare to "irregular war" to a Cold War counterinsurgency legacy.[87] Despite following the logic of Vietnamization, and officially exiting the Philippines, the United States continues to train and support the Philippine militarization project to corral and eliminate enemies of the state. Even as the military-industrial complex operates on a logic of creating the most up-to-date weapons of mass destruction and the most intelligent, technologized arsenal, the new insurgencies in the front lines of the war against terror are "best" fought "by having the local population do it themselves."[88] In the Philippines, this shift has meant increasing reliance on and training of the Philippine National Army and the Philippine National Police, particularly in its renewed war against Muslim rebels in the southern region of Mindanao.[89]

United States Special Forces now conduct "Security Assistance Trainings" for the Armed Forces of the Philippines in order to refine their counter-terrorism capabilities: some of this instruction comes straight from the lessons taught at the JEST camp.[90] In the context of the rearticulation of contemporary U.S. global military formations around the rubric of flexibility, the conversion of Subic and the JEST camp into a tourism complex may be cause for nostalgia for "the way things were" on the part of visiting former soldiers or JEST guides, but it also signals to the joint logics of post-Vietnam U.S. military restructuring and the ascendancy of neoliberal governance. When we take into account the long history of U.S. militarization of native bodies and spaces, then, ecotourism as an alternative and sustainable practice of consumption is laid bare as an inheritor of militarized ideologies about indigenous lands and people.

The JEST camp is the perfect example of this updated collaboration. It operates on two levels to support this renewed partnership: first, as a training ground for the Philippine counterparts of the U.S. military and, second, as a public relations coup for the pleasures of militarism and tourism. Its contemporary manifestation as a tourist attraction erases the latent violence of its remilitarization, making it innocent—just about being a weekend Rambo—or even about American "love" in a continuing age of empire. In the context of the Philippinization of the U.S. military presence in the Philippines, the tourist pedagogies of the JEST camp teach much more than jungle survival skills to tourists. In making the survival skills of mass warfare into harmless tourist entertainment, the JEST tour desensitizes its visitors to the military's violence and its historic use of everything at its disposal to accomplish its goals. Camouflaged by the articulations between indigeneity, ecotourism, and playing soldier, the JEST tour frames the historical military occupation by the United States and its contemporary remilitarization as benevolent and mutually beneficial. The JEST guide becomes evidence of a sensitive military that values marginalized indigenous Filipino knowledge. The brutal history of pacification, along with the divide-and-conquer method by which the militarization of the indigenous became thinkable, is replaced by an image of a forward-thinking and benevolent U.S. military. In contrast to this image, the Philippine state and its corporate partners never quite live up to the kind of modern and efficient management that the U.S. military wielded in consideration of indigenous Filipinos. Moreover, the JEST experience helps produce tourist subjects that are complicit with the myth of demilitarization, even as the garrison state increases its brutal campaign against Filipinos. In other words, the Philippines can claim its independence from U.S. military occupation even as it continues to receive aid to suppress its dissident subjects.

Tourism as JEST's new face masks its alternative clientele: the local military and police forces (and visiting U.S. soldiers) who continue to take training sessions in jungle survival. While its guides operate on the register of tourism, the JEST camp has once again been recruited to provide trainings to the Philippine military and police forces whose job it is to secure the Philippine garrison state. Lunesto Bulatao describes the rise in popularity of the overnight tour — among visiting U.S. soldiers and their Filipino trainees.[91] The updated U.S.-Philippine military configuration bonds through the sharing of weaponized indigenous skills. American soldiers come to JEST for refresher courses every two to three months during their mutual training exercises, arranging the visits through the U.S. embassy. Bulatao remembers a group of about ten American soldiers who were escorted by their Philippine Navy hosts: "Nagpapalitan sila ng alaman" (They exchanged knowledge), as if to say that Filipino soldiers claimed Aeta skills as Filipino military knowledge in exchange for U.S. military aid.[92] Philippinization has also meant that the Philippine military and police forces acquire this training in jungle survival to better fight the enemy—in this case, the Muslim separatists and political and peasant insurgents. Juan Denito notes that in the middle to late 2000s, the JEST guides regularly counted on Philippine National Police academy trainees for overnight forest training because it was required for their survival curriculum. The camp has also taken on the Philippine Military Academy and the Philippine military: "Wala na yung 'kano. Pinoy na" (There are no more Americans. It is now Filipinos).[93] He mentions that the last time the Philippine Military Academy came, they brought two hundred people — so many that the guides could not handle the capacity and had to split them in groups. For the most part, the tourist and military curricula overlap: campers and soldiers learn to fend for themselves on overnight stays in the deep jungle with minimum technological aid. Prohibited from bringing food, they hunt and forage for themselves and make their own shelter. There are lethal differences. For this new military clientele, Juan Denito emphasizes that "iba ang training — mga booby traps. Ayaw naming itraining ang civilian" (the training is different — booby traps. We don't want to teach those skills to civilians). The instructors teach skills that involve "gubat talaga" (the actual forest), rather than the exhibit they have revised for tourist consumption.[94] The JEST camp, belying its new incarnation as an ecotourism destination, returns to its roots to once again train paramilitary and military forces how to be Rambo. The flexible remilitarization of the JEST guides fits into a long legacy of translating indigenous skills, knowledge, and people into weapons, intelligence, and soldiers, testifying to how the U.S. military's "formerly held culture of facility with irregular war" uses "Indians to fight Indians" in the varied landscapes of conflict today.[95] Tourism pleasures of "playing Rambo" and going native are pivotal parts of this "irregular warfare."

In my interviews with the JEST guides, they profess their desire for the return of the American regime despite the regular living they are earning in Subic Freeport. During the American occupation of Subic, they feel, they had more job security, more respect from the military administrators, and more established relationships with their clientele. Julio Denito felt that during the American military occupation, the JEST guides were more appreciated and treated with respect and as equals: "Mahal na mahal nila kami" (They loved us very much). The same kind of community, he feels, does not exist with transient tourists or Filipino military trainees.[96] One of them states a wish for their return as "If the military comes back, we'll be here."[97] This desire for imperial love ironically frames the U.S. military as a kinder, more giving authority, producing more intimate and human connections than the hyperalienation of neoliberalism. This seeming fantasy, a wish for remilitarization, however, is already being carried out, and with the assistance of the JEST guides themselves. The wish for the return of the United States is evidence of the successful maneuver of Philippinization: the native has taken on the values of the colonizer, even as the U.S.-Philippine collaboration operates on a leaner and meaner model.

In the spring of 2011, following the tsunami and nuclear meltdown that devastated northern Japan, the media reported rumors of the U.S. military returning to Subic. In lieu of the delayed military buildup plans for Guam, the former Philippine home of the U.S. military was eyed as a possible substitute for troops being transferred from Japan. The fact that a return to the Philippines was even imaginable is due in part to the kinds of ideological and cultural work carried out by a supposedly postmilitary neoliberal economy. The Olongapo major James Gordon, part of the Gordon dynasty that has ruled the area, confirmed that U.S. senators Daniel Inouye and Thad Cochran did indeed take a tour of the facilities "to see the success of the free port," and "were amazed by what they saw." Regarding the possibility of the U.S. military's return, Gordon quipped, "Of course we would welcome it. We want two economies here — one that is freeport–based and the other [which relies on support services] to the military. They can coexist here."[98] In the JEST camp, such coexistence has long been the rule of law.

INSECURITIES, TOURISM, AND TERROR

As it enters the second decade of the twenty-first century, the United States finds itself in a new episode of what has been a continuous state of war. While Iraq and Afghanistan are the heated loci of the "global war against terror" launched in the days following the 9/11 Al-Qaeda attacks on the Twin Towers and the Pentagon, U.S. militarism has extended and reinforced its extraterritorial reach around a world that has been even more rigidly remapped into "us" and "them." This conclusion offers a short meditation on the intimacies between security, terror, and tourism that link Hawai'i and the Philippines to new American occupations. It tracks the formations of knowledge and subjectivities generated by the convergence of tourism and militarism to illuminate the insecurities of the New World Order.

TOURIST CITIZENSHIP

The 9/11 attacks were not a singular phenomenon. Although the predominant symbolic and economic effects of 9/11 centered on the collapsing Twin Towers in the financial capital of the world, the four planes that went down that day embodied the fragility of Western technological superiority and the vulnerability of the largest, best-equipped military in the world. The symbolic power of modernity and mobility—the huge metal bodies of 747 jets—ramming inexorably, repeatedly, in slow motion, from different angles, into the towers of capitalism—went beyond an attack on the built foundational myths of industrial and finance capital, to cause panic in a hyperresponsive travel industry. The largely marginalized attack on the Pentagon, the central headquarters of the U.S. military, likewise unveiled the vulnerability of the U.S. military machine and its inability to secure global mobility. Following the attacks, the immediate shutdown of airports around the world crippled globalized economies: aside from the serial World Trade Center reel, media coverage focused on the countless stranded travelers who were unable to leave or return home, symbols of how the attacks interrupted tourism's system of perfect exchange. Tourism around the world, still sluggish from the impact of the Asian financial crises of 1997 and 1998, took a collective nosedive. For the first time since 1982 (the year of the second oil crisis, martial law in Poland, the Falklands War, and the Israel/Lebanon conflict), the worldwide number of international tourist arrivals decreased.[1]

The symbolic work of insecurity carried out by the weaponization of American and United Airlines jets, however, had been carried out repeatedly before this 2001 cataclysm on much smaller scales and on different shores. In the Philippines, in particular, terrorism became unequivocally tied to the lack of freedom to travel safely, triggering a state of indiscriminate counterinsurgency. In its territories, the tourist, the primary symbol of Western mobility and development, had been the repeated target of kidnappings and other violence. Targeting Western—mostly American—tourists for the international publicity they would bring, the Abu Sayyaf group carried out audacious, nose-thumbing maneuvers that were smaller-scale versions of the 9/11 attacks. In May 2001, armed men kidnapped seventeen people, including three Americans and fourteen Filipinos, from a posh resort on the island of Palawan. The same group had also raided a diving resort in Malaysia a year before, kidnapping a group of vacationing foreigners. Although other kidnappings and village raids involving more hostages had occurred prior to these, they did not garner the same kind of international media attention that kidnapping foreigners did. Even then, without and before the spectacular results of 9/11, many of these acts remained regional and were chalked up to a domestic tradition of militant political dissent or local thuggery. At most, these localized attacks brought the Philippines international notoriety for being the home of tourist kidnappers as well as for its drawn-out struggle to get rid of Muslim extremists in the south. After 9/11, these kidnappings and bombings of airports, buses, hotels, and resorts took on a different meaning. By violating the contract between tourist and host, these attacks wreaked havoc with an incipient and struggling Philippine tourist industry, unsettled assumptions about native hospitality rooted in colonial master-servant encounters, and refused the abstracting geographies of tourism.[2]

What is often lost in the carnage of these horrific attacks is the memory of an almost systematic targeting of tourist sites by terrorist attacks. The bombings in the Philippines and elsewhere have not been limited to tourist sites, yet a significant number of them—such as the March and April 2003 bombings of an international airport in Davao, Mindanao; the resort bombings in Bali on October 2002 and 2005, and in Egypt in April 2006; and the Marriott and Ritz-Carlton hotel bombings in Jakarta in 2003 and 2009—have targeted infrastructures necessary to tourism.[3] What does it mean when the political battle over the New World Order is fought through and in planes, airports, resorts, hotels, and tourists? Assaulting the different aspects of the tourism industry, while an effective media stunt, also bore the symbolic weight of despair, powerlessness, and social critique, albeit in a violent and often indecipherable manner. Aimed at places and people seemingly unconnected with terrorist concerns, these attacks were that much more monstrous and irrational. This is not to condone the violence of terrorism, but to understand the method behind the ways it made tourists into targets.[4]

Shortly after the May 2001 kidnappings in Palawan, I visited the island on one of my first research trips. I deliberately chose to stay in one of the more posh resorts on the coast, but because I was coming in from farther north where I had done some other fieldwork, I skipped the airport service and came to the resort on a *banca*—a motor-powered outrigger that I had hired as a kind of water "taxi." As the banca approached the all-inclusive resort, armed security men with machine guns yelled at the terrified banca operator, who assured them that we were friendly, that his passengers had reservations. Unhappy at our breach of protocol, and suspicious of tourists who did not fit the bill, officials subjected our entry to an interrogation of sorts. It was never more clear to me as I faced the barrel of a gun that terror and tourism were intimately and violently intertwined. By breaking the tourist-host contract, the kidnappers had made clear that assumptions of tourist safety were violable and that certain protections extended to tourist subjects could be revoked at any moment. The tourist kidnappings—aside from the media spectacle they generated—produced a critical statement about the social relations of tourism. In the states of poverty where economic austerity measures and structural adjustment policies have disenfranchised and impoverished people, tourism's conspicuous consumption and mobility stand out in almost obscene contrast. The romance of hospitality is often belied by the harsh realities of its industry and its patronizing ideologies. Cast as the representatives—the cultural ambassadors—of their nations, tourists come to symbolize their "hostile or unsympathetic governments."[5] Because tourism is simultaneously a poster child for benevolent exchanges of culture and currency *and* inequitable and exploitative neocolonial relations, targeting it illuminated—if briefly—the insecurities and resentments generated by neoliberal economic policies that it epitomized: the gendered and racialized personal and national humiliations of service jobs on the one hand and the tourist's unfettered consumption of places and cultures on the other.

Of course, in the aftermath of the bombings, the tourist, and not the terrorist, was martyred. The tourist was cast as the innocent subject of leisure whose right to move freely and safely exemplified the ideologies of neoliberal governance; having paid for their freedom to travel and "the right to disregard native concerns and feelings" tourists were entitled to "the right to spin their own web of meanings."[6] In the post 9/11 world, tourists were reentrenched as the universal liberal subject whose mobility, modernity, and gift of economic hope needed to be secured against the encroachments of barbarism.[7] In the Philippines, the U.S. military reinforced its state-to-state collaborations against the Muslim "problem" in the southern Philippines: contradicting her claim that poverty was the primary cause of unrest and terrorism, President Gloria Macapagal-Arroyo embraced a $100 million package of U.S. military aid (supplemented by a $29 million economic package) and ratcheted up her military budget to bolster her police state.[8] As the Philippine secretary of defense Angelo Reyes eloquently put it: "The damage from Abu Sayyaf is not to the military . . . [but] to economic climate, investments, tourism and trade. That's the reason we have to finish them off."[9] To secure the safety of the endangered tourists, whose arrivals had dropped by 5.3 percent in the wake of the Abu Sayyaf and 9/11 attacks, the Philippines deployed one thousand police officers specifically to tourist hot spots and ramped up its ongoing war against Filipino citizens of interest such as Muslim insurgents, peasants, and political dissidents.[10]

Using the promise and benevolence of the tourist's gifts to engender support for the governance of a garrison state, the Macapagal-Arroyo regime cast abject and unruly populations as the obstacles to an abstracted idea of national security, prosperity, and peace, clearing the way for ethnic cleansing.[11] Once again reterritorialized as an American laboratory for technologies and techniques of surveillance, discipline, and war, the Philippines hosted U.S. troops in its land and waters with the Balikatan ("shoulder-to-shoulder") military exercises that signaled an eerie return to training colonial Philippine Scouts to hunt down the renegade Philippine revolutionaries during the Philippine-American War and the U.S. military purge of Muslim tribes in Mindanao during American colonial rule.[12] During the colonial era, American authorities fixated on reported incidents of "madness" and fanaticism that were ascribed to an innate, corrupted Muslim nature in order to "portray the imposition of their authority as a positive duty," underwriting military rule in the southern Philippines.[13] This lost history of colonial intimacy and violence underwrites the Balikatan exercises today, as Filipino soldiers are sent in to control and discipline "out-of-control" Filipino bodies. As much as the kidnappings of tourists were exposed in the international media to justify domestic and international military intervention in Mindanao, the corresponding atrocities committed by U.S. and Filipino soldiers alike remain underpublicized.[14] In contrast to the tourist's martyrdom and elevation to citizenship, the state-sanctioned ethnic cleansing of Muslims and Filipinos who have been deemed enemies of the state is subsumed under the logics of national security.[15] They must be "finish[ed] off" to secure paradise for its true paying subjects.

ALOHA PATRIOTISM

Cleaning house for visiting guests was likewise a priority in Hawai'i, though not nearly in as dramatic a fashion. Even before the insecurities of 9/11, tourist safety and comfort took precedence in local politics, redefining island publics as zones for tourist consumption.[16] Jeremy Harris, who was the mayor of Honolulu in the late 1990s, pioneered the cleanup of the Waikīkī beachfront, where tourist-centered crime was perceived to threaten the golden egg of the local economy. Harris embarked on a campaign that respatialized Waikīkī as a tourist zone, including an educational push to enlighten locals about the benefits of tourism (a kind of aloha training), with the renovation of the dilapidated Waikīkī boardwalk as a primary way to showcase the shopping and scenery along this famous stretch of tropical beach.[17] What locals had reterritorialized as their own space, in other words, was gentrified into a zone where tourist-local encounters could be managed and domesticated. Seizing the opportunity created by a "crisis" in crime, Harris framed the desires of the visitor population and the tourism industry as essential to local survival and well-being, remapping Waikīkī in tourist terms and selectively including Native and local culture to enhance an atmosphere of exoticism.[18]

In the new Waikīkī, the dated hotels, stores, and restaurants were renovated and made more upscale to appeal to the shopping tourists, with an emphasis on higher-end consumption and a chic, urban, modern tropical ambiance. Kuhio Avenue, once the back alley of Waikīkī, had its sidewalks widened, and a beach patrol was assigned the task of preventing thefts, giving directions, and generally keeping order. The tropics were literally re-created in the image of hospitality. A hundred thousand cubic yards of sand upgraded the beach, which had eroded to concrete. Hundreds of palm and tropical trees were planted along the sidewalks and the median strip, bringing a lushness to the desolate concrete jungle. In these improved tropics, Native Hawaiians were invited insofar as they contributed to the tourist experience: demonstrations of weaving, hula, musical performances, and even a sunset torch lighting—complete with young men in traditional dress blowing conch shells—demarcated the tourist's pleasures as the defining interests in this space.[19] Sculptures of Native Hawaiians such as Duke Paoa Kahanamoku and Prince Jonathan Kuhio share the boardwalk with more anonymous surfing and frolicking figures, rendering the contested indigenous history of Waikīkī into background props for tourist-friendly snapshots. Street names were changed to play up an indigenous and exoticized history, even as actual Native Hawaiians were increasingly marginalized from the space.[20] Cleaning up and modernizing Waikīkī Beach stood in stark contrast with the neglect of other beach spaces: in the nontourist zones such as Makaha on the leeward side of the island, increasing numbers of homeless Native Hawaiians and Pacific Islanders, pushed out by the real estate and tourism development boom, created their transient accommodations in tent cities on the sand.

In the sanitized and secured tourist zone of Waikīkī, encounters between locals and tourists are mediated by the tourist-centric values of the space. One of Harris's projects in this vein was "Sunset on the Beach," an event aimed at visitors to Waikīkī but also meant to lure more of the right kinds of locals to the beach. The monthly or bimonthly event included live local entertainment on a stage, a free outdoor movie on a thirty-foot screen at sunset, and stalls serving food from area businesses. The "food-music-movie fest" has been taken up and sponsored by the local tourist interests—in particular, the hotels and restaurants that line the beach strip in Waikīkī—in order to generate more visitor attractions. In the managed theater of Waikīkī's nightly torch lightings and hula shows, Sunset on the Beach exemplifies a rare contact zone between locals and tourists, but one nonetheless that is generated for tourist comfort. The millions of dollars pumped into the careful transformation of Waikīkī successfully revived the flagging tourism industry, remapping the space into a premier consumer paradise. Waikīkī's gentrification, to a less brutal degree, illuminates how tourist desires come to shape local spaces, interactions, and politics.

As Waikīkī was the site of a restored and secured tropics where tourist mobilities had precedence, it was no surprise that the beach staged a performance of aloha patriotism, or the translation of tourism freedoms into national interests, shortly after the 9/11 attacks. With its tourist economy sensitive to the new insecurities of the post-9/11 era, its massive military installations on alert, and its long-standing embrace of World War II history as the state's defining property, Hawai'i rallied to link its historical experience of victimization, triumph, and vigilance to 9/11's trauma, remapping Hawai'i in affective proximity with what some were calling the new Pearl Harbor. Waikīkī's newly secured and renovated tropical zone was the perfect staging ground for a performance of state-to-state affiliation that also designated Hawai'i as national property. At Sunset on the Beach, the featured films were regularly prefaced by an advertisement for aloha patriotism. This prefeature short wedded a dramatic national anthem score with an equally dramatic and sentimental tribute to national unity. Scenes of a brave nation pulling together after the terrorist attacks were juxtaposed with aerial, helicopter-shot images of the USS *Arizona* Memorial and the military Pacific Cemetery at Punchbowl, connecting 9/11 to December 7, 1941. At the same time that it militarized the deaths of New York civilians, the film short also made clear that this militarization extended only insofar as the World War II deaths in Hawai'i were understood within the framework of the sacrifice of innocence as the price of paradise and freedom. Gently swaying, hula-loving, multicultural youth—offering a somber and affective performance dedicated to the 9/11 victims—further fortified the ties between icons of Hawai'i tourism's "soft primitivism," the safety of tourist travel, a narrative of American innocence and tolerance, and the few good men that defend the security of a tropical island in the middle of the Pacific. Inviting the tourists and local residents who were viewing the film to identify their corporeal tropical pleasures (island breezes on their skin, warm sun setting on the horizon, the Pacific Ocean a few steps away, feet buried in the sand) with a threatened but responsive national body, the film's aloha patriotism tied consumer freedom to military security. The visual language of the film—drawing from evocative slow-motion hula dances; breezes rustling the tops of palm trees; and a panoramic, sweeping shot over rugged coastlines and island topography—is at last a euphoric celebration of the secured tropics as tourist commodity.

At the same time that this film short was being played with regularity at Sunset on the Beach in 2002–3, the political machinery was in motion to invade Iraq. Such as it was, the end of the patriotic minimovie was met by approving cheers, indicating its success in producing complex and simultaneous identifications with the militarization of paradise, the expanding global war against terror, and the freedoms of the tourist-citizen. Cloaking the impending war in sentimentality and images of exotic and peaceable paradise, the film abstracted Native Hawaiian land, people, culture, and history into the visual currency of tourism, obscuring the long-standing conditions of U.S. military occupation on the islands—the same conditions that the United States would re-create in Iraq. The gentrification of Waikīkī as a tourist zone symbolized the desired fate for Iraq not as tropical paradise, but as occupied, disciplined, American territory.

For Hawai'i and the Philippines, what securing paradise makes clear are the contours of the New World Order and for whom the project of security is undertaken. In the military-tourism spaces that this book has lingered over, the consolidation of tourist citizenship and aloha patriotism delineates which subjects have the freedom to travel at the expense of the mobility of other populations and just what kinds of encounters are most imaginable or possible in these tropics. Such encounters—because of their radically unequal natures—are always contestable in violent, creative, or other means. That is, they are themselves generative of critique and alternative ways of seeing. Just as Rosca and Trask offer unsettling juxtapositions of militarism and tourism within the same image to open up questions about partnerships and circuits of collaboration, I hope that what this book has done is to not spoil the next holiday of its readers. Rather, it is my desire that this book inspires a different way of seeing that understands the pleasures of tourism as both part of the success and potential interruption of empire.

NOTES

INTRODUCTION

This book uses modern Hawaiian orthography, which uses diacritical marks for Hawaiian-language terms: the ʻokina (ʻ) marks a glottal stop and the kahakō is a macron indicating a long vowel sound. I do not italicize Hawaiian words, as they are not foreign to Hawaiʻi. When quoting directly from sources, however, I have preserved the spelling of original sources for historical accuracy.

1. Lyons, *American Pacificism*, 8.
2. Gerhardt, "America's Pacific Century?"
3. I borrow the phrase from Isaac, *American Tropics*, to contrast the constant pull of American imperial desire against a historiographical will to amnesia.
4. Williams, *Marxism and Literature*, and Berger, *Ways of Seeing*.
5. On the differential mobilities that make up empire, see Ballantyne and Burton, *Moving Subjects*.
6. Haraway, "The Cyborg Manifesto," 168.
7. Enloe, *Maneuvers*, 68.
8. Enloe, *Globalization and Militarism*.
9. "Liberalization with a Human Face," World Tourism Organization, www.world-tourism.org/liberalization/menu.htm (accessed May 9, 2004). The website points out that this program follows the UN Millennium Development Goals as well as the Global Code of Ethics on fair trade and poverty alleviation of the United Nations' World Tourism Organization (UNWTO). On the uneven economic relations fostered between countries that send tourists, and those less-developed economies for whom tourism is a prescription, see Kincaid, *A Small Place*; Nash, "Tourism as a Form of Imperialism"; Mowforth and Munt, *Tourism and Sustainability*; and Britton, "The Political Economy of Tourism in the Third World."

10. Endy, *Cold War Holidays*; Klein, *Cold War Orientalism*.

11. See Johnson, *The Sorrows of Empire*, 23–24. See also Bacevich, *The New American Militarism*, and Giroux, "War on Terror."

12. McClintock, *Imperial Leather*, 26.

13. Ibid., 21–26.

14. See, e.g., Enloe, *Bananas, Beaches, and Bases*; Enloe, *Maneuvers*; Sturdevant, *Let the Good Times Roll*; Moon, *Sex among Allies*; Sakai, "On Romantic Love and Military Violence"; Barstow, *War's Dirty Secret*; Tanaka and Brownmiller, *Japan's Comfort Women*; and Shibusawa, *America's Geisha Ally*.

15. On the romantic overtones of security, within a discussion of the political-libidinal economies that frame U.S.-Philippine relations, see Tadiar, *Fantasy-Production*.

16. G. White, "Remembering Guadalcanal"; White and Lindstrom, *The Pacific Theater*; Teaiwa, "bikinis and other s/pacific n/oceans."

17. I borrow the term *militourism* from Teaiwa, "Militarism, Tourism and the Native."

18. Said, *Orientalism*, and *Culture and Imperialism*; Manderson and Jolly, *Sites of Desire, Economies of Pleasure*.

19. See Strachan's genealogy of paradise in *Paradise and Plantation*; and Cohen's exploration of nationalism and tourism in *Take Me to My Paradise*.

20. Skwiot's *The Purposes of Paradise* is a detailed study of tourism policy and imaginative power in Cuba and Hawaiʻi.

21. Merrill's *Negotiating Paradise* examines U.S. tourism in Latin America as a mode of cultural and consumer expansion alongside diplomacy.

22. See, in contrast to my focus on this hegemonic formation, Hauʻofa, "Our Sea of Islands."

23. The geographical specificity of this project attends to the call for a "critical regionalism" in Wilson, "Towards an 'Asia/Pacific Cultural Studies.'" While the paradises invoked in this book are limited for the most part to Hawaiʻi and the Philippines for reasons of time and expertise, American tropics in the Asia and the Pacific—such as Guam, Okinawa, Vietnam, the Marshall Islands, and American Samoa—and those outside the region—such as Puerto Rico and Cuba—are also key locations of the global American tourist-military complex. See also Tripp, "Contentious Divide," for a specific study of the Korean demilitarized zone.

24. Shigematsu and Camacho, "Introduction," xviii. I use the term "Native Hawaiian," or "Kanaka Maoli" to refer to people indigenous to Hawaiʻi. Where referring to Native Hawaiians (or other indigenous people), I use the term "Native" with an uppercase "N" to distinguish indigenous people from indigenous things such as native plants or animals. I also use "native" with a lowercase "n" as an adjective or noun to refer to a general population from an area who are not necessarily indigenous to that area.

25. Not to be confused with the recently inaugurated Philippine President Benigno "Noynoy" Aquino III. "Ninoy," his father, was an outspoken critic of the Marcos regime.

26. See Diller and Scofidio, *Back to the Front*, which looks at the tourism of war but centralizes European World War II sites as its objects of inquiry.

27. Lyons, *American Pacificism*.

28. Wilson, *Reimagining the American Pacific*, xi.

29. On population decline in Hawai'i, see Stannard, *Before the Horror*. For an early history of Hawai'i to the 1887 Reciprocity Treaty, see Osorio, *Dismembering Lāhui*.

30. Merry, *Colonizing Hawai'i*; Silva, *Aloha Betrayed*.

31. The 1848 Māhele legally transformed the Hawaiian system of land tenure from its traditional communal usage to a private property system, pitting Native Hawaiians, who were unfamiliar with private property, against savvy real estate developers. Asian plantation workers, who were imported as labor, were not allowed to own land. See Kame'eleihiwa, *Native Land and Foreign Desires*.

32. These reconnaissance missions had started as early as 1840. See Kent, *Hawaii*, 53–54.

33. U.S. Senator Albert J. Beveridge, Address to the Senate, Congressional Record, Senate, 56th Congress, 1st session, January 9, 1900, 704–12.

34. On early Spanish colonial cultures, particularly the complex dynamics of Catholic conversion and translation in the Philippines, see Rafael, *Contracting Colonialism*.

35. An economically and geographically overstretched Spanish empire had been undergoing a long, slow slide since the sixteenth century, punctuated by big losses to a revolutionary South America and Central America in the early 1820s. See also Ileto, *Pasyon and Revolution*.

36. Hoganson, *Fighting for American Manhood*.

37. Silva, *Aloha Betrayed*.

38. Many historians of this period suggest that Spain, in order not to lose face to Filipino insurgents—who were starting to make inroads in their revolutionary war—handed the islands over to a more powerful "enemy." Pérez Jr., *The War of 1898*, outlines this fate for Cuba.

39. Silbey, *A War of Frontier and Empire*, 27.

40. The Senate passed the Newlands Resolution in lieu of a treaty, which had the same result. See Kent, *Hawaii*, 67. On the multifaceted methods of Native Hawaiian resistance, see Silva, *Aloha Betrayed*.

41. Jacobson, *Barbarian Virtues*.

42. Pratt, *Imperial Eyes*.

43. See Urry, *The Tourist Gaze*.

44. Silva, *Aloha Betrayed*.

45. Johnson, *The Sorrows of Empire*, 44. On O'ahu, Fort Shafter, Fort Ruger, Fort Armstrong, Fort DeRussy, Fort Kamehameha, Fort Weaver, and Schofield Barracks were constructed soon thereafter, as part of a vision to surround the island with "a ring of steel." See Kajihiro, "The Militarizing of Hawai'i," 172.

46. Linn, *Guardians of Empire*.

47. Feeney, "Aloha and Allegiance," 221. See also Kajihiro, "The Militarizing of Hawai'i."

48. On the sex industry and Hawai'i militarization, see Bailey and Farber, *The First Strange Place*.

49. Ibid., 40. On hula tours and its exotic iconography, see Adria Imada, *Aloha America*.

50. The early sex industry that serviced the military in Hawai'i actually imported

mostly white women to serve the white soldiers who served in the military due to the warnings from elite, Native Hawaiian, and Asian settler communities. See Bailey and Farber, *The First Strange Place*.

51. On public health campaigns in the Philippines, see W. Anderson, *Colonial Pathologies*. On the colonial origins of contemporary Filipino/a nursing, see Choy, *Empire of Care*. See also Edmund, *Leprosy and Empire*.

52. See Go, "Introduction."

53. Trask, in "Settlers of Color and 'Immigrant' Hegemony," traces the doubled colonization of Native Hawaiians: first at the hands of European and American business concerns, then by Asian settlers. See also Cooper and Daws, *Land and Power in Hawai'i*, which outlines the rise of the Democratic Party in Hawai'i as led by the labor-supported Japanese settlers.

54. See Goldstone on the contribution of American Express traveler's checks to globalization and "democratization" in *Making the World Safe for Tourism*. See also Löfgren, *On Holiday*, and Yano, *Airborne Dreams*, which traces the cultural history of Pan American Airlines and its early assistance of the U.S. military. Yano identifies the feminized tropics of Hawai'i and the labor of Japanese-speaking Asian American women as flight attendants as key elements in the cosmopolitan training of Japanese tourists.

55. Kim, *Ends of Empire*. See also Endy, *Cold War Holidays*, and Klein, *Cold War Orientalism*.

56. Saranillio, "Seeing Conquest."

57. Lyons, *American Pacificism*, 152.

58. Craig Gima, in "Hawai'i Sixth in Federal Spending," *Star Bulletin*, July 23, 2009, tracks 2008 federal spending in Hawai'i, which comprises mostly military funds, as just behind tourism and real estate at $15 billion.

59. Kent, *Hawaii*, 180.

60. Hosek, Litovitz, and Resnick, *How Much Does Military Spending Add to Hawaii's Economy?* The disparity in numbers depends on whether the funds' purchasing power is calculated into the indirect jobs, goods, and services produced by the initial federal funds. The total percentage of federal funds spent on defense in Hawai'i has decreased from 46.2 percent in 1990 to 38.5 percent in 2000, but the total amount of both defense and nondefense spending has increased. In 2009 federal defense spending contributed $12.2 billion while 2010 visitor expenditures contributed $10 billion.

61. Verikios, "Philippines' Sustainable Growth Benefits Tourism," *Travel Daily News* website, June 27, 2007. Its wider economic impact is forecasted at 9.9 percent in 2012: see World Travel and Tourism Council, "Travel and Tourism Economic Impact 2012: Philippines," 3, www.wttc.org.site_media/uploads/downloads/philippines2012.pdf (accessed December 11, 2012).

62. During President Gloria Macapagal-Arroyo's first three years, her counterinsurgency strategy received 1,500 percent more U.S. military assistance as had the previous administration (for a total of $246 million). See Marina Walker Guevara, "Sustaining an Unpopular Regime," The Center for Public Integrity, May 31 2007, www.publicintegrity.org/2007/05/31/5763/sustaining-unpopular-regime

(accessed December 11, 2012). For 2012 numbers, see Manuel Mogato, "U.S. Triples Military Aid to Philippines in 2012," Reuters, May 12, 2012.

63. See, e.g., Clinton, "America's Pacific Century," for the secretary of state's declaration of Asia as the principal area for U.S. politics in the foreseeable future.

64. Export figure is from Carter, "United States Commits to Strengthening Asia-Pacific Trade," America-Engaging the World, June 17, 2010, newzealand.usembassy.gov /us_pacific_trade.html (accessed December 11, 2012). In an interesting note, the United States Pacific Command notes that the Asia/Pacific region weighs in with a whopping 35 percent share of U.S. trade—worth $548 billion (compared to 19 percent with the European Union, 20 percent with Canada, and 18 percent with Latin America). Its updated website notes more generally that "the 36 nations that comprise the Asia-Pacific region are home to more than 50% of the world's population, three thousand different languages, several of the world's largest militaries, and five nations allied with the U.S. through mutual defense treaties. Two of the three largest economies are located in the Asia-Pacific along with ten of the fourteen smallest, www.pacom.mil (accessed June 20, 2010).

65. Caldicott, *The New Nuclear Danger*; Hartung, *How Much Are You Making on the War, Daddy?*

66. Johnson, *The Sorrows of Empire*, 55–65; Cohen, "History and the Hyperpower." Data on the amount of military spending are from Sköns et al., "Military Expenditure."

67. See the United States Pacific Command website, www.pacom.mil.

68. World Travel and Tourism Council, The Review 2011, www.wttc.org/site_media /uploads/downloads/WTTC_Review_2011.pdf (accessed July 25, 2011); World Tourism Organization, "Asia Rose Again as a Fast Growing Region," World Tourism Organization, www.unwto.org/regional/south_asia/News/fastgrowing.htm (accessed May 8, 2007).

69. Taleb Rifai, Deputy Secretary-General of UNWTO, as quoted in World Tourism Organization, "Asia Rose Again as a Fast Growing Region."

70. "Transforming U.S. Army Pacific," 4.

71. For examples of these sociocultural forms, see Gillem, *America Town*, and Lutz, *Homefront*.

1. MANIFEST DESTINATIONS

1. Clifford, *Routes*, 39.

2. Said, *The World, the Text, and the Critic*.

3. Rosca, *State of War*, 67. Throughout the rest of this chapter, citations to this work are within parentheses.

4. See Elaine Scarry's *The Body in Pain* on torture, war, and language.

5. Sharpe, *Allegories of Empire*, 21.

6. Weeks and Meconis, *The Armed Forces of the USA in the Asia-Pacific Region*, 17.

7. Ibid., 26–27. The Asia-Pacific allies were seen as important, even though Europe was the focus of primary tensions during this time. It continues to be a critical region for the buildup of nuclear weapons, development of war scenarios, and hosting of geostrategic military sites. See also Smith, "Shifting Terrain."

8. Aparicio and Chavez-Silverman, *Tropicalizations*; Hereniko and Wilson, *Inside Out*.

9. Césaire, *Discourse on Colonialism*, 77.

10. Kim, *Ends of Empire*, 99.

11. Césaire, *Discourse on Colonialism*, 77.

12. A. Kaplan, *The Anarchy of Empire in the Making of U.S. Culture*, 23, 48.

13. See, e.g., Calhoun, Cooper, and Moore, *Lessons of Empire*.

14. Celoza, *Ferdinand Marcos and the Philippines*; Wurfel, *Filipino Politics*.

15. Bello, Kinley, and Elinson, *Development Debacle*, 198. See also Youngblood, "Philippine-American Relations under the 'New Society.'"

16. Rosca's novel is divided in three parts (the Book of Acts, the Book of Numbers, and the Book of Revelations), with the first and third sections set in the late stages of the Marcos dictatorship and the middle section a dizzying biblical accounting of centuries of deranged colonial begetting in the bloodlines of the prominent families from which the three protagonists hail.

17. Belinda Aquino, *The Politics of Plunder*.

18. Neumann, "Tourism Promotion and Prostitution," 182.

19. On gender, sexuality, and empire, see Stoler, *Carnal Knowledge and Imperial Power*; McClintock, *Imperial Leather*; and Tadiar, *Fantasy-Production*.

20. Tadiar, *Fantasy-Production*, 42–50.

21. McCoy, "Dark Legacies."

22. Testimonies from Marcos-era victims came to light during the August–September 1992 Honolulu trial pertaining to the civil lawsuits brought against the Estate of Ferdinand Marcos.

23. Sakamoto, *Asia, Militarization and Regional Conflict*.

24. Foucault, *"Society Must Be Defended."*

25. The estimated numbers differ and are clearly politicized, but conservative estimates start at at least 20,000 military and 200,000–500,000 civilian casualties. Other figures top 1 million total casualties.

26. On the Philippines as a global source of exported labor, see R. Rodriguez, *Migrants for Export*, and Parreñas, *Servants of Globalization*. On Philippine oligarchy politics, see B. Anderson, "Cacique Democracy in the Philippines."

27. Trask, "Nostalgia: vj-Day," 21. All poems by Trask discussed in the chapter are from the collection *Night Is a Sharkskin Drum*.

28. See Kent, *Hawaii*, and Cooper and Daws, *Land and Power in Hawai'i*.

29. Trask, "Nostalgia: vj Day," 22.

30. Dominant figures in labor union organizing at the turn of the century, Japanese, Chinese, and Filipino plantation workers began to make inroads into the political and economic scene of Territorial Hawai'i, which had previously been controlled by Native Hawaiians and white Americans. They contrasted themselves and their working-class politics with a Republican Party dominated by haole elites in the post–World War II era, vaulting themselves into the public eye through a familiar rhetoric of citizenship earned through military heroism. See especially Fujikane and Okamura, *Asian Settler Colonialism*, and Turnbull and Ferguson, *Oh, Say, Can You See?* 155–98.

31. "Make Hawaii a State," score, circa 1950s. Hawaiian Collection, Hamilton Library, University of Hawai'i at Mānoa.
32. Turnbull and Ferguson, "Military Presence/Missionary Past," 96.
33. Trask, "Nostalgia: VJ Day," 22–23.
34. Imada, *Aloha America*.
35. Trask, "Dispossessions of Empire," 35. See also Trask, *From a Native Daughter*, and in particular, the chapter "These Lovely Hula Hands." Prostitution is a recurring theme in Trask's meditations on tourism: her poem "Colonization," in the collection *Light in the Crevice Never Seen*, accuses Native Hawaiians and others of "selling identity/for nickels/and dimes/in the whorehouses of tourism."
36. Trask, "Lahaina, 1995," 18–19.
37. Trask, *From a Native Daughter*, 140.
38. See especially Bederman, *Manliness and Civilization*; Hoganson, *Fighting for American Manhood*; and A. Kaplan, *The Anarchy of Empire in the Making of U.S. Culture*.
39. O'Toole, *The Spanish War*; Brown, *The Correspondents' War*.
40. See Jacobson, *Barbarian Virtues*.
41. Davis wrote for the *New York Times* later in his career after having paid his dues as a special correspondent at the turn of the century. Feeney, "Aloha and Allegiance," 68, notes that the elite Hawai'i publication *Paradise of the Pacific* celebrated and catalogued the arrivals of U.S. military ships and personnel as part of its regular reportage.
42. Davis, "Our Conquests in the Pacific," 13.
43. Ibid.
44. Ibid., 14.
45. Ibid., 17.
46. Ibid., 18.
47. See Pratt, *Imperial Eyes*. See also Wexler, *Tender Violence*, on how American women's photography during this period domesticated imperial violence.
48. See, e.g., Silva, *Aloha Betrayed*, and Mililani B. Trask, "Hawaiian Sovereignty."
49. Davis, "Our Conquests in the Pacific," 88–89.
50. Ibid., 90.
51. See, e.g., Love, *Race over Empire*, which takes on the complex imperial landscape of racism in the U.S. imperial project.
52. Davis, "Our Conquests in the Pacific," 255.
53. T. White, *Our New Possessions*.
54. The first quote is from ibid., 1:143. The second quote, from ibid., 4:649, characterizes his opinion on the Blount report, which amounted to a condemnation of the U.S. political and military support for the overthrow.
55. Ibid., 1:143.
56. Ibid., first quote, 1:156; second quote, 1:241.
57. Ibid., 4:631.
58. See Love, *Race over Empire*, and Horsman, *Race and Manifest Destiny*.
59. Ashcroft, Griffiths, and Tiffin, *The Empire Writes Back*.

2. SCENIC HIGHWAYS, MASCULINITY, MODERNITY, AND MOBILITY

1. Transportation networks in the Philippines have facilitated trade in natural resources, especially as part of the logging and mining booms during the Marcos era. See Broad and Cavanagh, *Plundering Paradise*, and van den Top, *The Social Dynamics of Deforestation in the Philippines*.

2. *Ministry of Public Works and Highways: Annual Report*, 1. In the "precrisis" portion of Marcos's administration (1965–71), he took credit for building 31,816 kilometers of roads and 33,998 meters of bridges. According to the report, from 1972 to 1980, he added 209 meters of bridges and constructed and improved 490 kilometers of roads.

3. Celoza, *Ferdinand Marcos and the Philippines*.

4. Department of Tourism, *Department of Tourism and Philippine Tourism Authority Information Manual*, 5. President Diosdado Macapagal (1961–65), Marcos's predecessor and the father of the recent president Gloria Macapagal Arroyo, was the first to deregulate Philippine trade with President Kennedy's and the IMF's support, launching the Philippines into the cycle of debt dependence in which it is still mired today. See Scipes, "Global Economic Crisis, Neoliberal Solutions, and the Philippines."

5. Department of Tourism, *Department of Tourism and Philippine Tourism Authority Information Manual*, 17.

6. Hannam, Sheller, and Urry, "Editorial: Mobilities, Immobilities and Moorings."

7. Clifford, *Routes*, 23. See also Sheller and Urry, *Tourism Mobilities*.

8. Césaire, *Discourse on Colonialism*, 77.

9. Corpuz, *The Colonial Iron Horse*, 23.

10. Ibid., 3.

11. As suggested by General Arthur MacArthur, Douglas MacArthur's father and one-time military governor-general of the Philippines, in an April 8, 1902, hearing before the U.S. Senate Committee on the Philippines. Corpuz, *The Colonial Iron Horse*, 108.

12. As quoted in Corpuz, *The Colonial Iron Horse*, 27. From 1909 to 1934, more than 400 kilometers of roads and 7,500 kilometers of "new 'first class' highways" were built under the supervision of the U.S. engineering project.

13. Wilcox, *Through Luzon on Highways and Byways*, 30–31.

14. I will refer to the road as Kennon Road throughout this chapter for consistency and clarity.

15. Reed, *City of Pines*, xxiv–xxv; Corpuz, *The Colonial Iron Horse*, 143.

16. Designed by Daniel Burnham, the architect who planned the 1893 St. Louis Exposition's "White City," Baguio City also functioned as a built exemplar of civilized urban planning in the colonies, reflecting Burnham's pro-imperialist and racist sentiments.

17. W. Cameron Forbes opined: "The Americans are the best workers. They are sent to the tops of the cliffs and the most dangerous places. Next come the negroes, and then the Japanese. The Filipinos so far are the worst. They are afraid of heights and rolling rocks, etc., and justly. Few days pass without casualty." Quotation from

Forbes, "Notes on Early History of Baguio," reprinted from *Manila Daily Bulletin*, 1933: 7. See also Afable, *Japanese Pioneers in the Northern Philippine Highlands*.

18. Finin, *The Making of the Igorot*, 59.

19. Corpuz, *The Colonial Iron Horse*, 135–38. Finin notes that the American road-building project, particularly the Benguet Road, was a catalyst for community formation despite the abuses suffered by the workers at the hands of the foremen.

20. William H. Taft, in personal letter to Secretary of War Elihu Root, July 14, 1900, and from Taft Annual Report (November 15, 1903) as quoted in Resurreccion-Andrada, "Notes on the History of Camp John Hay," 31, 43. See also Reed, *City of Pines*, 89.

21. Corpuz, *The Colonial Iron Horse*, 155.

22. The average citizen was priced out: "The resort was of little value to the average citizen. The rail/bus fares to Baguio were extremely high. The 280 km. (174 mi.) trip itself was uncomfortable" (Halsema, *E. J. Halsema*, 171).

23. W. Cameron Forbes, "Notes on Early History of Baguio," reprinted from *Manila Daily Bulletin*, 1933: 3–4.

24. "As you ride over this road, you would never imagine the difficulties in the con-struction and maintenance of this road, owing to the torrential rains which cause great landslides. . . . Up to the present—with bridge improvements, widening, maintenance, and so forth—the cost of this strip of road is probably around five million dollars." Quoted in J. E. H. Stevenot, "Our Trip to Baguio and Return," 19.

25. Baguio, Philippines Summer Resort brochure of Manila-Baguio Train Service by Manila Railroad Company, 1928: 1.

26. From an anonymous travelogue written by a British traveler to the Philippines in 1924, "discovered" in London in 1977 and published in 1991: *In the Land of the Headhunters*, 23.

27. L. Wilson, *The Skyland of the Philippines*, 4–5.

28. Erlyn Alcantara interview.

29. This exposure paralleled, of course, the ways in which Igorot life and people had already been exhibited in the metropole in venues such as the 1904 St. Louis Columbian Exposition. See also Mitchell, *Colonising Egypt*, on the production of colonial space and ways of seeing.

30. Anonymous, *In the Land of the Headhunters*, 84.

31. Nakahara, "A Trip to the Philippines," 27.

32. Philippine Act No. 636 appropriated "a wide tract of land as a military reserva-tion" that eventually became Camp John Hay.

33. Reed, *City of Pines*, 137.

34. Reports of Philippine Commission and Forbes journals, 1904, 1913, as pointed out by Erlyn Alcantara and Patricia Afable, in untitled ms., n.d., 26.

35. Reed, *City of Pines*, xviii.

36. Ostelius, *Islands of Pleasure*, preface, 107.

37. Stephens, "Baguio: A Natural High," *Off Duty*, March 1979, 25.

38. Ibid.

39. Vizmanos, *Martial Law Diary and Other Papers*, 8.

40. Alcantara interview.

41. From "The City of Baguio" website, cityofpines.com/baguiokennon/kennon.html (accessed December 11, 2012).

42. Ibid.

43. Alcantara interview. See also Vincent Cabreza and Elmer Kristian Dauigoy, "5 Dead, 1 Hurt in Kennon Road Accident," *Inquirer.Net*, March 6, 2011; "Rains Trigger Landslides along Kennon Road in Benguet," GMA *News*, April 4, 2010.

44. de Villa, *Luzon by Car*, 95.

45. Bula-at, "Indigenous Women's Struggles."

46. Gonzalez, "Headhunter Itineraries."

47. Urry, *The Tourist Gaze*, 2–3.

48. On the particular focus in Hawai'i tourism on Native bodies, see Desmond, *Staging Tourism*.

49. "Army Activities Resulting in Benefits to the Territory of Hawaii."

50. Ibid., 9.

51. Bureau of Public Roads, "Report on Extension of National System of Interstate and Defense Highways within Alaska and Hawai'i."

52. Ibid.

53. Pushed through from start to finish by Dan Inouye — then congressman, later a perennial senator — the project was initially budgeted at a few hundred thousand dollars.

54. Other federally funded "interstates" on O'ahu are the following: (1) H-1, which connects the Hawai'i National Guard at Diamond Head to Barbers Point Naval Air Station, with off-ramps to Pearl Harbor and Hickam Air Force Bases; and (2) H-2, which links the Pearl Harbor/Hickam complex with Schofield Barracks in the middle of the island. See also the transcript of the documentary by Kubota, "H-3"; Hawai'i Department of Transportation, "Hawaii's Interstate H-3 Freeway"; and Highway Planning Commission, "Federal-Aid Highway System."

55. Hawai'i Department of Transportation, "Hawaii's Interstate H-3 Freeway," 2.

56. Hawai'i Department of Transportation, "Scenic Roads and Parkways Study."

57. Ibid., 1.

58. Ibid., 3.

59. Ibid., 4, 13.

60. Kubota, "H-3," 5–28; Hawai'i Department of Transportation, "Hawaii's Interstate H-3 Freeway," 2.

61. As a project, it pioneered the need for environmental impact statements that were designed to protect and preserve natural and cultural resources under the National Environmental Policy Act.

62. Near the end of the H-3's contentious litigation period, it set the precedent of having federal bodies overrule local processes for environmental protections and indigenous cultural sovereignty. See Coffman, "The H-3 Chapter in the Island Edge of America," and Ziegler, "Highway Wars."

63. Sanders, "H3."

64. The 1986 congressional testimony was a rare exception.

65. Gladys Pualoa interview.

66. Dawn Wasson interview.

67. Wasson interview.

68. Pualoa interview.

69. Ibid.

70. Grant, *Glen Grant's Chicken Skin Tales*, 157–60.

71. Gordon, *Ghostly Matters*.

72. Kameʻeleihiwa, *Native Land and Foreign Desires*.

73. Cruz, "From Resistance to Affirmation, We Are Who We Were," examines the contemporary Hawaiian sovereignty movement with attention to history.

74. Coffman's account of the H-3 fight notes that this was not the first time that the anti-H-3 coalition had used this line of argument: the archaeological site in contention had been initially discovered in 1982, but at that time the sovereignty movement had focused its efforts on reclaiming the island of Kahoʻolawe from navy bombing.

75. Pualoa interview.

76. Desmond, *Staging Tourism*, 4.

77. Governor Ben Cayetano, quoted in Hawaiʻi Department of Transportation, "Hawaii's Interstate H-3 Freeway," ii.

78. Hawaiʻi Department of Transportation, "Hawaii's Interstate H-3 Freeway," 3.

79. Brasswell, "Pride and Partnership," 2.

80. Hawaiʻi Department of Transportation, "Hawaii's Interstate H-3 Freeway," 4; Sanders "H3," 2.

81. Sanders, "H3," 2.

82. Ibid.

83. Brasswell, "Pride and Partnership," 4.

84. Hawaiʻi Department of Transportation, "Hawaii's Interstate H-3 Freeway," ii.

85. Ray Bert, "Paradise Crossed," *Civil Engineering Magazine*—ASCE 68:7 (July 1998): 42.

86. Helen Altonn and Pat Omandam, "H-3 Gets Green Light Today," *Honolulu Star-Bulletin*, December 12, 1997: 2.

87. Pualoa interview.

88. Bases Conversion Development Authority, "15 Years at the Forefront of Development: Creating New Engines of Growth," 2007 Annual Report, www.bcda.gov.ph/file_attachments/0000/0167/BCDA_AR_07.pdf (accessed December 12, 2012).

3. NEOLIBERATION AND U.S.-PHILIPPINES CIRCUITS OF SACRIFICE AND GRATITUDE

1. Flanagan, *Corregidor*; Breuer, *Retaking the Philippines*.

2. Santos, Hofmann, and Bulawan, "Prostitution and the Bases."

3. Following World War II and Philippine independence in 1946, the United States and the Philippines negotiated and signed the Military Bases Agreement, which essentially was a hundred-year lease that allowed the U.S. military to continue to occupy the Philippines. This was amended in 1966, with stipulations that the lease would run out in 1991.

4. For feminist critiques of the institutionalization of sex work by the military that look at the Philippines, see Enloe, *Bananas, Beaches, and Bases*, and Sturdevant, *Let the Good Times Roll*.

5. The proliferation of investor guides to Subic is an indicator of its changing status. Examples include Sycip, Gorres, Velayo and Company Research Division, *Doing Business in the Subic Special Economic and Freeport Zone* (Manila: Sycip Gorres Velayo & Company, 1995), and Joaquin Cunanan and Co., *Subic Bay Freeport, Philippines: A Guide for the Foreign and Local Investors* (Philippines: Joaquin Cunanan & Co./Price Waterhouse,1993).

6. See, for instance, Kirk and Okazawa-Rey, "Demilitarizing Security." See also Moon, *Sex among Allies*, which offers a detailed discussion of the Korean state's collusion with the U.S. military at the expense of the lives of Korean women dependent on base economies.

7. Frank G. Wisner, speech at the fiftieth anniversary commemoration of the fall of Corregidor, May 6, 1992, U.S. Information Service, American embassy, Manila, Philippines.

8. Tadiar, *Fantasy-Production*, 15.

9. Congressman Stanley Fish's speech is excerpted in the very short-lived journal *Bataan*, published in Washington, D.C., as "In the War: Bataan Remembered," *Bataan* 1:2 (May 1943): 7.

10. Frank Moss, statement, U.S. Information Service, American embassy, Manila, Philippines, December 7, 1962.

11. See Morris, *Corregidor*.

12. Diaz, "Deliberating 'Liberation Day,'" examines how "Liberation Day" celebrations in Guam reproduce feelings of obligations and continued dependence on U.S. military and economic hegemony.

13. See Boyce, *The Philippines*.

14. Lumbera, "From Colonizer to Liberator."

15. See the Subic Community website: www.sbma.com.

16. During Gordon's administration as mayor of Olongapo City, some of his more memorable slogans were "Bawal ang tamad sa Subic" (Lazy people are not allowed in Subic) and "Bawal ang tanga sa Subic" (Stupid people are not allowed in Subic).

17. A much-televised dramatic standoff between Gordon and a new appointee to head the Subic Bay Metropolitan Authority occurred during former president Joseph Estrada's term, in which Gordon barricaded himself and his supporters in a bid to keep his position at Subic, staging a patriarchal drama on the national media stage.

18. C. Kaplan, *Questions of Travel*.

19. Gonzalez, "Military Bases, 'Royalty Trips.'"

20. See Sturdevant, "Who Benefits?," which points out Richard Gordon's key role in disciplining the laboring bodies of Filipina workers during his stint as the head of the Subic Bay Metropolitan Authority.

21. Enloe, *Bananas, Beaches, and Bases*, 39.

22. For findings on the prostitution industry that cropped up in Olongapo and Angeles—the sites of Subic and Clark, respectively—see Hilsdon, *Madonnas and Martyrs*.

23. Tadiar, *Fantasy-Production*.

24. See Shalom, *The United States and the Philippines*.

25. Sergio Osmeña, as quoted in "Aircraft Carrier Bataan Signifies U.S. Pledge to Redeem Philippines," *Bataan* 1:9 (December 1943): 8.

26. Jose Besana, "America Must Take Filipinos into Its Heart, Romulo Says," *Bataan* 2:4 (July 1944): 9.

27. Carlos Bulosan, "Carlos Bulosan Urges Naming of Committee to Study Needs of Filipinos in United States," *Bataan* 2:2 (May 1944): 8.

28. Frank Church and Gale McGee, statement, U.S. Information Service, American embassy, Manila, Philippines, December 7, 1962.

29. Emmet O'Neal, statement, U.S. Information Service, American embassy, Manila, Philippines, October 12, 1964.

30. For American tourists as "unofficial ambassadors" to postwar Europe under Marshall Aid, see Endy, *Cold War Holidays*.

31. Klein, *Cold War Orientalism*. Harry W. Frantz argued that tourism would create "international goodwill and neighborliness," and convert planes from bombers to tourist transportation, aiding in state-level diplomacy. See "Manila Destined to Play Important Part in World-Wide Drama, Frantz Says," *Bataan* 2:4 (July 1944): 7.

32. Tadiar, *Fantasy-Production*, 27.

33. Miranda, *The Political Economy of ASEAN Development*.

34. Corregidor figures in Marcos's early years in two ways: first as a scandal that exposed his ambitions for a "garrison state" and second as a symbol of his soldierly brotherhood with the United States. The first, labeled the Jabidah Massacre, allegedly involved the mutiny and massacre of Muslim troops being secretly trained by Philippine and U.S. Special Forces personnel on Corregidor to recover the territory of Sabah from Malaysia, and the Marcos-ordered court-martial for the soldiers involved in the massacre, despite his key role in their training to begin with. This event marked the beginnings of opposition to Marcos, with Senator Benigno "Ninoy" Aquino charging that the purpose of these covert military operations on Corregidor was actually to "form the shock troops of his cherished garrison state." Conboy, *South-East Asian Special Forces*, 30; Aquino, *A Garrison State in the Make and Other Speeches*.

35. Hamilton-Paterson, *America's Boy*.

36. Goldstone, *Making the World Safe for Tourism*.

37. Diaz, "Deliberating 'Liberation Day.'" On World War II veteran commemorations and the transnational memories of the war, see White, "Remembering Guadalcanal."

38. Art Matibag interview.

39. Guerrero, "Hero Island Corregidor," *Freeman Magazine*, April 1993: 28–29.

40. Taylor, "Corregidor Revisited," *Mabuhay Magazine*, June 1991: 38–44.

41. Rates are based on a 2011 schedule.

42. Fujitani, White, and Yoneyama, "Introduction," in *Perilous Memories*, 5–6.

43. Armando Hildawa interview.

44. Matibag interview. This is a sentiment echoed by some of the guides I interviewed as well, who state that Corregidor is "more of a U.S. place than a Filipino place" (Stella Cordoba interview).

45. Cordoba interview.

46. Hildawa interview.

47. Corregidor Foundation, *Corregidor Island: Historical Treasures, Diverse Adventures*, brochure, n.d.

48. The small nurses' memorial is an exception that reflects a revisionist correction to Corregidor's masculine historiography.

49. Aluit, *Corregidor*, 125.

50. President Ferdinand Marcos, Pacific War Memorial plaque, June 24, 1968.

51. See Fujitani, White, and Yoneyama, "Introduction," in *Perilous Memories*, which addresses the alternative forms of periodization and spatialization of World War II in the region.

52. See Wexler, *Tender Violence*.

53. An article in the *Philippine Daily Inquirer*'s Sunday "Lifestyle" section gives an account of the nascent tourism on Corregidor, with a few digs at the irony of the Filipino-American Friendship Park: "Never mind if the colonizer has yet to fully honor the Filipino veterans' invaluable contributions to the war effort with a compensation package at par with their American comrades." See Alex Y. Vergara, "The Fall and Rise of Corregidor," *Philippine Daily Inquirer*, March 11, 2001: G-1, G-4.

54. Campomanes, "Casualty Figures of the American Soldier and the Other," 142.

55. See, for instance, Valor Tours, Ltd., a group based in California that caters to war-site enthusiasts.

56. After his release as a prisoner of war, he claimed to have returned to guerrilla fighting, although the veracity of his war narrative was increasingly questioned and exposed in the 1980s.

57. E. P. Romualdez, "The Shrine Stands," *Sunday Times Magazine*, October 3, 1971: 18–20.

58. The program includes a list of awardees of the Distinguished Conduct Star for "Gallantry in Action," which cites Lieutenant Ferdinand E. Marcos for his "conspicuous courage before an armed enemy and his intrepidity in the face of death."

59. Brokaw, *The Greatest Generation*.

60. Hawes, *The Philippine State and the Marcos Regime*; Bureau of National and Foreign Information, Philippines, *The Philippine Economy in the Mid-Seventies*.

61. See, e.g., "GABRIELA Says No to VFA," GABRIELA press release, February 13, 1998, members.tripod.com/~gabriela_p/6-pressreles/980213_vfa.html.

62. The Critical Filipina and Filipino Studies Collective, "The War against the People: U.S. Scholars Denounce Killings in the Philippines and Calls for a World-Wide Action," March 28, 2005, www.habi-arts.org/articles/article.php?id=8 (accessed October 4, 2012).

63. Hilsdon, *Madonnas and Martyrs*, 96–97.

64. "US Marines 'Raped Filipina Woman,'" BBC News, November 3, 2005, http://news.bbc.co.uk/2/hi/asia-pacific/4403134.stm (accessed November 17, 2005).

65. Burgonio and Contreras, "6 US Marines Held for Rape," *Inquirer News Service*, November 4, 2005.

66. For more detail on these rape cases, see, e.g., Lacsamana, *Revolutionizing Feminism*.

67. Rosca, "Rape Case Exposes U.S. Domination of Philippine Government."
68. Task Force Subic Rape, "Rape and the VFA," briefing paper, 2006: 1–8.

4. REMEMBERING PEARL HARBOR, REINFORCING VIGILANCE

1. See Valene L. Smith's study of the interrelationship between war and tourism, "War and Tourism," and Weaver, "Tourism and the Military."
2. According to the U.S. Navy website, the goal of programs such as the Distinguished Visitors Program is to "increase awareness of the Navy's mission and highlight the tremendous service of our people" to help support a robust military budget, www.navy.mil/navydata/nav_legacy.asp?id=165; Eugene R. Fidell, president of the National Institute of Military Justice, states that these kinds of programs "absolutely [have] to do with funding weapons programs." Quoted in John Kifner, "Despite Sub Inquiry, Navy Still Sees Need for Guests on Ships," *New York Times*, April 23, 2001.
3. On Oʻahu, 85,718 acres out of 382,148 "belong" to the military. In the islands as a whole, the U.S. military's "partnership in aloha" helps to secure 5.7 percent of the total land area of Hawaiʻi. Ocean territory is also included, although usually not noted. Data are from Kajihiro, "A Brief Overview of Militarization and Resistance in Hawaiʻi."
4. On how national history is refracted through Hawaiʻi-specific locales such as museums, burial sites, films, and war memorials, see Ireland, *The U.S. Military in Hawaiʻi*.
5. On the competing cultures of commemoration between the United States and Japan in the Mariana islands, see Camacho, *Cultures of Commemoration*.
6. The Valor in the Pacific National Monument was established in 2008 by President George W. Bush and encompasses other sites in California and Alaska. To avoid confusion with this larger entity, I will refer to Hawaiʻi's portion of the monument as the Pearl Harbor military-tourism complex.
7. On the nationalism of American historiographies of the Pacific War, see T. Fujitani, White, and Yoneyama, "Introduction," in *Perilous Memories*.
8. See, for instance, Osorio, "Memorializing Puʻuloa and Remembering Pearl Harbor," which recounts Native epistemologies that illustrate Pearl Harbor's colonial naming and military occupation as part of the process of Native Hawaiian dispossession.
9. The 2008 dedication of the World War II Valor in the Pacific National Monument occurred on December 5, just a few days short of another Pearl Harbor Day.
10. With the renovation of the entire complex, the ways in which these sites are now packaged as a bundle—whereby the free admission tickets for the *Arizona* Memorial must now be procured at the same place as the paid tickets for the auxiliary attractions—suggest that it is being marketed along the lines of a broader historical "park" experience.
11. On death and tourism, see Goss, "The Souvenir and Sacrifice in the Tourist Mode of Consumption"; Lennon and Foley, *Dark Tourism*; and Lippard, "Tragic Tourism," in *On the Beaten Track*.

12. For a cinematic explanation of white masculine melodrama in cinema, see Eagle, "Making a Spectacle of Himself."

13. See also Goss, "'From Here to Eternity.'"

14. For multiculturalism and the military, see McAlister, *Epic Encounters*.

15. One park ranger noted that she received questions about why Japanese tourists came to the memorial because it was clearly a site that had U.S. perspectives in mind. Sheryl Broderick interview.

16. See Stannard, *Honor Killing*, for an in-depth history of race in 1930s Hawai'i.

17. Benjamin, "Theses on the Philosophy of History," 255.

18. See Kosasa, "Searching for the 'C' Word."

19. See, e.g., Mills, *A Trip through Hawaii's Military History*.

20. Ali, Ferguson, and Turnbull, "Rethinking the Military in Hawaii." Military strategists such as J. G. Walker (rear-admiral, U.S. Navy) argued that a naval station in the Hawaiian islands was "an absolute necessity, as it would give our Government the command of the Pacific." United States Navy Department, "Letter from the Acting Secretary of the Navy, in response to Senate resolution of January 19, 1895, transmitting reports of the preliminary survey of Pearl Harbor, Hawaiian Islands," executive document no. 42, Fifty-Third Congress, third session, Washington, D.C., 1895.

21. Ali, Ferguson, and Turnbull, "Rethinking the Military in Hawaii," and Vanbrackle, "Pearl Harbor from the First Mention of 'Pearl Lochs' to Its Present Day Usage," 1–6. Schofield's report urged the United States to treat with the Hawaiian kingdom for a cession of Pearl Harbor "deeded free of cost" in exchange for the removal of tariffs on Hawaiian sugar in the U.S. market, which was eventually solidified through the Reciprocity Treaty of 1887 (Stickney, "Early History of Pearl Harbor," 2–4). Kajihiro names the officers in "The Militarizing of Hawai'i."

22. Slackman, *Remembering Pearl Harbor*, 11. In response to an annexation attempt by Great Britain, Judd asked the naval officers of the USS *Constitution* to assess Honolulu's defenses against "foreign aggression" and received an answer that pointed out the "vast importance" of Pearl Harbor. A hydrographic and topographic survey completed and published in 1875 "produced a profound impression upon the government at Washington" and urged "the adoption of some measure through which the islands might pass to the control of the United States" (Vanbrackle, "Pearl Harbor from the First Mention of 'Pearl Lochs' to Its Present Day Usage," 8). See also the Department of the Navy Naval Historical Center, "The U.S. Navy in Hawai'i, 1826–1945: An Administrative History," a website that refers to a letter from Lieutenant F. W. Curtis to Dr. C. P. Judd, the Hawaiian Minister of Foreign Affairs, Department of the Navy Naval Historical Center, Washington, D.C., www.history.navy.mil/docs.wwii/pearl/hawaii-2.htm (accessed December 14, 2012).

23. Stevens, *American Expansion in Hawai'i 1842–1898*, 188. Queen Lili'uokalani's diary entry was from September 26, 1887.

24. Prior to this, repetitions of "rescue" and "aid" had already been played out with Pearl Harbor's strategic importance as a backdrop. In 1874, U.S. Marines landed and arrested demonstrators who were supporting the election of Queen Emma in

her race with David Kalākaua. See Turnbull and Ferguson, *Oh, Say, Can You See?*, 103, and Ali, Ferguson, and Turnbull, "Rethinking the Military in Hawaii," 2.

25. Vanbrackle, "Pearl Harbor from the First Mention of 'Pearl Lochs' to Its Present Day Usage," 13–14.

26. White, "Moving History," 710. White argues that despite the differences between the old and new films, they both "represent variants of a common national 'mytho-history'" (723).

27. By the film's end, American "mytho-history" is flexible enough to stretch its embrace to the enemy portrayed so ruthlessly. Japan's defeat, its protracted postwar militarization and occupation by the United States, the fact that the military installation it currently hosts in Okinawa is one of the biggest in Asia, and its continued international collaboration with the United States—these points all operate to momentarily abstract Japan's World War II role as the enemy. On other controversial memorializations of World War II sites and artifacts, see Yoneyama, "For Transformative Knowledge and Postnationalist Public Spheres," and Boyer, "Whose History Is It Anyway?"

28. Slackman, *Remembering Pearl Harbor*, 66.

29. Lenihan, *Submerged Cultural Resources Study*, suggests that "without the dead aboard, the site would be less compelling—empty memorials do not have the drawing power of tombs" (178).

30. Dan Inouye, the same politician who secured the pork-barrel funds for the construction of the H-3, also acquired the funding for the visitor center.

31. There was a 300 percent rise in the numbers of people visiting the *Arizona* Memorial between 1962 and 1976: from 178,872 to 585,953 (Slackman, *Remembering Pearl Harbor*, 83).

32. On the memorialization of key wars to formation of national identity and myths, see Mayo, *Memorials and Political Landscape*.

33. Delgado, "Recovering the Past of USS *Arizona*," 77.

34. Marilyn Nelson interview.

35. White, "Moving History," 742.

36. Indeed, with the past of the United States and its continued military occupation of various Asian and Pacific sites, Asians and Pacific Islanders have already experienced the kind of U.S. militaristic ideology that they consume at the *Arizona* Memorial and, in many ways, have already been recruited into U.S. military geographies.

37. USS *Bowfin* Submarine Museum and Park website, www.bowfin.org.

38. Brandon Bosworth, "Commanding the Mighty Mo," *Midweek*, December 3, 2008; Olena Heu, "Mighty Mo Celebrates 4 Millionth Visitor," KHON, www.khon2 .com/news/local/story/Mighty-Mo-celebrates-4-millionth-visitor/quC_pC -7mEytqGEpCJG71g.cspx?rss=1803 (accessed December 14, 2012).

39. Based on the 2011 fee schedule. The battleship tour is forty-five dollars.

40. From the USS *Missouri* Memorial website, www.ussmissouri.com.

41. USS *Missouri* Memorial Association, Battleship *Missouri* Overnight Encampment Program Guide, Honolulu, n.d. The program was made possible initially

with funding from the Hawai'i Tourism Authority, and it hosts over seventeen thousand children from around Hawai'i every year in its broader educational programs.

42. Since it was decommissioned for the second time in 1992, removed from the navy's ship registry, and donated by the navy to the nonprofit USS *Missouri* Memorial Association in 1998, the Mighty Mo has risen again as a popular tourist destination.

43. The quotes are from the website, but the guides often point out this targeting power.

44. "Japan Defense Chief: 'It Is Outrageous,'" *Honolulu Star-Bulletin* (online edition), February 16, 2001, archives.starbulletin.com/2001/02/16/news/story1.html (accessed December 14, 2012); "Navy Tightens Rules on Civilians Aboard Subs," *Honolulu Star-Bulletin* (online edition), February 16, 2001; "Families View *Ehime Maru* Debris," *Honolulu Star-Bulletin* (online edition), February 16, 2001; Gregg K. Kakesako, "Inquiry Focuses on *Ehime Maru* Location Data," *Honolulu Star-Bulletin* (online edition), March 6, 2001, archives.starbulletin.com/2001/03/06/news/index .html (accessed December 14, 2012); Gregg K. Kakesako, "Waddle Gets Reprimand, but Is Allowed to Retire," *Honolulu Star-Bulletin* (online edition), April 24, 2001, archives.starbulletin.com/2001/04/24/news/story4.html (accessed December 14, 2012).

45. Kakesako, "Inquiry Focuses on *Ehime Maru* Location Data." See also the website for the Pacific Fleet, www.cpf.navy.mil.

46. See Paik and Mander, *The Superferry Chronicles*.

47. See Turnbull and Ferguson's chapter 6 on Daniel Inouye, in *Oh, Say, Can You See?* The quotes are from a KHON June 18, 2008, airing of Hawai'i Star's Special *Plumeria and Steel: Partnership in Aloha* preceded by a "Fit to Fight" segment on the naval shipyard's history (essentially an extended infomercial on the military), which was hosted by local news anchors who conclude, after showing the community volunteerism of military troops, that "the military plays a positive role in our state."

5. THE MACHINE IN THE GARDEN

Thanks to Jonna Eagle, who suggested the title of Leo Marx's seminal work on technology and the American pastoral for this chapter.

1. T. C.'s helicopter, the Hughes 500D, was the civilian version of the OH-6 military helicopter. See "Civil, Military Demands Spur Helicopter Growth Surge," *Aviation Week & Space Technology*, September 29, 1975: 30.

2. Magnum is a former Navy SEAL and Office of Naval Intelligence officer and T. C. is a former Marine helicopter pilot; the other two are an ex-marine door gunner and an ex–British Army sergeant major and intelligence officer.

3. The show won two Emmys (thirteen nominations), two Golden Globes (eleven nominations), one Edgar, and six People's Choice Awards. The final episode was watched by 50.7 million viewers, and remains one of the most watched television finales of all time. It has been in syndication in many foreign markets since its original run.

4. In the case of *Hawaii Five-O*, the usual villains were Cold War international secret agents or organized crime syndicates.

5. Virilio, *War and Cinema*, 104.

6. Kaplan, "Mobility and War," 406.

7. United States General Accounting Office, "Defense Acquisitions," 1.

8. See Hauʻofa's "Our Sea of Islands" for a critique and counternarrative of how Pacific Islands are seen as insignificant.

9. Marx, *The Machine in the Garden*.

10. Blackmore, "Rotor Hearts," 94.

11. Marx, *The Machine in the Garden*, 343.

12. Scholars of journalism and war have challenged the conventional narrative of the media as a major contributor to the domestic antiwar sentiment that derailed the U.S. war effort in Southeast Asia. See, e.g., Hallin, *The "Uncensored War,"* and Sherer, "Vietnam War Photos and Public Opinion."

13. For more on Vietnam and news media coverage, see Berg, "Losing Vietnam."

14. The most famous photograph, taken by United Press International photographer Hubert van Es, was mislabeled then, and subsequently, as taking place at the U.S. embassy in Saigon rather than at an apartment building that happened to be the resident of CIA and USAID agents. See R. Chiles, *The God Machine*, 190.

15. See Blackmore, "Rotor Hearts."

16. The interest of the U.S. military in helicopter technology was piqued after successful World War II operations in Burma, China, and the South Pacific but finally "took off" with the development of turbine power (Chiles, *The God Machine*, 150, 157–59).

17. Leary, *Perilous Missions*; Robbins, *Air America*. See also Dickey Chapelle, "Helicopter War in South Viet Nam," *National Geographic*, November 1962: 722. Air America used both planes and helicopters.

18. Chinnery, *Vietnam*, 6–7; Chiles, *The God Machine*, 161.

19. Chinnery, *Vietnam*, 58. American military interests and investment in developing helicopter technology began shortly after World War I (Chiles, *The God Machine*, 62).

20. Chiles, *The God Machine*, 150.

21. Mason, *Chickenhawk*.

22. As quoted in Chiles, *The God Machine*, 161.

23. Richard Pyle, "Saigon Quartet," *Vanity Fair* online, December 1999, www.vanityfair .com/magazine/archive/1999/12/burrows199912 (accessed December 14, 2012). See also Chapelle, "Helicopter War in South Viet Nam," 722.

24. Chiles, *The God Machine*, 172, 192. See also Ralph Blumenthal, "U.S. Copter Pilots Taking Some of Worst Fire of War," *New York Times*, February 12, 1973, and Gross, *Rattler One-Seven*, 42.

25. Berg, "Losing Vietnam."

26. Jack Raymond, "It's a Dirty War for Correspondents, Too," *New York Times Magazine*, February 13, 1966. On the 1971 incident, see Pyle, "Saigon Quartet."

27. Virilio, *War and Cinema*, 1.

28. Chiles, *The God Machine*, 190–92; "Saigon Copter Lands on Another in Stampede to U.S. Ship's Deck," *New York Times*, April 30, 1975.

29. On Vietnam in television and film, see Anderegg, *Inventing Vietnam*.

30. Michael Klein, in "Cultural Narrative and the Process of Re-collection: Film, History and the Vietnam Era," notes that Hollywood took up Vietnam in the postwar era, having produced only John Wayne's *The Green Berets* (1968) during the war, exorcising its demons through film. See also Novelli, "Hollywood and Vietnam," and Muse, *The Land of Nam*. The proliferation of memoirs of Vietnam veteran memoirs also led to a robust narrative presence of helicopter pilots. See, in addition to the ones already cited above, Flanagan, *Vietnam above the Treetops*, and Ballentine, *Gunbird Driver*.

31. In addition to the panoply of independent and studio films on the Vietnam War, including those just mentioned, in the 1990s a small body of documentaries focused on the helicopter experience, such as *Of Heroes and Helicopters: The Life and Times of the Helicopter Pilot in Vietnam* (1993) and *Wings over Vietnam* (1998).

32. Virilio, *War and Cinema*, 34; italics in original.

33. Rowe, "'Bringing It All Back Home,'" 212. See also Turner, *Echoes of Combat*, for an account of how the war affects the American psyche.

34. Mark Thompson, "Why Flying Choppers in Afghanistan Is So Deadly," *Time.com*, September 27, 2009. Some video footage is included on Internet news sites, supplementing text with visual images, such as in Karen DeYoung and Ernesto Londono, "Nine U.S. Troops Killed in Helicopter Crash in Afghanistan," *Washington Post*, September 21, 2010.

35. W. J. Hennigan and Ralph Vartabedian, "Bin Laden Raid Reveals Another Elusive Target: A Stealth Helicopter," *Los Angeles Times*, May 7, 2011; Ray Rivera, Alissa J. Rubin, and Thom Shanker, "Copter Downed by Taliban Fire: Elite U.S. Unit among Them," *New York Times*, August 6, 2011. Several scholars have commented on the reanimation of Native American icons as in code names for U.S. military targets (such as "Geronimo" for the Bin Laden mission). The use of helicopters—which have often been named after Native American nations and tribes—compounds the irony. See the next chapter for "using Indians to fight Indians."

36. Helicopter tours on Kaua'i have fairly generic flight paths. Today, most leave from the Lihue Airport helipad, fly along the Hoary Head Mountain Range to Hanapepe Valley, home to waterfalls and tropical rainforests. They then hover over Olokele and Waimea Canyons, the latter of which features Wai'alae Falls and the Alaka'i Swamp. The Na Pali coast is next, followed by the Hanalei Bay and a small detour through Princeville, a high-end resort area, before heading to the Mount Wai'ale'ale Crater ("the wettest spot on Earth"), and Wailua Falls and finally back to Lihue.

37. Island Helicopter tours brochure, Blue Hawaiian Helicopter brochure, Jack Harter Helicopters brochure, circa 2007–8.

38. Paul Proctor, "Hawaii Helicopter Tours Rebound after Gulf War Dip," *Air Transport* 135:13 (September 30, 1991): 35.

39. State of Hawai'i Department of Business, Economic Development, and Tourism, "Majority of Visitors Call Their Hawai'i Experience Excellent," October 18, 2007.

40. Proctor, "Hawaii Helicopter Tours," 35.

41. Lucy Jokiel, "Kaua'i's Unfriendly Skies," *Hawai'i Business*, July 1, 1987, www

.highbeam.com/doc/1G1–5124077.html (accessed December 14, 2012); James T. Yenckel, "The Downside of Going Up," *Washington Post*, December 17, 1989.

42. State of Hawai'i Department of Transportation, Airports Division, Hawai'i Aviation website, hawaii.gov/hawaiiaviation/hawaii-airfields-airports/kauai/lihue-airport (accessed December 14, 2012).

43. F. Kenneth Stokes, "Choppers Still Safe Despite Deaths," *Honolulu Advertiser*, April 13, 2007.

44. Wood, *Displacing Natives*; Desmond, *Staging Tourism*.

45. Williamson, "Woman Is an Island."

46. See, e.g., typical prose such as "SHE'S ALMOND-EYED, honey-skinned and raven-haired. She glides up to you and slips a fragrant lei of vividly colored flowers around your neck. . . . 'Aloha,' she murmurs. She doesn't so much say it as sigh it" (Sid Fassler, "Paradise Awaits Kauai's Visitors," *Globe and Mail*, October 6, 1984).

47. H. Trask, *From a Native Daughter*, 136–37.

48. County of Kaua'i website, www.kauai-hawaii.com. This text is often lifted and used by other tourist-oriented businesses on the island.

49. "The Garden Isle Kaua'i: A Journey of Discovery," *Pleasant Hawai'i Magazine*, March–April 2008.

50. Jerry Hulse, "Traveling in Style: A Primal Piece of Paradise," *Los Angeles Times*, March 19, 1989.

51. "Introduction," *101 Things to Do on Kauai*, February–June 2003.

52. Robert Trumbull, "What's Doing on Hawaii's Neighbor Islands," *New York Times*, December 19, 1982.

53. County of Kaua'i 2010 County Demographics, www.kauai.gov. This number includes Hawaiians who are part Native.

54. Baptiste, "Message from the Mayor," in "Kaua'i—Hawaii's Island of Discovery," Discover Kaua'i—Official Tourism Site of the Island of Kaua'i, www.kauai-hawaii .com/mayorspage.html (accessed April 19, 2004).

55. As a sugar plantation island, Kaua'i was the site of the infamous 1924 Hanapepe massacre, a deadly confrontation between Kaua'i police and striking plantation workers.

56. Charles Lockwood, "Kauai: Hawaii's Own Garden of Eden," *Christian Science Monitor*, March 18, 1986.

57. Jack Harter ad in *101 Things to Do on Kauai*, February–June 2003.

58. "Uniquely Kauai," *101 Things to Do on Kauai*, February–June 2003.

59. Janne Apelgren and Christopher Reynolds, "I Love the Sound of Choppers in the Morning," *Sunday Age*, November 28, 1993.

60. Hawai'i has appeared in films since the earliest Edison photographers passed through Honolulu on their way to film the Spanish-American War in the Philippines in 1898. For other films that established Hawai'i in popular cinematic culture, see *From Here to Eternity* (dir. Fred Zinnerman, 1953), *South Pacific* (dir. Joshua Logan, 1958), *In Harm's Way* (dir. Otto Preminger, 1965), *Hawaii* (dir. George Roy Hill, 1966), and *Tora! Tora! Tora!* (dir. Richard Fleischer, Kinji Fukasaku and Toshio Masuda, 1970).

61. See, e.g., Elvis Presley's *Blue Hawaii* (1961) and *Paradise, Hawaiian Style* (1966).

See Wood, *Displacing Natives*, Wilson, *Reimagining the American Pacific*, and Ireland, *The U.S. Military in Hawai'i*, for studies of Hawai'i in film.

62. Incidentally, *South Pacific* was filmed in Kaua'i.
63. George Cruys, "'Coptering Kauai," *Pacific Travel News*, October 1982.
64. Blackmore, "Rotor Hearts," 94.
65. The most popular music are songs or scores associated with Hawai'i films (such as Disney's 2002 *Lilo and Stitch*, or *Raiders of the Lost Ark*) or by recognizable Hawai'i artists (such as Israel Kamakawiwo'ole).
66. The description of the tour is a composite narrative built from actual and recorded tours that I went on in 2008, and video samples from company websites.
67. For an indigenous genealogy of this area, see Andrade, *Hā'ena*.
68. Reasoner, "During the Viet Nam War," www.nixwebs.com/Search9/helitac/harry reasoner.htm.
69. As quoted in Lucy Jokiel, "Kaua'i's Unfriendly Skies," *Hawai'i Business*, July 1, 1987, www.highbeam.com/doc/1G1-5124077.html (accessed December 14, 2012).
70. "Uniquely Kauai," *101 Things to Do on Kauai*, February–June 2003. Safari Tours, Sunshine Helicopters, and Blue Hawaiian Tours are among those that tout the military experience of their pilots and mechanics.
71. Blue Hawaiian Helicopters brochure.
72. Safari Helicopter tour brochure. The same text is repeated in print ads.
73. Cook, *Kaua'i, The Garden Island*, 109.
74. "Policy Recommendations of Tour Helicopters," Kauai Helicopter–community Relations Project Report, Kaua'i, Hawai'i, July 1988.
75. James Gilden, "Copter Crashes Put Focus on Sightseeing Tour Safety," *Los Angeles Times*, March 25, 2007; Associated Press, "Hawai'i: Kauai Helicopter Crash Kills 4," *Los Angeles Times*, March 9, 2007.
76. "Breaking News—Kauai Copter Crash: The Most Dangerous Place for Whirlybirds on Earth," Hawaiirama Website, March 2007, hawaiirama.com/2007/03/breaking-news-kauai-copter-cra (accessed June 15, 2011).
77. Safari helicopters brochure, emphasis mine.
78. "Introduction," *101 Things to Do on Kauai*, February–June 2003.
79. See Kaplan and Kelly, "Dead Reckoning."
80. Kelly and Quintal, "Cultural History Report of Makua Military Reservation and Vicinity," 38–39.
81. Lind, "The Captive Valley of Makua," 8–9.
82. Kelly and Quintal, "Cultural History Report of Makua Military Reservation and Vicinity," 45–46.
83. Ibid., 46.
84. "Final Environmental Impact Statement: Military Training Activities at Mākua Valley Reservation, Hawai'i," U.S. Army Environmental Command, Aberdeen Proving Ground, MD & U.S. Army Corps of Engineers, Honolulu Engineer District, June 2009, ES-3, 2–38–49.
85. Virilio, *War and Cinema*, 26; italics in the original.
86. Protect Kaho'olawe 'Ohana website, www.kahoolawe.org.
87. "Hyland Says Navy Needs Kahoolawe," *Honolulu Advertiser*, October 31, 1969.

In the article, Admiral John Hyland, the commander of the U.S. Pacific Fleet, is quoted as saying that "it's the only place around anywhere that is suitable. I think the island is of very little use for anything else."

88. "Navy May Spend $2 Million on Kahoolawe 'Bomb Island,'" *Honolulu Advertiser*, March 13, 1964.

89. Protect Kahoʻolawe ʻOhana website, www.kahoolawe.org; Lyle Nelson, "Kahoolawe Test to Simulate Nuclear Blast," *Honolulu Star-Bulletin*, December 21, 1964; "Atomic-Age Navy Tests Its Strength," *Honolulu Star-Bulletin*, May 21, 1966; "Kahoolawe Isle under Heavy Marine Fire," *Honolulu Star-Bulletin*, April 4, 1967.

90. Harry Moskos, "A Visit to Kahoolawe," *Honolulu Star-Bulletin*, August 28, 1968; "Navy Calls Operation Sailor Hat a Rocking Success," *Honolulu Star-Bulletin*, June 24, 1965.

91. Blackford, *Pathways to the Present*.

92. "Navy Bombers Rattle Mauians," *Honolulu Star-Bulletin*, January 8, 1969; "Navy Still Trying to Ease Problem," *Sunday Advertiser, Star-Bulleting & Advertiser*, March 30, 1969.

93. "Admiral Says Navy Needs Target Isle," *Honolulu Advertiser*, January 14, 1969.

94. See Lind, "The Captive Valley of Makua."

95. Jan Tenbruggencate, "Tour of Kahoolawe Turns Up Some Predictions," *Honolulu Advertiser*, June 8, 1970.

96. Keith Haugen, "Carvalho Wants to Build Kahoolawe County Park," *Honolulu Star-Bulletin*, June 8, 1970; "Kahoolawe's Promise" (editorial), *Honolulu Advertiser*, June 9, 1970.

97. Kahoʻolawe Island Reserve Commission website, kahoolawe.hawaii.gov.

98. Ibid.

99. Dorrance, "The U.S. Army on Kauaʻi, 1909–1942."

100. Bui, "When the Forest Became the Enemy," 11–55.

101. See the United States Department of Veteran Affairs website for a more complete list of Agent Orange test sites, www.publichealth.va.gov.

102. Beverly Deepe Keever, "University Vulnerable to Pitfalls of Secret Experiments," (editorial), *Star Bulletin.com*, Sunday March 27, 2005, archives.starbulletin.com /2005/03/27/editorial/specia12.html (accessed December 14, 2012).

103. Motooka et al., "Control of Hawaiian Jungle with Aerially Applied Herbicide," 18. The Esteron Brush Killer tested in these experiments was made up of a mixture of 2,4-dichlorophenoxyacetic acid, which makes up Agent Orange.

104. Suehisa et al., "Defoliation of Tropical Jungle Vegetation in Hawaii." However, the fact that bulldozers and other vehicles used for trail cutting were able to access the plots and mark them for tagging belies this rationale.

105. Suehisa et al., "Defoliation of Tropical Jungle Vegetation in Hawaii," 60.

106. The aptly but chillingly named Operation Ranch Hand ran from 1962 to 1971.

107. Beverly Deepe Keever, "University Vulnerable to Pitfalls of Secret Experiments" (editorial), *Star Bulletin.com*, Sunday March, 27, 2005, archives.starbulletin. com/2005/03/27/editorial/specia12.html (accessed December 14, 2012). See also Bettie Wallace, "Agent Orange: Men Sprayed in Kauai Tests," *Ka Leo O Hawaiʻi*, February 3, 1986, which is the original breaking news story from the University of

Hawai'i's student newspaper, which tracks the tragic result of the testing on participating UH employees and the subsequent illegal storage of the chemicals after the experiment.

6. PLAYING SOLDIER AND GOING NATIVE

All translations from Tagalog are mine.

1. See Teaiwa, "Militarism, Tourism and the Native."
2. Roberto Reyes, "Rainforest Trek in Subic," *Mabuhay Magazine*, August 1993, 31–34.
3. The filmic Rambo originally hails from the David Morrell novels about a seventeen-year-old American sent to fight in the Vietnam War.
4. It is no accident that Leonardo DiCaprio's character in the ecotourism adventure film *The Beach* also takes on military aspects when he "goes rogue" on a tropical island.
5. Bederman, *Manliness and Civilization*. For scholarship on the Vietnam War's damage to and the subsequent rehabilitation of American manhood, see Faludi, *Stiffed*, and Jeffords, *The Remasculinization of America*.
6. Robert H. Reid, "Former US Marine Instructors Now Instructing Tourists," *Philippine Star*, August 17, 1994.
7. Mowforth and Munt, *Tourism and Sustainability*, 1.
8. deKadt, *Tourism*.
9. Banerjee, "Who Sustains Whose Development?"
10. Mies and Shiva, *Ecofeminism*, 264–65.
11. Bandy, "Managing the Other of Nature," 560.
12. Deloria, *Playing Indian*.
13. Navajo, or Diné peoples, were culturally matrilocal and traditionally a hunter/ gatherer, not a warrior, society.
14. It is worth noting that the Navajo and their language were particularly militarized through their code work in World War II.
15. Dunlay, *Wolves for the Blue Soldiers*.
16. Heidler and Heidler, *Indian Removal*; Wallace, *The Long Bitter Trail*.
17. Bederman, *Manliness and Civilization*; Haraway, "Teddy Bear Patriarchy," 35.
18. Roosevelt, *Theodore Roosevelt*, 62. Italics in original.
19. Pratt, *Imperial Eyes*.
20. Drinnon, *Facing West*.
21. Gedacht, "'Mohammedan Religion Made It Necessary to Fire.'"
22. Kramer, *The Blood of Government*, points out that racist taxonomies were not cleanly relocated from one site to another and that new contexts made for unfamiliar realities of race, and thus newly invented racial models (29, 102–4, 124–30, 139, 144–45).
23. Drinnon, *Facing West*, 299.
24. Quoted in ibid., 288.
25. Mojares, *The War against the Americans*. See also Rodriguez, *Suspended Apocalypse*, on the American colonial roots of Filipino genocide as the condition of Filipino American identity.

26. Meixsel, "American Exceptionalism in Colonial Forces?," 163. Meixsel estimates that 75 percent of the 4,165 Americans who died had perished from disease.
27. Linn, "The US Army and Nation Building and Pacification in the Philippines," 85.
28. They were supervised, of course, by white American commissioned officers. Silbey, *A War of Frontier and Empire*, 113–14; Linn, *The Philippine War, 1899–1902*, 128.
29. Quoted in Holman, "Seminole Negro Indians, Macabebes, and Civilian Irregulars," 29.
30. Campbell, "'Making Riflemen from Mud.'"
31. Holman, "Seminole Negro Indians, Macabebes, and Civilian Irregulars," 30.
32. Linn, *The U.S. Army and Counterinsurgency in the Philippine War, 1899–1902*, 25, 50.
33. The exact official status of the scouts was never clear. Scouts who had served for long periods were denied pensions upon retirement, reflecting this ambivalence toward native troops.
34. Kramer, *The Blood of Government*, 114.
35. Linn, *The U.S. Army and Counterinsurgency in the Philippine War, 1899–1902*, 110.
36. Linn, *Guardians of Empire*, 14, 23. See Hoganson, *Fighting for American Manhood*, on the gender politics leading to and structuring the Philippine-American War.
37. Abinales, "An American Colonial State."
38. Finin, *The Making of the Igorot*, 49–50.
39. Kramer, *The Blood of Government*, notes that pitting people from the Mountain Region against the "lowlanders" who tended to be Tagalog played into historic divisions and enmities among different Filipino people, and presented a domestic army to battle possible Tagalog insurrection.
40. Befitting their status as "auxiliary" or "irregulars," their position vis-à-vis the regular army was never clearly articulated, and benefits and pensions for which U.S. troops were eligible did not extend to Filipinos.
41. Hawai'i also had its own Colonial Army.
42. The Philippine Scouts were fully incorporated into the Regular Army in 1920, according to Campbell, "'Making Riflemen from Mud,'" 3. The Philippine Scouts, however, were not treated equally and were paid less than their American counterparts. See Linn, *Guardians of Empire*, 245.
43. Kramer, *The Blood of Government*, 320–21.
44. Kerkvliet, *The Huk Rebellion*; Entenberg, "Agrarian Reform and the Hukbalahap."
45. Newton, "The Seeds of Surrogate Warfare."
46. Wong, "Pursuing the Soldier-Rebels," 12–13.
47. Gobrin and Andin, "Development Conflict," 6.
48. Wong, "Pursuing the Soldier-Rebels," 13.
49. Quoted in Young, *The Vietnam Wars*, 82.
50. The Philippines served as a filmic location for Vietnam War films, most famously *Platoon* and *Apocalypse Now*.
51. Graciano Duero interview.
52. See also Salvador Dimain's interview in Shimizu, *Orphans of Pinatubo*, 318–28.
53. Salvador Dimain in Shimizu, *Orphans of Pinatubo*, 318.
54. Lunesto Bulatao interview.

55. Bulatao interview.
56. Duero interview.
57. Monico Dimain interview.
58. Salvador Dimain in Shimizu, *Orphans of Pinatubo*, 318.
59. Ibid., 319.
60. Duero interview.
61. Salvador Dimain in Shimizu, *Orphans of Pinatubo*, 319.
62. Duero interview.
63. Newton, "The Seeds of Surrogate Warfare," 3–4.
64. Juan Denito interview, 2007.
65. Julio Denito interview.
66. Juan Denito interview, 2007.
67. Alfredo Viernes interview.
68. Dimain interview.
69. Julio Denito interview; Bulatao interview.
70. Juan Denito interview, 2007.
71. Viernes interview. Eighty thousand houses were damaged and eight thousand were totally destroyed. More than one hundred thousand people had to evacuate, and damage in millions of dollars was caused by the eruption (Shimizu, *Orphans of Pinatubo*, xi). The death toll numbers around five hundred (Brillantes, "The Philippines in 1991").
72. Salvador Dimain in Shimizu, *Orphans of Pinatubo*, 324.
73. Juan Denito interview, 2007.
74. Bulatao interview.
75. Duero interview.
76. As quoted in Shimizu, *Orphans of Pinatubo*, 8. See also Gobrin and Andin, "Development Conflict," 6–7. Of the total Philippine population of seventy-five million, about 10–12 percent are considered indigenous peoples and have retained aspects of precolonial life.
77. Juan Denito interview, 2007.
78. Julio Denito interview.
79. Robert H. Reid, "Former US Marine Instructors Now Instructing Tourists," *Philippine Star*, August 17, 1994.
80. The following description is based on notes from intermittent observations of the mini jungle demonstration over the course of two years, spanning 2007–8.
81. Duero interview.
82. Reid, "Former US Marine Instructors Now Instructing Tourists," 39.
83. Juan Denito interview.
84. Gobrin and Andin, "Development Conflict," 6–7.
85. Juan Denito interview, 2007.
86. Birtle, *U.S. Army Counterinsurgency and Contingency Operations Doctrine, 1860–1941*, 116.
87. Campbell, "'Making Riflemen from Mud,'" iii.
88. Ibid., 6.

89. Majul, *The Contemporary Muslim Movement in the Philippines*.

90. Training on March 2003 in the Zamboanga peninsula was provided as part of Operation Enduring Freedom–Philippines.

91. Bulatao interview.

92. Ibid.

93. Johnny Denito interview, 2008.

94. Ibid.

95. Campbell, "'Making Riflemen from Mud,'" iii.

96. Julio Denito interview.

97. Susan Kreifels, "If the Military Comes Back, We'll Be Here," *Star-Bulletin*, May 28, 1997.

98. Robert Gonzaga, "Return of US Forces to Subic Possible," *Philippine Daily Inquirer*, April 28, 2011.

CONCLUSION: INSECURITIES, TOURISM, AND TERROR

1. World Travel Organization, "Tourism Proves as a Resilient and Stable Economic Sector," press release, Madrid, June 18, 2002.

2. See, e.g., Ness, "Tourism-Terrorism."

3. Richter and Waugh, "Terrorism and Tourism as Logical Companions."

4. Sönmez, "Tourism, Terrorism, and Political Instability."

5. Richter and Waugh, "Terrorism and Tourism as Logical Companions," 235.

6. Bauman, *Postmodern Ethics*, 179.

7. Balce and Rodriguez, "American Insecurity and Radical Filipino Community Politics after 9/11."

8. White House, Office of the Press Secretary, "Joint Statement between the United States of America and the Republic of the Philippines," November 20, 2001, www.whitehouse.gov; IBON Foundation, "2002 National Budget: Is GMA Gearing Up for War?" press release, IBON Foundation, Inc., 2002, www.ibon.org.

9. Eric Schmitt, "Plan of U.S. Troops in Philippines Hits Snag," *New York Times*, March 1, 2003, www.nytimes.com/2003/03/01/international/asia/01FILI.html. See also terrorism's ideological goals of delegitimizing governments by making them look incapable of guaranteeing security (Hall and O'Sullivan, "Tourism, Political Stability and Violence").

10. "1,000 Cops to Guard Key Tourist Spots, Says Dick," *Manila Times*, January 30, 2002; "Gordon: ME Tension May Boost Tourism," *Philippine Star*, September 26, 2002.

11. Berlant, *The Queen of America Goes to Washington City*, 175.

12. On the Philippines as a military laboratory, see McCoy, *Policing America's Empire*.

13. Eduardo Ugarte, "Muslims and Madness in the Southern Philippines," 17.

14. Karapatan—a human rights watchdog organization—has documented countless violent acts, murders, and destruction of property carried out by the Macapagal-Arroyo administration and the U.S. military against Muslims in the southern Philippines, as well as by the Philippine military throughout the archipelago.

15. D. Rodriguez, *Suspended Apocalypse*.

16. See Pizam and Mansfeld, *Crime, Tourism and International Security Issues.*
17. Kaomea, "A Curriculum of Aloha?"
18. Chesney-Lind and Lind, "Visitors as Victims."
19. Marek, "Waikiki Virtual Reality."
20. Wood, "Echo Tourism," in *Displacing Natives*, 85–102.

BIBLIOGRAPHY

INTERVIEWS BY AUTHOR

Alcantara, Erlyn. May 30, 2003.

Broderick, Sheryl, national park ranger, USS *Arizona* Memorial. March 6, 2003.

Bulatao, Lunesto, JEST guide. July 2, 2007.

Cordoba, Stella, Corregidor guide. June 26, 2007.

Denito, Juan "Johnny," JEST guide. July 5, 2007, and December 19, 2008.

Denito, Julio "July," JEST guide. July 6, 2007.

Dimain, Monico, JEST guide. December 19, 2008.

Duero, Graciano, JEST guide. July 6, 2007.

Gawe, Peter, senior tourism operations officer, Department of Tourism, Cordillera Administrative Region. May 29, 2003.

Hildawa, Armando, Corregidor guide. July 12, 2007.

Martinez, Daniel, site historian, USS *Arizona* Memorial. March 6, 2003.

Matibag, Art, retired colonel and executive director of the Corregidor Foundation. June 25, 2007.

Nelson, Marilyn. February 12, 2003.

Pualoa, Gladys. March 10, 2007.

Viernes, Alfredo, JEST guide. July 5, 2007.

Wasson, Dawn. February 26, 2007.

SECONDARY SOURCES

Abinales, Patricio. "An American Colonial State: Authority and Structure in Southern Mindanao." In *Vestiges of War: The Philippine-American War and the Aftermath of an Imperial Dream, 1899–1999*, ed. Angel Velasco Shaw and Luis H. Francia. New York: New York University Press, 2002: 89–117.

Afable, Patricia, ed. *Japanese Pioneers in the Northern Philippine Highlands*. Baguio City, Philippines: Filipino-Japanese Foundation of Northern Luzon, 2004.

Alcantara, Erlyn, and Patricia Afable. Untitled ms. about Kennon Road. ca. 2002.

Ali, Mehmed, Kathy Ferguson, and Phyllis Turnbull. "Rethinking the Military in Hawaii." The Office for Women's Research, Working Papers Series, University of Hawai'i, 1992–93.

Althusser, Louis. "Ideology and Ideological State Apparatuses." In Lenin and Philosophy and Other Essays, trans. Ben Brewster. New York: Monthly Review Press, 1971: 127–86.

Aluit, Afonso J. Corregidor. Manila: Galleon Publications, 2003.

Anderegg, Michael, ed. Inventing Vietnam: The War in Film and Television. Philadelphia: Temple University Press, 1991.

Anderson, Benedict. "Cacique Democracy in the Philippines: Origins and Dreams." New Left Review 1:69 (May–June 1988): 3–31.

Anderson, Warwick. Colonial Pathologies: American Tropical Medicine, Race, and Hygiene in the Philippines. Durham: Duke University Press, 2006.

Andrade, Carlos. Hā'ena: Through the Eyes of the Ancestors. Honolulu: University of Hawai'i Press, 2008.

Anonymous. In the Land of the Headhunters: Being an Account of a Summer Holiday in Baguio. Manila: Fullmoon Publishing, 1991.

Aparicio, Frances R., and Suzanna Chavez-Silverman, eds. Tropicalizations: Representations of Latinidad. Lebanon, N.H.: Dartmouth College Press, 1997.

Aquino, Belinda. The Politics of Plunder: The Philippines under Marcos. Manila: Great Books Trading, 1987.

Aquino, Benigno S. A Garrison State in the Make and Other Speeches. Manila, Philippines: Benigno S. Aquino Jr. Foundation, 1985.

"Army Activities Resulting in Benefits to the Territory of Hawaii." Series F. Road Construction. Subject 1: Military and Federal Aid Roads. Control Division, Hq AFMIDPAC, 1946.

Ashcroft, Bill, Gareth Griffiths, and Helen Tiffin, eds. The Empire Writes Back: Theory and Practice in Post-Colonial Literatures. 2nd ed. New York: Routledge, 2002.

Bacevich, Andrew. The New American Militarism: How Americans Are Seduced by War. New York: Oxford University Press, 2005.

Bailey, Beth, and David Farber. The First Strange Place: Race and Sex in World War II Hawai'i. Baltimore: Johns Hopkins University Press, 1992.

Balce, Nerissa, and Robyn Rodriguez. "American Insecurity and Radical Filipino Community Politics after 9/11." Peace Review 16:2 (June 2004): 131–40.

Ballantyne, Tony, and Antoinette Burton. Moving Subjects: Gender, Mobility, and Intimacy in an Age of Global Empire. Urbana: University of Illinois Press, 2009.

Ballentine, David A. Gunbird Driver: A Marine Huey Pilot's War in Vietnam. Annapolis: Naval Institute Press, 2008.

Bandy, Joe. "Managing the Other of Nature: Sustainability, Spectacle, and Global Regimes of Capital in Ecotourism." Public Culture 8 (1996): 539–66.

Banerjee, Subhabrata Bobby. "Who Sustains Whose Development? Sustainable Development and the Reinvention of Nature." Organization Studies 24:1 (2003): 143–80.

Barstow, Anne Llewellyn. War's Dirty Secret: Rape, Prostitution, and Other Crimes against Women. Cleveland: Pilgrim Press, 2001.

Bauman, Zygmunt. *Postmodern Ethics*. London: Routledge, 1993.

Bederman, Gail. *Manliness and Civilization: A Cultural History of Gender and Race in the United States, 1880–1917*. Chicago: University of Chicago Press, 1995.

Bello, Walden David Kinley, and Elaine Elinson. *Development Debacle: The World Bank in the Philippines*. San Francisco Institute for Food and Development Policy, 1982.

Benjamin, Walter. "Theses on the Philosophy of History." In *Illuminations*, ed. Hannah Arendt, trans. Harry Zohn. New York: Schocken Books, 1968: 253–64.

Berg, Rick. "Losing Vietnam: Covering the War in an Age of Technology." In *From Hanoi to Hollywood: The Vietnam War in American Film*, ed. Linda Dittmar and Gene Michaud. New Brunswick: Rutgers University Press, 1990, 41–68.

Berger, John. *Ways of Seeing*. London: British Broadcasting Corporation and Penguin, 1973.

Berlant, Lauren. *The Queen of America Goes to Washington City: Essays on Sex and Citizenship*. Durham: Duke University Press, 1997.

Birtle, Andrew James. *U.S. Army Counterinsurgency and Contingency Operations Doctrine, 1860–1941*. Washington, D.C.: U.S. Army Center for Military History, 1998.

Blackford, Mansel. *Pathways to the Present: U.S. Development and Its Consequences in the Pacific*. Honolulu: University of Hawai'i Press, 2007.

Blackmore, Tim. "Rotor Hearts: The Helicopter as Postmodern War's Pacemaker." *Public Culture* 15:1 (2003): 90–102.

Boyce, James K. *The Philippines: The Political Economy of Growth and Impoverishment in the Marcos Era*. New York: Palgrave Macmillan, 1993.

Boyer, Paul. "Whose History Is It Anyway? Memory, Politics, and Historical Scholarship." In *History Wars: The Enola Gay and Other Battles for the American Past*, ed. Edward T. Linenthal and Tom Engelhardt. New York: Metropolitan, 1996: 115–39.

Brasswell, Barbara. "Pride and Partnership: Completing the Interstate H-3." *Public Roads Online*, May/June 1998, www.fhwa.dot.gov/publications/publicroads.

Breuer, William B. *Retaking the Philippines: America's Return to Corregidor and Bataan, October 1944–March 1945*. New York: St. Martin's Press, 1986.

Brillantes, Alex B. "The Philippines in 1991: Disasters and Decisions." *Asian Survey* 32:2 (February 1992): 140–45.

Britton, Stephen. "The Political Economy of Tourism in the Third World." *Annals of Tourism Research* 9 (1982): 331–58.

Broad, Robin, and John Cavanagh. *Plundering Paradise: The Struggle for the Environment in the Philippines*. Berkeley: University of California Press, 1993.

Brokaw, Tom. *The Greatest Generation*. New York: Random House, 1998.

Brown, Charles H. *The Correspondents' War: Journalists in the Spanish-American War*. New York: Charles Scribner's Sons, 1967.

Bui, ThiPhuoung-Lan. "When the Forest Became the Enemy and the Legacy of American Herbicidal Warfare in Vietnam." Ph.D. diss., Harvard University, 2003.

Bula-at, Leticia. "Indigenous Women's Struggles: The Chico Dam Project and the Kalinga Women," ed. and trans. Bernice See. Presented at the NGO Forum of the Fourth World Conference on Women, 1995, cpcabrisbane.org/Kasama/1996/V10n2/Innabuyog.htm.

Bureau of National and Foreign Information, Philippines. *The Philippine Economy in*

the Mid-Seventies: Development for the New Society. Manila: Department of Public
Information, 1976.

Bureau of Public Roads, Department of Commerce. "Report on Extension of National
System of Interstate and Defense Highways Within Alaska and Hawai'i." Washington, D.C.: United States Government Printing Office, 1960.

Caldicott, Helen. The New Nuclear Danger: George W. Bush's Military-Industrial Complex. New York: New Press, 2002.

Calhoun, Craig, Frederick Cooper, and Kevin W. Moore, eds. Lessons of Empire:
Imperial Histories and American Power. New York: The New Press, 2006.

Camacho, Keith Lujan. Cultures of Commemoration: The Politics of War, Memory, and
History in the Mariana Islands. Honolulu: University of Hawai'i Press, 2011.

Campbell, James D. "'Making Riflemen from Mud': Restoring the Army's Culture of
Irregular Warfare." U.S. Army War College Civilian Research Project, U.S. Army
War College, Penn., April 2007.

Campomanes, Oscar V. "Casualty Figures of the American Soldier and the Other:
Post-1898 Allegories of Imperial Nation-Building as 'Love and War.'" In Vestiges
of War: The Philippine-American War and the Aftermath of an Imperial Dream 1899–
1999, ed. Angel Velasco Shaw and Luis H. Francia. New York: New York University Press, 2002: 134–62.

Celoza, Albert F. Ferdinand Marcos and the Philippines: The Political Economy of Authoritarianism. New York: Praeger Publishers, 1997.

Césaire, Aimé. Discourse on Colonialism. New York: Monthly Review Press, 2001.

Chesney-Lind, Meda, and Ian Lind. "Visitors as Victims: Crimes Against Tourists in
Hawaii." Annals of Tourism Research 13 (1986): 167–91.

Chiles, James R. The God Machine: From Boomerangs to Black Hawks. The Story of the
Helicopter. New York: Bantam Books, 2007.

Chinnery, Philip D. Vietnam: The Helicopter War. Annapolis: Naval Institute Press,
1991.

Choy, Catherine Ceniza. Empire of Care: Nursing and Migration in Filipino American
History. Durham: Duke University Press, 2003.

Clifford, James. Routes: Travel and Translation in the Late Twentieth Century. Cambridge: Harvard University Press, 1997.

Clinton, Hillary. "America's Pacific Century." Foreign Policy (November 2011): 56–63.

Coffman, Tom. "The H-3 Chapter in the Island Edge of America." Unpublished manuscript. University of Hawai'i Hamilton Library, Hawaiian Collection, n.d.

Cohen, Colleen Ballerino. Take Me to My Paradise: Tourism and Nationalism in the
British Virgin Islands. New Brunswick: Rutgers University Press, 2010.

Cohen, Eliot. "History and the Hyperpower." Foreign Affairs 83:4 (July–August 2004):
49–63.

Conboy, Kenneth. South-East Asian Special Forces (Elite). Oxford: Osprey Publishing,
1991.

Cook, Chris. Kaua'i, The Garden Island: A Pictorial History of the Commerce and the
Work of the People. Virginia Beach: Donning Company, 1999.

Cooper, George, and Gavan Daws. Land and Power in Hawai'i: The Democratic Years.
Honolulu: University of Hawai'i Press, 1990.

Corpuz, Arturo. *The Colonial Iron Horse: Railroads and Regional Development in the Philippines, 1875–1935.* Quezon City: University of the Philippines Press, 1999.

Cruz, Lynette Hiʻilani. "From Resistance to Affirmation, We Are Who We Were: Reclaiming National Identity in the Hawaiian Sovereignty Movement 1990–2005." Ph.D. diss., University of Hawaiʻi, Mānoa, 2003.

Davis, Oscar King. "Our Conquests in the Pacific." *New York Sun*, May–December 1898, c. Sun Printing and Publishing Assoc., 1898, c. New York: Frederick A. Stokes Company, 1899.

deKadt, E., ed., *Tourism: Passport to Development?* Oxford: Oxford University Press, 1979.

Delgado, James P. "Recovering the Past of USS *Arizona*: Symbolism, Myth and Reality." *Historical Archaeology* 26:4 (1992): 69–80.

Deloria, Philip J. *Playing Indian.* New Haven: Yale University Press, 1998.

Department of Tourism. *Department of Tourism and Philippine Tourism Authority Information Manual.* Manila: Department of Tourism, September 1975.

Desmond, Jane. *Staging Tourism: Bodies on Display from Waikiki to Sea World.* Chicago: University of Chicago Press, 1999.

de Villa, Jill Gale. *Luzon by Car: Day Trips from Manila and Baguio.* Manila: Devcon I.P., 1982.

Diaz, Vicente. "Deliberating 'Liberation Day': Memory, Culture and History in Guam." In *Perilous Memories: The Asia-Pacific War(s)*, ed. T. Fujitani, Geoffrey M. White, and Lisa Yoneyama. Durham: Duke University Press, 2001: 155–80.

Diller, Elizabeth, and Ricardo Scofidio, eds. *Back to the Front: Tourisms of War.* Princeton: Princeton Architectural Press, 1994.

Dimain, Salvador. "Jungle Survival Training: Instructor's Pride in Being an Ayta." In *Orphans of Pinatubo: The Ayta Struggle for Existence*, by Hiromo Shimizu. Manila: Solidaridad Publishing House, 2001: 318–28.

Dorrance, William H. "The U.S. Army on Kauaʻi, 1909–1942." *Hawaiian Journal of History* 32 (1998): 155–69.

Drinnon, Richard. *Facing West: The Metaphysics of Indian-Hating and Empire-Building.* Norman: University of Oklahoma Press, 1997.

Dunlay, Thomas W. *Wolves for the Blue Soldiers: Indian Scouts and Auxiliaries with the United States Army.* Lincoln: University of Nebraska Press, 1982.

Eagle, Jonna K. "Making a Spectacle of Himself: White Masculinity, Melodrama, and Sensation in the American Cinema, 1898–1999." Ph.D. diss. Brown University, 2006.

Edmund, Rod. *Leprosy and Empire: A Medical and Cultural History.* Cambridge: Cambridge University Press, 2007.

Endy, Christopher. *Cold War Holidays: American Tourism in France.* Chapel Hill: University of North Carolina Press, 2004.

Enloe, Cynthia. *Bananas, Beaches, and Bases: Making Feminist Sense of International Politics.* Berkeley: University of California Press, 1989.

———. *Globalization and Militarism: Feminists Make the Link.* New York: Rowman and Littlefield, 2007.

————. *Maneuvers: The International Politics of Militarizing Women's Lives*. Berkeley: University of California Press, 2000.

Entenberg, Barbara. "Agrarian Reform and the Hukbalahap." *Far Eastern Survey* 15:16 (August 14, 1946): 245–48.

Faludi, Susan. *Stiffed: The Betrayal of the American Man*. New York: Harper Perennial, 2000.

Feeney, Paulette. "Aloha and Allegiance; Imagining America's Paradise." Ph.D. diss. University of Hawai'i, Mānoa, 2009.

"Final Environmental Impact Statement: Military Training Activities at Mākua Valley Reservation, Hawai'i." Vol. 1. U.S. Army Environmental Command, Aberdeen Proving Ground, Md., and U.S. Army Corps of Engineers, Honolulu Engineer District, June 2009.

Finin, Gerard. *The Making of the Igorot: Contours of a Cordillera Consciousness*. Quezon City: Ateneo de Manila Press, 2005.

Flanagan, E. M. *Corregidor: The Rock Force Assault*. Novato, Calif.: Presidio, 1995.

Flanagan, John F. *Vietnam above the Treetops: A Forward Air Controller Reports*. New York: Praeger, 1992.

Foucault, Michel. *"Society Must Be Defended": Lectures at the Collège de France, 1975–1976*, trans. David Macey. New York: Picador, 2005.

Fujikane, Candace, and John Okamura, eds. *Asian Settler Colonialism: From Local Governance to the Habits of Everyday Life*. Honolulu: University of Hawai'i Press, 2008.

Fujitani, T., Geoffrey M. White, and Lisa Yoneyama, eds. *Perilous Memories: The Asia-Pacific Wars*. Durham: Duke University Press, 2001.

Gedacht, Joshua. "'Mohammedan Religion Made It Necessary to Fire': Massacres on the American Imperial Frontier from South Dakota to the Southern Philippines." In *Colonial Crucible: Empire in the Making of the Modern American State*, ed. Alfred W. McCoy and Francisco A. Scarano. Madison: University of Wisconsin Press, 2009: 397–409.

Gerhardt, Tina. "America's Pacific Century?: APEC Summit in Hawaii Seeks to Implement Free Trade Agreement of the Asia Pacific Region." *Common Dreams*, November 11, 2011.

Gillem, Mark. *America Town: Building the Outposts of Empire*. Minneapolis: University of Minnesota Press, 2007.

Giroux, Henry A. "War on Terror: The Militarising of Public Space and Culture in the United States." *Third Text* 18:4 (2004): 211–21.

Go, Julian. "Introduction: Global Perspectives on the U.S. Colonial State in the Philippines." In *The American Colonial State in the Philippines: Global Perspectives*, ed. Julian Go and Anne L. Foster. Durham: Duke University Press, 2003: 1–42.

Gobrin, Gerardo, and Almira Andin. "Development Conflict: The Philippine Experience." Quezon City, Philippines: Katipunan ng mga Katutubong Mamamayan ng Pilipinas and Minority Groups International, November 2002.

Goldstone, Patricia. *Making the World Safe for Tourism*. New Haven: Yale University Press, 2001.

Gonzalez, Vernadette Vicuña. "Headhunter Itineraries: The Philippines as Dream Jungle." *Global South* 3:2 (2009): 144–72.

———. "Military Bases, 'Royalty Trips' and Imperial Modernities: Gendered and Racialized Labor in the Postcolonial Philippines." *Frontiers: A Journal of Women Studies* 28:3 (summer 2007): 28–59.

Gonzalves, P. "Structural Adjustment and the Political Economy of the Third World." *Contours* 7:1 (1979): 33–39.

Gordon, Avery. *Ghostly Matters: Haunting and the Sociological Imagination*. Minneapolis: University of Minnesota Press, 1996.

Goss, Jon. "'From Here to Eternity': Voyages of (Re)Discovery in Tourist Landscapes of Hawai'i." In *New Geographies*, ed. Deborah Woodcock. Department of Geography, University of Hawai'i, 1999: 153–78.

———. "The Souvenir and Sacrifice in the Tourist Mode of Consumption." In *Seductions of Place: Geographical Perspectives on Globalization and Touristed Landscapes*, ed. Carolyne Cartier and Alan A. Lew. London: Routledge, 2003: 48–62.

Grant, Glen. *Glen Grant's Chicken Skin Tales: 49 Favorite Ghost Stories from Hawai'i*. Honolulu: Mutual Publishing, 1988.

Gross, Chuck. *Rattler One-Seven: A Vietnam Helicopter Pilot's War Story*. Denton, Tex.: University of North Texas Press, 2004.

Hagedorn, Jessica. *Gangster of Love*. New York: Penguin, 1996.

Hall, C. M., and V. O'Sullivan. "Tourism, Political Stability and Violence." In *Tourism, Crime and International Security Issues*, ed. A. Pizam and Y. Mansfeld. New York: Wiley, 1996: 105–21.

Hallin, Daniel C. *The "Uncensored War": The Media and Vietnam*. Berkeley: University of California Press, 1986.

Halsema, James. *E. J. Halsema: Colonial Engineer*. Quezon City: New Day Publishers, 1991.

Hamilton-Paterson, James. *America's Boy: A Century of United States Colonialism in the Philippines*. New York: Henry Holt, 1999.

Hannam, Kevin, Mimi Sheller, and John Urry. "Editorial: Mobilities, Immobilities and Moorings." *Mobilities* 1:1 (March 2006): 1–22.

Haraway, Donna. "The Cyborg Manifesto: Science, Technology and Socialist Feminism in the Late Twentieth Century." In *Simians, Cyborgs and Women: The Reinvention of Nature*. New York: Routledge, 1991: 149–81.

———. "Teddy Bear Patriarchy: Taxidermy in the Garden of Eden, New York City 1908–1936." In *Primate Visions: Gender, Race, and Nature in the World of Modern Science*. New York: Routledge, 1989: 26–58.

Hartung, William D. *How Much Are You Making on the War, Daddy? A Quick and Dirty Guide to War Profiteering in the Bush Administration*. New York: Nation Books, 2004.

Hau'ofa, Epeli. "Our Sea of Islands." *The Contemporary Pacific* 6 (1994): 147–61.

Hawai'i Department of Transportation. "Hawaii's Interstate H-3 Freeway." Hawai'i Department of Transportation, 1997.

———. "Scenic Roads and Parkways Study." Vol. 1. State of Hawai'i Department of Transportation, Highways Division, 1965.

Hawes, Gary. *The Philippine State and the Marcos Regime: The Politics of Export*. Ithaca, N.Y.: Cornell University Press, 1987.

Heidler, David S., and Jeanne T. Heidler. *Indian Removal: A Norton Casebook*. New York: W. W. Norton, 2007.

Hereniko, Vilsoni, and Rob Wilson. *Inside Out: Literature, Cultural Politics and Identity in the New Pacific*. New York: Rowman and Littlefield, 1999.

Highway Planning Commission. "Federal-Aid Highway System State of Hawaii: Re-evaluation and Recommendation." State of Hawai'i Department of Transportation Highways Division, January 1964.

Hilsdon, Anne-Marie. *Madonnas and Martyrs: Militarism and Violence in the Philippines*. Manila: Ateneo de Manila University Press, 1995.

Hoganson, Kristin. *Fighting for American Manhood: How Gender Politics Provoked the Spanish-American and Philippine-American Wars*. New Haven: Yale University Press, 2000.

Holman, Victor. "Seminole Negro Indians, Macabebes, and Civilian Irregulars: Models for the Future Employment of Indigenous Forces." M.A. thesis, U.S. Army Command and General Staff College, Ft. Leavenworth, Kans., 1995.

Horsman, Reginald. *Race and Manifest Destiny: The Origins of American Racial Anglo-Saxonism*. Cambridge: Harvard University Press, 1981.

Hosek, James, Aviva Litovitz, and Adam C. Resnick. *How Much Does Military Spending Add to Hawaii's Economy?* Santa Monica, Calif.: RAND Corporation, 2011.

Ileto, Reynaldo Clemeña. *Pasyon and Revolution: Popular Movements in the Philippines, 1840–1910*. Quezon City: Ateneo de Manila University Press, 1979.

Imada, Adria. *Aloha America: Hula Circuits Through the U.S. Empire*. Durham: Duke University Press, 2012.

Ireland, Brian. *The U.S. Military in Hawai'i: Colonialism, Memory and Resistance*. New York: Palgrave Macmillan, 2011.

Isaac, Allan Punzalan. *American Tropics: Articulating Filipino America*. Minneapolis: University of Minnesota Press, 2006.

Jacobson, Matthew Frye. *Barbarian Virtues: The United States Encounters Foreign Peoples at Home and Abroad, 1876–1917*. New York: Hill and Wang, 2001.

Jeffords, Susan. *The Remasculinization of America: Gender and the Vietnam War*. Bloomington: Indiana University Press, 1989.

Johnson, Chalmers. *The Sorrows of Empire: Militarism, Secrecy, and the End of the Republic*. New York: Owl Books, Henry Holt, 2004.

Kajihiro, Kyle. "A Brief Overview of Militarization and Resistance in Hawai'i." DMZ-Hawai'i / Aloha 'Aina Paper, March 1, 2007, www.dmzhawaii.org/wp-content /uploads/2008/12/overview-military-in-hawaii-mac-small-with-funderspdf.pdf.

———. "The Militarizing of Hawai'i: Occupation, Accommodation and Resistance." In *Asian Settler Colonialism: From Local Governance to the Habits of Everyday Life*, ed. Candace Fujikane and Jonathan Y. Okamura. Honolulu: University of Hawai'i Press, 2008: 170–94.

Kame'eleihiwa, Lilikalā. *Native Land and Foreign Desires: Pehea Lā E Pono Ai?* Honolulu: Bishop Museum, 1992.

Kaomea, Julie. "A Curriculum of Aloha? Colonialism and Tourism in Hawai'i's Elementary Textbooks." *Curriculum Inquiry* 30:3 (2000): 319–44.

Kaplan, Amy, *The Anarchy of Empire in the Making of U.S. Culture.* Cambridge: Harvard University Press, 2003.

Kaplan, Caren. "Mobility and War: The 'Cosmic View' of Air Power." *Environment and Planning A* 38:2 (2006): 406.

———. *Questions of Travel: Postmodern Discourses of Displacement.* Durham: Duke University Press, 1996.

Kaplan, Caren, and Raegan Kelly. "Dead Reckoning: Aerial Perception and the Social Construction of Targets." *Vectors Journal,* vectors.usc.edu/projects/index .php?project=11.

Kelly, Marion, and Sidney Michael Quintal. "Cultural History Report of Makua Military Reservation and Vicinity." Mākua Valley, Oʻahu: Bernice P. Bishop Museum, April 1977.

Kent, Noel. *Hawaii: Islands under the Influence.* Honolulu: University of Hawaiʻi Press, 1993 [1983].

Kerkvliet, Benedict J. *The Huk Rebellion: A Study of Peasant Revolt in the Philippines.* 2nd ed. New York: Rowman and Littlefield, 2002.

Kim, Jodi. *Ends of Empire: Asian American Critique and the Cold War.* Minneapolis: University of Minnesota Press, 2010.

Kincaid, Jamaica. *A Small Place.* New York: Farrar, Straus and Giroux, 1988.

Kinzer, Stephen. *Overthrow: America's Century of Regime Change from Hawaiʻi to Iraq.* New York: Henry Holt and Company, 2006.

Kirk, Gwyn, and Margo Okazawa-Rey. "Demilitarizing Security": Women Oppose U.S. Militarism in East Asia." In *Frontline Feminisms: Women, War, and Resistance,* ed. Marguerite R. Waller and Jennifer Rycenga. New York: Garland, 2000:159–72.

Klein, Christina. *Cold War Orientalism: Asia in the Middlebrow Imagination, 1946–1961.* Berkeley: University of California Press, 2003.

Klein, Michael L. "Cultural Narrative and the Process of Re-collection: Film, History and the Vietnam Era." In *The Vietnam Era: Media and Popular Culture in the U.S. and Vietnam.* London: Pluto Press, 1990: 3–37.

Kolodny, Anne. *The Lay of the Land: Metaphor as Experience and History in American Life and Letters.* Chapel Hill: University of North Carolina Press, 1975.

Kosasa, Karen. "Searching for the 'C' Word: Museums, Art Galleries, and Settler Colonialism in Hawaiʻi." In *Studies in Settler Colonialism: Politics, Identity, and Culture,* ed. Fiona Bateman and Lionel Pilkington. New York: Palgrave Macmillan, 2011: 153–68.

Kramer, Paul. *The Blood of Government: Race, Empire, the United States and the Philippines.* Philippine ed. Manila: Ateneo de Manila Press, 2006.

Kubota, Gary. "H-3: A Question of Direction." Transcript of documentary, Honolulu: Hawaiʻi, 1975.

Lacsamana, Anne E. *Revolutionizing Feminism: The Philippine Women's Movement in the Age of Terror.* Boulder: Paradigm Publishers, 2012.

Leary, William M. *Perilous Missions: Civil Air Transport and CIA Covert Operations in Asia.* Tuscaloosa: University of Alabama Press, 1984.

Lenihan, Daniel. *Submerged Cultural Resources Study: USS Arizona Memorial and Pearl*

Harbor National Historic Landmark. Professional Papers no. 23, Santa Fe: South-
west Cultural Resources Center, 1989.

Lennon, John, and Malcolm Foley. *Dark Tourism: The Attraction of Death and Disaster*.
London: Continuum, 2000.

Lind, Ian. "The Captive Valley of Makua: 42 Years of Military Occupation." *Ka Huliau*,
May–June 1983: 8–9.

Linn, Brian McAllister. *Guardians of Empire: The U.S. Army and the Pacific, 1902–1940*.
Chapel Hill: University of North Carolina Press, 1997.

———. *The Philippine War, 1899–1902*. Lawrence: University Press of Kansas, 2000.

———. *The U.S. Army and Counterinsurgency in the Philippine War, 1899–1902*. Chapel
Hill: University of North Carolina Press, 1989.

———. "The US Army and Nation Building and Pacification in the Philippines."
In *Armed Diplomacy: Two Centuries of American Campaigning*. Fort Leavenworth,
Kans.: Combat Studies Institute Press, 2003: 77–90.

Lippard, Lucy R. "Tragic Tourism." In *On the Beaten Track: Tourism, Art, and Place*.
New York: The New Press, 1999.

Löfgren, Orvar. *On Holiday: A History of Vacationing*. Berkeley: University of California
Press, 1999.

Love, Eric Tyrone Lowery. *Race over Empire: Racism and Imperialism, 1865–1900*.
Chapel Hill: University of North Carolina Press, 2004.

Lumbera, Bienvenido. "From Colonizer to Liberator: How U.S. Colonialism Suc-
ceeded in Reinventing Itself after the War." In *Vestiges of War: The Philippine-
American War and the Aftermath of an Imperial Dream, 1899–1999*, ed. Angel Velasco
Shaw and Luis H. Francia. New York: New York University Press, 2002: 193–203.

Lutz, Catherine. *Homefront: A Military City and the American Twentieth Century*. Boston: Beacon Press, 2001.

Lyons, Paul. *American Pacificism: Oceania in the U.S. Imagination*. New York: Routledge, 2006.

MacCannell, Dean. *The Tourist: A New Theory of the Leisure Class*. Berkeley: University
of California Press, 1999.

Majul, Cesar Adib. *The Contemporary Muslim Movement in the Philippines*. Berkeley:
Mizan Press, 1985.

Manderson, Lenore, and Margaret Jolly. *Sites of Desire, Economies of Pleasure: Sexuali-
ties in Asia and the Pacific*. Chicago: University of Chicago Press, 1997.

Marek, Serge A. "Waikiki Virtual Reality: Space, Place and Representation in the
Waikiki Master Plan." M.A. thesis, University of Hawai'i, 1997.

Marx, Leo. *The Machine in the Garden: Technology and the Pastoral Ideal In America*.
Oxford: Oxford University Press, 1967.

Mason, Robert. *Chickenhawk*. New York: Viking Press, 1983.

Mayo, James. *Memorials and Political Landscape: The American Experience and Beyond*.
New York: Praeger, 1988.

McAlister, Melani. *Epic Encounters: Culture, Media, and U.S. Interests in the Middle East
since 1945*. Berkeley: University of California Press, 2001.

McClintock, Anne. *Imperial Leather: Race, Gender and Sexuality in the Colonial Conquest*. New York: Routledge, 1995.

McCoy, Alfred W. "Dark Legacies: Human Rights under the Marcos Regime." Paper presented at the "Legacies of the Marcos Dictatorship." University of Wisconsin, Madison / Ateneo de Manila University Conference, September 20, 1999. Quezon City: Office of Research and Publications, Ateneo de Manila University, September 20, 1999: 131–40.

——. *Policing America's Empire*. Madison: University of Wisconsin Press, 2009.

Meixsel, Richard. "American Exceptionalism in Colonial Forces? The Philippine Scout Mutiny of 1924." In *Colonial Armies in Southeast Asia*, ed. Karl Hack and Tobias Rettig. New York: Routledge, 2006: 162–84.

Merrill, Dennis. *Negotiating Paradise: U.S. Tourism and Empire in Twentieth-Century Latin America*. Chapel Hill: University of North Carolina Press, 2009.

Merry, Sally Engle. *Colonizing Hawai'i: The Cultural Power of Law*. Princeton: Princeton University Press, 2000.

Mies, Maria, and Vandana Shiva. *Ecofeminism*. Melbourne: Spinifex Press, 1993.

Mills, Barbara. *A Trip through Hawaii's Military History: Exploring the U.S. Army Museum of Hawaii*. Hawai'i Army Museum Society, 2000.

Ministry of Public Works and Highways: Annual Report. Manila: Ministry of Public Works and Highways, 1982.

Miranda, Felipe B. *The Political Economy of ASEAN Development: The Philippines under Marcos*. Manila: Social Weather Stations, 1986.

Mitchell, Timothy. *Colonising Egypt*. Cambridge: Cambridge University Press, 1988.

Mojares, Resil B. *The War against the Americans: Resistance and Collaboration in Cebu, 1899–1906*. Manila: Ateneo de Manila Press, 1999.

Moon, Katherine H. *Sex among Allies: Military Prostitution in U.S.-Korea Relations*. New York: Columbia University Press, 1997.

Morris, Eric. *Corregidor: The American Alamo of World War II*. New York: Cooper Square Press, 1988.

Mosse, George L. *Fallen Soldiers: Reshaping the Memory of the World Wars*. New York: Oxford University Press, 1990.

Motooka, P. S., S. F. Saiki, D. L. Plucknett, O. R. Younge, and R. E. Daehler. "Control of Hawaiian Jungle with Aerially Applied Herbicide." *Down to Earth* 23:1 (1967): 18–22.

Mowforth, Martin, and Ian Munt. *Tourism and Sustainability: New Tourism in the Third World*. London: Routledge, 1998.

Muse, Eben J. *The Land of Nam: The Vietnam War in American Film*. Lanham, Md.: Scarecrow Press, 1995.

Nakahara, Zentoku. "A Trip to the Philippines: Early Impressions of a Japanese Visitor, First Trip, 1936." Reprinted in "Kennon Road Commemoration Program." Baguio City; n.p., 1991.

Nash, Dennison. "Tourism as a Form of Imperialism." In *Hosts and Guests: The Anthropology of Tourism*, ed. Valene Smith. Philadelphia: University of Pennsylvania Press, 1989: 37–52.

Ness, Sally Ann. "Tourism-Terrorism: The Landscaping of Consumption and the Darker Side of Place." *American Ethnologist* 32:1 (2005): 118–40.

————. *Where Asia Smiles: An Ethnography of Philippine Tourism*. Philadelphia: University of Pennsylvania Press, 2003.

Neumann, A. Lin. "Tourism Promotion and Prostitution." In *The Philippines Reader: A History of Colonialism, Neocolonialism, Dictatorship, and Resistance*, ed. Daniel B. Shirmer and Stephen Rosskamm Shalom. New York: South End Press, 1987: 182–86.

Newton, Richard D. "The Seeds of Surrogate Warfare." In *Contemporary Security Challenges: Irregular Warfare and Indirect Approaches*. Hurlburt Field, Fla.: The JSOU Press, 2009: 1–18.

Novelli, Martin. "Hollywood and Vietnam: Images of Vietnam in American Film." In *The Vietnam Era: Media and Popular Culture in the US and Vietnam*, ed. Michael Klein, 107–24. London: Pluto Press, 1990.

Olson, John, ed. *The Philippine Scouts*. Daly City, Calif.: Philippine Scouts Heritage Society, 2002.

Osorio, Jonathan Kay Kamakawiwoʻole. *Dismembering Lāhui: A History of the Hawaiian Nation to 1887*. Honolulu: University of Hawaiʻi Press, 2002.

————. "Memorializing Puʻuloa and Remembering Pearl Harbor." In *Militarized Currents: Toward a Decolonized Future in Asia and the Pacific*, ed. Setsu Shigematsu and Keith L. Camacho. Minneapolis: University of Minnesota Press, 2010: 3–14.

Ostelius, Hans. *Islands of Pleasure*. London: George Allen and Unwin, 1963.

O'Toole, G. J. A. *The Spanish War: An American Epic 1898*. W. W. Norton, 1986.

Paik, Koohan, and Jerry Mander. *The Superferry Chronicles: Hawaiʻi's Uprising against Militarism, Commercialism and the Desecration of the Earth*. Honolulu: Koa Books, 2008.

Parreñas, Rhacel Salazar. *Servants of Globalization: Women, Migration and Domestic Work*. Stanford: Stanford University Press, 2001.

Pattullo, Polly. "The Holiday and Its Makers: The Tourists." In *Last Resorts: The Cost of Tourism in the Caribbean*. 2nd ed. New York: Monthly Review Press, 2005.

Pérez, Louis A., Jr. *The War of 1898: The United States and Cuba in History and Historiography*. Chapel Hill: University of North Carolina Press, 1998.

Pizam, Abraham, and Yoel Mansfield, eds. *Crime, Tourism and International Security Issues*. Chichester, England: John Wiley and Sons, 1996.

Pratt, Mary Louise. *Imperial Eyes: Travel Writing and Transculturation*. New York: Routledge, 1992.

Rafael, Vicente L. *Contracting Colonialism: Translation and Christian Conversion in Tagalog Society under Early Spanish Rule*. Ithaca, N.Y.: Cornell University Press, 1988.

Reasoner, Harry. "During the Viet Nam War." ABC News commentary, February 16, 1971, www.nixwebs.com/Search9/helitac/harryreasoner.htm.

Reed, Robert R. *City of Pines: The Origins of Baguio as a Colonial Hill Station and Regional Capital*. Baguio City, Philippines: A-Seven Publishing, 1999.

Resurreccion-Andrada, Bona Elisa. "Notes on the History of Camp John Hay." In *Camp John Hay: How It All Began . . . Where It Is Bound*, ed. Lucris Carina Agnir-Paraan and Alice Buenviaje-Wilder. Baguio City: John Hay Poro Point Development Corporation, 2000.

Richter, L. K., and W. L. Waugh Jr. "Terrorism and Tourism as Logical Companions."

In *Managing Tourism*, ed. S. Medlik. London: Butterworth-Heinemann, 1991: 318–27.

Robbins, Christopher. *Air America: From WWII to Vietnam. The Explosive True Story of the cia's Secret Airline*. New York: Avon, 1985.

Rodriguez, Dylan. *Suspended Apocalypse: White Supremacy, Genocide and the Filipino Condition*. Minneapolis: University of Minnesota Press, 2009.

Rodriguez, Robyn Magalit. *Migrants for Export: How the Philippine State Brokers Labor to the World*. Minneapolis: University of Minnesota Press, 2010.

Roosevelt, Theodore. *Theodore Roosevelt: An American Mind. A Selection from His Writings*, ed. Mario DiNunzio. New York: Penguin, 1995.

Rosca, Ninotchka. "Rape Case Exposes U.S. Domination of Philippine Government." *Socialism and Liberation* 4:3 (March 1, 2007), www2.pslweb.org/site/News2?page=NewsArticle&id=12121&news_iv_ctrl=2245, accessed May 17, 2012.

———. *State of War*. New York: W. W. Norton, 1988.

Rowe, John Carlos. "'Bringing It All Back Home': American Recyclings of the Vietnam War." In *The Violence of Representation: Literature and the History of Violence*, ed. Nancy Armstrong and Leonard Tennenhouse. London: Routledge, 1989: 197–218.

Said, Edward. *Culture and Imperialism*. New York: Vintage Books, 1994.

———. *Orientalism*. New York: Vintage, 1978.

———. *The World, the Text, and the Critic*. Cambridge: Harvard University Press, 1983.

Sakai, Naoki. "On Romantic Love and Military Violence: Transpacific Imperialism and U.S.-Japan Complicity." In *Militarized Currents: Toward a Decolonized Future in Asia and the Pacific*, ed. Setsu Shigematsu and Keith L. Camacho. Minneapolis: University of Minnesota Press, 2010: 205–21.

Sakamato, Yoshikazu. *Asia, Militarization and Regional Conflict*. Tokyo: United Nations University Press, 1988.

Sanders, Craig. "h3: The Island Interstate." *Public Roads Online* 57:1 (summer 1993): www.fhwa.dot.gov/publications/publicroads/93summer/p93su16.cfm.

Santos, Aida, Cecilia Hofmann, and Alma Bulawan. "Prostitution and the Bases: A Continuing Saga of Exploitation." Manila: Coalition against Trafficking in Women in Asia Pacific, 1998. catwap.wordpress.com/resources/speeches-papers (enter article title in Search box).

Saranillio, Dean. "Seeing Conquest: Colliding Histories and the Cultural Politics of Hawai'i Statehood." Ph.D. diss., University of Michigan, 2009.

Scarry, Elaine. *The Body in Pain: The Making and Unmaking of the World*. New York: Oxford University Press, 1985.

Scipes, Kim. "Global Economic Crisis, Neoliberal Solutions, and the Philippines." *Monthly Review* 51:7 (1999), monthlyreview.org.

Shalom, Stephen R. *The United States and the Philippines: A Study of Neocolonialism*. Philadelphia: Institute for the Study of Human Issues, 1981.

Sharpe, Jenny. *Allegories of Empire: The Figure of Woman in the Colonial Text*. Minneapolis: University of Minnesota Press, 1993.

Sheller, Mimi, and John Urry, eds. *Tourism Mobilities: Places to Play, Places in Play.* London: Routledge, 2004.

Sherer, Michael D. "Vietnam War Photos and Public Opinion." *Journalism Quarterly* 66:2 (summer 1989): 391–95.

Shibusawa, Naoko. *America's Geisha Ally: Reimagining the Japanese Enemy.* Cambridge: Harvard University Press, 2006.

Shigematsu, Setsu, and Keith L. Camacho. "Introduction: Militarized Currents, Decolonizing Futures." In *Militarized Currents: Toward a Decolonized Future in Asia and the Pacific,* ed. Setsu Shigematsu and Keith L. Camacho. Minneapolis: University of Minnesota Press, 2010: xv–xlviii.

Shimizu, Hiromo. *Orphans of Pinatubo: The Ayta Struggle for Existence.* Manila: Solidaridad Publishing House, 2001.

Silbey, David J. *A War of Frontier and Empire: The Philippine-American War, 1899–1902.* New York: Hill and Wang, 2007.

Silva, Noenoe. *Aloha Betrayed: Native Hawaiian Resistance to American Colonialism.* Durham: Duke University Press, 2004.

Sköns, Elizabeth, Samuel Perlo-Freeman, Carina Solmirano, and Noel Kelly. "Military Expenditure." In *sipri* (*Stockholm International Peace Research Institute*), www.sipri.org/research/armaments/milex.

Skwiot, Christine. *The Purposes of Paradise: U.S. Tourism and Empire in Cuba and Hawai'i.* Philadelphia: University of Pennsylvania Press, 2010.

Slackman, Michael. *Remembering Pearl Harbor: The Story of the U.S.S. Arizona Memorial.* Honolulu: Arizona Memorial Museum Association, 1984.

Smith, Sheila. "Shifting Terrain: The Domestic Policies of the U.S. Military Presence in Asia." East-West Special Reports. Honolulu: East-West Center, 2006.

Smith, Valene L. "War and Tourism: An American Ethnography." *Annals of Tourism Research* 25:1 (1998): 202–27.

Sönmez, Sevil F. "Tourism, Terrorism, and Political Instability." *Annals of Tourism Research* 25:2 (1998): 416–56.

Stannard, David E. *Honor Killing: Race, Rape and Clarence Darrow's Spectacular Last Case.* New York: Penguin, 2005.

———. *Before the Horror: The Population of Hawai'i on the Eve of Western Contact.* Honolulu: University of Hawai'i Press, 1989.

Stein, Rebecca L. *Itineraries in Conflict: Israelis, Palestinians, and the Political Lives of Tourism.* Durham: Duke University Press, 2008.

Stevenot, J. E. H. "Our Trip to Baguio and Return." Philippine Commonwealth Committee Baguio Trip for the Congressional Party, November 9 and 10, 1935.

Stevens, Sylvester K. *American Expansion in Hawai'i 1842–1898.* Harrisburg Archives Publishing Company of Pennsylvania, 1955.

Stickney, H. L. "Early History of Pearl Harbor" (photocopy), n.d., Hamilton Library, University of Hawai'i at Mānoa.

Stimpson, Catherine. "Foreword." In *Manliness and Civilization: A Cultural History of Gender and Race in the United States, 1880–1917,* ed. Gail Bederman. Chicago: University of Chicago Press, 1995: xi–xii.

Stoler, Ann Laura. *Carnal Knowledge and Imperial Power: Race and the Intimate in Colonial Rule*. Berkeley: University of California Press, 2002.

Strachan, Ian Gregory. *Paradise and Plantation: Tourism and Culture in the Anglophone Caribbean*. Charlottesville: University of Virginia Press, 2002.

Sturdevant, Saundra Pollack. *Let the Good Times Roll: Prostitution and the U.S. Military in Asia*. New York: The New Press, 1993.

———. "Who Benefits? U.S. Military, Prostitution, and Base Conversion." In *Frontline Feminisms: Women, War, and Resistance*, ed. Marguerite R. Waller and Jennifer Rycenga. New York: Garland, 2000:141–58.

Suehisa, Robert H. David F. Sakai, Otto R. Younge, and Donald L. Plucknett. "Defoliation of Tropical Jungle Vegetation in Hawaii." Final Report. May 1, 1967–June 30, 1968. Department of Agronomy and Soil Science, University of Hawaiʻi and Department of the Army, Fort Detrick, Md.

Tadiar, Neferti Xina M. *Fantasy-Production: Sexual Economies and Other Philippine Consequences for the New World Order*. Hong Kong: Hong Kong University Press, 2004.

Tanaka, Yuki, and Susan Brownmiller. *Japan's Comfort Women: The Military and Involuntary Prostitution during War and Occupation*. New York: Routledge, 2002.

Teaiwa, Teresia. "bikinis and other s/pacific n/oceans." *The Contemporary Pacific* 6:1 (1994): 87–110.

———. "Militarism, Tourism and the Native: Articulations in Oceania." Ph.D. diss., University of California, Santa Cruz, 2001.

"Transforming U.S. Army Pacific." Torchbearer: National Security Report, June 2009.

Trask, Haunani-Kay. "Colonization." In *Light in the Crevice Never Seen*. Corvallis, Oregon: Calyx, 1994: 64–66.

———. *From a Native Daughter: Colonialism and Sovereignty in Hawaiʻi*. Repr. ed. Honolulu: University of Hawaiʻi Press, 1999.

———. *Night Is a Sharkskin Drum*. Honolulu: University of Hawaiʻi Press, 2002.

———. "Settlers of Color and 'Immigrant' Hegemony: 'Locals' in Hawaiʻi." In *Asian Settler Colonialism: From Local Governance to the Habits of Everyday Life*, ed. Candace Fujikane and Jonathan Y. Okamura. Honolulu: University of Hawaiʻi Press, 2008: 45–65.

Trask, Mililani B. "Hawaiian Sovereignty." *Amerasia Journal* special issue: "Whose Vision? Asian Settler Colonialism in Hawaiʻi." 26:22 (2000): 31–36.

Tripp, Jeffrey A. "Contentious Divide: The Cultural Politics of the Korean Demilitarized Zone, 1953–2008." Ph.D. diss., University of Hawaiʻi, Mānoa, 2010.

Turnbull, Phyllis, and Kathleen Ferguson. "Military Presence / Missionary Past: The Historical Construction of Masculine Order and Feminine Hawaiʻi." *Social Process in Hawaiʻi* 38 (1997): 94–107.

———. *Oh, Say, Can You See? The Semiotics of the Military in Hawaiʻi*. Minneapolis: University of Minnesota Press, 1999.

Turner, Fred. *Echoes of Combat: Trauma, Memory and the Vietnam War*. Minneapolis: University of Minnesota Press, 2001.

Ugarte, Eduardo. "Muslims and Madness in the Southern Philippines." *Pilipinas: A Journal of Philippine Studies* 19 (fall 1992): 1–23.

United States General Accounting Office. "Defense Acquisitions: Steps Needed to Ensure Interoperability of Systems That Process Intelligence Data." A Report to the Chairman, Committee on Armed Services, House of Representatives, March 2003.

Urry, John. *The Tourist Gaze*. 2nd ed. Thousand Oaks, Calif.: Sage, 2002.

Vanbrackle, Joseph D. "Pearl Harbor from the First Mention of 'Pearl Lochs' to Its Present Day Usage." Honolulu: Public Information Office, 1955: 1–6.

van den Top, Gerhard. *The Social Dynamics of Deforestation in the Philippines: Actions, Options and Motivations*. Copenhagen: NIAS Press, 2003.

Verikios, Michael. "Philippines' Sustainable Growth Benefits Tourism." *Travel Daily News*, June 27, 2007.

Virilio, Paul. *War and Cinema: The Logistics of Perception*. London: Verso Books, 1989.

Vizmanos, Danilo. *Martial Law Diary and Other Papers*. Manila: Ken, 2003.

Wallace, Anthony F. C. *The Long Bitter Trail: Andrew Jackson and the Indians*. New York: Hill and Wang, 1993.

Weaver, Adam. "Tourism and the Military: Pleasure and the War Economy." *Annals of Tourism Research* 38:2 (2011): 672–89.

Weeks, Stanley B., and Charles Meconis. *The Armed Forces of the USA in the Asia-Pacific Region*. London: I. B. Tauris, 1999.

Wexler, Laura. *Tender Violence: Domestic Visions in an Age of U.S. Imperialism*. Chapel Hill: University of North Carolina Press, 2000.

White, Geoffrey. "Moving History: The Pearl Harbor Film(s)." *Positions* 5:3 (1997): 709–44.

———. "Remembering Guadalcanal: National Identity and Transnational Memory-Making." *Public Culture* 7 (1995): 529–55.

White, Geoffrey, and Lamont Lindstrom, eds. *The Pacific Theater: Island Representations of World War II*. Honolulu: University of Hawai'i Press, 1989.

White, Trumbull. *Our New Possessions*. Vols. 1–4. Philadelphia: A. J. Holman, 1898.

Wilcox, Willis Bliss. *Through Luzon on Highways and Byways*. Philadelphia: Franklin Book Company, 1901.

Williams, Raymond. *Marxism and Literature*. Oxford: Oxford University Press, 1977.

Williamson, Judith. "Woman Is an Island: Femininity and Colonization." In *Studies in Entertainment*, ed. Tania Modleski. Bloomington: Indiana University Press, 1989: 111–18.

Wilson, Laurence Lee. *The Skyland of the Philippines*. Baguio: Baguio Printing and Publishing, 1953.

Wilson, Rob. *Reimagining the American Pacific: From South Pacific to Bamboo Ridge and Beyond*. Durham: Duke University Press, 2000.

———. "Toward an 'Asia/Pacific Cultural Studies': Literature, Cultural Identity, and Struggle in the American Pacific." *Studies in Language and Literature* 7 (August 1996): 1–18.

Wong, Pak Nung. "Pursuing the Soldier-Rebels: Governing Military Rebellions in the Contemporary Congo, Sierra Leone and the Philippines." Working paper No. 163, Asia Research Centre, Murdoch University, Australia, April 2010.

Wood, Houston. *Displacing Natives: The Rhetorical Production of Hawai'i*. Lanham, Md.: Rowman and Littlefield, 1999.

Wurfel, David. *Filipino Politics: Development and Decay*. Ithaca, N.Y.: Cornell University Press, 1991.

Yano, Christine. *Airborne Dreams: Nisei Stewardesses and Pan American World Airways*. Durham: Duke University Press, 2010.

Yoneyama, Lisa. "For Transformative Knowledge and Postnationalist Public Spheres: The Smithsonian Enola Gay Controversy." In *Perilous Memories: The Asia-Pacific Wars*, ed. T. Fujitani, T., Geoffrey M. White, and Lisa Yoneyama. Durham: Duke University Press, 2001: 323–46.

Young, Marilyn B. *The Vietnam Wars, 1945–1990*. New York: HarperPerennial, 1991.

Youngblood, Robert L. "Philippine-American Relations under the 'New Society.'" *Pacific Affairs* 50:1 (spring 1977): 45–63.

Ziegler, Rick. "Highway Wars: The Stop H-3 Trilogy." Unpublished manuscript, University of Hawai'i Hamilton Library, Hawaiian Collection, 2003.

INDEX

Abu Sayyaf, 90, 216, 218
activism: against militarism, 80, 112, 175; for Native Hawaiian issues, 26, 32, 70–77; by peasants in the Philippines, 193; against Philippine martial law, 22, 26, 56. *See also* dissent
Aeta, 182–88, 193–213
Afghanistan, 24, 159, 215
Agent Orange, 177–78
Aguinaldo, Emilio, 43, 45, 56, 190–91
Air America, 154, 170
airmobilities, 149, 157–58, 165, 167, 173
Alamo, 88, 96
Allies: narratives about, 87–90, 95, 98, 101, 108, 111, 118; war efforts of, 15, 84, 92, 96, 140
aloha, 35, 38–39, 144, 219
aloha patriotism, 221–22
Al-Qaeda, 215
Angeles, 81, 84, 236n22
antiterrorism, 8, 20. *See also* counterinsurgency; counterterrorism
APEC (Asia Pacific Economic Cooperation), 3, 17, 103, 112
Aquino, Benigno, Jr., 8, 237n34
Aquino, Corazon, 8, 96
Armed Forces of the Philippines, 114, 211
Asian Development Bank (ADB), 27, 89
Asian financial crisis, 103, 216
Asian settlers, 34, 39, 123–26, 129, 228n50, 228n53

Asia Pacific Economic Cooperation (APEC), 3, 17, 103, 112
Aspiras Highway, 51–52, 64
Associated Press, 153–56
authenticity, 3; of natives or indigenous people, 59–60, 63, 66, 202, 209; of travel experience, 60, 62–66, 136, 160, 209

Baguio, 19, 50–66
Balikatan exercises, 219
Barking Sands, 176, 179
Bataan: commemorations of, 19, 88, 92–95, 109–10, 133; legacies of, 90, 94–96, 109, 112, 114; tourism in, 84–86, 90–92, 102, 108–14, 135; and World War II, 14, 83–85, 92–93, 99
Bataan Death March, 84, 104, 109, 111
Battle of Manila Bay, 45, 83
Bayonet Constitution, 10
benevolence, 14, 219; discourses of, 3, 25, 53, 76–77, 85, 112–13, 211; of the United States, 2, 19, 24, 101, 112
Benguet Road, 54–55, 233n19. *See also* Kennon Road
bin Laden, Osama, 159
Bishop Museum, 71, 73, 75, 77
Black Hawk Down, 159
brotherhood: colonial relations as, 16, 54, 112; as metaphor for interstate relations, 87, 103–4, 114; military as a,

brotherhood (*continued*)
93–95, 100, 104–6, 111. *See also* fraternity

Bulatao, Lunesto, 194–95, 199, 212

Bush, George W., 5, 20, 90, 175, 239n6

Camp John Hay, 61–62, 66

capital, 27, 50, 216; culture as, 98; influence of, 20, 186, 201; investment of, 25, 28, 49, 90, 112, 193; logics of, 50, 112; protection of, 5, 17, 68, 113

capitalism, 216; benefits of, 16, 32, 163, 185; and consumption, 6, 94, 185; dominance of, 3, 87; exploitation and, 28, 53; formations of, 25, 86, 181; interests of, 10, 130

Catholic Church, 8, 10, 227n34

Cavite, 43, 83

Cayetano, Ben, 76, 78

Cesaire, Aimé, 25–26, 50

China, 10, 15, 17

citizenship, 33–34, 92–93, 126, 219, 222, 230n30

civilians, 154, 203, and colonialism, 14, 56, 126; as militarized, 116, 124, 126, 143, 156–57, 221; sacrifices of, 126, 134, 221; and travel, 1, 12–13, 56, 61, 121, 143, 212

civilization, 166, 184–85; as colonial project, 31, 43–44, 53–55, 80, 189, 191; discourses of, 92, 160–67, 171, 187, 189

Clark Air Base, 8–9, 17, 19, 193. *See also* Clark Air Field

Clark Air Field, 84–86. *See also* Clark Air Base

Clark Freeport, 85, 111–12, 116, 209

Clinton, Bill, 103–4

Cold War: alliances during, 19, 26, 92, 94, 181, 193; critiques of, 19, 23, 181; economic policy of, 5, 15, 19, 25, 27, 88 (*see also* development: as Cold War strategy); in Hawai'i, 15–16, 24, 32–34, 69–70, 151, 163, 172, 176; ideologies of, 6, 25, 94, 133, 163; interventions during, 14, 16, 24–26, 151, 172 (*see also* Korean War; Vietnam War); militarization during, 5, 15–16, 24, 151, 163, 172,

176, 193; in the Philippines, 15–16, 27, 92, 94, 181, 193

Colonial Army, 192

commemoration, 60; geopolitics of, 101, 111, 118–19, 121, 239n5; and the state, 93, 118; and veterans, 237n37; of World War II, 33–37, 46, 88, 92, 101–5, 115, 141

commodification, 64; of identity, 35–39, 74, 161, 183, 186, 204, 208, 210; of places, 24, 28, 65, 115, 161, 171, 178, 222

Communism, 24, 93–94, 181, 193

conquest, 6, 31, 63, 80, 127, 142, 161

constructive colonialism, 14, 23–25, 53–57

consumer culture, 64, 120, 185; as global, 31, 44, 186, 220; and literature, 21–23, 29; logics of, 149, 184, 187, 222; and multiculturalism, 32, 121; U.S. doctrine of, 94, 226n21. *See also* tourism: as consumer practice

Cordilleras, 52, 55, 59, 61–62, 65–66. *See also* Mountain Province; mountain region

Corregidor, 14, 19, 83–118, 133

Corregidor Foundation, 96, 98

cosmopolitanism: of natives, 66, 72; of tourism, 1, 39, 61, 65, 182, 185, 201, 210, 228n54

counterinsurgency, 193–94, 210, 216, 228n62. *See also* counterterrorism

counterterrorism, 113, 211. *See also* counterinsurgency

Cuba, 7, 11, 44, 226n23

Dambana ng Kagitingan, 109–11

Davis, Oscar King, 41–46, 53, 83

decolonization, 15–16, 32

defense spending, 16–17, 39, 69–70, 79, 115–16, 128. *See also* foreign aid

demilitarization, 91, 211–12

Denito, Juan "Johnny," 197–99, 201, 208–9, 212

Denito, Julio, 197, 203, 213

Department of Defense (U.S.). *See* U.S. Department of Defense

Department of Tourism (Hawai'i). *See* Hawai'i Visitors Bureau; State of Hawai'i Department of Tourism

Department of Tourism (Philippines). *See* Philippine Department of Tourism; Philippine Ministry of Tourism

development, 6, 65; as Cold War strategy, 5, 8, 19, 25, 27–28; discourses of, 6, 43, 187, 216; in the Philippines, 49, 112, 200, 208–9; tourism as strategy of, 5, 8, 17, 28, 94, 187, 216

Diamond Head, 41, 143, 234n54

Dimain, Monico, 195, 198

Dimain, Salvador, 195–96, 198

discipline, 169, 219; as gendered, 13, 27, 37, 53, 55, 78, 236n20; knowledge production as, 16, 78; as a military act, 5, 22, 29, 31, 149, 151, 219; as mode of colonial management, 13, 50, 53–57, 62, 78, 219, 222; as sexualized, 13, 27, 29

discovery, 46, 76, 142, 160; as a gendered act, 6–7, 31; narratives of, 20, 40–41, 46, 58–59, 77, 161

"Dispossessions of Empire," 37–39

dissent, 27–28, 50, 75–76, 112, 181, 194, 216, 218

Distinguished Visitors Program, 143, 239n2

Dole, Sanford B., 41, 131

Duero, Graciano, 195–96, 199

ecotourism, 208; critiques of, 186–87, 211; marketing of, 160, 178, 182, 185–86, 201–2, 213; values of, 184–86, 188, 210–11

Ehime Maru, 142–44

Eisenhower Interstate and Defense Highway System, 69

empire: American, 11, 46, 50, 159–60, 192, 194, 211 (*see also* U.S. colonialism; U.S. imperialism); apparatuses of, 12, 25–26, 40, 47, 150; gendered logics of, 9, 46, 90, 230n19; Japanese, 129; labor of, 12, 44, 46; romance of, 57–58; Spanish, 11, 84; theorizations of, 23–27, 36–37, 42–46, 223

environmentalism, 70–71, 76, 160, 186–87, 189

exceptionalism, 135, 150

exoticization, 24, 37, 46, 63, 171, 220

export processing zone, 112. *See also* Clark Freeport; freeport; special economic zone; Subic Freeport

Faas, Horst, 156

Fantasy Island, 166–67

feminism, 19, 26, 46, 235n4

fictions, 19–21; as built, 25, 73; of colonialism and empire, 25–26, 40, 46, 75; as method, 22–23, 30

Filipinas, 19, 28, 31, 112–14; 236n20. *See also* Macapagal-Arroyo, Gloria; Rosca, Ninotchka

Filipino-American Friendship Park, 104–6

Filipino Americans, 33–34, 97, 248n25

Filipino Heroes Memorial, 97, 104, 106

Filipinos, 4, 88, 95, 218; as Balikbayan, 97–98; as elites, 11, 30, 56, 62, 87, 89–90, 182, 186, 192; as laborers, 12, 28–29, 55–56, 201, 208, 228n51; as organizers, 194, 230n30; in Philippine military, 212–13, 219; racialization of, 44, 55, 59, 93, 191–92; as revolutionaries, 11, 43–44, 65, 106, 181, 190–91, 194 (*see also* Aguinaldo, Emilio); as soldiers in World War II, 33–34, 91, 101, 104, 107–9, 111, 238n53; state violence against, 22, 28, 30, 112, 193, 212, 218; struggles of, 8, 89, 112, 181; as tourist attractions, 59–60, 62, 183, 201–8; as tourists, 2, 62, 97–98, 201, 203, 216–17; in the United States, 34, 92, in U.S. colonial military, 62, 190–94 (*see also* Philippine Scouts); U.S. colonial violence against, 31, 45, 61, 248n25

First World, 21, 29, 186–87

Forbes, W. Cameron, 57, 61, 232n17

foreign aid, 17, 30, 94–95, 218

442nd regiment, 126

fraternity: as metaphor for interstate relations, 1, 6, 19, 54, 84–87, 181, 201; of military, 7, 33–34, 95, 101, 104, 181. *See also* brotherhood

Igorot, 60, 66
IMF (International Monetary Fund), 5, 27–28, 89, 112, 186, 200
Indian Removal Act, 189
Indians, 153, 189–90, 193, 213, 244n35
Indian scouts, 189
Indian Wars, 30, 189–90
indigeneity, 74, 183, 200, 202, 208, 211
indigenization, 20, 62
indigenous people, 10, 34–35, 59, 184–86; commodification of, 66, 68, 74, 186, 220; cultural practices and knowledge of, 20, 38, 71–80, 181–83, 192, 195–202, 208–11 (*see also* genealogy: of the indigenous); militarization of, 20, 179–83, 188–202, 209, 211–13; and politics of resistance, 65, 70, 72; representations of, 80, 127, 129, 162, 187; rights of, 26, 70, 200, 208–9. *See also* Aeta; Indians; Kanaka Maoli; Native Hawaiians
Indigenous People's Rights Act, 200
Indochina, 153. *See also* Laos; Southeast Asia; Vietnam
innocence, 7, 29, 85, 221; of military, 102–3, 107, 126, 130, 133–35; narratives of, 19, 116–17, 126, 132, 135, 222; of tourists, 121, 152, 211, 218; of United States, 14, 118–19, 131, 222
Inouye, Daniel, 34, 76, 213, 234n52, 241n30
insecurity, 20, 215–19, 221
International Monetary Fund (IMF), 5, 27–28, 89, 112, 186, 200
interoperability, 149–51, 173, 176, 179
Iraq, 159, 215, 222
irregular warfare, 190–91, 210, 213
islandness, 31, 37, 108, 149–51, 161–65, 171–75, 179
Iwo Jima, 94, 140

Japan, 3, 9, 34, 138, 213; attack on Pearl Harbor, 14, 69; imperialism by, 14, 106, 119, 124–25, 129–30, 192; and invasion of the Philippines, 62, 84, 87, 90, 94, 103, 108; military of, 14, 62, 84, 87, 96, 103, 108–9, 124–25; military

spending of, 17; people of, 39, 60, 97, 105, 124, 143, 232n17 (*see also* tourists: Japanese as); Philippine relations with, 98, 106; U.S. occupation of, 15, 213, 241n27; World War II defeat of, 33–34, 117, 140, 142
Japan Bank for International Cooperation, 81
Japanese Americans: in Hawai'i, 15, 34–35, 39, 70, 123, 126; as veterans, 33–34, 97, 121, 133
Japanese Friendship Garden, 97. *See also* Japanese Garden of Peace
Japanese Garden of Peace, 104–6. *See also* Japanese Friendship Garden
Japanese Imperial Army, 96. *See also* Japan: military of
JEST (Jungle Environment Survival Training), 182–88, 195, 198–214
Johnson, Lyndon B., 154, 173
joint military exercises, 86, 90, 114, 212. *See also* Balikatan exercises
journalists, 12, 19, 24–26, 40–42, 83, 152–56. *See also,* Davis, Oscar King; Faas, Horst; Huet, Henri; Reasoner, Harry; Rosca, Ninotchka; White, Trumbull
Jungle Environment Survival Training (JEST), 182–88, 195, 198–214
jungle school, 20, 182–83, 195–99, 201, 203, 206, 208
jungle, 164; as combat zone, 109, 150, 154–55, 158, 178, 190, 194–95; as military training site, 176–78, 182, 195–98, 212; as tourism destination, 184, 187–88, 204–8, 212; urban space as, 51, 184, 220
Jurassic Park, 164–67

Kaho'olawe, 172–75, 235n74
Kaho'olawe Island Reserve Commission, 175–76
Kalākaua, 10, 241n24
Kalalau valley, 163, 166
Kanaka Maoli, 129, 226n24. *See also* Native Hawaiians
Kaua'i, 20, 149–52, 159–79. *See also* Garden Island

Kaua'i Agriculture Research Station, 178
Kaua'i Department of Tourism, 161–62
Kennedy, John F., 154, 232n4
Kennon, Lyman, 55
Kennon Road, 19, 50–70, 77, 79
Kingdom of Hawai'i, 9–10, 34, 130; over-
throw of, 11, 26, 32, 116, 118, 131; repre-
sentations of overthrow of, 20, 34, 42,
45, 78, 80, 118, 127–28; resistance to
overthrow of, 12. *See also* sovereignty:
of Hawai'i
Ko'olau Mountains, 19, 67–68
Korean War, 15, 24, 140, 154, 157, 174

labor, 7, 31, 80, 210; in colonial era, 44,
55–56, 59; as discursive or ideological,
8, 44, 46, 92, 111, 116, 118; as gendered
or racialized, 6, 38, 208; migrant, 12,
19, 31, 34, 55–56, 69, 201; in service
economy, 28–29, 192, 195, 197
land, 41–43, 46, 80, 135, 142, 222; Aeta
claims to, 193–95, 199–200, 208–9;
colonial attitudes regarding, 12, 25, 40,
162; exploitation of, 65–66, 77, 112; as
feminized, 6–7, 38, 53, 75, 161; military appropriation of, 13, 24, 54, 116,
173–79, 193–95, 233n32; Native Hawaiian claims to, 10, 15, 33–34, 70–75, 119,
129, 175–76; as source of conflict, 7,
9–11, 70, 91, 181, 189; stewardship of,
175, 186, 189, 208–9, 211; theft of, 10,
32, 46, 72, 78, 118, 123
land reform, 91, 181
Laos, 152, 156
liberalization, 5, 20, 89
liberation: ideologies of, 19, 27, 31, 46,
116; World War II narratives of, 2, 30,
84–90, 93, 95–107, 111–12
Lihue, 160, 167
Lili'uokalani, 11, 13, 116, 130–31
Luzon, 53, 65, 81, 83, 99, 181, 190–91

Macabebe, 190
Macapagal-Arroyo, Gloria, 218–19, 228n62
MacArthur, Douglas, 2, 84, 88, 98–100,
108
Magnum, P.I., 147–50, 164

Mākua Valley, 172–75
Malinta Tunnel, 97, 108
Manawaoipuna Falls, 166
manifest destination, 23–27, 29, 32–33,
39–40, 45, 47
Manifest Destiny, 23, 25, 31, 35
Manila, 8, 62, 81, 94, 103, 185, 190; as
colonial destination, 42–45; as departure point, 51–52, 58, 64, 97–98
Manila Bay, 11, 83
Marcos, Ferdinand: coup against, 8–9,
106; martial law administration of,
21–22, 26–31, 51, 63, 65, 95–96,
226n25, 230n16, 230n22; modernization policies of, 27–28, 49–52, 63,
65–66, 80, 89, 112, 232nn1–2; political
career of, 93–96, 109–11, 237n34; war
commemorations by, 95, 101, 109–10.
See also martial law: in the Philippines;
New Society
Marcos, Imelda, 8–9
Marcos Highway, 50–51. *See also* Aspiras
Highway
martial law: in Hawai'i, 126, 173–74; in the
Philippines, 2, 22, 26–28, 31, 95, 109;
in Poland, 216
masculinity, 53, 90, 171; and authorship,
19, 25; and empire, 6, 40, 46, 55, 58;
of heroism, 15, 20, 95, 98, 120–21; of
indigenous men, 20, 183, 185, 187–88,
208–10; in international relations, 1,
6–7 (*see also* brotherhood: as metaphor for interstate relations; fraternity: as metaphor for interstate relations); of military, 1, 4, 12, 85, 95,
113–14, 210; of military sacrifice, 20,
34, 37, 85, 98, 101; and technology, 19,
77, 150, 153, 169; of tourist or traveler,
1, 4, 12, 58, 91, 114, 161, 183–87; and
the United States, 9, 26, 120
*M*A*S*H*, 157
Maui, 160–61, 164, 175
Middle East, 168, 170
Midway, 14, 94
Mighty Mo, 139–42. *See also* USS *Missouri*
militarism, 176, 192, 215; as beneficial,
60, 94, 111, 113, 201–2; critiques of,

neoliberalism, 8, 213; discourses of, 111, 118, 148, 183, 186; as economic strategy, 84, 86, 90, 185, 201, 210, 213; as U.S. foreign policy, 3, 88, 113, 218. *See also* governance: neoliberal mode of

neoliberation, 88–90, 95, 97, 111–14, 116

New People's Army, 65, 193

New Society, 28–29, 51, 63. *See also* Marcos, Ferdinand

New World Order, 6, 7, 24, 183, 215, 217, 222

Night Is a Sharkskin Drum, 26, 33

9/11, 17–18, 20, 90, 114, 144, 215–22

Nixon Doctrine, 196

North Atlantic Treaty Organization, 94

North Korea, 17, 144

North Vietnam, 154–56, 188

nostalgia: about colonialism, 62–63, 65, 103; about military past, 20, 86, 88, 91–92, 98, 114, 117, 120, 126, 132, 199, 211 (*see also* "Nostalgia: VJ Day"); about premodernity, 12, 78

"Nostalgia: VJ Day," 33–37

Oʻahu, 11, 67, 142; as militarized, 19, 116, 125, 129, 172–73, 176, 227n45, 234n54; as tourist site, 115, 147–49, 160–61

Officer's School of the Philippine Constabulary, 61. *See also* Philippine Military Academy

Okinawa, 14, 24, 94, 140, 188, 226n23, 241n27

Olongapo, 89, 203; legacies of U.S. military in, 201, 213, 236n16, 236n22; as site of U.S. military base, 84, 86

Operation Ranch Hand, 178

Operation Rolling Thunder, 155

pacification, 6, 50; discourses of, 27, 30, 50, 177; as Philippine state strategy against Filipinos, 1, 29, 30; as U.S. colonial military strategy in the Philippines, 30–31, 54, 58, 61, 183, 188–91, 211

Pacific Aviation Museum, 117, 119, 121, 135

Pacific Cemetery (Punchbowl), 221. *See also* Punchbowl Cemetery

Pacific Missile Range Facility (PMRF), 176–79

Pacific War Memorial, 94–95, 97, 101–4

Pacific War Memorial Museum, 102–4

Palawan, 216–17

Pampanga, 52, 81, 190–93

paradise, 47; as Cold War product, 16, 24, 27, 32–36; exclusions of, 77–79; as fantasy, 7–9, 24, 33, 72, 161; as gendered, sexualized, or racialized, 7, 9, 13, 27, 35, 37, 46, 161; imagery of, 7, 13, 32, 115, 221–22; as interchangeable, 176; as multicultural, 32, 34–35, 77, 123, 135; as object of securing, 40, 61, 86, 131, 172; as tourism marketing strategy, 20, 46, 70, 95, 117, 161–62, 170–71; and violence, 22–24, 27, 31, 143, 158, 219. *See also* tropics

patriotism, 34, 117. *See also* aloha patriotism

Pearl Harbor, 39, 92, 183, 131, 221; attack on, 14, 69, 88, 93, 115–19, 125–27; history of, 10, 13–14, 116, 125–27, 130; as military base, 16, 36, 69, 115, 140, 142–43, 234n54; tourism in, 36, 114–145 (*see also* Pearl Harbor military-tourism complex). *See also* Puʻuloa

Pearl Harbor military-tourism complex, 114, 117–20, 135, 143–44

peasants, 155, 181, 193–94, 212, 218

Pentagon, 215–16

People Power Revolution, 8, 106

Philippine Airlines, 184, 188, 203

Philippine-American War, 18–19, 100, 107, 249n36; as U.S. imperialism, 11, 40–41, 44, 106; violence of, 13, 30, 45, 189, 193, 219

Philippine Department of Tourism, 49, 66, 90–91, 96. *See also* Philippine Ministry of Tourism

Philippine Military Academy, 61–62, 66, 193, 212

Philippine Ministry of Tourism, 28, 95. *See also* Philippine Department of Tourism

Rosca, Ninotchka, 24, 46, 222; *State of War*, 21–23, 26–33, 114

sacrifice, 6, 143; discourses of military acts of, 32, 126; as justification for military occupation, 116–18, 133–34, 144; as justification for neoliberal governance, 112–13; rewards for, 34, 95, 101, 123–24, 134; of soldiers during war, 16, 57, 96, 109–11, 136–39, 175; World War II and discourses of, 15, 85, 87–88, 221; World War II and tourisms of, 19–20, 83–85, 91–92, 100–101, 104–11, 119–20, 131–36
Saigon, 153, 155, 157
Sangley Point, 43, 83
scenic highway, 19, 50–51, 54, 56–57, 61–62, 68–71, 80, 83
security, 1, 16, 62, 80, 215, 251n9; definitions of, 5–6, 14; militarism and 6, 8, 79, 114, 116–17, 119; military as guarantor of, 4, 143–44, 222; national, 5–6, 17–19, 24, 175, 219; partnerships in, 85, 90, 103; of tourism and travel, 5, 45, 50, 116; U.S. Cold War discourses of, 5, 94, 101, 152; as U.S. justification for intervention or occupation, 8, 24, 46, 130
segregation, 20, 91, 107, 125
sentimentality, 14, 16, 34, 37, 65, 84, 86–88, 111, 120, 221–22
sightseeing, 57, 59, 66–68, 80, 148–49, 163, 178
soldiers, 67, 130, 150, 168; as agents of U.S. imperialism, 42, 53–54, 61, 90, 125, 129, 189, 219; at duty, 140–41; in film and television, 158–59; in literature, 22, 27–31, 34, 36–37, 184, 188; media coverage of, 42, 153–57, 184–85; playing at being, 20, 136, 182–83, 187, 203–12; recruitment of, 3, 90, 190–92; and sexual violence, 13, 22, 27–29, 113–14; as symbol of U.S. power, 4, 9, 31; as tourists, 1–4, 42, 61–62, 86, 90–91, 109, 113, 174; training of, 153, 181–83, 188, 192–93, 195–99, 211–13, 237n34. *See also* sacrifices: of soldiers during war

Southeast Asia, 16; hill stations of, 54, 61; people of, 194, 196; as theater of war, 151, 153–54, 157–58, 173–74, 194, 196, 243n12. *See also* Indochina; Laos; Vietnam
South Pacific, 163–64, 170
South Vietnam, 154, 178
souvenir, 2, 44–45, 103, 125, 130, 167, 205–6
sovereignty, 1, 39, 187; of Kingdom of Hawaiʻi, 9–11, 32, 116, 127, 130; of Native Hawaiians, 15, 26, 34, 37, 119, 126, 130; of Philippines, 10, 113; politics of, 26, 70–71, 73, 175, 235nn73–74
Spain, 11–12, 43, 45, 56; colonialism by, 9–10, 53, 83–84, 190
Spanish-American War, 11, 88, 100, 189, 245n60; press reports about, 40, 44–45
special economic zone, 19, 81, 84, 89, 91, 208. *See also* Clark Freeport; export processing zone; freeport; Subic Freeport
stability, 5–6, 85, 114; military as guarantor of, 1, 17, 31, 37, 86, 113, 185; violence and, 29
Stallone, Sylvester, 184, 188
statehood, 27, 32–35, 37, 116
State of Hawaiʻi Department of Tourism, 69, 78–79
State of Hawaiʻi Department of Transportation, 69, 70, 76–79
State of War, 21–23, 26–33, 114
structural adjustment, 6, 28, 89, 218. *See also* International Monetary Fund (IMF); liberalization; neoliberalism
structures of feeling, 4, 19, 149
Stryker Brigade, 174
Subic: military history of, 205, 213, 236n22; as site of neoliberalism, 116, 201, 208–9, 211, 236n5, 236nn16–17; territory of, 186, 188, 195, 197, 202. *See also* Subic Bay; Subic Freeport
Subic Bay, 84–86, 89, 90, 103, 111–12, 194, 200
Subic Bay Metropolitan Authority, 86, 201, 208, 236n6, 236n17

Subic Bay Naval Base, 17, 19, 84–86, 182, 184, 188, 193

Subic Freeport: American military history of, 202, 205, 208; conversion into, 85–86, 89–90, 103, 111–12, 182, 201, 208; tourism in, 20, 182, 185–88, 201, 208; violence in, 113–14

sublime, 58, 68, 75–80, 108, 111, 187

submarines, 117, 125, 136–38, 142. *See also* USS *Bowfin*; USS *Greeneville*

"Sunset on the Beach," 220–22

surveillance, 219; the military and, 179; roads and 19, 50–51, 54, 68; tourism and 66, 147, 149–50

sustainability, 185–87, 208, 210–11

sustainable tourism, 183. *See also* ecotourism

Tagalogs, 190–91, 249n39

target: of imperialism, 14, 23; military as, 156, 158; of military, 142, 145, 151, 156, 172–79, 244n35; tourists as, 216–17

targetability, 149, 173–75, 179

technology, 46, 79, 163, 171, 181; advances in, 15, 25, 30, 140, 177–79, 192; of affect, 120, 165; apparatuses of, 27, 51, 150; logics of, 50, 64, 187; as masculinized, 19, 78, 150, 153, 169; of military, 20, 57, 79, 139, 142, 148–49, 151–52, 170–71; of mobility, 4, 12, 68, 150; as primitive, 182, 198; superiority of, 55, 63, 77, 153, 156, 181, 215; of visuality, 147–50

terror, 215; acts of, 112, 216–18; states of, 3, 27, 29, 65, 112, 216–18

Third World, 21, 186–87

torture, 22–23, 27–33, 46, 190

tourability: as amenability to touring, 109, 149, 151–52, 161, 163, 171, 176, 178; and security, 45, 143, 152, 172

tourism, 189, 215; and class, 2, 15, 62–63, 95, 97, 162, 218; as Cold War strategy, 5–6, 15–16, 24, 32, 94, 133; as consumer practice, 5–6, 120–21, 142, 183–87, 204, 218–21; cultures of, 12, 18–20, 24, 47, 66; economy of, 4–5, 15–18, 88–89, 111–15, 186–87, 210, 216; and

exploitation, 5–7, 24, 28–29, 38–39, 218; gendered logics of, 4, 6–7, 37–38, 114, 161, 187; in Hawaiʻi, 7, 115–44, 148–50, 159–73, 176–78, 219–22; and history of relationship with militarism, 12–20, 24–25, 40, 45–57, 149–50, 172–73; as interdependent with militarism, 3–9, 27–37, 80, 83, 113–14, 143–44, 182–84; mass, 9, 13–15, 24, 63, 163; in the Philippines, 45, 57–66, 83–86, 94–112, 182–85, 201–12, 216–17; rhetoric or idiom of, 21–22, 30–31, 44–46, 58, 60, 66, 75; sexualized logics of, 6–7, 13, 24, 27, 114; and violence, 28–29, 113–14, 216–17

tourist gaze, 164, 204; as averted or impaired, 7, 101, 111, 152; objects of, 12, 78, 80, 186; resisting, 65

tourists, 67, 94, 96, 200, 213; colonial agents as, 12, 14, 41–45, 54, 57, 61, 189; and exploitation, 28–29, 38–39, 186–87, 218, 220; fantasies of, 13, 59–60, 78, 151, 184–88; Filipinos as, 2, 62, 97–98, 201, 203, 216–17; freedoms of, 50, 80, 111, 121, 135, 221–22; itineraries of, 52, 56–68, 78–79, 97–112, 116–44, 159–71, 182–83, 201–8 (*see also* mobility: of tourists and tourism); Japanese as, 9, 60, 97–100, 121, 123, 125, 134, 203; Koreans as, 134, 203; as modern, 62, 66, 78, 80, 218; violence against, 216–19. *See also* soldiers: as tourists

Trask, Haunani-Kay, 23–27, 32, 46, 161, 222; "Dispossessions of Empire," 37–39; *Night Is a Sharkskin Drum*, 26, 33; "Nostalgia: VJ Day," 33–37

trauma: of defeat, 3, 20, 150, 156, 159, 179; of 9/11, 221; of war, 134, 157, 169

travel: as method, 18, 21–23, 46

travel narratives, 12, 18, 50, 57–60, 63–64; journalism as, 41–46, 184; of military, 13, 130

travelogues. *See* travel narratives

triumph, 31, 120, 159; of technology, 55, 64, 76–77; in war, 94–95, 100, 105, 118, 138–39, 142, 221. *See also* victory tropicalization, 23–24, 45, 68, 151, 163–64

tropics, 30, 150, 159, 169; as American or colonial property, 3, 9, 46, 50, 152, 164; as fantasy, 12–13, 19, 25, 75, 167, 171, 222; as feminized or sexualized, 6–7, 24, 27–28, 33, 75, 172; as interchangeable, 147, 151, 168, 172, 174, 179, 195; as militarized, 117, 170, 125–26, representations of, 13, 25, 40, 45, 115, 164, 220–22; as space of imperial management, 14, 54, 64, 78, 177; violence and the, 21–23, 31. *See also* paradise

U.S. Air Force, 8, 174, 176, 195

U.S. Army, 56, 173, 176–77, 191

U.S. Army Corps of Engineers, 55, 57

U.S. colonialism, 19, 78; cultures of, 12, 40, 44–46, 76, 166, 171–72; fictions about, 25–28, 30–32; history of, 9, 13–14, 188–92, 219; legacies of, 103, 186–87; projects of, 14, 52–59, 61–62, 64–65, 181. *See also* constructive colonialism; U.S. imperialism

U.S. Congress, 13, 53, 127

U.S. Department of Defense, 17

U.S. imperialism, 3–4, 7–8, 14, 27, 106; cultures of, 19, 26, 40, 42, 92; fictions of, 42; history of, 8–12, 116, 128–30; as modern, 24–27, 50, 53–54 (*see also* constructive colonialism); projects of, 54; and war, 65, 106–7, 150, 231n51 (*see also* Philippine-American War, Spanish-American War, Vietnam War). *See also* U.S. colonialism

U.S. Marines, 127, 156, 185, 195–96, 240n24, 242n2

U.S. militarization, 2, 4, 6, 50; of Asia and the Pacific, 8, 15–18, 24, 116, 188, 241n27; Hawai'i history of, 10–17, 24, 172–79; and Hawai'i mobility, 68–69, 71, 79; and Hawai'i tourism, 115–17, 120, 124–30, 141, 147–52, 162–63, 221–22; logics of, 1, 7, 156, 171, 184; Philippine history of, 12–17, 24, 30, 53, 188–99; and Philippine tourism, 61–62, 83–87, 90–95, 101–14, 181–83, 209–14, 218–19

U.S. military: activism or resentment against, 1, 70, 112, 144, 175; alliances of, 85, 87, 90–91, 94–95, 181, 192–93, 218–19; as apparatus of colonialism, 12, 53; benefits from, 69, 79, 85, 144, 198–201, 210–11, 213–14; budget of, 16–17, 149; desires and interests of, 10, 12, 14, 20, 24, 35, 43, 128, 130; as guarantor of security, 14, 45, 86, 131; interventions of, 9–11, 131 (*see also* Vietnam War); itineraries of, 4, 12–13, 40, 62, 127, 130 (*see also* mobility: of military); as object of love, 205–6, 199, 211, 213; personnel of, 12–13, 42, 55, 148, 190, 199 (*see also* Native Scouts; Philippine Scouts; soldiers; veterans); policies of, 4–5, 14, 17, 182, 189–92, 196, 210–11, 213; and public relations, 14, 115, 134, 143–44; race and, 124, 131, 190 (*see also* segregation); recruitment by, 13, 190–92, 194–95; representations of, 32, 124–30, 184, 213; rights of, 10, 16, 118, 127; strength of, 15, 116–18, 210; training of or by, 86, 173–75, 182–83, 193–98, 208–9; vulnerability of, 24, 156, 159, 216

U.S. military bases, 18, 36, 46–47, 221; economies of, 81, 90, 111–14, 124, 185, 208, 210; in Hawai'i, 13, 69, 115–119, 127, 133–34, 142, 161 (*see also* Hickam Air Force Base; Pearl Harbor); Philippine history of, 13, 15, 43, 61, 84, 194–201; the Philippines and the economy of, 81, 84–89, 181–86, 208 (*see also* Clark Air Base; Subic Bay Naval Base); politics of, 9, 113–14, 129; return of, 84, 87–89, 114, 183, 198–99, 201; sexualized violence in, 1, 84, 113–14

U.S. military occupation, 17, 26, 187, 215; of Hawai'i, 13–19, 24, 42–45, 115–18, 127–31, 143–45, 172–79, 222; of Japan, 3; of the Philippines, 11, 14–15, 24, 44–45, 54, 57, 61, 84–91, 188–200

U.S. Navy, 92, 170; in Hawai'i, 174–76, 235n74; and overthrow of Kingdom of Hawai'i, 10, 116, 130–31; in the Spanish-American War, 83; at Subic

Bay Naval Base, 90, 195, 197–99; and tourism, 131, 134, 140, 142–43, 195, 197–99, 242n42

U.S. Pacific Command, 17, 24, 115, 133

U.S. Pacific Fleet, 16, 143, 247n87

U.S. Special Forces, 188, 196, 211

U.S.-Philippines Mutual Defense Treaty, 85

University of Hawaiʻi, 177–78

University of Hawaiʻi Department of Agronomy, 178

USS *Arizona*, 19, 115, 118, 131, 137–39

USS *Arizona* Memorial, 19, 35, 115–22, 129–36, 139, 142, 221

USS *Boston*, 11, 131, 142

USS *Bowfin*, 117, 121–22, 135–39, 141, 144

USS *Bowfin* Submarine Museum and Park, 117, 119, 136

USS *Greeneville*, 142–43

USS *Maine*, 11, 88

USS *Missouri*, 117–19, 121, 135–36, 139–42, 144

USS *Oklahoma*, 138

USS *Oklahoma* Memorial, 117, 119

valor: narratives of, 98, 101, 106, 119, 144, 151; tourisms of, 83, 85, 88, 91, 108, 119, 151

Valor in the Pacific National Monument, 117, 120, 239n9

veterans, 140, 170; of the Indian Wars, 30, 189–90; of the Vietnam War, 148, 169, 184, 238n53, 244n30; of World War II, 32–34, 36, 97, 105, 120, 123, 133, 237n37

VFA (Visiting Forces Agreement), 16, 85–86, 90–91, 113

victory, 3, 77, 89, 94–95; failure of technology as key to, 154, 158, 181; tourisms of, 102, 118, 135, 138–40, 142. *See also* triumph

Vietnam, 16, 226n23; people of, 156, 184, 188; as site of war, 148, 150, 153–57, 159, 182, 188; substitute terrain for, 151, 163, 168–79, 194–96

Vietnamization, 210

Vietnam War, 15, 18; combat training for,

194–97; in film and television, 157–58, 164–65, 168, 194, 248n3; tourisms of, 147–88; trauma of, 3, 20, 24, 248n5

vigilance: of military, 95, 103, 120, 133, 135, 140, 163; narratives of, 87, 118, 221; over women, 114

violence, 8, 118, 131, 137, 141, 143, 159, 171; as gendered or sexualized, 7, 84, 91, 113–14; of modernity, 79–80; as productive, 25, 31, 55; of and by the state, 21–22, 28, 30, 63, 91, 114; against tourists, 216–19

Visiting Forces Agreement (VFA), 16, 85–86, 90–91, 113

visuality, 19, 150–59, 172, 178. *See also* visual regimes

visual regimes, 147–49, 167, 174, 178–79. *See also* visuality

VJ Day, 34. *See also* "Nostalgia: VJ Day"

Waikīkī, as departure point, 67, 78; as site of tourism, 32, 36, 42, 74, 147, 162, 173, 219–22

war, 2, 44, 150, 189; cultures of, 20, 116, 158–59, 182–83, 229n4, 243n12; economy or industry of, 36, 115, 149, 154, 171; against the people, 112, 218; preparations for, 11, 42, 174, 195–96; territorializations of, 14, 16, 111, 159, 177, 219; tourisms of, 108–9, 116, 135, 143 (*see also* Bataan; Corregidor; Pearl Harbor: tourism in); state of war, 21–22, 28, 215; types of, 43, 37, 191, 198, 210, 213; violence of or in, 32, 65, 101, 106, 116, 138, 141–42, 158

War of 1898. *See* Spanish-American War

war zone, 57, 118, 159, 169

Washington, D.C., 3, 88, 92, 94, 152, 240n22

Wasson, Dawn, 72–75

weaponization, 149, 155–56, 182, 189, 195, 212, 216

White, Trumbull, 44–46, 53

white man's burden, 40, 53

Wilcox, Willis Bliss, 53–54

Wisner, Frank G., 87–88

women: activism by or for, 26, 32, 71–75,

women (*continued*)
78; as agents of U.S. empire, 14, 120, 134; commodification of, 38–9, 161; representations of, 21–23, 27–28, 31, 43, 60, 147, 161; violence against, 6–7, 21–23, 27–30, 112–14; writing by, 19, 21–39 (*see also* Rosca, Ninotchka; Trask, Haunani-Kay). *See also* Filipinas

World Bank, 5, 27–8, 65, 89, 112, 186, 200
World War I, 13, 191

World War II, 18; commemoration of, 33–37, 46, 88, 92–93, 101–5, 115, 141; history of, 14–15, 84, 119, 129, 140, 144; legacies of, 85, 88–89, 95–96, 116–17, 119, 126, 172–74; narratives of, 15, 118–20, 126, 221 (*see also* liberation: World War II narratives of; rescue: narratives of; sacrifice: discourses of); tourisms of, 19–20, 83–114, 116–44

Zambales Province, 193, 199